Weaving the American Catholic Tapestry

Weaving the American Catholic Tapestry

Essays in Honor of William L. Portier

EDITED BY

Derek C. Hatch

AND

Timothy R. Gabrielli

FOREWORD BY

David G. Schultenover, SJ

PICKWICK *Publications* · Eugene, Oregon

WEAVING THE AMERICAN CATHOLIC TAPESTRY
Essays in Honor of William L. Portier

Pickwick Publications
An Imprint of Wipf and Stock Publishers
199 W. 8th Ave., Suite 3
Eugene, OR 97401

www.wipfandstock.com

PAPERBACK ISBN: 978-1-4982-0279-4
HARDCOVER ISBN: 978-1-4982-0281-7
EBOOK ISBN: 978-1-4982-0280-0

Cataloguing-in-Publication data:

Names: Hatch, Derek C., editor | Gabrielli, Timothy R., editor | Schultenover, David G., foreword.

Title: Weaving the American Catholic tapestry : essays in honor of William L. Portier / edited by Derek C. Hatch and Timothy R. Gabrielli.

Description: Eugene, OR: Pickwick Publications, 2017 | Includes bibliographical references and index.

Identifiers: ISBN 978-1-4982-0279-4 (paperback) | ISBN 978-1-4982-0281-7 (hardcover) | ISBN 978-1-4982-0280-0 (ebook)

Subjects: LCSH: Portier, William L. | Catholic Church—Doctrines. | Hermeneutics—Religious aspects—Catholic Church | Catholic Church—United States—History.

Classification: BX1751.2 W40 2017 (print) | BX1751.2 (ebook)

Manufactured in the U.S.A.   03/24/17

Contents

Contributors

Michael J. Baxter teaches Religious Studies and is Assistant Director of the Catholic Studies Program at Regis University in Denver, Colorado.

Andrew D. Black is Regional Director for Baylor University's Texas Hunger Initiative in Lubbock, Texas.

William J. Collinge is Professor Emeritus of Theology and Philosophy at Mount St. Mary's University in Emmitsburg, Maryland.

Damian Costello is an Independent Scholar residing on the Navajo Nation.

Timothy R. Gabrielli is Assistant Professor of Theology at Seton Hill University in Greensburg, Pennsylvania.

Derek C. Hatch is Associate Professor of Christian Studies at Howard Payne University in Brownwood, Texas.

Michael F. Lombardo is Assistant Professor of Theology and Director of the University of Mary's Rome Program in Rome, Italy.

Patricia M. McDonald, SHCJ, is Academic Programme Director at the Pontifical Beda College in Rome, Italy.

Jeffrey L. Morrow is Associate Professor of Undergraduate Theology at Seton Hall University in South Orange, New Jersey.

David J. O'Brien is Loyola Professor of Catholic Studies Emeritus at College of the Holy Cross in Worcester, Massachusetts, and formerly University Professor of Faith and Culture at the University of Dayton in Dayton, Ohio.

Benjamin T. Peters is Associate Professor of Religious Studies at the University of Saint Joseph in West Hartford, Connecticut.

Anathea Portier-Young is Associate Professor of Old Testament at Duke Divinity School in Durham, North Carolina.

Susan K. Sack is Staff Chaplain and Pastoral Educator at Good Samaritan Hospital in Dayton, Ohio.

Matthew Shadle is Associate Professor of Theology and Religious Studies at Marymount University in Arlington, Virginia.

Fr. Charles J.T. Talar is Professor of Church History at the University of St. Thomas in Houston, Texas.

Sandra Yocum is University Professor of Faith and Culture at the University of Dayton in Dayton, Ohio.

Foreword

William Portier has spent a major part of his professional career describing and clarifying U.S. Catholicism and, more specifically, its relationship to Roman Catholic Modernism. It was in this role that I first met Bill and came to appreciate his broad, deep, and clear thinking on contested issues, such as the historiography of Americanism and Modernism, mainly through annual meetings of the Roman Catholic Modernism Working Group of the American Academy of Religion. This group had an exceptionally long run as AAR working groups go, largely because it produced a remarkable number of publications, to which Bill contributed substantially.

The group's productivity was mainly a result of timing: it was born in the heat of emanations from the Vatican archives' opening to qualified scholars for the period of Roman Catholic Modernism. This began in the late 1970s for the years of Leo XIII's reign, then progressively through the reigns of Popes Pius X, Benedict XV, on up (with certain restrictions for the years after 1939), and with Pope Francis now considering when to open the archives for the pontificate of Pope Pius XII.

While numerous publications on Modernism appeared prior to the onset of the Roman Catholic Modernism Working Group, conclusions were, at least with respect to the Vatican's role in the Modernist crisis, rather tentative and at times speculative, for two main reasons: (1) Pope Pius X's *motu proprio Sacrorum Antistitum* (1910) mandated that all ordained clergy and professors (ordained or not) of philosophy and theology annually take the Oath against Modernism; (2) Along with this oath, *Sacrorum Antistitum* also reaffirmed Pius X's mandate in *Pascendi Dominici Gregis* (1907), his encyclical condemning Modernism, that vigilance committees be established in every diocese worldwide to espy and report to Rome any evidence of tendencies toward what the Holy Office regarded as Modernism.

These two measures and their draconian enforcement generated an atmosphere of fear and anti-intellectualism in seminaries and Catholic schools of philosophy and theology until Pope Paul VI revoked them in 1967 following the close of Vatican II. Pope John XXIII called this council by famously opening a window and declaring, "I want to throw open the windows of the church so that we can see out and the people can see in." Until this opening, any adventurous research and writing on topics that tested the boundaries of church-mandated neo-scholastic theology was unlikely.

John XXIII and Vatican II, then, enabled scholars to search church archives seventy-five years after a given papacy for answers to questions raised by the censures, secrecy, and sealed documents of the Modernism period. With the progressive opening of the Vatican archives beginning in 1978 (for the papacy of Pius X), studies of salient questions regarding Modernism and anti-Modernism began. But I stress that whatever archival files scholars saw were only those they were allowed to see. No one but the archivists could know what other files might have been withheld for whatever reasons. Results of archival studies must therefore be considered tentative.

Diocesan archives follow the restrictions of Vatican archives. Thus Portier, in his research in U.S. church archives, worked under Vatican restrictions. Nevertheless, he, like his colleagues in the Roman Catholic Modernism Working Group, managed to produce enlightening narratives based on local archival research, the importance of which is indicated by the essays collected in this Festschrift.

In my consideration here of Portier's contribution to U.S. church and Modernist studies, I will restrict myself to his most recent monograph, *Divided Friends: Portraits of the Roman Catholic Modernist Crisis in the United States* (2013), not only because I like it best of all his writings but also because I find it to be his most significant contribution to the field. For Portier, along with fully aged scholarship came clarity enhanced by wisdom.

Little did Bill know that the words of his study and, for me, its essential message would find confirmation in Pope Francis's November 10, 2015 address to the church of Italy: "Church reform, then—and the church is *semper reformanda*— . . . does not exhaust itself in coming up with the umpteenth plan to change structures. Rather, it means to be grafted and rooted in Christ, allowing itself to be led by the Spirit. Then, with talent and creativity, anything is possible."[1]

---

1. Pope Francis, *Incontro con i rappresentanti del V Convegno Nazionale della Chiesa Italiana*, my translation.

What connection do I see between Francis's address and Portier's *Divided Friends*? C. J. T. Talar's conclusion to his essay in this Festschrift gives a strong clue. Talar rightly argues that Portier helped clean up the historiography of Modernism by clarifying its relationship to the slightly earlier "Americanist heresy" with which it was sometimes elided and blindly pinned on Isaac Hecker.

As Talar points out, pre-Portier "Phantom heresy historiography emphasized the practical nature of the errors that were identified as Americanism, and contrasted them with the more intellectual issues that were condemned in Modernism."[2] But post-Vatican-II revisionist historians—chiefly Portier and colleagues in the Modernism Working Group—"challenged this separation, arguing for greater continuity between Americanism and Modernism."[3] My own take on what I regard as Portier's most important contribution in his *Divided Friends* to a more valid historiography turns on the tragic element of what eventually separated Joseph McSorley from the other three priests, namely, his practice of a true Modernism over against their false Modernism.

Portier's argument progresses under the implications of his insistence that, as far as a true Modernism is concerned, church historian Louis Duchesne, and not Loisy, "is the key figure" of Modernism.[4] I myself connect this observation with the thought of true Modernist Friedrich von Hügel as found in his seminal *The Mystical Element of Religion*,[5] on which George Tyrrell, his true Modernist friend, was the primary interlocutor and adviser. For those of von Hügel's mind—among whom I would include McSorley but not the other "divided friends"—the mystical element of religion is fundamental and prior to the effort to explain it and develop its theology into doctrinal conclusions. In other words, the mystical element of religion effects what emerged as the early church's pathway to dogma, namely, the principle, *lex orandi, lex credendi*. That is, the mystical apprehension of divine mystery as shared by the church is what integrally leads to church dogma.

For von Hügel, disagreements (and sometimes heresies) arise as the result of two failures: (1) to properly balance what he calls the three elements of religion: the historical/institutional, the scientific/intellectual, and the mystical/experiential elements; and (2) to adequately enter into that third element, the mystical. This latter failure precludes balancing the three

---

2. Cf. below, 125.
3. Ibid.
4. Portier, *Divided Friends*, 34–35.
5. Von Hügel, *The Mystical Element of Religion*.

elements and so leads to an eccentric relationship with the church; whereas a balance of the three elements—with priority given to the mystical element—leads to a generosity of spirit that enables patient and compassionate broadening of the church's umbrella.

For me, the most insightful, if subtly stated, subtext to Portier's *Divided Friends* is the implication that McSorley departed from his three long-time friends precisely over Catholicism's mystical element. He embraced it; they did not. This embrace enabled him to maintain a generous spirit toward those with whom he disagreed, and allow them, however painfully for himself, to take a different road.

Those who enter into William Portier's oeuvre graced with shimmering sacramental vision will not be surprised that his colleagues adorned him with this Festschrift.

David G. Schultenover, SJ

Henri de Lubac Professor of Historical Theology
Marquette University

Acknowledgments

"Theology is indeed a practice of friendship." These are the words that Bill Portier wrote inside Derek's copy of *Divided Friends*. This Festschrift, which is dedicated to the life and work of Portier himself, also extends from friendship. The editors met as students in a doctoral seminar led by Portier at the University of Dayton in August 2006. Since then, our paths have become closely woven together through our families, work responsibilities, job applications, and conference presentations. In truth, this friendship has crossed confessional boundaries as it has brought together a Catholic and a Baptist within the communion of Christ's cosmic love and in shared appreciation of Bill's work.

We would like to thank several groups of people. First, we owe a debt to our fellow travelers in the doctoral program at UD (some of whom were in that first seminar with Portier and some of whom are featured in this volume). Without these people, our own scholarly journeys would certainly be impoverished: Gary Agee, Louis Albarran, Wes Arblaster, Andy Black, Damian Costello, Michael Cox, Coleman Fannin, Tim Furry, Susanna Cantu Gregory, Jason Hentschel, Satish Joseph, Michael Lombardo, Dan Martin, Justin Menno, Herbie Miller, Matthew Minix, Jeff Morrow, Maria Morrow, Sharon Perkins, Ben Peters, Biff Rocha, Sue Sack, Katherine Schmidt, Matthew Shadle, Adam Sheridan, Ethan Smith, Nikki Coffey Tousley, and Justin Yankech.

Further, a project of this sort is definitely a labor of love. As such, many people have worked to help make it a reality. Foremost on this list is Sandra Yocum. Throughout the development of this book, her guidance and advice has been invaluable. In similar fashion, Vince Miller aided in planning for the volume's creation. We are additionally grateful for the generous support of the University of Dayton's Department of Religious Studies (under the leadership of Daniel Thompson) and the College of Arts & Sciences (directed first by Paul Benson, then Jason Pierce). Jim Heft granted permission for a revised version of Dave O'Brien's Marianist Award lecture to be published in this volume. Moreover, we are grateful for the gracious and thorough editorial work of Albert Liberatore of EditsMadeEasy, Jessi Jordan's enthusiastic proficiency in pursuing bibliographic and archival information, and Ian Bush's skill and creativity in developing promotional materials for the book. Of course, a collaborative work of this nature cannot exist without contributors, and we are thankful for the work of the authors within this volume. The excellence of their scholarship is a further tribute to their friendship with Bill.

We would also like to thank our families for their support. Bringing this project to fruition has involved significant time and effort, and we have welcomed three additional children to our respective families as time has elapsed. So, for the love, friendship, and patience of our spouses Sarah and Jessica, as well as our children Sofia, Philip, Simon, Lidia, Joseph, Leo, and Rebekah, we are ever thankful.

Finally, this Festschrift stands on our abiding friendship with William Portier, a man who has taught us a great deal about how to love theology and see it within the life of the pilgrim church. We are always reminded of the ways that he has shaped our academic vocations: through scholarly interests, selecting course readings for our own students, and even classroom mannerisms. We embody our gratitude as better theologians and better teachers because of his formation and friendship.

Derek C. Hatch & Timothy R. Gabrielli

Pentecost 2016

Introduction

DEREK C. HATCH AND
TIMOTHY R. GABRIELLI

If you really want to rankle Bill Portier, float the assertion that a theological focus on American Catholicism is "narrow." Or, better, that the American Catholic Church did not make any real contributions to theology in the nineteenth century and the first decades of the twentieth century. As more than one colleague or graduate student who has traveled down that path with Portier can surely attest, the result is an earful. This is because Portier has a spent a career taking seriously his location as an American Catholic theologian, convinced that all theology is woven within a cultural context. Thus Rahner's theology is as much about post-World-War-II Germany and Schillebeeckx's is as much about the Netherlands in the middle of the twentieth century, as John Courtney Murray's is about the U.S. in the Cold War era. However, because U.S. Catholic theology underwent extensive "colonization" by its European counterpart in the decades following the Second Vatican Council, we tend to forget that beyond Murray stands a host of bearers of the Catholic theological tradition in America.[6]

By 1987, Portier was convinced that, in his words, "I am by training and deep conviction an *historical* theologian (can there really be any other kind?), I assume that one's religious thought is intimately related to one's religious life and is best interpreted faithfully when placed in its concrete historical setting."[7] To do American Catholic theology is to work to under-

6. Portier, *Divided Friends*, 326.
7. Portier, "John R. Slattery (1851–1926), Missionary and Modernist," 9.

stand our forbearers and, for that matter, our contemporaries in the U.S. Catholic Church who have lived, prayed, and thought through being Catholic in this cultural-national matrix, *mutatis mutandis*, and so to understand something about God. And since at bottom, theology is "a more or less disciplined form of reflection on the Christian life,"[8] this work to grasp, to know, to commune is always located, never disembodied.

To take seriously one's location as an American Catholic theologian involves a kind of *ressourcement*, a return to the oft-overlooked theological contributions by American Catholics throughout the history of the United States. Before Murray there were Hecker and Brownson, McSorley and Slattery, Gigot and Driscoll, Rudd, Day, Michel, Falls, de Hueck, Furfey, and many others. If these figures are not often seen as key resources for American Catholic theology, it is because our approach to theology remains too narrow. Many American Catholic thinkers of the nineteenth century fit the mold of the patristic pastor-scholar, addressing questions ad hoc in a land where Catholic universities had yet to be established. Therefore, they were not considered worthy contributors to theological discourse in the European university-centered model. Then, between 1910 and 1965, "one theological school, modern neo-Scholasticism (or manual Thomism) with its center in Rome, came perilously close to being identified with the faith."[9] The exclusive reign of neo-scholasticism meant that creative thinkers often inhabited places and realms of discourse not strictly dubbed "theological." While certain contemporary scholars yearn for the ostensible stability and unquestionable clarity that this theological narrowing enabled,[10] it undoubtedly marginalized other Catholic theological voices that in many cases were life-giving for the mystical body of Christ.

Portier's historical-theological project, so ably explicated by William Collinge in the opening essay of this volume, is one of faithfully bearing "the burden of the dead" in order to illuminate our present.[11] Neo-scholasticism responded to, among other intellectual and cultural developments, the fear of relativism incited by the advent of critical history. This is a legitimate and real fear. However, the *ressourcement* response (and here we include the European early-twentieth-century movement typically so named, but also U.S. Catholic theology like Portier's) gives voice to those who have suffered and whose lives bear witness to our inability to remain neutral (methodological-

8. Portier, *Tradition and Incarnation*, 148.

9. Portier, *Divided Friends*, 368.

10. Portier, "Thomist Resurgence."

11. For an overview and examination of how Portier understands "the burden of the dead," see *Divided Friends*, Chapter 3.

ly or otherwise). As Portier wrote in 1987, "The most rhetorically persuasive arguments against historical relativism as a theoretical position are ethical ones addressed to us in our neutrality by mice who have elephants standing on their tails."[12] Beyond describing the contours of the elephant or the plight of the mouse, U.S. Catholic theology à la Portier seeks to find a religiously usable past for both sustenance and critique in the present.

"There is no separation of Church and baseball," concludes James T. Fisher, upon reflection on his rebellious childhood in which he exchanged devotion to Roberto Clemente at the Forbes Field sanctuary for his Catholic upbringing.[13] As Fisher grew, he observed sprawling Eucharistic congresses celebrated on the Pirates' diamond, which reminded him that American Catholic urban, ethnic identity was lived in and through cultural incarnations such as baseball. Therefore, a good measure of the embodied task of American Catholic theology involves sorting through mediation as inculturation. In other words, that "concrete historical setting," cited by Portier, mediates God to us, sometimes in surprising ways. For Portier, insights flow freely from Bob Dylan and Bruce Springsteen as from the baseball diamond. In light of the Incarnation, how could it be otherwise? Nevertheless, imperial domination calls for rebuke wherever it rears its ugly head.[14] The church works in and through its setting, undertaking the hard work of inculturation: seeking the *logos*, as did St. Paul in Athens, while discerning elements that must be rejected, as did the apostle in Corinth or Philippi.

In the esteemed tradition of the Festschrift, this volume is a tribute to Portier's work in its theological depth and range. Yet, from its inception we have been concerned to lightly shape it as a suitable introduction to the study of American Catholicism at the advanced undergraduate or graduate levels. As such, students of Catholic theology, American Catholic studies, and even American religious history will find its essays of interest. Rather than creating hard divisions between areas of study, this volume, following Portier's vision, sees history, theology, biblical interpretation, and cultural studies as fields that are not wholly separated from one another. Not entirely different from the medieval emphasis on theology as the queen of the sciences, these disciplines exist in a mutually beneficial and illuminating relationship. When woven together, a greater whole emerges. Like the tattooed circus performer in Flannery O'Connor's short story, "Parker's Back," the result is not a haphazard patchwork of events, people, and their voices,

---

12. Portier, "John R. Slattery (1851–1926), Missionary and Modernist," 10.

13. Fisher, "Seeking a Way Home."

14. See Portier, "Heartfelt Grief." On "inculturation" in the U.S. context see Portier, "Americanism and Inculturation."

but instead, "one intricate arabesque of colors."[15] Scripture, tradition, reason, and experience become not unlike the warp and woof of the tapestry, interwoven and inseparable from one another. This volume, then, reflects that interdisciplinary approach, which illuminates the tapestry of American Catholicism in its multifaceted character. Not only does it tell the story of American Catholicism, but it also reflects on, contends with, and extends the work of Bill Portier.

After Collinge's opening essay, the rest of the volume is divided into three major sections, each with a diverse array of essays. These sections provide a set of handles for understanding and discussing American Catholic life and thought. While they are certainly not mutually exclusive, they do approach the subject from three distinct perspectives. It is also notable that they figure prominently in Portier's work.

The first major section, "Reflecting on the Word of God," centers on the ways in which the rise of biblical studies, and the discussions found within that field, have shaped American Catholicism. Anathea Portier-Young offers reflections on the nature of wisdom from the Old Testament, noting how treatments of the modernist crisis in American Catholicism might be affected by such insights and how Portier's work as a whole attends to the importance of the search for wisdom. Jeffrey Morrow outlines the history of Catholic interaction with historical-critical biblical scholarship from the late-nineteenth century to the present. As this history unfolds, he argues that the groundwork has been laid for the future development of an "evangelical Catholic biblical scholarship." Patricia McDonald, while also concerned with the state of biblical scholarship under the conditions of the modernist crisis, focuses her attention on the work and enduring relevance of Francis Gigot, a Sulpician who embraced critical study of Scripture during this time.

The second major section, "Inculturating the Catholic Tradition," offers a larger set of essays aimed at exploring the ways in which Catholic thought has taken shape in the American context. Andrew Black engages questions of sanctity and catholicity within American Catholicism by way of the life of Orestes Brownson and the popular *All Saints* collection compiled by Robert Ellsberg, inquiring whether there can be any joining of these two disparate voices. David O'Brien revisits his 2005 Marianist Award lecture concerning the trajectory of Catholic Americanism. In dialogue with Portier's work on "evangelical Catholics," he calls for a "renewed Americanism" in both theory and practice. C.J.T. Talar's essay examines the early life of Abbé Félix Klein, detailing how this French priest stands at the center of a crisis across

15. O'Connor, "Parker's Back," 514.

the Atlantic Ocean, especially his contributions to the "phantom heresy" historiography of Americanism. Michael Lombardo outlines the contours of the "Italian Problem" that stemmed from the increase in Italian immigration to the U.S. at the turn of the twentieth century, noting its significance for studying American Catholicism. Benjamin Peters discusses Catholic voices in favor of conscientious objection and how American Catholicism has received these voices, especially after the Second World War. After providing this historical and theological overview, he offers some insights concerning the present and future state of Catholic radicalism. Susan Sack's essay considers the American reception of the work of Pierre Teilhard de Chardin, noting both its convergence with the optimism of the 1960s and its divergence with that optimism when the events of the decade grew much more alarming.

The third major section, "Exploring Faith and Reason in the Body Politic," consists of four essays echoing Portier's perspective that neither faith nor reason exist in a vacuum. Thus, their intersection is always both political and theological. Damian Costello discusses the *Requerimiento*, a text read by Spanish conquistadors who arrived in the New World. As Costello details, while this text may initially seem to underwrite an ecclesial sanction of royal expansion, it actually provides a significant theological and political service to the Spanish crown rather than to the church. Derek Hatch examines the legacy of American Jesuit John Courtney Murray since his death in 1967. Mapping Murray onto two prevalent ideologies of contemporary American Catholic life, he finds these "two Murrays" to be largely unhelpful. Turning to French philosopher Maurice Blondel, Murray's full legacy and an alternative trajectory for American Catholicism emerges. Matthew Shadle focuses on the role of Catholic social teaching in the American political landscape. He notes that the common appeal to "public reason" requires attention to historically contingent concerns, a task that is increasingly difficult in our time. Michael Baxter offers an essay that extends from his earlier piece, "Writing History in a World Without Ends," which discussed American Catholic historiography in absence of a shared teleology. While the first essay critiqued the prevalent account of the story of American Catholicism, this essay gestures toward what a history of American Catholicism might look like if final ends are in view.

The volume concludes with a treatment of Paulist Joseph McSorley's writings on prayer by Sandra Yocum. While this concluding essay may seem strangely located, it in fact sews up the entire volume with a central concern of Portier's life—that the story of American Catholicism is not one merely of self-described Catholics in a land called America. Instead, it is about the pursuit of holiness within the ever-shifting landscape of the

United States. Because his pursuit of holiness and historical scholarship guided him through the modernist crisis, McSorley emerges as the hero of Portier's magnum opus *Divided Friends*. Yocum's essay, with its focus on prayer, charts a path forward in both theology and sanctity for Portier's fellow travelers and this volume's readers.

It is only fitting that a volume in honor of Portier, who has spent the last thirteen years at the University of Dayton forming the next generation of theologians in American Catholic life and thought, be suited for the classroom. Undoubtedly instructors will find the most effective ways to make use of the volume in their courses. They will find some essays that take in-depth looks at moments or figures germane to the study of American Catholic history (e.g., those by McDonald, Talar, and Costello), some essays that take a thematic approach (e.g., those by Morrow, O'Brien, and Shadle), and others that explore creative intersections in the American Catholic context (e.g., those by Black, Lombardo, and Baxter). Collectively, the essays represent an introduction to major themes, figures, and methods in American Catholic historical theology. Each essay could be used as a launching pad for further research into the particular topic and its surrounding issues and questions, or as an entryway into the thematic questions of the relationship between theology and history.

It is with great joy that we offer these essays written in Bill's honor. Portier's dedication to the constructive retrieval of American Catholic sources has done a great service to the church. Readers will observe that the research in this volume is deeply indebted to his gift.

Searching for the *Logos* in America

William L. Portier as Historical Theologian

William J. Collinge

The Making of an Historical Theologian

"When people ask me if I'm an historian or a theologian," William L. Portier wrote in 2005, "I usually say that I'm an historical theologian and then ask, Can there be any other kind?"[1] Two autobiographical narratives Portier published that year tell in brief how he arrived at this point.[2] In 1960 he entered the Missionary Servants of the Most Holy Trinity, passing through high school seminary and college seminary in years that straddled Vatican II. Little theology was then taught to high school and minor seminarians; one "got to" theology on the graduate level, after two years of philosophy. Such theology as existed was in the mold of the neo-scholasticism of the period after *Pascendi Dominici Gregis*, the 1907 encyclical that condemned "Modernism." This theology was defiantly anti-historical, presenting itself as based on timeless principles of epistemology and metaphysics.

When his class did get to theology, it was 1968. Portier's professors were, he says, "all keen on what German philosophers called 'historicity'"[3]

---

1. Portier, "From Historicity to History," 70.
2. Ibid. and Portier, "Confessions of a Fractured Catholic Theologian."
3. Portier, "From Historicity to History," 65.

and Bernard Lonergan called "historical-mindedness," the recognition that terms and propositions must be understood against the background of the thought-frameworks and practices of their time period and that something like an act of translation is required in order to incorporate them into our own frameworks or to reject them as untrue. The question of historicity was a specific form of a yet broader theological question: "A signature focus of our generation has been on the subjective conditions of believing, the subjective and historical mediations of religious truth."[4]

The trouble was that "between 1968 and 1980, Catholic theology in North America was awash in a sea of Europeans."[5] Karl Rahner, Yves Congar, and Edward Schillebeeckx were not themselves sufficiently articulate about the way their theologies reflected the conditions of postwar Germany, France, and the Netherlands, respectively. And, in the hands of American Catholic theologians of the time, their world became simply the "modern world," in which supposedly we all live.[6]

"One day," at the University of Toronto in the 1970s, Portier says, "while reading Isaac Hecker for a paper on 'Americanism' it hit me that 'U.S.' and 'Catholic' defined the particular forms and terms in which I had and would come to know God. U.S. Catholicism was the site, the location or standpoint, from which I would think theologically."[7] But this insight itself had a context. Portier had already written a master's thesis on Black Theology, with the title "An Examination of the Contemporary Theological Task: Toward a Suitable Method for a Specifically American Theology," focusing on James Cone. He had also heard the lectures of Hans-Georg Gadamer at The Catholic University of America and had taken to heart his tradition-based epistemology, which held that meaning and truth emerge within inherited traditions of thought and practice and must be understood in their context.

Toronto supplied two remaining missing pieces. One was American Catholic history. That paper on Americanism led to Portier's dissertation, "Providential Nation: An Historical-Theological Study of Isaac Hecker's 'Americanism,'" completed in 1980 under the supervision of Harry McSorley.[8] And a seminar by Daniel Donovan on the Modernist crisis opened the line of research that has led Portier to *Divided Friends: Portraits of the Roman Catholic Modernist Crisis in the United States*.

---

4. Portier, *Divided Friends*, 13.

5. Portier, "Confessions," 121. The Canadian Lonergan, who taught in Rome for much of his career, was only a partial exception.

6. Portier, "From Historicity to History," 66.

7. Portier, "Confessions," 121.

8. Portier, "Providential Nation."

Foundational and Doctrinal Theology

Theology as Contextual

The other missing piece was the critical Marxist theory of the Frankfurt School, which Portier encountered in classes taught by Gregory Baum and which he appropriated largely through its use in the work of Edward Schillebeeckx. To the hermeneutics of philosophers such as Gadamer, critical theory adds the insight "that the interpretation of any tradition likely involves systematic distortions of communication in the interests of those who have power and privilege."[9] For Schillebeeckx, "This means that faithful interpretation becomes, in significant measure, a function of ethical and political commitment to act in a way that will minimize systemic distortion."[10] Any thinker who assumes the permanent validity of the present socio-political order or the prevailing idea of the demands of reason does so at the cost of those who have suffered and died needlessly for that order and those demands.[11] Schillebeeckx provides a model of the sort of contextual theology that Portier wishes to pursue:

> Contextual theologians in Europe and North America give critical attention to the relationship of theological ideas to the particular situatedness of theologians as embodied persons in social and economic settings in particular cultures and places at particular times. The voices and experiences of those who suffer unjustly in and from such concrete settings provide theologians with an epistemological corrective for their own points of view as creatures of the modern West.[12]

Contextual theologies give a new shape to classical problems such as the relation of faith and reason and of grace and nature. Reason is no longer understood in an eighteenth-century Enlightenment manner—carried over into the neo-scholasticism of the nineteenth and twentieth centuries—as a matter of invariant structures that can adjudicate what is or is not meaningful and true. Instead, reason itself, though it includes invariant structures, has a history, or histories, and incorporates local forms of common sense. Moreover, the Frankfurt school reminds us that what is considered to be reasonable in a given time and place may well reflect distorted power relationships and be in need of criticism in that respect. On the other hand,

9. Portier, "Interpretation and Method," 26.

10. Ibid., 27.

11. Ibid., 31.

12. Portier, "Mysticism and Politics and Integral Salvation," 258.

since revelation has entered history, the history of reason can be expected to reflect the presence of revelation, in some sense enlightening and elevating reason, as Thomas Aquinas said. If you substitute "nature" for "reason" and "grace" for "revelation," all the above still holds. The theological anthropology that largely replaced neo-scholasticism in Catholic theology, taking the "subjective turn" and beginning from the human person as the recipient of grace and the hearer of the Word, tended, despite its awareness of historicity, toward an abstract idea of "modern man" or the "modern world" that obscured its home in postwar Western Europe. In particular, missing from most accounts of reason and nature was the role of politics.

Tradition

Portier's one book-length treatment of foundational and doctrinal theology, *Tradition and Incarnation*, shows his contextual approach at work: "If it is true that inquirers always ask questions out of a tradition, then their inquiries will always be perspectival, i.e., located somewhere. Further, if understanding is indeed contextual, then the absolutely objective, neutral observer is not only illusory but represents a fundamental misunderstanding about inquiry."[13] *Tradition and Incarnation* presents itself as a textbook in theology, complete with a claim (to seduce the unwary) that its fourteen chapters match the fourteen weeks of a typical semester. But it is a textbook in somewhat the way that Vladimir Nabokov's *Pale Fire* is a poem and commentary. It is in fact a theological argument, even an apologetic argument, for the reasonableness of Catholic faith in the contemporary American academy. Elsewhere, I have spoken of it as an exercise in inculturation,[14] in Pope John Paul II's sense, of a presentation of the Christian message in a way that is intelligible within a culture and a challenge to that culture from the standpoint of Christian revelation. Here the culture is that of the American academy and, more broadly, the contemporary American society from which our students hail. Portier stands consciously within two traditions, captured by John Drummond in the image of Pittsburgh.[15] The contemporary American Catholic theologian stands in the Ohio, downstream from Point Park, where the Allegheny of the Catholic religious tradition flows into the Monongahela of the academic tradition, with its mountain sources in the Greeks and the Enlightenment.

13. Portier, *Tradition and Incarnation*, 5.

14. Collinge, Review of *Tradition and Incarnation*, 78.

15. Drummond, "Downstream from Pittsburgh." He is referring to modern Catholic colleges and universities, not specifically to theologians.

Portier uses a Gadamerian notion of tradition to argue for the legitimacy of theology within the academy. Following Gadamer, he argues that all claims to truth make sense only within traditions. An epigraph from Gadamer highlights the Enlightenment's "prejudice against prejudice itself," and Portier goes on to argue that the Enlightenment ideal of the solitary, disengaged inquirer is a fiction, though sometimes a useful fiction. In fact, the relevant contrast is between those who are aware of the influence of tradition, as Catholic theologians are, and those who are not.[16] The Gadamerian argument is something like the positive moment of inculturation, presenting Christian theology as a legitimate humanities discipline, "part of the conversation among the humanities and sciences."[17] The negative moment comes when Portier challenges assumptions prevalent in the academy, both methodological, in regard, for instance, to its dismissal of tradition, and substantive, in regard to such issues as its rejection of the possibility of miracles.[18]

It would be a mistake to think that Portier simply takes Gadamer and applies his idea of tradition to Catholic theology as an instance.[19] It is characteristic of Portier's thought to deny that you have to get your philosophy right before you can do theology. That was the error of the neo-scholastics, who attempted an autonomous philosophy based upon a complete and unchanging "pure nature," unaffected by history and the presence of grace in history. Philosophy can help us understand and explain the theological idea of tradition, but the theological idea stands on its own, normed ultimately by the revelation it transmits.

One component of the Catholic tradition is the authority of popes and bishops: "Catholic theologians remain committed to the teaching office (*magisterium*) of the church in its episcopal, conciliar, and papal forms. They hold that this teaching office originates in the apostolic tradition, along with the scriptures, and that it has the trust of interpreting the word of God for the sake of the church's unity in faith."[20] This point is not prominent in *Tradition and Incarnation*, but it is central to Portier's view of theology as an activity within an ecclesial tradition. He develops it most fully in a 1982 article, "Theology and Authority," responding to David Tracy's *The Analogical Imagination*. In this article the argument is hypothetical, couched

---

16. See, for instance, *Tradition and Incarnation*, 168.

17. Ibid., 2.

18. Ibid., 305–25.

19. Portier, Review of *Inventing Catholic Tradition*. In this review, Portier criticizes Tilley for doing something like this (though not with Gadamer).

20. Portier, *Tradition and Incarnation*, 143.

in terms of questions and possibilities, but there is little doubt it is Portier's own. If, as Catholic tradition and Portier assert, church authorities have "a mission from Jesus Christ to teach in his name,"[21] it is in principle possible for them to intervene in theological disputes not simply to contribute to the ongoing conversation but to close off discussion, reject a position as unacceptable, or something similar. Tracy appears to hold that "if carried on with intelligence and integrity," with sufficient attention to a range of points of view, theology "will correct itself and arrive at relatively adequate interpretation" of classic texts and other sources.[22] Church authorities should sit on the sidelines while academic debate converges on truth and dismisses error. Tracy's position has affinities with a prevalent view in the modern academy: "From the modern point of view, actions of church authorities such as those described above appear as invasions of privacy which interfere with freedoms of inquiry and religion which are basic to the Enlightenment heritage."[23] But if church authorities have a mission from Jesus to teach in his name, then "exercises of ecclesiastical authority in regard to theological opinion cannot be dismissed *a priori* as unwarranted interference in the integrity of the academic progress."[24] This does not mean that such interventions are always timely, fair, or accurate. As will be clear from this essay, "timely," "fair," and "accurate" are not terms by which Portier would characterize *Testem Benevolentiae* or *Pascendi Dominici Gregis*. But ecclesiastical interventions cannot be ruled out in principle as foreign to the practice of theology in the academy. This position underlies Portier's defense of the requirement, imposed by Pope John Paul II's apostolic constitution *Ex Corde Ecclesiae* (1990), that Catholics teaching theology in a Catholic university obtain a *mandatum* (authorization) from the local bishop.[25]

Incarnation: Jesus-Flavored Ice Cream

The "Incarnation" half of *Tradition and Incarnation* is subtitled "Jesus as the Heart of Theology." Although there is much philosophy in the first half of the book, Portier takes seriously the idea that theology starts with Christian revelation, and that Christian revelation is centered in Jesus Christ. "In Jesus' life and teaching . . . we find God revealed. We find what God has to say

21. "Theology and Authority," 595.

22. Ibid., 594.

23. Ibid., 596.

24. Ibid., 606. In quoting, I changed the modality of this sentence. Portier expresses it as a possibility, but the burden of his argument is that it is, in fact, the case.

25. See, for instance, "Reason's 'Rightful Autonomy.'"

to us . . . Jesus' revelation of the Father is not just in his teaching but in his very being, in everything he says and does."[26] When we think of incarnation, of God made human, we must let Jesus be the norm for our ideas of divinity and humanity: "In order to believe in the incarnation, we must allow it to reshape our ideas of what God is and what a human being is."[27] Thus, the book begins with a chapter on the "Great Questions," questions which students of any, or no, religious persuasion can be brought to raise about their lives, but it concludes with a section on how the resurrection of Jesus not only answers our great questions but challenges our typical hopes for what the answers will be.

How do we know Jesus? Portier does not attempt to get behind scripture to the "historical Jesus" or to go straight to the Gospels. Ultimately, we know Jesus through tradition, a tradition which incorporates the memory of the Christian community, including its written scriptures, and which can be developed and enriched through modern scholarship. The second half of the book begins not with scripture or scholarship but with the great creedal and doctrinal statements of the councils of Nicaea I, Constantinople I, Ephesus, and Chalcedon, which are central to church tradition. In turn, Portier begins his account of academic Gospel scholarship by situating it in academic traditions originating in the Enlightenment. His hope—his Pittsburgh, Drummond might say—is to produce a "historical-theological portrait of Jesus" that achieves four goals:

> (1) to take seriously modern suspicions about the historical reliability of the New Testament sources; (2) to interpret the sources in a way that is both historically plausible and defensible, as well as; (3) compatible with the traditional expressions of the church's faith about Jesus; (4) to present a religiously compelling portrait of Jesus capable of functioning religiously in the lives of contemporary people.[28]

Portier's Christocentrism becomes yet more prominent in his work after *Tradition and Incarnation*. A portion of a 2012 article traces Portier's growing estrangement from Schillebeeckx in favor of Henri de Lubac, whom he elsewhere calls "the pivotal figure in twentieth-century Catholic theology."[29] The issue is the idea of a "world of grace," a commonplace in

---

26. Portier, *Tradition and Incarnation*, 82–83.

27. Ibid., 201.

28. Ibid., 249–50. These goals are presented as the goals of chapter 11, but really they are goals of chapters 11–14, his entire treatment of the biblical picture of Jesus.

29. Portier, "Twentieth-Century Catholic Theology and the Triumph of Maurice Blondel," 105.

theology after Vatican II. "At stake is the centrality of Christ and whether Christ is indeed the 'prime analogate,' as it were, for a sacramental or incarnational understanding of the world as graced. How should we understand the senses in which the 'world' is graced? In Susan Wood's summary, at issue between de Lubac and Schillebeeckx is how grace is present in the world: 'within the temporal order by creation or through the Christ event mediated through the Church sacramentally.'"[30] Despite the centrality of Christ to Schillebeeckx, as shown in his massive volumes *Jesus* and *Christ*, his thought, Portier says, shows "a certain tendency to displace Christ" in favor of creation and history.[31] With de Lubac, Portier takes his stand in the Christocentrism of section 22 of *Gaudium et Spes*, summed up in the opening line of Pope John Paul II's first encyclical, *Redemptor Hominis* (1979): "The Redeemer of man, Jesus Christ, is the center of the universe and of history."[32] He expresses his position in a memorable image:

> The phrase "nature and grace" is misleading from the start because it tends to suggest that we begin with two externally related realities that we must then connect. In my attempts to teach this piece of theology to twenty-year-olds, I have come upon a crude analogy . . . To clarify the significance of a modern theology of nature and grace, I compare a relatively autonomous nature or reason to vanilla ice cream. The Christian life adds chocolate Jesus sprinkles to the vanilla ice cream, or, in the cases of really holy people, chocolate Jesus syrup . . . Recovering the Augustinian dimension of St. Thomas, proponents of the so-called *nouvelle théologie* [such as de Lubac] tended to think of grace as *transforming* nature rather than being superadded to it. Similarly, St. Thomas thought that reason could be transformed by the light of faith or the light of glory. Rather than vanilla ice cream with chocolate Jesus sprinkles, then, we would have Jesus-flavored ice cream.[33]

30. Portier, "What Kind of a World of Grace?" 143–44.

31. Ibid., 145.

32. Pope John Paul II, *Redemptor Hominis* §1. In a paper, "Jesus and the World of Grace, 1968–2014," presented at the 2014 annual convention of the Catholic Theological Society of America, Portier looks to the New Testament Christological hymns for a way forward: "A strong contextual reading of the New Testament hymns to Christ connecting him to creation and the cosmos brings together the orders of creation and redemption, relating creation to the Christ-event in its fullness."

33. Portier, "Adam Smith with Jesus Sprinkles."

American Catholic Theology, Catholic Theology of America

Henri de Lubac and his colleagues in the *nouvelle théologie* movement of the 1930s and 1940s understood themselves to be engaging in a process of *ressourcement*, "retrieving the sources," going back to the styles of thought and practice found in the Bible, the ancient and early-medieval Christian writers, and the early liturgical tradition. Portier understands his research in American Catholic theology in a similar way. He is not simply adding to the historical record but engaging with thinkers of the past in order to do historically minded theology in the present.[34] In Portier's project, America is not only the location of the theology to be recovered, but also to a significant degree its subject. What is "the religious significance of the American reality"?[35] How should American Catholics interpret and evaluate their distinctive national traditions?

Isaac Hecker

Portier's project begins with Isaac Hecker (1819–1888), the subject of his 1980 doctoral dissertation, a man whom the *Atlantic* described in 1864 as "preparing the ancient ark of the Catholic Church for conversion to steam power."[36] Originally a Methodist, Hecker undertook a spiritual quest that led through New England Transcendentalism and the Brook Farm community to entry into the Catholic Church in 1844. Ordained a Redemptorist priest, he left the Redemptorists to found the Missionary Society of St. Paul the Apostle, known as the Paulists, in 1858, the aim of which was the evangelization of the United States. Under the initial influence of Orestes Brownson, Hecker developed the idea, dating from the Puritans and widespread in American Protestantism at the time, of the United States as having a God-given messianic mission to the world. In Hecker's version, America was destined by God to be converted to Catholicism and to be God's agent for the conversion of Europe, even the whole world. The Paulists would play a central role in this process.[37]

Serious engagement with Hecker's ideas by theologians, however, was impeded by their association with the "Americanism" censured by Pope Leo XIII in the letter *Testem Benevolentiae* in 1899. The relation of Hecker to *Testem Benevolentiae* is complicated, as Hecker's thought was refracted

34. Portier, "Catholic Theology in the United States, 1840–1907," 318, 331.

35. Portier, "Americanism," 55.

36. Quoted in Portier, *Isaac Hecker*, 3.

37. Ibid., 84–94.

after his death, first through the leading "Americanists," Archbishop John Ireland, Bishop John J. Keane, and then Monsignor (later Bishop) Denis O'Connell; then through the Americanists' disciples in France; and finally through *Testem Benevolentiae* itself. The writing and speeches of the Americanists, Portier says, "reveal a characteristic ideology of near-mythic proportions. The world had entered upon a new democratic age. The U.S., with its institution of separation of church and state, embodied the spirit of the new age . . . To American Catholicism fell the messianic mission of leading the Catholic Church into the new age. With the adoption of this world view, the Americanists had bought uncritically into the ambivalent Puritan idea of American election."[38]

Hecker became the center of controversy when the Paulist Walter Elliott's *Life of Father Hecker* (1891) was translated into French and published in 1897 with an enthusiastically Americanist preface by Abbé Félix Klein. This sparked *Etudes sur l'Américanisme: Le Père Hecker, est-il un saint?* an "often tastelessly overstated negative reply" by Charles Maignen, a French monarchist hostile to the political liberalism of the Americanists.[39] Maignen conducted "a vehement attack on the persons and ideas of Keane, Ireland, and [James Cardinal] Gibbons,"[40] melding them into the figure of Hecker. Maignen's attack informed the understanding of Americanism held by the neo-scholastic authors of *Testem Benevolentiae*, which "condemned[41] the notion that the church should adapt to the age in essentials, and, more specifically, that the church should imitate contemporary states by introducing greater individual liberty."[42] Some purported consequences regarding the church and the relation of nature and grace were then censured. In concluding, Pope Leo, adopting a distinction from O'Connell, acknowledged the legitimacy of political Americanism, distinguishing it from theological Americanism. This last distinction was exploited by Klein and others to argue that Americanism was, in Klein's term, a "phantom heresy" that existed only in the minds of its opponents. No one in the United States really held the censured opinions, they said. Rather, Hecker and his followers were dedicated to the political institutions of the United States and to the concrete shape of American Catholicism. They were not theologians at all.

---

38. Portier, "Americanism," 54.

39. Portier, "Isaac Hecker and *Testem Benevolentiae*," 21.

40. Portier, "Americanism," 55.

41. A rare use of "condemned" in this context. Portier almost always prefers "censured."

42. Portier, "Americanism," 53.

To retrieve Hecker's theology, therefore, Portier must disentangle it from its representations by (1) the Americanists, (2) *Testem Benevolentiae*, and (3) the "phantom heresy" historians. He argues in his dissertation[43] that *Testem Benevolentiae* and Hecker were working from different theological frameworks, those of neo-scholastic theology and American empirical theology, respectively. He argues that the statements of Hecker and of *Testem* are not directly in contradiction with each other, but also not isolated from one another in their separate theological frameworks. Rather, it requires a complicated hermeneutical process in order to bring them into relation with each other. Perhaps the central insight is that when *Testem* speaks of nature and grace, it has in mind the neo-scholastic *natura pura*, abstractly conceived apart from all influence of grace, while Hecker is speaking of concrete persons acting in a history that is already shaped by the presence of grace. "Hecker did not regard the founders or the inheritors of American republicanism as purely or merely natural men and women."[44] God's Holy Spirit was working through them. The thesis of Portier's dissertation is that Hecker's "view of 'America' as a 'providential nation' . . . provides the theological basis for his religious affirmation of the American fact."[45]

Portier treats Hecker's thought as an early form of historically minded theology, sensitive to its American context, though lacking the methodological sophistication of later efforts. It is influenced by American Protestantism and by Catholic Romantic theology in Europe, in particular by traditionalism, which meant something quite different in the nineteenth century from what it meant in the twentieth. Traditionalism posited a revelation of God to Adam and Noah and never altogether lost by their descendants. Moreover, God's providence never ceased to govern human history, and for centuries God educated humans through the church. Thus, for Hecker, "the legitimate aspirations of the age toward liberty have been inspired by centuries of education in the school of Christianity."[46] And human beings, never entirely cut off from God's grace, are capable of self-government, contrary to what many nineteenth-century European Catholics were saying. "Hecker affirmed American civilization on theological grounds and emphasized individual liberty and self-reliance based on the authentically discerned impulses of the Holy Spirit."[47] Discernment is not limited to the spiritual life of the individual soul; it extends to history as well. A process of discern-

---

43. And in briefer form in "Isaac Hecker and *Testem Benevolentiae*."

44. Ibid., 30.

45. Ibid., 23 and 45 nn. 31–32.

46. Ibid., 31.

47. Ibid., 25.

ment, subordinate to the authority of the church as in the classic treatments of spiritual discernment, is required in order to identify the movements of God's Spirit in history.

This means that Hecker cannot uncritically affirm whatever happens in history as God's will. In particular, the prevailing American religious pluralism must yield to a conversion of the nation to Catholicism. "Hecker wanted to convert America to Catholicism because he thought that only Catholic theology and its view of human nature could ground, secure, and direct the individual liberties fostered by American political institutions."[48] As Hecker said, "Our people are young, fresh, and filled with the idea of great enterprises; the people, who, of all others, if once Catholic, can give a new, noble, and glorious realization to Christianity; a development which will go even beyond the past in achievements of zeal, in the abundance of saints, as well as in art, science and material greatness. The Catholic Church alone is able to give unity to a people, composed of such conflicting elements as ours, and to form them into a great nation."[49] This point illustrates the negative or critical side of inculturation as described, that is, the moment in which the gospel challenges the culture rather than adapting to it.

Americanism and Modernism: *Divided Friends*

Divided Friends (2013) is Portier's most substantial contribution to American Catholic history thus far. It is primarily a work of history, but at the same time it is "a theologian's narrative meditation on the relationship between theology and history."[50] It tells the stories of two pairs of divided friends, all priests: John R. Slattery (1851–1926) and Denis J. O'Connell (1849–1927), and William Laurence Sullivan (1872–1935) and Joseph McSorley (1874–1963). Slattery and Sullivan left the Catholic Church in the wake of the Modernist crisis, while O'Connell and McSorley remained. All were affected, in varying degrees, by the intellectual currents that gave rise to Americanism and by the legacy of Hecker.

Like "Americanism," the term "Modernism" was put into circulation by the Vatican's response. But unlike *Testem Benevolentiae*'s limited and cautious censure of Americanism, *Pascendi Dominici Gregis*, issued by Pope Pius X in 1907, knitted a disparate collection of theological ideas into "Modernism," a "synthesis of all heresies," and denounced it in apocalyptic terms. Prior to *Pascendi*, the theologians and scholars associated

48. Portier, "Inculturation as Transformation," 114.

49. Quoted in ibid., 116.

50. Portier, *Divided Friends*, 13.

with Modernism did not consider themselves part of a movement or call themselves "Modernists";[51] what they had in common was a desire to adapt Catholic thought to contemporary philosophical emphasis on subjective experience and to contemporary historical consciousness, especially modern biblical criticism and critical church history. All were critical of the neoscholasticism that was dominant in Rome.

Pascendi called for the establishment of "committees of vigilance" against suspected Modernists in every diocese. In a sort of autoimmune frenzy, they denounced one Catholic author and teacher after another—including at least two future popes—to Rome under suspicion of Modernism. Many lost academic and ecclesiastical appointments and suffered the ruin of their careers. From 1910 to 1967, priests, seminarians, and theology faculty were required to take an Oath against Modernism. Portier finds himself unable fully to account for the vehemence of the anti-Modernist reaction,[52] but he ascribes much of it to political concerns. "The connections between freedom in politics," demanded in modern liberalism, "and freedom in intellectual life," demanded by those associated with Modernism, "were clear to the Roman authorities," who understood, better than the Americanists, that "modern political freedoms tend to undermine . . . religious authorities."[53]

Divided Friends does not grapple in depth with the first-order theological issues raised by Modernism, the way Portier does with Americanism in his writings on that subject, but I think it argues three main theses *about* theology. First, clearing away the "phantom heresy" historiography (for which McSorley bears some responsibility)[54] enables us to see continuity between Americanism and "Modernism" in the United States, as theological efforts to address the issue of "how to conceive the presence and exercise of a spiritual power in a pluralist society."[55] The Americanists' efforts to transform Catholic thought through engagement with American culture created the institutional environments for a "theological effervescence"[56] between 1889 and 1907, in which critical biblical and historical scholarship, explorations of evolutionary theory and modern social sciences, and other elements of "modernism" could flourish. Chief among them was The

---

51. After *Pascendi*, Sullivan accepted the label, as did Alfred Loisy and George Tyrrell, the two leading European figures associated with Modernism.

52. Portier, *Divided Friends*, 48.

53. Ibid., 15.

54. Ibid., 24–26, 350–52.

55. Colin, *L'Audace et le soupçon*, 269, quoted in Portier, *Divided Friends*, 15, translated by Portier.

56. Portier, *Divided Friends*, 200.

Catholic University of America, founded in 1889, where both McSorley and Sullivan studied.

Second, *Pascendi*, though it had "a devastating impact on Catholic theology . . . in the United States,"[57] did not extinguish it. Between 1907 and 1962, academic theology, especially in seminaries, was confined to a rigid neo-scholasticism, but theological engagement with contemporary culture continued in at least three contexts: (1) the social sciences and social ethics; (2) Catholic medievalism and the Catholic Renaissance in philosophy, literature, history, and other fields; and (3) history and church history.[58] McSorley played a part in the first and third of these.

Third, recovery of American theology in the nineteenth and early-twentieth centuries may provide a better way forward for U.S. Catholic theologians than either "the massive European colonization of Catholic theology in the U.S. that followed in the wake of" Vatican II or today's attempts to engage with "local theologies in non-Western languages in which most U.S. Catholics have no competence."[59]

Perhaps we could add a fourth. McSorley emerges as the hero of the book. In his *The Sacrament of Duty* (1909), Portier finds a model for theologians in times of conflict with church authorities. The model consists of "holiness and history."[60] Study the history of the church, which tells us what has happened and what can happen; meanwhile, hold firmly to a center in prayer and sacramental practice, conduct apologetics by living the best Christian life one can, and remain faithful to the Holy Spirit, who guides both individual Christians and church authorities.

Americanism and the Americanist Tradition:
From Providential Nation to Evil Empire?

Portier's attitude toward Americanism has changed over the years. In a 1984 article, he depicts the Americanist episode of the nineteenth century as "a case study in the relationship between Catholicism and American culture."[61] He sets out three possible "myths" that can guide American Catholics' thoughts and actions on this question. According to the first, the "myth of the Catholic left [of the 1960s and 1970s], the nation 'America'

57. Ibid., 30.

58. Ibid., 325–46.

59. Ibid., 326, 13.

60. Ibid., 322. On McSorley, holiness, and history, see Sandra Yocum's essay, chapter 15 in this volume.

61. Portier, "The Future of 'Americanism,'" 49.

is the evil empire whose demonic power must be resisted at every turn by those who are true Christians."[62] The second myth continues the tradition of American messianism. It is characteristic of American neoconservatives, among whom Portier singles out Michael Novak, who "comes perilously close to erecting the obvious goods of the form of government of the United States into some form of religious absolute which we can use any means to defend."[63] The third is a "liberal" myth, which "appeals to the symbols of Enlightenment faith in reasoned public discourse as it comes to us from the founding fathers."[64] This myth, Portier holds, is complex enough to "have room for the prophetic witness who calls the nation to true repentance,"[65] and, with that proviso, Portier endorses it.

The icon of the liberal myth is John Courtney Murray (1904–1967), an American Jesuit whose *We Hold These Truths* (1960) argued that there was a basic fit between the Catholic natural law tradition and the fundamental principles of American political discourse, and whose defense of religious liberty was central to the Second Vatican Council's acceptance of it. Ideas such as these, which resemble those of Hecker and the nineteenth-century Americanists, led writers in the "public theology" debate of the 1980s to champion a Murray positioned within the "Americanist tradition."[66] In a series of articles beginning in 1993, Portier engages with Murray's thought in the context of rival claims about the Americanist tradition, and he moves from the liberal myth to a position closer to what in 1984 he had called the "myth of the Catholic left."[67]

In "Inculturation as Transformation: The Case of Americanism Revisited" (1993), of which Portier says "Murray is more the occasion than the subject,"[68] Portier begins to speak of Hecker and Americanism in terms of inculturation. Hecker and the Americanists of the nineteenth century emphasized both moments of inculturation, the drive to adapt the church and

62. Ibid.

63. Ibid., 50.

64. Ibid.

65. Ibid., 51.

66. According to Mary Doak, the proponents of public theology advocated that theology should do two or three things: (1) "address issues of society, politics, and culture theologically," (2) "articulate this theology in a manner accessible to a wider population," not a narrow church or academic audience, and (3), according to some theologians, do so in a manner "consistent with the demands of religious freedom in a pluralistic democracy" (Doak, "Table Fellowship," 202–3). The idea of situating Murray within the "Americanist tradition" originates with Pelotte, *John Courtney Murray*.

67. On Catholicism in the public square, see Matthew Shadle's essay, chapter 13 in this volume.

68. Portier, "Inculturation as Transformation," 109.

its message to American culture, and the need to challenge the culture from the standpoint of Christian faith. Late-twentieth-century writers on the Americanist tradition who lay claim to the legacy of Murray, exemplified by the liberal Dennis McCann and the neoconservative George Weigel,[69] appropriate the first, "accommodationist" aspect of the Americanist tradition but overlook its "transformationist" side.[70]

"Americanism and Inculturation: 1899–1999" (2000) sharpens Portier's argument that inculturation, rather than Americanism or Americanization, is the proper theological framework for understanding Catholicism in the United States. After reviewing contemporary treatments of "the Americanist tradition" and the "triumph of Americanism,"[71] Portier considers the possibility that "Americanism" might be an "*idea* in the sense that [John Henry] Newman describes in *An Essay on the Development of Christian Doctrine* (1845, 1878)," that is, a complex of ideas associated with a "leading idea" and subject to growth and development as well as to the risk of corruption.[72] "If there is an Americanist tradition," Portier says, "its leading idea is an unabashed sense of the true but yet to be fully realized fit between American institutions and a Catholic natural law world view."[73] But nineteenth-century Americanism and, still more, its putative twentieth-century descendants, tend toward an uncritical acceptance of American social, political, and economic structures. Portier cites David Schindler, who criticizes contemporary neoconservative Americanism as "a moral blank check written to the order of the United States of America,"[74] and Michael Baxter, who indicts the entire Americanist narrative as a story of "accommodation to un-Christian elements of the existing political and cultural order."[75] Baxter suggests "a counter-narrative from the perspective of what he calls Evangelical Catholicism," represented especially by Dorothy Day and the Catholic Worker movement.[76] Portier acknowledges a change in his own thinking: "John Courtney Murray and Dorothy Day have been arguing in

---

69. Portier's examples are McCann, *New Experiment in Democracy* and Weigel, *Catholicism and the Renewal of American Democracy*.

70. Portier, "Inculturation as Transformation," 112. On Murray and his American Catholic legacy, see Derek Hatch's essay, chapter 12 in this volume.

71. Portier cites R. Scott Appleby, "The Triumph of Americanism, Common Ground for U.S. Catholics in the Twentieth Century."

72. Portier, "Americanism and Inculturation," 151.

73. Ibid., 148.

74. Ibid., 150, referring to Schindler's "*Communio* Ecclesiology and Liberalism."

75. Ibid., quoting Baxter, "In Service to the Nation."

76. Portier, "Americanism and Inculturation," 150–51. For some preliminary notes on the shape of such a counter-narrative, see Baxter's essay, chapter 14 in this volume.

my head for many years. Day's voice grows louder now and the arguments of Schindler and Baxter sound increasingly convincing."[77] Later, however, in *Divided Friends,* Portier notes that the figure of Joseph McSorley, heir to the Americanists yet spiritual director to Dorothy Day and instrumental in the founding of the *Catholic Worker* newspaper, complicates the picture.[78]

Portier's advocacy of inculturation as an interpretive framework for U.S. Catholic history explicitly joins his historical work to the Christocentrism of his systematic theology. Inculturation, an idea based on the incarnation of the Word of God in Jesus, "privileges Christ."[79] Employing this theological category, "historians can both search for the 'seeds of the Word' in American culture and, at the same time, discern critically the forms of nationalism and individualism which might conceal them."[80] A narrative of U.S. Catholic history would then "have to include both the Americanists' transforming vision of their country's conversion and the conservative critique of the Americanists' culture capitulation. The voices of Dorothy Day and John Courtney Murray would both have to be heard, not in some final theoretical synthesis, but in serious searching for Christ the Logos hidden within our conflicted love for what we call freedom."[81]

In a 2006 article, Portier takes on Murray directly and, along with him, the "public theology" approach "for which Murray stands as symbolic inspiration or totem."[82] In *We Hold These Truths,* Murray interprets the First Amendment as "articles of peace" between the state and the churches, rather than as concealing a free church theology or a form of secularism. This enables him to argue that Catholics can embrace it wholeheartedly rather than grudgingly. American Catholics may therefore engage with "civility" in American political discourse. Reflecting the then-popular theme of "the end of ideology,"[83] Murray wrote, "In America, we have been rescued from the disaster of ideological parties." Americans, in his view, agreed on a "final view of man and society," while continuing to argue about means.[84] Portier refers to Murray's approach as a "theology of manners," but he holds that it "required that he practice simultaneously a theology of containment. A

77. Ibid., 155.

78. Portier, *Divided Friends*, 335.

79. Portier, "Americanism and Inculturation," 157.

80. Ibid., 158.

81. Ibid., 159.

82. Portier, "Theology of Manners as Theology of Containment," 84.

83. The title of a 1960 book by Daniel Bell.

84. Murray, *We Hold These Truths*, 82, quoted in Portier, "Theology of Manners as Theology of Containment," 90. The page references from *We Hold These Truths* are from the reprinted 2005 edition, and therefore differ from Portier's original citation.

Catholic embrace of the end of ideology required the suppression of Catholic voices who contested the postwar consensus."[85] Murray freely admitted that the United States was now, in the postwar period, an "imperialism."[86] Catholics, operating as public intellectuals, could employ natural law discourse to help it be a moral empire rather than an evil one. In this context, "It fell to Murray to discredit the voices who did not take postwar American empire for granted," notably Catholic pacifists such as Dorothy Day and Paul Hanly Furfey.[87]

Portier proceeds to examine Vatican II's Declaration on Religious Liberty, *Dignitatis Humanae* (1965), of which Murray, a theological *peritus* ("expert" or advisor) at the council, was a principal but not the only author. Portier supports Murray's, and the document's, affirmation of religious freedom but also accepts David Schindler's theological critique of Murray's natural law defense of it. Once again, the central issue is nature and grace. Schindler argues that Murray works from a nature-grace dualism like that of the neo-scholastics. In Portier's words, "The question is whether we are primitively open to God . . . or primitively indifferent to God such that we look pretty much the same whether our final end is added on or not."[88] According to Schindler, the latter is Murray's position, while the former is that of Henri de Lubac, which both Schindler and Portier regard as better suited to undergird a theology of the relation between the church and the state. In a concluding paragraph, Portier gives thanks "first to God the Holy Spirit and then to John Courtney Murray, S.J.,"[89] for *Dignitatis Humanae* and its promise "before the world" that the Catholic Church will not "use coercion to promote Jesus and his gospel."[90] He concludes, however, "It is time to listen to those silently corrected voices offering a more radical critique of our nation and our culture than Murray's example allows."[91]

During the time when Murray was articulating his principles for civil discourse, one of those "silently corrected voices," Dorothy Day, went to jail four times for antiwar protests. Her witness against war is a primary reason her voice has grown louder in Portier's head. Though he has written

---

85. Portier, "Theology of Manners as Theology of Containment," 95.

86. Murray, *We Hold These Truths*, 212, quoted in Portier, "Theology of Manners as Theology of Containment," 95.

87. Portier, "Theology of Manners as Theology of Containment," 96.

88. Ibid., 101.

89. Ibid., 105.

90. Ibid., 102.

91. Ibid., 105. On the importance of these voices for American Catholicism, see Benjamin Peters's essay, chapter 9 in this volume.

little on war,[92] Portier is a lifelong pacifist. His wife, Dr. Bonita Portier, traces his pacifism to the impact of World War II on his family.[93] Portier's father, a medic, witnessed great suffering and developed illnesses that led to partial disability; his father's brother, Roy, was killed; and other family members suffered at least at second hand. She thinks the experience led him to ask, "Who could kill another mother's child, another father's son?" or, I would add on the basis of his lectures and conversations, "Could Jesus or anyone who wishes to be like Jesus ever do such a thing?" William and Bonita Portier were active in demonstrations against the Vietnam War in the 1960s and 1970s, and against U.S. military actions in Central America in the 1980s; briefly, around 1971, they lived in the Dorothy Day Catholic Worker House in Rochester, New York. Though William Portier chose the path of scholarship over that of activism, a concern that the United States has become a permanent war state colors his treatment of the public role of its Catholic citizens.

In a symposium published in 2008, Portier responds to the question, "Can a Christian be a (devoted) citizen of the polis (even in a time of war)?"[94] He notes that the question reflects the Aristotelian ideal of civic discourse in a polis, an ideal of which Murray and the public theologians were fond. He acknowledges that Emmitsburg, Maryland, where he lives for part of every year, "is close to a polis." But "the United States is more like a Hobbesian Leviathan" or "an imperial plutocracy" "than an Aristotelian polis."[95] Elsewhere he responds to Lieven Boeve's defense of "correlationist" versus "anti-modern" theologies, including those of John Milbank and David Schindler, by siding with the anti-modernists. Portier surmises that he differs from Boeve not on matters of theological principle but on contingent "judgments about the particularities of our present time of upheaval."[96] "What, for example, am I as an American to make of the intrinsic connection between tradition and context if my context is an empire that makes war without end?"[97]

---

92. I am aware of two articles. "Are We Really Serious When We Ask God to Deliver Us from War?" (1996) argues that the division between just-war and pacifist approaches reflects theologies that separated nature and grace, and that in the concrete order just-war and pacifism may be converging. "If the pope has not said, 'Just War No More!' he has come very close" (62). "'Good Friday in December'" (2009) traces the opposition, on just-war grounds, of Joachim V. Benson, MSSsT, to U.S. entry into World War II.

93. Dr. Bonita J. Portier, e-mail message to author, 8 July 2014.

94. Portier, "Heartfelt Grief," 349.

95. Ibid., 353, 355. I have combined two similar statements into a single sentence.

96. Portier, "Does Systematic Theology Have a Future?," 147.

97. Ibid., 140.

Evangelical Catholicism

"Isaac Thomas Hecker was an evangelical Catholic," David O'Brien wrote in 1983.[98] In this respect, Portier thinks, Hecker points the way forward for American Catholics and American Catholic theologians.

"Evangelical Catholicism" is one of three styles that O'Brien identifies in Catholic public discourse in American society.[99] The others are the civil "republican" style, represented by the first Catholic bishop in the United States, John Carroll (1735–1815) and by John Courtney Murray, and the "immigrant" style, which challenges the dominant society from the margins, nourished by and defending an immigrant subculture.

The American Catholic immigrant subculture, which flourished in the first half of the twentieth century, came to an end at the time of, though mostly not because of, Vatican II. A system of schools and other institutions had cultivated a distinctive religious way of life, with shared symbols, practices, and patterns of thought. The best description of it of which I am aware appears in Richard Rodriguez's *Hunger of Memory*;[100] Rodriguez's Mexican-American West Coast religious formation differed only in minor details from Portier's Italian-American East Coast formation and my Irish- and German-flavored Midwestern formation. Today the decisive fact for American Catholicism is the collapse of the subculture, the victim of its own success. The Catholic schools of the subculture educated their pupils to succeed in American society, and as alumni they did succeed, moving to the suburbs and becoming demographically no different from other Americans.[101] But now American Catholics live within a "culture of religious pluralism in which diversity . . . is perceived as the normal and desirable state of things."[102] Rather than fostering religious discourse seeking consensus in the public square, as was Murray's ideal, it tends to exclude religion from public life and to confine it to a "private" sphere. Such conditions "tend to deform Christianity insofar as it is ecclesial and incarnate in a culture."[103]

In "Here Come the Evangelical Catholics," which has attracted more attention than anything else he has published, Portier argues that the

---

98. O'Brien, "An Evangelical Imperative," 90.

99. O'Brien, *Public Catholicism*, 242–52.

100. Rodriguez, *Hunger of Memory*, 75–110.

101. Portier, "Here Come the Evangelical Catholics," 46. The experience of Hispanic-American Catholics today is somewhat different; among them the "immigrant" style survives to a degree.

102. Machacek, "The Problem of Pluralism," 157–58, quoted in Portier, "Here Come the Evangelical Catholics," 62–63.

103. Portier, "Here Come the Evangelical Catholics," 42–43.

contemporary culture of pluralism has helped to give rise to "Evangelical Catholicism" among young people. An evangelical style is grounded in personal conversion and expresses itself in witness. It arises from "the plain desire to share the faith and the riches one has found in Jesus."[104] Evangelical Catholics are attracted to what is distinctively Catholic, such as the pope and eucharistic adoration, and are fond of displaying Catholic identity markers in public. Their religious identity is personally chosen or reaffirmed, not absorbed from a subculture. It sets them consciously apart from the culture around them. Portier finds this style not only in young Catholics but also in some older ones, such as Pope St. John Paul II. Portier also sees it developing in some movements in theology, for instance, the younger theologians in David Schindler's *Communio* circle and the Catholic graduate students of Stanley Hauerwas, among whom is Michael Baxter.

In 2003, Portier found an intellectual home in the doctoral program in theology at the University of Dayton, with its focus on the U.S. Catholic experience. There he works to educate a new generation of Catholic theologians to be Christ-centered and evangelical, ecclesial rather than individualistic. They are to be grounded in the Catholic and American traditions while critically aware of the limitations of these traditions and the distortions borne by them, and to do theology in dialogue with Catholicism around the globe and with other Christians, American evangelical Protestants in particular. It is a generation that can find its models in Isaac Hecker and William L. Portier.

104. Portier, "Jesus 2000!"

Part 1

Reflecting on the Word of God

2

The Search for Wisdom

ANATHEA PORTIER-YOUNG

In 1971, my father, William Portier, wrote "Epithalamium" for his soon-to-be-bride, Bonita Krempel. He sang this song for her at their wedding, and he later sang it at the weddings of his three children:

> Come minstrels from the cities deep
> With songs from every side,
> And harlequins from underneath
> The faces where you hide.
>
> Beggars bring your magic brew
> And ladies bring your wine,
> And we will feast upon the lawn
> Of your life and of your time.
>
> I've come home from a sailing trip
> To bring you a surprise.
> Been hearing rumors of innocence,
> And forgiveness shall arise.
>
> The sun will marry to the moon,
> The earth will kiss the sky.
> God bless the bride and keep the groom
> And may all your sons be wise.[1]

1. Portier, "Epithalamium."

This celebration of love and innocence is also a celebration of wisdom, whose intimacy with God brings forth all of creation and dwells within its surprising details. I detect wisdom's feast within the wedding feast and life of my mother and father. They formed and taught their children in the life-long search for wisdom to which Proverbs calls its readers.

My father's academic career embodies this search as well. Moreover, his most recent book, *Divided Friends: Portraits of the Roman Catholic Modernist Crisis in the United States,* chronicles this same search within the lives of four figures in American Catholicism.[2] At its heart were questions about "how we know and believe in God," including what Edward Schillebeeckx termed "the relation between experience and concept."[3] Portier argues that this question persists today. It is at the heart of theology and at the heart of my own field, biblical studies. The present essay explores the relation between human subjectivity and divine revelation through an examination of the search for wisdom in Proverbs and Job.

I argue that Proverbs and Job portray wisdom as object, subject, faculty, praxis, and path. Wisdom is the object of searching, a treasure and tree of life to be held fast. Wisdom is also a speaking subject who invites all to her feast and to a life of searching that is relational and moral. The paradoxical experience of wisdom as both transparent and hidden permeates the multifold testimony to the search for wisdom in Proverbs and Job. At the same time, the gift of wisdom forms a bridge between humans and God, enabling human relationship with God and human participation in divine creativity and knowing.

Wisdom as Object

"Search out [wisdom] like a hidden treasure . . . and you will find knowledge of God" (Prov 2:4–5).[4] The sages who contributed to the book of Proverbs say that wisdom is a precious riddle and the promise of untold wealth, buried beneath the surface of things, hiding behind and within mundane, everyday surroundings. And yet she didn't come to be buried there by accident: someone has hidden wisdom within creation, within the workings of the world, within the rhythms and patterns of everyday life, of relationships, of seasons, of human nature, of the order of the cosmos. To find that hidden treasure is to find knowledge of the one who hid her within creation:

2. Portier, *Divided Friends.*

3. Quoted in Portier, *Divided Friends,* xix.

4. Unless otherwise noted, translations are the author's own.

God the creator, who has given wisdom out of God's own mouth and into creation, even into human hearts (2:6, 10).

What would a person pay for this treasure? Here is the advice of Israel's sages: "Get [or acquire, or buy] wisdom; at the cost of all you have, get understanding" (Prov 4:7 NAB). "How much better to acquire wisdom than gold!" (16:16 NAB). "Get [acquire, buy] truth and do not sell it: wisdom, instruction, understanding" (23:23). Israel's sages spoke of wisdom as an object to search for and find, to get, or buy, and never sell. This object was more precious than gold, silver, or fine gems, better than a bank account, real estate, or rare commodities. The message is: trade everything else away, if you can just get wisdom.

But wisdom is more than a commodity, and more than a mystery hidden in the dirt. Proverbs 3 again directs hearers to search for wisdom. "Fortunate is the one who finds wisdom" (Prov 3:13). But what the happy sage finds is no dusty jewel buried away from human sight. He finds a tree, a vital source of life at the heart of creation. This wisdom-tree lives and grows from the soil. Her roots reach down into the earth, her trunk rises toward the sun, and her dewy branches embrace the creatures of earth and heaven. "She is a tree of life to those who grasp her" (3:18 NAB). This organic metaphor takes the reader back to Eden, back to the source of all that lives. Here we behold the vital and abundant fruitfulness of creation. Here wisdom, verdant tree, sustains, nourishes, and grants life. She offers this gift to whoever should hold fast to her. To "grasp" in this sense is an act of effort, reaching out, choosing, and holding on; it is also an act of cognition and understanding.[5]

Israel's sages knew that wisdom was more than a treasured object to be found or bought, for she was also a living tree. Yet the sages knew wisdom also as a speaking, inviting, teaching subject, who could say to humankind: "The one who finds me, finds life" (8:35).[6]

---

5. Cf. Isa 56:4, 6, where the same hiphil plural participle of *ḥzq* is used to describe "holding fast" to the covenant. In Neh 10:30 this form similarly describes how the people joined with (held fast to) one another in entering into the covenant. In Neh 4:10, 15 the same form is used simply of holding spears. Van Hecke argues that a "universal framework of how people understand their own cognition" "underlie[s] the Classical Hebrew concepts" of cognition ("Searching for and Exploring Wisdom," 147–48). Part of this framework "structures ideas or insights as entities, often as physical objects that can be localized in a spatial environment" (147). He cites as an example the English metaphor of "grasping" a concept. Van Hecke goes on to argue that the search for wisdom (as locatable, graspable object) builds on this basic conceptual framework.

6. Kamp, "World Building in Job 28," emphasizes Wisdom as acting subject even in the poem of Job 28, though scholars have sometimes resisted seeing a personification of wisdom in this passage. Kamp pays attention to the change in wording between 28:12 and 28:20. Both verses inquire about wisdom's location and the source of

Wisdom as Subject and Faculty

Proverbs personifies the figure of wisdom as a woman who occupies public spaces and addresses a bustling humanity: "Wisdom cries aloud in the street, in the open square she raises her voice. Down the crowded ways she calls out, at the city gates she utters her words" (1:20–21 NAB).[7] Wisdom knows that people are looking for her and does not hide. Instead, she shouts out her invitations and rebukes in the crowded spaces, at the crossroad spaces and gates where people bump into and past one another, conduct their business, come in and go out. These are the places where people make choices and pass judgments. She does not whisper, but raises her voice loud so anyone can hear her. She holds out her hands so all can see what is in them: "Long life is in her right hand; in her left are riches and honor" (3:16 NAB).

In Proverbs 8 Wisdom again appears in the public square to call out her invitation and appeal to humankind (8:4). She invites even the simple and the fool to hear her words and receive her teaching, counsel, advice, and strength. She proclaims that she, Wisdom, is the governing principle of society, the foundation of justice, and the source of wealth, honor, and prosperity. She also invites her hearer back in time, before creation, to reveal that she is the beginning of God's ways, poured forth before the earth, brought forth before creation, attending and animating God's work and playing on the surface of the earth (8:22–31). Wisdom was God's artisan, a master-worker, God's architect and builder. And because God founded the earth by Wisdom (3:19), so by Wisdom the depths break open, and the clouds drip down dew, until the water of insight and understanding permeates and sustains the whole earth. Just as these waters sustain the earth, so to

---

understanding. But a shift occurs between v. 12 and v. 20. Verse 12 asks "Where can wisdom be found?" Verse 20 asks, "Whence does wisdom come?" Kamp observes that "Instead of showing man searching for the places of wisdom, the first clause of 28:20 shows another perspective. It starts from the point of view of wisdom" (315). In light of his cognitive linguistic analysis, Kamp concludes that the reader "no longer regards wisdom as an object, but as a subject." For Kamp, this shift orients the reader toward a "religious and moral attitude" (318). The search for wisdom is intersubjective and thereby moral.

7. Proverbs's portrait of woman Wisdom is counterbalanced by a personification of woman Folly. Moreover, throughout the book of Proverbs Wisdom is closely associated with the ideal wife (she is a mighty householder, like the woman in Proverbs 31), just as Folly is closely associated with dangerous "Other" women. On the gendering of Wisdom, see Camp, *Wisdom and the Feminine in the Book of Proverbs*; Newsom, "Woman and the Discourse of Patriarchal Wisdom"; Fontaine, "The Social Roles of Women in the World of Wisdom"; McKinlay, *Gendering Wisdom the Host*; and Webster, "Sophia: Engendering Wisdom in Proverbs, Ben Sira, and the Wisdom of Solomon."

humankind Wisdom offers her feast. She summons, invites, and spreads her table: they have only to listen to her words to receive the gift of life (9:1–11).

As portrayed in Proverbs, this offer of life and salvation is no abstract promise. As Roland Murphy has emphasized, Wisdom promises a secure life here and now, in its concrete dimensions, including wealth, honor, and longevity.[8] For the sage, each of these gifts mediates divine blessing.[9] Wisdom holds out that life and blessing as a gift from God. Yet the sages also believed that to grasp this gift requires human effort, discipline, attention, and obedience. To put it another way: Wisdom issues a summons, and invites humans to respond.[10] Wisdom calls humans into an active, committed, lifelong relationship.[11]

There are two parts to her summons: (1) the one who would get wisdom, and so have life, must be always engaged in the search;[12] and (2) this one must be committed to the life of justice and honesty that Wisdom teaches. The search for wisdom, and the life in wisdom, is relational and moral.[13] It is at its core a search for and a living into relationship with God, with humanity, and with creation.

8. Murphy, *The Tree of Life*, 29.

9. In *The Tree of Life*, Murphy calls them "sacramentals."

10. Walter Brueggemann has emphasized the theme of summons and human response; see *In Man We Trust*.

11. Cf. Davis, *Proverbs, Ecclesiastes, and the Song of Songs*, 64: "Wisdom can be sought and found only as a relationship is 'found'—when we prepare our hearts for receiving the gift of the other, when we attend carefully to the responsibilities that relationship entails." Davis calls attention to the language of "mutual seeking" in Wis 6:14–16 (ibid., 65).

12. In analyzing the imagery of path in Prov 2:8, Davis observes: "Wisdom and understanding come only to those who persist in walking that way, step by step, day after day" (ibid., 36).

13. Proverbs repeatedly emphasizes interpersonal relationships and social mores. In her discussion of the personified figure of Wisdom in Proverbs, Claudia Camp asserts, "the most fundamental point made by these poems is that wisdom is *not* an abstract concept but a way of being that is at its heart relational and holistic" ("Woman Wisdom as Root Metaphor," 45, cited in Fretheim, *God and World in the Old Testament*, 208). For Fretheim, Wisdom is "the 'relational infrastructure' of creation." He elaborates on the search for wisdom this way: "In and through a discernment of the many and various interrelationships that God has built into the created order, one may be more closely attuned to God's will for that world and act accordingly" (*God and World in the Old Testament*, 209). On the relational dimension of Job's ethics, see also Crenshaw, *Old Testament Wisdom*, 7. Job 28 puts special emphasis on relation with the earth. See Habel, "Implications," 294–96. Habel identifies earth as a "subject whose voice is mediated through Wisdom to the Earth Community" (295), and with whom we are challenged to relate (296). He asks, "Are we not moving beyond the traditional model of a subject seeking wisdom by analyzing an object to an interaction between subjects?" (296).

(1) The search. The one who would get wisdom must open her eyes, look around, and look closely: the sage will watch daily at Wisdom's gates, waiting at her doorposts for new insight to emerge (Prov 8:33–34). But this sage does not wait passively: she is looking, investigating, thinking. As she investigates nature, she disciplines and exercises her mind, develops her common sense, attends to experience, trains her virtues.[14] She learns to think analogically, to infer from the visible to the invisible, from the created to the mind of the creator. She also asks questions—simple questions and hard questions—and she tugs at them, pushes on them, moves through them to deeper understanding, or to more fundamental questions. She receives the tradition of her elders and reveres it; she also tests it, investigating even the words that are handed down to her by her parents and teachers. She perceives contradictions and she interrogates them, seeking to discern the conditions in which each saying, each teaching, can be true, and challenging and testing them to learn in what ways they are false. As her search continually reshapes her thinking, so she continually reshapes the very traditions she inherits. As she teaches these traditions and habits of thought to her children and students, she invites the next generation to take up the search.

(2) The moral dimension. If the sage I have described sounds like a scientist, philosopher, or university professor, she is what my own institution would call a "Professor of the Practice": Wisdom is both theoretical and practical, and the sage's work of discernment is foundational for a life of just praxis.[15] The emphasis on virtue, justice, and the moral life permeates the book of Proverbs. Within the Hebrew Bible, nearly a third (66 out of 206) of the total occurrences of the adjective ṣaddîq, "righteous" or "just," occurs in the book of Proverbs. In Proverbs this adjective ṣaddîq is frequently used in parallel with "good"; both are contrasted with the wicked or guilty. The noun "righteousness" (ṣĕdāqâh) occurs in Proverbs eighteen times out of a total of 157, or 11% of its total occurrences in the Hebrew Bible. Proverbs contains twelve references to "truth" ('emet) and eleven to "loyalty," or ḥesed. The book repeatedly emphasizes the necessity of honest testimony and gentle speech, and warns against the dangers of anger and revenge. Twice the book condemns false weights and measures (Prov 20:10, 23; cf. 16:11), and Proverbs repeatedly instructs Wisdom's student to care for the poor and the needy (14:21, 31; 19:17; 22:9; 28:27; 29:7; 31:9). The book is

14. Crenshaw insists that "[t]he goal of all wisdom was the formation of character" (*Old Testament Wisdom*, 3). See the important study of Brown, *Character Is Crisis*.

15. Geller argues that "scholarly distinctions between 'practical' wisdom (*Lebensweisheit*) and 'speculative' wisdom would have seemed deeply false to the ancients. The theme of wisdom as an intellectual tradition was the unity of order" ("Where is Wisdom?," 170).

concerned above all else with laying out clear and persuasive guidance for the moral life.[16]

Creative Wisdom

As the sage seeks wisdom, shapes her virtues, and shapes and hands on the very wisdom tradition that will lead others on the path of virtue, she engages in what Carol Newsom has called a "life of moral creation."[17] If wisdom is the founding principle and animating force of God's initial work of creation and continues to govern and animate all that God has made, then the sage who patterns her own life according to wisdom participates in God's creative praxis. To put it another way, human practice of wisdom becomes a mirror of God's creativity.

A playful double meaning in Hebrew underscores this connection. Many proverbs pun or play on sound and meaning, and Proverbs portrays Wisdom herself *at play* in creation—playing alongside God—from the very beginning.[18] Ellen Davis argues that in light of Wisdom's play and delight in creation and in humankind, "playfulness is part of the proper human response to God." The sages' delight in the play of language participates in divine delight.[19] Here the double meaning lies in the Hebrew verb *qnh*, commonly rendered "get" or "acquire" in translations of the book's injunctions to "get wisdom." But *qnh* can also mean "to create." The verb occurs fourteen times in Proverbs, and in all but one occurrence (the exception is 20:14, where it means "to buy" something at the market) the object of the verb is wisdom, understanding, knowledge, or insight.[20] In all but one instance (8:22), the subject is human, sometimes the audience, "an intelligent man," even "a fool." The plain meaning of *qnh* in these verses is "get," "acquire," or even "buy," and not "create."

But Proverbs 8:22 presents a distinctive case. Wisdom is again the object, but now God is the subject. Does Wisdom say, "the Lord *acquired* me first, his way, before his works, long ago"? Or does she say, "the Lord *created* me first, his way, before his works, long ago"? The verb is the same verb (*qnh*) that is translated elsewhere in Proverbs as "get" or "acquire." In

16. Crenshaw, *Old Testament Wisdom*, 4.

17. Newsom, "Dialogue and Allegorical Hermeneutics," 304.

18. For a detailed study of wordplay in Proverbs, see McCreesh, *Biblical Sound and Sense.*

19. Davis, *Proverbs, Ecclesiastes, and the Song of Songs*, 69.

20. Prov 1:5; 4:5 (x2), 7 (x2); 8:22; 15:32; 16:16 (x2); 17:16; 18:15; 19:8; 20:14; 23:23.

this instance, however, NRSV and NAB distinguish God's action and relationship to wisdom from human action and relationship to wisdom by two distinct translations. Throughout Proverbs, humans as "get" or "acquire" wisdom. In Proverbs 8:22, God creates (NRSV) or begets (NAB) wisdom. Other translations recognize (for example, those of Norman Habel and KJV) that by using the same verb to speak of God's primordial relationship with Wisdom and human's perennial charge, the writers of Proverbs convey a deep affinity between God's relationship to Wisdom and that of humans.[21] We will see later on that the book of Job exploits this ambiguity in the riddling hymn to wisdom in chapter 28.[22]

Wisdom as Human Creative Skill: Exodus

Before we consider Job 28, we will briefly consider the way the word "wisdom" is used in another biblical text to identify human creative skill and artistry. The word for "wisdom," ḥokmâh, is used eight times in the book of Exodus, always with the meaning of exceptional skill and mastery of a craft. These are the only instances of the word ḥokmâh in the entire Pentateuch or Torah. The first reference to wisdom in Exodus, at 28:3, is to those the Lord has endowed with wisdom to make the priestly vestments, including the jeweled ephod, in order to consecrate Aaron to the priesthood. What is noteworthy here is that (1) God gives the gift of wisdom; (2) wisdom is creative skill; (3) wisdom is required to clothe and consecrate the high priest who will serve as cultic intermediary between Israel and the Lord. This God-given human creativity enables humans to approach God, serve God, offer gifts to God, and receive guidance from God. To put it more succinctly: in this text, God's gift of wisdom empowers humans for relationship with God.

---

21. Habel translates the verb qnh as "acquire" in both cases, with the understanding that humans and God are both engaged in the same activity ("The Implications of God Discovering Wisdom in Earth," 294). The KJV understands the verb in 8:22 in a manner more or less consistent with its other uses in Proverbs: "The LORD possessed me in the beginning of his way."

22. Claus Westermann identifies the poem as a riddle (*The Structure of the Book of Job*, 135). Scholars are equally occupied by the riddles within the poem (e.g., "where will wisdom be found?") as by the riddles of the poem itself (Hill, "Job in Search of Wisdom," 37). The following questions rank high among the puzzles that occupy scholars: What is the poem's function in its present setting? Who is the speaker? Has the poem been displaced from a location later in the book? Is 28:28 original to the poem, or a later pious redaction? For a discussion of recent scholarship, see Newsom, "Re-considering Job," 161–64.

This theme is continued in the chapters that follow. The remaining seven instances of the term "wisdom" in Exodus occur in chapters 31, 35, and 36 and describe the exceptional gifts of the artisans who create the tabernacle and its furnishings. We first hear of Beṣalel, whom God has "filled with divine spirit, with ability, intelligence, and knowledge in every kind of craft, such that he can conceive of designs in order to make . . ." or "do" (Exod 31:3). Like *qnh*, this verb "to make" or "do" (*ʿśh*) is a word sometimes used in describing God's own creative activity (e.g., Gen 2:4; Jer 32:17; Jonah 1:9). Here God inspires human creativity. Beṣalel, Oholiab, and their team of artisans receive wisdom from God in order to construct the tabernacle and its furniture. They will design and make the tent of meeting—i.e., the place where God and humans meet—as well as the ark (sign of God's presence), the mercy seat, the table, the lampstand (source of illumination, also symbolically connected with the tree of life),[23] the altar of incense and the altar of burnt offering, the basins, the priestly vestments, and the oil of anointing. God's gift of wisdom now empowers not only the crafting of the priestly vestments, but the design and crafting of the cultic space that both mirrors God's cosmos and mediates God's presence to the people. The hearts of the artisans are stirred to do this creative work (Exod 36:2); they carry out their work in accordance with God's commands (36:1). In a similar way, Exodus draws our attention to women who, "in wisdom," weave cloths for the tabernacle and bring these as offerings, as their hearts move them (35:26). In Exodus, wisdom inspires the creative activity of both women and men.

I call attention to these passages from Exodus advisedly: they are not part of the wisdom literature, they seem to use the term "wisdom" somewhat differently from what we see in the wisdom books Proverbs and Job, and they prescribe a type of Yahwistic piety largely absent from the classical

---

23. In her dissertation, Carol Meyers examines the form, thematic identification, and symbolic value of the tabernacle menorah; see *The Tabernacle Menorah*. The lampstand has the form of a stylized tree (84). In Meyers' analysis of the tree symbolism, she notes that "the sacred quality of trees lies in the fact of their embodiment of the life principle. . . . Since the ultimate source of this life that renews is found within divine creation, trees become imbued with the divine power that has deigned to impart life and regeneration within the mundane sphere" (95). Meyers examines associations of the tree motif with fertility and eternal life, as well as the motif of "the divinity revealed in the tree," linking the latter with the cosmic tree motif (143). She concludes that the tabernacle lampstand serves not only as symbol of life but also as a symbol and assurance of God's sustaining presence (180). Meyers does not explore connections with Wisdom as tree of life in her dissertation, but the multiplex associations of Wisdom as animating force within creation, means to long life and good name, mode of revelation, and mediator of divine presence suggest significant parallels and overlap in the function and meaning of the tabernacle lampstand and that of the image of Wisdom as tree of life.

biblical wisdom literature. But the use of the term "wisdom" in the Exodus texts helps us to see, from a slightly different angle, certain dimensions of wisdom that I have highlighted already, and certain dimensions that we will see developed further in the book of Job. In Proverbs as in Exodus, God is the source and originator of wisdom. Both texts emphasize the practical and creative dimension of wisdom, though in different ways. In Proverbs it is ethical, relating to the practice of virtues; in Exodus it is religious, relating to the worship life of the community. Yet we should not press that distinction too far. In both cases wisdom is the necessary bridge that mediates divine presence to humankind.

Wisdom as Object, Subject, Faculty, Praxis, and Path

With this in mind, we can ask, in their search for wisdom, what exactly were the sages looking for? Is it enough to say that they sought insight, understanding, and even life itself? Wisdom is many things and one thing. I highlight five: (1) Wisdom is an object of knowing—namely the principles of creation and of human living;[24] (2) Wisdom is a speaking, summoning subject; (3) Wisdom is a faculty of discernment sages seek to cultivate; (4) Wisdom is a praxis, or an art of living;[25] and (5) Wisdom is a way or a path bridging the gulf between humans and God.[26] That is, the sages sought nothing less than God, and God's presence in, with, and for creation.[27]

For those who seek wisdom, wisdom is the search itself, for wisdom is the habit and faculty of examining, investigating, plumbing the depths, questioning, testing, and handing on.[28] Wisdom is also the habit and faculty of discerning, judging, choosing what is right.[29] This search for wisdom is

---

24. Hill distinguishes between what he calls the objective sense and subjective sense of Wisdom ("Job in Search of Wisdom," 36).

25. For Crenshaw, Wisdom is also "an attitude toward reality, a worldview" (*Old Testament Wisdom*, 10).

26. Habel focuses on wisdom as "way" (*derek*) ("Implications," 286). In an earlier essay Habel explored the meaning of way as path for life ("The Symbolism of Wisdom in Proverbs 1–9," 131–57), but in the later essay understands the term more in the sense of "driving characteristic," "law," or "code."

27. Crenshaw, "In Search of Divine Presence," 365–66.

28. See Aitken, "Lexical Semantics and the Cultural Context of Knowledge in Job 28," 133, 155.

29. Crenshaw defines wisdom this way: wisdom is "the reasoned search for specific ways to ensure personal well-being in everyday life, to make sense of extreme adversity and vexing anomalies, and to transmit this hard-earned knowledge so that successive generations will embody it" (*Old Testament Wisdom*, 3).

characterized by a fundamental openness to the world that recognizes the dynamic nature of lived reality and the autonomy of creation.[30]

As the object of knowing, wisdom is understood to be the guiding principle of creation, the order of the cosmos and the principle directing human life within it. For Norman Habel, wisdom is the design, the governing principle or mystery behind all the ways of creation.[31] Klaus Koch identified this governing principle as one of act and consequence. In Koch's view this one principle animated both natural processes of cause and effect and divine retributive justice. Thus, for Koch, Proverbs portrays a rational God who dispassionately punishes evil and rewards good.[32] For Hans H. Schmid, wisdom was the one order unifying not only the cosmic realm but also social and political reality. The wise ordered their own conduct in harmony with the universe, and creation provided the unitary and universal framework for the cosmic, social, and political realms.[33] Each of these proposals has clear merits. Yet we must be careful not to reduce wisdom as object of knowing to a system or a principle.[34] Throughout the wisdom tradition, wisdom's playfulness repeatedly comes to the fore. Wisdom is hardly fixed or frozen.[35] Terence Fretheim writes eloquently of wisdom's dynamism: "Woman Wisdom opens up the world rather than closes it down; she is always ready to take new experience into account, recognizing that God may be about new things for new times and places. Such is the life of a genuine Creator."[36] In

---

30. Murphy, *The Tree of Life*, 113–14. As Murphy writes, "The cosmos was not a machine that was wound up at creation and then let go." For a fuller treatment, see Murphy, "The Hebrew Sage and Openness to the World." See also Von Rad, *Wisdom in Israel*, 301.

31. Habel, "Of Things Beyond Me," 142.

32. Summary of Koch in Murphy, "The Hebrew Sage," 116. For bibliographic references and further discussion, see ibid., 129 n. 21. Koch first laid out this theory in "Gibt es ein Vergeltungsdogma im alten Testament." An English version is available in Crenshaw, *Theodicy in the Old Testament*, 57–87.

33. Murphy, "The Hebrew Sage," 117; Crenshaw, "In Search of Divine Presence," 363–64. See Schmid, "Schöpfung, Gerechtigkeit und Heil," translated into English as "Creation, Righteousness, and Salvation," in Anderson, *Creation in the Old Testament*, 102–17. Crenshaw articulates a view close to Schmid's, affirming the close connection between creation and justice in the Wisdom literature. But for Crenshaw it is not creation that is of primary concern, but rather "order, righteousness, and justice" ("In Search of Divine Presence," 363–64).

34. According to Davis, the image of Wisdom at play in Proverbs 8:30–31 "excludes any theological view that the universe is a closed system operating according to fixed laws" (*Proverbs, Ecclesiastes, and the Song of Songs*, 68).

35. Cf. Fretheim, *God and World*, 209–10, 218.

36. Ibid., 218. Elsewhere he emphasizes that Wisdom's portrayal as *person* reveals her to be "dynamic, creative, developing, truly interactive, full of life, and genuinely

this understanding, Wisdom is living, organic, and artistic. She is a tree and a fountain. She is not only an architect, but also a chef and a mixer of wine.

The productive tension between the ordered and organic qualities of wisdom finds a parallel in the speech of Job's interlocutor Zophar. Zophar proposes that wisdom or understanding (*tûšîyyâh*) is "two-sided" (Job 11:6). Norman Habel argues that the two sides revealed in Zophar's speech are wisdom's qualities as simultaneously "manifest" and "hidden."[37] As much as we are able to seek out and know, there remain deep things of God we cannot know. Though we can investigate, count, measure, and learn the extent of earthly terrain, we are helpless to fix a limit to God's ways, and there will always be much we fail to comprehend (11:7).[38]

A key word in biblical treatments of the "search" for wisdom (and the search that *is* wisdom) is the verb *ḥqr*, often translated to "search." The term is perhaps better translated as "investigate": it typically means not to look for something, but to search something thoroughly to determine its limits and contents.[39] The verb is used, for example, to describe the act of spying out a land to determine its strengths, weaknesses, and boundaries.[40]

But this kind of investigation necessarily fails when applied directly to God. According to one psalmist God's greatness is unsearchable (*'ên ḥēqer*)—its limit cannot be determined (Ps 145:3).[41] In Job 5:9 and 9:10 we are told there is no searching God's great deeds. Humans cannot count them because they are without number. In Job 34:24 it is God's shattering of the mighty that is unsearchable and unaccountable. We begin to see that the frustrated search for understanding in the book of Job relates explicitly to Job's own experience of God. According to the tale, by God's own admission God has shattered Job without cause. Will God be held accountable for Job's suffering? Will God abide by the "rules" or the "governing causal principle"

---

relational with every living creature" (209).

37. Habel insists on the translation "two-sided" rather than "many-sided." Habel identifies these two sides as the "manifest" and the "hidden" ("Of Things beyond Me," 148).

38. Fretheim writes: "Those in search of wisdom will always be finding ever new dimensions of reality to be studied and will always be at least one step behind" (*God and World*, 210).

39. The essays by Van Hecke ("Searching for and Exploring Wisdom") and Aitken ("Lexical Semantics") both offer detailed studies of the term. Aitken argues that the basic meaning of the term is "examine," while Van Hecke argues for a core meaning of "explore," from which its other meanings are derived.

40. Examples of this meaning can be found at Judg 18:2 and 2 Sam 10:3 (along with its parallel in 1 Chr 19:3). Cf. also Jer 46:23 and Ezek 39:14.

41. Aitken notes that God is never the object of the verb *ḥaqar* ("Lexical Semantics," 134).

of God's own creation? Have the sages correctly discerned these rules and principles at all? If human experience is also human experience of God's way and will, how will humans interpret the experience of injustice? How will humankind respond when the search for divine presence reveals seeming absence, or worse, divine injustice? Where, then, does wisdom come from?

Job 28

Job 28 offers a powerful meditation on human inability to search out and find wisdom's place. The poem claims that humans cannot locate wisdom's place or source in creation in the same way that they have so cunningly found the sources of silver and bronze and gems. That is to say, it is precisely when wisdom is viewed solely as faculty (human knowing or skill) or object (something to be dug up) that the search fails. In the final portion of this essay I focus on Job 28, to see how the poem presents wisdom not merely as faculty or object but as praxis and as path to God.

The poem begins by affirming that even precious silver has its place where it comes forth, its sources that humans can seek out and exploit (Job 28:1). Humans have learned the processes for purifying gold, and know how to extract iron from the earth (28:2). In pursuit of these ores humans have searched to the farthest limits of the earth, deep into darkness and stone, fixing a limit and putting an end even to the subterranean darkness of the mine shaft (28:3–4). We see miners, the lowly and forgotten ones, hanging low in shafts, trembling as they work, far from habitation, far from the path of travelers (28:4).

And next the poet paints an image of the turmoil within the earth (28:5).[42] Earth, who sustains human life with the gift of bread, is, *beneath* her surface, overturned, churned up as though with a raging fire. The language and imagery of "overturning" and fire recalls the destruction of Sodom and Gomorrah, cities that became a wasteland because of human greed and the willingness to exploit others for personal pleasure (Gen 19:25; Deut 29:22). With this vivid image the poet suggests that this great display of human craft and technological mastery is destructive rather than creative art. In this search for ores and gems there is no wisdom to be found.

Though humans have discerned and discovered places that eye of eagle and foot of proud lion have not found (Job 28:7–8), they have traded the search for God's order and will for profit. In so doing they have substituted

---

42. I credit my former student Rev. Mel Baars O'Malley (Duke M.Div., 2008) for teaching me to read Job 28 in this way through her work in the class Intermediate Hebrew Poetry, Spring 2007.

exploitation for justice. This exercise of human skill does violence to creation, as humans send forth their hand with flinty tool to carve channels into rock, tunneling through the roots of mountains, uprooting them, destroying their foundations, even binding up wisdom's waters beneath the earth to gain unhampered access to precious gems and metals (28:9–10).

What was hidden now comes to light, but it is not wisdom (28:11). For all this ingenuity, for all this skill and craft and cunning, in all this technology and the plumbing and sounding of the depths of the earth, where is wisdom to be found? (28:12). "No human knows her place or her measure," comes the reply (28:13). She cannot be bought with gold or silver (28:15–16). She is concealed from human eyes (28:21). She is not in the sky, or the birds would have seen her (28:21). She is not in the place of death deep below; they have only heard about her (28:22). God, the poet tells us, discerns her way (28:23). God is the one who knows her place. God knows because God looks, and God's gaze encompasses all that is upon the earth, even to the limits of earthly existence, beneath all the heavens. God sees (28:24).

Here in the book of Job, God is the observant sage who attends to what God has made.[43] God set weight and measure and decree for wind and water and rain and thunder (28:26). In God's creating, we are told, "at that time, God saw her, and he took her measure, he established her, and he searched her" (28:27). God sought to know the full measure and extent of wisdom.[44] God saw her with attentive and discerning eyes. God counted her, and so established her. In God's work of creation God comes to know Wisdom in her fullest measure. God models here for humankind a path to wisdom: not through destruction, but through creation, artistry, and attention. Indeed, Carol Newsom has argued that in Job 28 humans do have access to wisdom, but only insofar as humans cease to regard wisdom solely as object. Rather, humans can find wisdom "only if they also know it through a mode comparable to God's creative activity, that is, through a life of moral creation."[45] In the poem's concluding verse God reminds humankind of the fundamental starting point for the search for wisdom: fear of God. "Fear of the Lord, [God] said to humanity, this is wisdom. Turning aside from evil is understanding" (28:28).

---

43. Referring to this passage, Habel calls YHWH "the supreme sage" ("Implications," 295).

44. Van Hecke, "Searching for and Exploring Wisdom," 160: "While men explore (ḥāqar) the whole earth without ever locating wisdom, God can not only locate wisdom, but can also measure wisdom's inner extent and explore (ḥāqar) it to the full."

45. Newsom, "Dialogue and Allegorical Hermeneutics," 303–4.

Conclusion

Humans arrive at fear of God through awareness of human limitations: what Maria Taranto calls the "wisdom of unknowing," or the wisdom that comes from a recognition of and response to human limitation.[46] With this recognition humans can discern their place in creation, not at its center but in its midst.[47] So too humans can see that wisdom is not buried in the deep but permeates all the earth, for she is the way of all creation.[48] Through this awareness God invites humankind into a life of free, artistic, and attentive moral creation in relationship with God and all that God has made. If the sage finds wisdom, the sage will also find God.

Wisdom is object and subject, accessible and hidden. It is the praxis by which we seek understanding of God, world, and human life. It is guiding principle. It is creativity and art, participation in God's creating and knowing.

In 1893 John Ireland declared in Baltimore's Cathedral of the Assumption that the church had a duty "to stimulate the age to deeper researches" and to leave "untouched no particle of matter that may conceal a secret . . . no act in the life of humanity, that may solve a problem."[49] Despite his optimism, then as now, the findings of biblical criticism challenged cherished teachings of the church.[50] The condemnation of modernism in the 1907 encyclical *Pascendi Dominici Gregis* included a caricature of so-called modernist biblical scholarship, including textual criticism, source and redaction criticism, and composition history, that was "in opposition to

---

46. Taranto, "Facets of Wisdom," 6, 15–16, cited in Dailey, "The Wisdom of Job," 50–52. Dailey brings Taranto's psychological and developmental analysis of wisdom to bear on the book of Job. Taranto argues "that wisdom involves a recognition of and response to *human limitation*" ("Facets of Wisdom," 15–16, cited in Dailey, 51).

47. Ellen Davis has suggested that "the search for wisdom is a search for the proper human place in the divinely established order" (*Proverbs, Ecclesiastes, and the Song of Songs*, 6). For Geller, chapter 28 addresses the relationship between humanity, God, and nature. Yet Geller still sees humankind close to the center: "Man dominates over nature, he stands closer in wisdom to God than any other creation, but still he can offer no challenge to God so far as obtaining the ultimate knowledge of natural order is concerned" ("'Where is Wisdom?,'" 173). I argue rather that the poem deconstructs the notion of human domination: it is in fact destruction, and is no true kind of mastery. Humans can only get wisdom by turning their attention to creation as subject rather than object, as Habel argues.

48. Habel, "Implications."

49. Ireland, *The Church and Modern Society*, 1:116, quoted in Portier, *Divided Friends*, 31–32.

50. Ibid., 39.

Catholic faith."[51] The encyclical paints a sharp dichotomy between objective knowledge, arguments, and articles of faith, on one hand, and subjective reasoning, appeals to experience, and claims to knowing, on the other. Toward the conclusion of his book *Divided Friends*, Portier writes that the stories of John R. Slattery, Denis J. O'Connell, William L. Sullivan, and Joseph McSorley "show the moral and religious complexities involved in pioneer attempts to deal with the subjective conditions of religious meaning and truth in an ecclesial world normed by one-sided theological objectivity and conceptualism."[52] In this essay I have shown that for the sages of Israel, wisdom, as object and subject, was the dynamic force that might bridge this divide, even as it forms a bridge between humans and God.

51. Pope Pius X, *Pascendi Dominici Gregis* §34.
52. Portier, *Divided Friends*, 363.

3

The Fate of Catholic Biblical Interpretation in America

Jeffrey L. Morrow

Gerald Fogarty writes, "In the early years of the American republic, the Catholic community in the United States had neither the numbers nor the resources for undertaking serious scholarship."[1] The situation was different shortly after the 1884 Third Plenary Council of Baltimore, which issued the famous *Baltimore Catechism*. In the late-nineteenth century some Catholic biblical interpretation can easily be described as scholarship—scholarship that was accompanied by other intellectual trends, influenced by the Americanist controversy and the subsequent modernist crisis.[2] In light of these developments, we must say that the solemn condemnation of Modernism in 1907 by Pope St. Pius X as the "synthesis of all heresies" occasioned a directional change for American Catholic biblical scholarship.[3] More than half a century later, however, the Second Vatican Council eliminated the formal ecclesiastical infrastructure that Pius X had erected to combat Modernism, thereby opening up new possibilities for Catholic biblical scholars and giving rise to what is typically thought of as "modern

---

1. Fogarty, *American Catholic Biblical Scholarship*, 1.

2. On the *Baltimore Catechism* and the Third Plenary Council of Baltimore see Rocha, "'De Concilio's Catechism.'"

3. Pope Pius X, *Pascendi Dominici Gregis* §39. Throughout the chapter, I follow William Portier's practice of using "Modernism" (with initial capital) to refer to the diverse intellectual trends *Pascendi* depicted as a single organized movement. When referring to the events and figures caught up in the controversy, I will use the term "modernist" (lower case initial). For more on these issues, see Portier, *Divided Friends*, 3–37.

Catholic biblical scholarship." In this new era, Catholic biblical interpretation was accorded its rightful place as genuine scholarship in the broader community of exegetes.

Three significant events, then, suggest a periodization for examining this topic: the Third Plenary Council of Baltimore (1884), the formal condemnation of Modernism (1907), and the Second Vatican Council (1962). Though not characterized by any one event, the 1990s mark still another sea change in regard to American Catholic biblical scholarship. In considering this fourth and final period, I will pay special attention to one growing trend within Catholic biblical scholarship: what I call "evangelical Catholic biblical scholarship."

Before 1884: Early Years

What is good for the clergy must be good, also, for the laity. Be assured that if you become a Catholic you will never be forbidden to read the Bible. It is our earnest wish that every word of the Gospel may be imprinted on your memory and on your heart.

—BISHOP JAMES GIBBONS, 1876[4]

Mathew Carey, a Catholic who, in Philadelphia, successfully published the *Douay Catholic Bible* in English, was also the "largest American producer of Bibles in the first two decades of the nineteenth century."[5] We do not know much about Catholic Bible reading practices from the eighteenth century to the middle of the nineteenth century, but the available evidence indicates that at least some of America's Catholics were reading Bibles. In a letter to Carey, Fr. John Carroll, months before becoming the first American Catholic bishop, wrote that he still hoped to see the Douay Bible "in the hands of our people, instead of those translations, which they purchase in stores & from Booksellers in the Country."[6] Commenting on this letter, historian Michael Carter points out that Carroll "asserts that Catholics were buying Protestant Bibles from American booksellers, and thus either unaware or unconcerned with prohibitions emanating from Rome regarding unreliable (by Catholic standards) translations of the Bible into the vernacular." Further, "Carroll's

---

4. Bishop James Gibbons, quoted in Noll, "Bishop James Gibbons," 96.
5. Gutjahr, *An American Bible*, 23. On Carey, see Carter, "Under the Benign Sun."
6. Carroll to Carey, 30 January 1789, quoted in Carter, "Under the Benign Sun," 448.

concern suggests that Catholics were involved in private Bible study," more so than is often supposed.[7]

As is obvious from Carroll's remarks, precisely which Bible Catholics used was quite important. A number of nineteenth-century anti-Catholic incidents involved public schools, which allowed only Protestant Bibles to be used, thus creating a conflict for Catholic school children who were only permitted by the church to use Catholic Bibles.[8] Prior to these controversies, there was no major demand for printing Catholic Bibles, as can be seen by the fact that Carey was their only producer (and in limited quantity, at that) until roughly the mid-1820s—the time of the first major influx of Catholic immigrants from Europe. By the mid-nineteenth century, however, seven separate publishers in the U.S. produced thirty-nine different editions of the Catholic Bible.[9]

The Twin Cyclones of Americanism and Modernism: 1884–1907[10]

Academic biblical scholarship on the part of American Catholics, located primarily in the seminary and university settings, begins at the close of the Third Plenary Council of Baltimore in 1884. Though still entrenched in the pastoral concerns of newly arriving immigrants, it was at this time that some priests engaged in a more academic consideration of biblical interpretation as they instructed seminarians in the United States. This biblical scholarship was concurrent with the rise of Americanism and Modernism. Fogarty explains that "Americanism and biblical scholarship were . . . separate movements. But there were essential similarities, both in the theologies, which underlay each, and in the close, and sometimes complex, personal relationships, that existed between proponents of either issue."[11] The Ameri-

---

7. Carter, "Under the Benign Sun," 448.

8. McGreevy, *Catholicism and American Freedom*, 7–15, 30–33, 37–42; and Dolan, *The American Catholic Experience*, 263–64, 267, 269–70, 276.

9. Gutjahr, *An American Bible*, 126. For valuable information on Catholic publishing in the U.S. during the nineteenth century, see Cadegan, "Running the Ancient Ark by Steam"; see also O'Connor, "American Catholic Reading Circles," on literacy and reading habits of Catholics in the U.S. at the end of the nineteenth century. The evidence of Catholic biblical interpretation at the popular level during this time period—found in preached homilies, parish missions, and Catholic immigrants struggling with life in America—unfortunately has not yet been uncovered by scholarly research.

10. The cyclone metaphor is taken from the letter of James F. Driscoll to Charles A. Briggs of 8 December 1907, quoted in Portier, *Divided Friends*, 3.

11. Fogarty, *American Catholic Biblical Scholarship*, 76.

canist controversy and the modernist crisis form the context in which Catholic biblical scholars worked at the end of the nineteenth century and throughout the first several decades of the twentieth. Although Pope Leo XIII's *Testem Benevolentiae* did not censure Americanism until 1899 and Pius X did not condemn Modernism until 1907, the trends to which they were responding existed much earlier. For example, Bishop Francis Kenrick, seeking in the 1850s to improve upon an English translation of the Catholic Bible for Americans, was already engaged with certain trends in historical criticism.[12] Meanwhile, by the 1880s, Catholic priests in the U.S. had begun engaging issues surrounding Darwinian evolution, as well as other topics later associated with Modernism.

In Europe at this time the seeds of Modernism were beginning to germinate, and Americans were involved as well. The English Baron Friedrich von Hügel was engaged in a series of what he regarded as transformative conversations in France, which led him to become a major player in the modernist controversy.[13] The Irish-English Jesuit George Tyrrell, who was later excommunicated as a Modernist along with Alfred Loisy, reflected in 1885 that he was dissatisfied with the official Catholic theology as it stood, and he began to see a need to reform it by transforming it.[14] In the same year the American Josephite priest John Slattery commenced a life-changing correspondence with "a well-read woman" who gave him the works of Darwin. This correspondence raised many questions that would have a profound impact on his life, ultimately leading to the abandonment of his priesthood.[15] Denis O'Connell, who introduced Slattery to "the Americanist orbit," became personally acquainted with fellow Americanist leader John Ireland for the first time in 1884.[16] O'Connell emerged "as chief strategist and campaign organizer for the Americanist initiative to Europe" during his time in Rome as the rector of the North American College, and served as the "center of this reform energy" of Catholics who desired "to modernize the church politically and intellectually."[17]

William Portier notes, "In the chronicle of Catholicism's protracted and ambivalent struggle with liberal secular states, the modernist crisis emerges

---

12. Gutjahr, An *American Bible*, 129; and Fogarty, *American Catholic Biblical Scholarship*, 14–16, 23, and 32.

13. O'Connell, *Critics on Trial*, 51–53.

14. Ibid., 112.

15. Portier, *Divided Friends*, 33, 70–76. The phrase in quotation marks is taken from J.R. Slattery's "How My Priesthood Dropped from Me" (1906), quoted in Portier, *Divided Friends*, 70.

16. Ibid., 75–76, quoted phrase from 76.

17. Ibid., 125–27.

as one in a continuing series of Catholic openings to the age. But it is the pivotal opening that gives shape to twentieth-century Catholic theology."[18] This is also true specifically with regard to Catholic biblical scholarship, in the U.S. and in Europe. In the world of biblical scholarship, new and controversial ideas were afoot, and Catholic biblical scholars were swept up in the Americanist controversies and the related modernist crisis as they sought to employ methods that focused upon historical context.[19]

Inspired by Ernest Renan's lectures on biblical criticism, Alfred Loisy decided in 1884 to pursue the goal of achieving the highest level of expertise in biblical scholarship while formally studying Assyriology. Loisy's work on the Bible exerted a tremendous influence not only on Europeans like von Hügel, but also in the United States.[20] For example, the American Joseph Bruneau, SS, studied with Loisy in France and, upon his return, drew on Loisy's scholarship in his teaching at St. Joseph's Seminary in Dunwoodie.[21] Moreover, Loisy began a budding friendship with O'Connell while the latter was on the continent.[22]

The Dominican biblical scholar and founder of the *École Biblique* in Jerusalem, Marie-Joseph Lagrange, who challenged Loisy's works, was another towering figure during this time period.[23] Both scholars appropriated historical-critical biblical methodologies in their exegesis and were under suspicion during the pontificates of Leo XIII and Pius X. Loisy was excommunicated while Lagrange suffered in remaining a faithful son of the church. It was in this context that Leo XIII promulgated the first papal encyclical to deal with the Bible, *Providentissimus Deus* (*PD*), in 1893. The encyclical was largely a response to the work of Loisy, although he was not explicitly named in it.[24]

In his work on the modernist crisis in the U.S., Portier situates that conflict within a broader political context involving the Catholic Church's relationship with modern states.[25] That history is also an important backdrop to the development of American Catholic biblical scholarship lead-

18. Ibid., 14.

19. Ibid., 31–37.

20. On Loisy's biblical scholarship, see Morrow, "Alfred Loisy's Developmental Approach to Scripture," and Talar, "Innovation and Biblical Interpretation."

21. McDonald, "Biblical Scholarship," 116; and Fogarty, *American Catholic Biblical Scholarship*, 51–55, 64–65, 71–72, 174–80.

22. Fogarty, *American Catholic Biblical Scholarship*, 47–48.

23. See Montagnes, *Le Père Lagrange*.

24. See Beretta, "La Doctrine romaine de l'inspiration de Léon XIII à Benoît XV (1893–1920)," 52–55; and Hill, "Leo XIII, Loisy, and the 'Broad School,'" 40, 46.

25. Portier, *Divided Friends*, 7–12, 80.

ing up to and during the modernist controversy. A much broader focus on the history of modern biblical scholarship in general, stretching back to the late-medieval and early-renaissance periods, reveals equally important political matrices. In the seventeenth, eighteenth, and nineteenth centuries these form the context within which the advent of modern biblical criticism should be understood. Delegitimizing the authority of the Bible was a way of delegitimizing the authority of the church in favor of the authority of the state, and critical methods provided a way to systematize doubt about the accuracy and, consequently, the sanctity of the biblical text.[26]

Shortly after *PD*, the Fourth International Catholic Scientific Congress was held in 1897 in Fribourg. It brought together some of the most important Catholic intellectuals who were engaging with and appropriating modern trends and methods, from Darwinian evolution to modern historical biblical criticism. Those present included Lagrange, O'Connell, and John Zahm. Evolution and modern biblical criticism were both parts of the multifaceted modernist trend: Zahm spoke on evolution and Lagrange on Pentateuchal criticism; Von Hügel, although not present, had a paper read on source criticism.[27]

In 1898, five years after *PD*, Pope Leo set up an investigative commission that resulted in his censure of Americanism. Fogarty remarks, "At the time, few of the progressives either in Europe or in the United States probably saw any connection between the condemnation of Americanism and the growing opposition against the biblical exegetes. Yet, the reactions to both movements continued to run parallel to each other."[28] The trends Leo targeted as problematic in Americanism—one thinks especially of the church adapting to the spirit of the times—were similar to what would appear in Pius's condemnation of Modernism a mere eight years later. Further, these trends were related to concerns about Catholic biblical exegesis. The magisterium saw historical-critical methods of biblical interpretation as fundamentally Protestant, and indicted their practitioners with having granted authority to state government over and against the Catholic Church. From this perspective, Catholic biblical scholars who embraced such methods were regarded with suspicion.

Henri Hyvernat stands as a noteworthy example of a biblically interested scholar who was not targeted by Catholic critics of Modernism. His escape from scrutiny was due, at least in part, to his focus on philology.

---

26. For a brief treatment of the overarching history of modern biblical criticism in this vein, see Morrow, "The Politics of Biblical Interpretation."

27. Beretta, "Les Congrès scientifiques internationaux des catholiques (1888–1900)," and Fogarty, *American Catholic Biblical Scholarship*, 58–65.

28. Fogarty, *American Catholic Biblical Scholarship*, 70–71.

Hyvernat, who shared a teacher with Loisy, was a friend and former class-mate of Lagrange, and in 1897 he became the first professor at the recently founded Catholic University of America. Here he began the department that would later be named the Department of Semitic and Egyptian Languages and Literatures. His careful work, especially in Coptic and Syriac, made him justly famous. Hyvernat was careful to keep out of the thorny issues in biblical exegesis and theology that embroiled so many of those involved in biblical studies during these tumultuous times. Like both Loisy and La-grange, Hyvernat had superb training in languages and literatures of the ancient Near Eastern world. At Catholic University, Hyvernat's attention to the languages and cultures of the biblical time period influenced American Sulpician biblical scholars, encouraging attention to the historical setting of the text. Hyvernat's students included James F. Driscoll, SS, when he was in Rome, and then Edward Arbez, SS, while Hyvernat was in Washington.[29]

After the condemnation of Modernism, the academic work of many such scholars went underground. They rightly feared the ramifications—condemnations, censures, loss of jobs, etc.—that had befallen their col-leagues accused of the "synthesis of all heresies." Fogarty underscores that "The condemnation of Americanism . . . had an even more direct effect on the development of American Catholic biblical scholarship. It created an environment of theological reaction and of intellectual slumber."[30] The example of Henry Poels, appointed to Catholic University as Old Testament professor in 1904, is a case in point. The Dutch Poels became the sole Cath-olic biblical scholar operating in the U.S. who was formally censured and removed from his position. The focal point of the controversy with Poels was that he held the popular scholarly assumption that the final form of the Pentateuch dated from after Moses' time and that it came from multiple sources. This widely-assumed-and-argued scholarly position was formally challenged in the Pontifical Biblical Commission's (PBC) 1906 statement on the Mosaic authorship of the Pentateuch.[31]

Amid controversy, Poels was dismissed from the Catholic University of America in 1910.[32] Poels was asked to swear an oath, in which he ac-cepted the decrees of the PBC. He spoke with Rafael Cardinal Merry del Val y de Zulueta about the oath, explaining the only interpretation of the oath

---

29. Griffith and Blanchard, "Henri Hyvernat (1858–1941)"; Nuesse, *The Catho-lic University of America*, 54, 57; Kauffman, *Tradition and Transformation in Catholic Culture*, 206; and Ellis, *The Formative Years of The Catholic University of America*, 350.

30. Fogarty, *American Catholic Biblical Scholarship*, 76–77.

31. Pontifical Biblical Commission, "De mosaica authentia Pentateuchi."

32. Fogarty, *American Catholic Biblical Scholarship*, 80 and 83–119.

by which he would be willing to swear it. According to Poels, Merry del Val did not accept his interpretation of the oath as sufficient:

> He said that I had to testify under oath that I admitted *in foro interno* [in the internal forum] the truth of all those Decisions. My signing the formula would be understood to mean, first of all, a solemn affirmation of my personal belief—in conscience— that Moses was the author of the Pentateuch. Furthermore, he declared I had to teach the Decisions of the Biblical Commission as being part of my personal teaching.[33]

Merry del Val's recounting of this meeting is slightly different: "I said to Dr. Poels in this regard, that if he was not first intimately persuaded and convinced of the decisions of the Biblical Commission, he would not be able to teach according to their norms, because neither could his teaching be faithful, nor could he sincerely guarantee the orthodoxy of that teaching."[34] This is one example from the modernist controversy that exemplifies what scholars of that generation (in private writings), and of the next generation (in published writings), lamented. In Fogarty's words, the conflict "became more complicated than a contemporary soap opera."[35]

In July of 1907, the Supreme Sacred Congregation of the Roman and Universal Inquisition (now the Sacred Congregation for the Doctrine of the Faith) issued *Lamentabili Sane Exitu*. September of the same year saw Pius X's promulgation of *Pascendi*. These documents appeared in the midst of a stream of sixteen PBC statements (spanning 1905–1915) that dealt with various issues and concerns related to the historicity and authorship of biblical books. The sheer number of these documents indicates the concern with which the magisterium viewed the development of certain trends in regard to Catholic biblical exegesis and its relationship to Modernism. This time period was one in which Catholic scholars sought to expand biblical knowledge by careful attention to the historical context of the Bible, but the time period ends with a rough stop to this investigation.

33. Quoted in Fogarty, *American Catholic Biblical Scholarship*, 106.
34. Quoted in ibid., 116.
35. Ibid., 102.

Fallout of the Modernist Crisis and Its Aftermath:
The Road to Vatican II, 1907–1965

The idea of God as author of a book is more contradictory, more absurd in itself, than that of the man-toad or of the snake-woman. It is a childish myth, as childish as the creation of the first man with clay, and the first woman with a rib from Adam.

— ALFRED LOISY, 1930[36]

The time period after *Pascendi* is often described as a nadir in Catholic biblical scholarship, when Catholic exegetes ducked their heads and either wrote pieces in support of the PBC's decisions or retreated to ancient Near Eastern philology and such cognate studies, while refusing to engage theologically with the Bible—excepting a Thomistic interpretation that was in keeping with the neo-scholastic norms of the day. Francis Gigot, one of the most important Catholic Bible scholars during this time, is one of these figures who began work prior to *Pascendi* and continued after it, but whose hermeneutic shows a marked turn. Whereas, prior to *Pascendi*, Gigot used historical criticism as had his instructor Loisy, afterwards, his writings were in line with the PBC's decisions, even when those decisions were contrary to what he had earlier written, e.g., on the question of the Mosaic authorship of the Pentateuch. Such turnabouts were not uncommon.[37]

The Oath against Modernism began to be ritually sworn in 1910. Portier maintains that the Oath "helped to create and sustain the intellectual atmosphere that characterized the years between *Pascendi* and Vatican II."[38] In that atmosphere, even future popes Benedict XV and John XXIII were suspected of Modernism. During his papacy, Pope Benedict XV made a number of changes, including suppressing Umberto Benigni's *Sodalitium Pianum*, the curial body which had "hunted Modernists under every tree."[39] However, his 1920 papal encyclical on Scripture, *Spiritus Paraclitus*, was viewed by many as more of the same, with its emphasis on more traditional forms of exegesis (such as that of the fathers and medieval theolo-

36. Loisy, *Mémoires*, 306, my own translation.

37. On Gigot see especially McDonald, "Biblical Brinkmanship" and Fogarty, *American Catholic Biblical Scholarship*, 120–39. See also McDonald's contribution to this volume for greater detail on Gigot's role.

38. Portier, *Divided Friends*, 42.

39. Ibid.

gians). McDonald labels the American Catholic biblical scholarly scene of the 1920s and 1930s "the silent time."[40] Exegetes were hesitant to question historical matters concerning Scripture that might go contrary to the official PBC decisions, and they did not engage Scripture theologically. During this time, Fogarty suggests, "Silence was the way of survival for even potential biblical scholars."[41] Joseph Ratzinger noted in 1993 that "The danger of a narrow-minded and petty surveillance is no figment of the imagination, as the history of the Modernist controversy demonstrates."[42]

During this "silent time," while Edward Arbez used Gigot's works in the classroom in St. Patrick's Seminary in California, he avoided publishing controversial research. But things began to change in 1936, with the emergence of the Catholic Biblical Association of America (CBA), which had Arbez as its first president.[43] The CBA became the first scholarly guild of American Catholic biblical scholars, who had been excluded from the larger Society of Biblical Literature (SBL).[44] The CBA was responsible for the publication of several important pieces of American Catholic biblical scholarship: *Catholic Biblical Quarterly* (the prestigious scholarly journal on the Bible), the famous *Jerome Biblical Commentary* (and the *New Jerome Biblical Commentary*), as well as the New American Bible translation. Already in 1937, at the CBA's first annual meeting, a paper was presented that addressed the Mosaic authorship of the Pentateuch; although the paper clearly and emphatically asserted that the Pentateuch is Mosaic, it also argued that additions and changes of some kind can be allowed.[45] Hesitancy remained, but Catholic biblical scholars were slowly becoming emboldened in their discussions.

In 1943, Pope Pius XII promulgated his papal encyclical on Scripture, *Divino Afflante Spiritu* (*DAS*), which has been viewed by many of these scholars as the "magna carta" of biblical interpretation, providing liberty to a field of scholarship that had been severely restricted. By 1948, some members of the CBA, perhaps feeling encouraged by *DAS*, showed their

40. McDonald, "Biblical Scholarship," 121.

41. Fogarty, *American Catholic Biblical Scholarship*, 196.

42. Ratzinger, *The Nature and Mission of Theology*, 66. See also Ratzinger's comments about his own teachers with respect to the difficulties faced by Scripture scholars, in "Kirchliches Lehramt und Exegese."

43. Kauffman, *Tradition and Transformation*, 207, 227–28, and 278; and Hill, "Reverend Edward P. Arbez, SS."

44. McDonald, "Biblical Scholarship," 122–23; and Fogarty, *American Catholic Biblical Scholarship*, 201, 204, and 222–80.

45. Fogarty, *American Catholic Biblical Scholarship*, 225.

"growing independence of dogmatic theology."[46] In the 1949 CBA meeting, "John L. McKenzie gave a paper on 'Polygenism and Exegesis,' in which he argued that, according to both *Divino Afflante Spiritu* and the commission's letter, polygenism was not clearly ruled out of legitimate Catholic exegesis."[47] McKenzie soon became one of the most significant Catholic biblical scholars on the American scene. He was instrumental in getting the CBA to discuss Old Testament themes, a topic the society was hesitant to broach at first because of the censures, excommunications, and other measures taken earlier in the century.

Fogarty identifies the 1950s as a period of "rapid change" in American Catholic biblical scholarship, and he names a number of factors for this: Pius XII's critique of recent trends in theology in his 1950 encyclical *Humani Generis*; what was perceived as "encouragement" from the PBC for Catholic scholars to pursue historical criticism, particularly in 1956; Joseph ("Butch") Fenton's neo-scholastic crackdown on a number of American Catholic theologians; and the death of Pius XII and subsequent election of John XXIII in 1958.[48]

As Fogarty tells the story, 1955–1962 became a sort of reenactment of the earlier controversy over Americanism as it affected biblical scholars in both periods; there was both development of academic ideas and the continued threat of condemnation over these ideas. Moreover, something similar was happening in Rome at the time, where scholars at the Pontifical Biblical Institute were experiencing both advancement and the concern of censure. The controversies in Rome were exhibited by the removal and then reinstatement of biblical scholars Max Zerwick, SJ and Stanislaus Lyonnet, SJ, as professors at the Institute.[49]

Fogarty remarks that by 1953,

> The CBA meetings were becoming increasingly technical and drawing more younger scholars. Gone were the days of less than a decade before where the CBA would also hear papers on more pastoral and catechetical issues. For the time, however, Old Testament scholars would have no difficulty as long as they remained within the confines of ancient Near Eastern languages. It was a different story, if they dealt directly with the composition and dating of the various books.[50]

46. Ibid., 247.
47. Ibid., 248.
48. Ibid., 250.
49. Ibid., 254–55 and 258–323.
50. Ibid., 256–57.

However, the 1956 CBA meeting dared to consider issues that would never have been discussed in prior years; it even assumed as factual a number of historical-critical conclusions, such as the division of Isaiah into three distinct parts.[51] The history of the College Theology Society (CTS) paints a similar picture. From 1960 to 1963 papers were presented at what was then known as the Society of Catholic College Teachers of Sacred Doctrine, by scholars such as McKenzie, Bruce Vawter, CM, Caroll Stuhlmueller, CP, Barnabas Ahern, CP, and Raymond Brown, SS. Vawter and McKenzie, in particular, enthusiastically engaged in the type of historical-critical exegesis that had been forbidden during the modernist controversy.[52] By the end of the 1950s McKenzie was lamenting the lack of sufficient historical and critical tools within theology.[53]

In his survey of the history of college theology in the U.S. Catholic world, Patrick Carey notes, "From the late 1950s to the end of the Second Vatican Council the discipline of college theology was in a period of transition."[54] In the context of "emerging historical consciousness" the Bible began to be studied not "for its explicit potential to form Christian character. It was studied phenomenologically to acquaint students with its message in its historical context."[55] What was going on was a transformation of Catholic theology, including biblical studies, which involved a major separation, as Carey points out:

> One of the chief characteristics of the academic approach was its separation from spiritual formation. The complete separation of teaching (conceived of as an exclusively intellectual enterprise) from religious or spiritual guidance in the Catholic college became institutionalized in the late 1960s and early 1970s in a large number of Catholic schools when campus ministry departments were established as the proper place for fostering religious life. The theology or religious studies departments became the domain of intellectual development—one separated from spiritual development. Theology became a phenomenological or humanistic or descriptive discipline that yearned for and sought academic respectability—a respectability that was built upon an understanding of academic theology as an exclusively rational enterprise.[56]

51. Ibid., 264–65.

52. Yocum Mize, *Joining the Revolution*, 36–39.

53. Carey, "College Theology in Historical Perspective," 257.

54. Ibid., 259.

55. Ibid., 260.

56. Ibid., 262–63.

Historical-critical methods of biblical interpretation became an important way to make the field of biblical study appear rational and scientific, deserving of study at an academic institution.

The PBC's 1964 instruction, *Sancta Mater Ecclesia*, embraced a version of form criticism that enabled Catholic biblical scholars to feel completely free to engage publically in these and similar historical-critical methods, even prior to the final form of Vatican II's Dogmatic Constitution on Divine Revelation *Dei Verbum* (*DV*). Space limits what can be said about the history of *DV*, but this watershed document of 1965 pulled together the history of Catholic magisterial thinking on the nature, inspiration, and interpretation of Scripture, as well as its relationship to tradition, and its role in the life of the church, and presented all of this in a new way, with new emphases. *DV* clarified that God's eternal Word is the source of revelation and comes down to us through Scripture and Tradition. *DV* §12 dealt with the thorny matter of biblical interpretation. Of course, this treatment included the centrality of interpreting the Bible in light of the "Spirit through whom it was written," with attention to the Bible's "content and coherence," and "taking into account the whole church's living tradition and the sense of perspective given by faith." But at the same time it took serioiusly the role of the Bible's human authors, and encouraged the biblical interpreter to pay attention to a whole host of matters that are always related to the study of any documents that humans write.[57] These human details included careful attention to the historical context, social and cultural contexts, linguistic and philological analyses, and literary genre. *DV* thus brought a seeming end to the roller-coaster years of, on the one hand, development and discovery, and on the other hand, enforced silence and accepted caution.

In the Wake of Vatican II: The Triumph of Historical Criticism and the Diversity of Methods: 1965–1995

I would be very happy if we had many exegetes like Father [Raymond] Brown.

—JOSEPH RATZINGER, 1988[58]

---

57. Translations from Tanner, *Decrees of the Ecumenical Councils.*

58. Ratzinger, "Foundations and Approaches of Biblical Exegesis," 595. I am indebted to Fr. Pablo Gadenz for this reference.

If anything can be said about the bulk of American Catholic biblical scholarship in the wake of Vatican II, it is that the portion of *DV* §12 that addresses historical-critical biblical interpretation has been followed very well by scholars, building upon the earlier trends we already discussed. Given the challenges faced in the period after the condemnation of Modernism, biblical scholars were eager, finally, to embrace the methods that had once been restricted. Scholars have generally been weaker in the other requirements that *DV* §12 mentions, such as attention to Scripture's content and unity, the church's living tradition, and the analogy of faith. This period saw the development of a plurality of methods for interpreting Scripture, including liberationist and feminist methods. Even with this new plurality, the historical-critical method remains the dominant trend in the American Catholic academy, as in biblical studies more broadly. Two of the most outstanding Catholic scholars in this period are, without a doubt, Raymond Brown, SS and Joseph Fitzmyer, SJ.

Both W. F. Albright students, Brown and Fitzmyer mastered the relevant and ancillary biblical languages.[59] As Fogarty notes, Albright "was the key figure in gaining recognition of American Catholic biblical scholarship in Protestant circles."[60] Fogarty observes how Catholic University of America's Patrick Skehan would take Albright's place at Johns Hopkins from time to time so that Albright could embark on archaeological excavations. Fitzmyer's work was exemplary in its use of Jewish sources (like the Dead Sea Scrolls) for understanding the New Testament and its background.[61] Brown rapidly became known as the foremost Catholic scholar of the New Testament in the western hemisphere. Like Fitzmyer, he situated the New Testament in its early Jewish context, and in particular he revolutionized the field of Johannine studies.[62]

Already by the end of the 1970s, American Catholic biblical scholarship had changed. Some Catholic Bible scholars were moving beyond historical criticism, opening up more space for theological exegesis, although initially this was not the traditional theological exegesis of pre-historical-criticism days, but rather exegesis of a more postmodern sort, with liberationist and feminist themes.[63] This period represents the ascendancy of

59. Witherup, "Raymond E. Brown," 3–4; and Donahue, "Joseph A. Fitzmyer," 65, 68.

60. Fogarty, *American Catholic Biblical Scholarship*, 243.

61. Donahue, "Joseph A. Fitzmyer."

62. Witherup, "Raymond E. Brown."

63. Examples of such scholarship can be found among the work of Sandra M. Schneiders, IHM, Elisabeth Schüssler Fiorenza, and Fernando Segovia. Although these scholars engage in biblical work that is historical-critical as well, they are leading

American Catholic biblical scholars in the broader academic community. No longer restricted in their resources and methods, American Catholic exegetes embraced historical-critical approaches previously associated with Protestants and earned due respect for their accomplished use of these methods.

We might speak of this movement of Catholic Bible scholars, with Brown among those at the forefront, as becoming ecumenical rather than specifically Catholic, much as the Society of Catholic College Teachers of Sacred Doctrine made an (in part) ecumenical move by changing its name to the College Theology Society.[64] These ecumenical concerns were not completely new, but divergent approaches to exegesis had plagued American Catholics from their earliest encounters with American Protestants.[65] Such ecumenism, and what Luke Timothy Johnson identifies as Catholic scholars' attempts to be accepted by non-Catholic scholars, can be understood in light of the earlier modernist controversy. In commenting briefly on the modernist controversy and the Catholic Church's antimodernist response (e.g., *Pascendi* and the early decisions of the PBC), Brown explains: "Since scholars were obliged to assent, such actions gave to the non-Catholic world the image of a monolithically fundamentalist Catholic attitude toward the Bible—an attitude where questions were not discussed by exchanging scientific opinion but were solved by unquestionable centralized authority. The vigorous ecclesiastical action taken in the 1920's [sic] against Catholic biblical scholars who deviated from these directives only reinforced the image."[66] It turned out that Catholics were as good at using historical and critical methods as everyone else. But in the decades to follow, some Catholic biblical scholars began to wonder if anything had been lost in the eager embrace of those methods that had so long been off limits for those who wanted to avoid the pain of censure and remain faithful to the magisterium.

---

examples of postmodern, feminist, and post-colonial. Catholic biblical scholarship. Thus, post-Vatican-II Catholic biblical scholarship is far more diverse than simply historical criticism.

64. On the CTS see Yocum Mize, *Joining the Revolution*, 64–67; and Carey, "College Theology in Historical Perspective," 262. Yocum Mize comments that, "The reason now for the omission of the word 'Catholic' had as much to do with including Catholics as it did with making a sincere effort at ecumenism. Catholics were now teaching religion at colleges and universities outside of the Catholic sphere" (65). This is not to say that it was not also a Catholic one, since ecumenism is closely bound up with Catholicism in the church post-Vatican II, but is not distinctly Catholic.

65. For how this played out in the nineteenth century especially, see, e.g., Noll, "Bishop James Gibbons."

66. Brown, *The Virginal Conception & Bodily Resurrection of Jesus*, 3–4.

One Contemporary Trend: Here Come the Evangelical Catholic Biblical Scholars, 1995–present

> Beyond historical-biblical criticism I see the fuller meaning of the text. This can be developed only by adding the theological. This is still exegesis. It still draws meaning from the text.
>
> —RAYMOND E. BROWN, SS, 1988[67]

> There has risen biblical theology, which is closely connected with exegesis.... [I]t aims at presenting, in a unified and systematic way, the origin and development of revealed doctrine in its successive stages.... This is perhaps the greatest progress exegesis has made in the course of centuries.
>
> —AUGUSTIN BEA, 1953[68]

In commenting on Benedict XVI's *Jesus of Nazareth* volumes, Canadian Cardinal Marc Ouellet has described the dawning of "a new era in theological exegesis."[69] What typifies Ratzinger's exegesis is found among a growing trend within some sectors of American Catholic biblical scholarship, namely, "evangelical Catholic" biblical exegesis. This form of scholarship utilizes traditional historical and philological analyses, but it is also sacramental/liturgical (paying attention to the church's living tradition), canonical (taking into account the content and unity of Scripture), and strives to work explicitly with reference to the church's rich dogmatic tradition (observing the analogy of faith). Among these scholars are both converts to Catholicism from primarily evangelical and Calvinist Protestant traditions, as well as Catholics who were formed after the Second Vatican Council (and, therefore, without the traumatic experiences of a climate of academic restriction).

These scholars have graduated from notable biblical studies programs across the globe, though mainly from those in the U.S. They include figures such as Michael Barber, Brant Pitre, and John Bergsma.[70] Moreover,

---

67. As recorded in Stallsworth, "The Story of an Encounter," 145. I am indebted to Fr. Pablo Gadenz for reminding me of this quotation.

68. Bea, "Progress in the Interpretation of Sacred Scripture," 71.

69. Ouellet, *The Relevance and Future of Vatican II*, 36.

70. E.g., see Barber, "Jesus as the Davidic Temple Builder"; Pitre, *Jesus, the*

these scholars are involved in wide-ranging projects to popularize their scholarship, and they have done so to a far greater extent than previous U.S. Catholic biblical scholars had. Perhaps most significant among this group of scholars is Scott Hahn, whose popular works have collectively sold millions of copies.[71] Hahn's work over the past two decades has proven incredibly diverse, with a surprising depth for its impressive breadth. Hahn has been uniquely able to synthesize and unite a variety of theological topics so often separated in the contemporary theological academy, e.g., Old and New Testament, theology, and exegesis.[72] In addition to scholarly studies in fundamental theology, liturgical theology, and Mariology, Hahn has published major exegetical studies on a vast array of biblical texts: Genesis, 1 and 2 Chronicles, Ezekiel, the Gospel of Luke and Acts, the Gospel of John, Galatians, and Hebrews.[73]

Conclusion

Though the work of Hahn and other evangelical Catholic biblical scholars obviously does not encompass the great diversity of Catholic biblical scholarship in recent years, it is a noteworthy trend due to its both popular and academic reach. Understanding the history regarding Catholic biblical interpretation that precedes this trend is crucial to understanding and acknowledging its influence. Because of the past struggles of Catholic biblical scholars, more recent scholars—most of them lay—have the freedom to publish academically and popularly without a constant fear of censure. There is room for debate and also room for commitment to past magisterial teachings; this commitment need no longer be seen as the result of unreflective obedience so much as careful consideration allowed by a great diversity of scholarly resources.

Tribulation, and the End of the Exile; and Bergsma, *The Jubilee from Leviticus to Qumran*. Other such scholars include William Bales, Pablo Gadenz, Timothy Gray, Leroy Huizenga, Steven Smith, Edward Sri, and Peter Williamson.

71. Hahn is a best-selling author with Doubleday, having sold over a half-million copies of several of his books. In addition to his edited *Catholic Bible Dictionary* and his co-edited *Ignatius Catholic Study Bible*, Hahn also wrote popular summaries of Scripture and introductory material. On Hahn, see Morrow, "Evangelical Catholics and Catholic Biblical Scholarship."

72. E.g., see Hahn, *Kinship By Covenant*; and Hahn and Wiker, *Politicizing the Bible*.

73. E.g., see Hahn, *Covenant and Communion*; Hahn, "Covenant, Oath, and the Aqedah"; Hahn, "Covenant, Cult, and the Curse-of-Death"; Hahn, "A Broken Covenant"; Hahn, "Biblical Theology and Marian Studies"; Bergsma and Hahn, "Noah's Nakedness"; and Hahn and Bergsma, "What Laws Were 'Not Good'?"

It is often painful and difficult to study the history of Modernism. Quoting French historian Émile Poulat, Portier reminds us:

> ". . . more than an abandoned river bed, the modernist crisis brings to mind a battle field, still mined, through which it is wise not to pass without taking precautions." . . . In the intellectual *cum* spiritual struggles of these figures, we sometimes recognize our own. I cannot remember them without a certain sadness. The modernist crisis makes the self-involving nature of theological inquiry unavoidable even to the obtuse. Remembering the modernist crisis takes on a certain moral cast that puts the inquirer at risk. One is drawn to take sides and to consider one's obligations.[74]

For more than three decades, keenly aware of "the burden of the dead," Portier has risked travel through this particular minefield. We should be attentive to the words of such a careful historical theologian and wise fellow traveler. Overreactions, anonymous denouncements, clandestine witch hunts—one is reminded especially of the work of the *Sodalitium Pianum*—actually occurred, some of which was clearly sinful, and should motivate the believing historian to make acts of reparation. At the same time, real dangers existed. Fr. Angelo Roncalli (the future Pope St. John XXIII) gives us a first-hand glimpse into his own thoughts of the time (1910):

> this wind of Modernism blows very strongly and more widely than seems at first sight, and that it may very likely strike and bewilder even those who were at first moved only by the desire to adapt the ancient truth of Christianity to modern needs. Many, some of them good men, have fallen into error, perhaps unconsciously; they have let themselves be swept into the field of error. The worst of it is that ideas lead very swiftly to the spirit of independence and private judgment about everything and everyone.[75]

Describing the conflict at the beginning of the twentieth century, Portier claims, "the modernist crisis ripped through Catholic intellectual life like a tragic storm. But its havoc cut to a level deeper than the merely intellectual. *Pascendi* forced people to take sides. Agonized personal decisions put colleagues at odds and set friend against friend. Censured priests questioned fellow clergy or pious laymen who escaped censure."[76] In looking at trends

---

74. Portier, *Divided Friends*, 38–39.

75. Pope John XXIII, *Journal of a Soul*, 175–76.

76. Portier, *Divided Friends*, 4.

from the history of American Catholic biblical scholarship, it becomes clear that this history is full of wounds—wounds which, for many, remain open and sore. The danger in such a context is further wounding, unintentional but also defensive. As a scholar and mentor Portier has embodied, and has encouraged among his students, an openness to dialogue. Such dialogue— charitable, with patient listening and attempts to understand the other—is essential if Catholic biblical scholarship in the U.S. is to proceed in a more charitable way than its past.[77]

77. I owe thanks to Biff Rocha and Maria Morrow for critiquing drafts of this chapter.

4

Staying with the Program

Studying the Word of God in Changing Times

—— Patricia M. McDonald, SHCJ ——

For faculty and students alike, the Theology Department at Mount St. Mary's in the 1990s was a fine place to continue one's education. It was there that my colleague, mentor, and friend, Bill Portier, introduced me to some of my Scripture-teaching forebears from the early-twentieth-century United States. I thus discovered the extent to which, even for a non-historian, putting some effort into historical research could provide salutary perspective to one's primary activities.

The classic coverage of Catholic biblical scholarship in the United States up to the Second Vatican Council (1962–65) is Gerald Fogarty's 1989 book, *American Catholic Biblical Scholarship*. Fogarty's treatment includes the four main turning points in recent biblical understanding, shared by the whole church. The first of these is Leo XIII's 1893 encyclical *Providentissimus Deus*, addressed to bishops and encouraging the study of Scripture in seminaries and academic institutions under their jurisdiction. It was followed all too soon by the anti-modernist legislation from Leo's successor, Pius X. The resulting repressive atmosphere perdured until 1943. In that year, Pius XII marked the fiftieth anniversary of *Providentissimus Deus* with the breakthrough *Divino Afflante Spiritu*, which promoted the use of the methods of modern biblical criticism, although strong resistance remained in some quarters until the Council was well underway. Fourthly came *Dei Verbum*, Vatican II's Dogmatic Constitution on Divine Revelation (1965): the "*Verbum*" in its title is Christ, the Word of God, to whom tradition and

Scripture, "flowing from the same divine wellspring" bear witness.[1] Those who interpret Scripture must take very seriously both its divine origin and the fact that it was written by human beings who belonged to their particular time and place.[2]

From our present vantage point it is hard to appreciate the extent of the transformation that has taken place in scriptural study by Catholics in the United States. From the early days of the republic until around the middle of the twentieth century, it took place almost entirely in the context of the formation of priests. In the first half of the nineteenth century, as diocese after diocese was established, each bishop wanted to ensure a supply of priests to succeed the foreign-born clergy he had managed to recruit. So he would establish a seminary in which he himself was likely to be the principal instructor of a handful of students. Most such initiatives were short-lived, although some developed into diocesan or regional seminaries, alongside others that had been founded and run by groups with particular expertise and experience of priestly formation.[3]

By 1893, when Leo wrote *Providentissimus Deus*, Georgetown and St. Mary's Seminary, Baltimore had been in existence for more than a century.[4] Baltimore's Archbishop John Carroll had been involved in the foundation of both. He entrusted St. Mary's to the Sulpicians, who were also in charge of Mount Saint Mary's Seminary in Emmitsburg, Maryland (from 1809 until 1826) and St. Charles College, a minor seminary established in 1848, originally in Ellicott City, Maryland, on land provided (in 1830) by Charles Carroll, a Maryland signer of the Declaration of Independence. Overseas, the American College of Louvain was founded by Martin Spalding in 1857, and the U.S. bishops established the North American College in Rome two years later. The Jesuits opened their seminary at Woodstock in 1869, and the Sulpicians began to offer priestly formation at St. John's Seminary, Brighton, Massachusetts, in 1884. The Catholic University of America was founded as a graduate institution in 1887 by the U.S. Catholic bishops, with the support of Leo XIII. There were also many high school seminaries sponsored by religious orders of men, to provide the necessary training for their own people.

In all of these institutions, the professors of Scripture tended to be priests from European countries, notably France, Ireland, Italy, and

1. Second Vatican Council, *Dei Verbum* §9.

2. Ibid., §12.

3. Viéban, "Ecclesiastical Seminary."

4. Georgetown now dates its foundation from 1789, although the original documents read 1788 and the first classes were held in 1792. The Sulpicians founded St Mary's, Baltimore, in 1791.

Germany. Their students were boys aspiring to be priests, seminarians, or (at CUA) young priests undergoing post-ordination studies. Fairly soon, financial constraints and the pressure to provide education for Catholic boys in the New World would move some of the seminaries to admit a wider student body and, eventually, to develop into many of today's Catholic colleges and universities.[5] As long as they were seminaries, however, priestly formation determined the curriculum and the limits of what could be taught.

The extent and nature of those limits depended very much on the time and place. To begin with, the signs were auspicious. The Third Plenary Council of Baltimore (1884), taking its cue from Roman concerns of the time, mandated seminary programs that were rigorous in their intellectual scope and content.[6] The preparatory seminary curriculum should include Christian doctrine, English, at least one other modern language, Latin (speaking and writing), Greek, natural sciences, and Gregorian chant. The major seminary was to devote two years to philosophy and four to theology, the latter of which was comprised of dogmatic and moral theology, biblical exegesis, church history, canon law, liturgy, and "sacred eloquence."[7]

During the following two decades or so, the program thus set out was developed with skill and enthusiasm in the United States. A key figure was the Irish-born Sulpician, John Baptist Hogan (1829–1901), who, as theological expert to John Williams, the Archbishop of Boston, had attended the 1884 Council within months of his arrival in the United States to be the founding rector of the Boston seminary, St. John's, Brighton. Hogan had already spent more than thirty years teaching dogma and moral theology to seminarians in Paris. Although not a Scripture specialist, he came to realize the importance of the recent developments in the field, especially in light of *Providentissimus Deus*, and he recognized the need to address the questions that biblical scholars were raising about topics that were traditionally the concern of theologians, such as inspiration and biblical inerrancy.[8] Equally importantly, Hogan was connected with a handful of younger French Sulpicians who had trained in Paris (at the Society's seminary at Issy and at the *Institut Catholique*) at a time when questions of historicity were becoming increasingly pressing. Scott Appleby credits Hogan with having recruited

5. In the 1740s, John Carroll and his cousin Charles were among the Catholic boys from Maryland sent to Europe to attend the Jesuits' school at St. Omer in French Flanders. See Spalding, "Most Rev. John Carroll."

6. See the Council's decree, *De Clericorum Educatione et Instructione*, and Talar, "Seminary Reform and Theological Method on the Eve of the Modernist Crisis."

7. See Fanning, "Plenary Councils of Baltimore."

8. See Hogan, *Clerical Studies*, a collection of articles about seminary education previously published in the *American Ecclesiastical Review* from 1891.

one of these, Francis Ernest Gigot (1859–1920), for the seminary in Brighton, where Gigot taught dogma and Scripture for four years from 1885, the year after its foundation.[9]

Gigot's Early Years

Francis Gigot, originally from Lhuant, near Bourges, studied first at the seminary in Limoges. He received the STB from the *Institut Catholique* in 1882, was ordained the following year, and obtained his licentiate, also in theology, in 1884. At some point, perhaps immediately after graduation, he would have completed the *solitude*, the required period of formation as a Sulpician, since it was as a Sulpician that Gigot was sent to the seminary in Boston in 1885. He was then in his mid-twenties.

At this time the church had no provision for specialized biblical studies: the *École Biblique* in Jerusalem was established in 1890, the Pontifical Biblical Commission in 1902, and the Biblical Institute in Rome not until 1909. But biblical questions were very much in the air, among educated people at large and within the church, and by the time that *Providentissimus Deus* appeared in 1893, Gigot was firmly established as a seminary teacher and in a position to respond to its challenges. One of these was to provide the necessary materials for students to learn biblical "Introduction," which Leo spelled out as "how to prove the integrity and authority of the Bible, how to investigate and ascertain its true sense, and how to meet and refute objections."[10] Gigot's engagement with this project is characterized by remarkable energy and skill.[11]

In the following years, he wrote two outlines of biblical history, one for each Testament (1897 and 1898), a two-volume *Outlines of a Life of Our Lord* (1896 and 1897), a *General Introduction to the Study of the Holy Scriptures* (1900), and a two-volume *Special Introduction to the Study of the Old Testament*: Part I, *The Historical Books* (1901) and Part II, *Didactic Books and Prophetical Writings* (1906). Even today these books are impressive, packed with detailed information that is made accessible by means of a synopsis that opens each chapter. Thus, the 606-page *General Introduction*

---

9. Appleby, *Church and Age Unite!*, 95.

10. Pope Leo XIII, *Providentissimus Deus* §13. See Hartdegen, "The Influence of the Encyclical *Providentissimus Deus*," 142.

11. Other contributions from the United States included Charles P. Grannan, *A General Introduction to the Bible*, and Anthony Maas, SJ, *The Life of Jesus Christ According to the Gospel History*. Grannan was one of the original twelve members of the PBC.

(which specifies in its preface that the historical-critical method will be used)[12] consists of four sections: Canon, Text and Versions, Hermeneutics of Sacred Scripture, and (first as an Appendix, but as a separate section from the second edition of 1901) Biblical Inspiration. Nineteen high-quality plates illustrate various forms of Hebrew script and a wide range of biblical manuscripts and versions: Hebrew (including a Samaritan Pentateuch), the fourth- and fifth-century major Greek uncial codices, a cursive Greek manuscript, Syriac, Coptic, and Latin versions, examples from Wycliffe and Tyndale, and nine versions of the English translation of Hebrews 1:1–9. By 1904, with the third edition nearly sold out, Gigot had produced an abridged edition of 347 pages for "colleges and other institutions where the larger work has but little chance to be adopted."[13] The abridgement still includes from the full version the list of nineteenth-century Catholic commentaries in German, French, English, and Latin. The fourth section (formerly "Inspiration") is now "Biblical Theopneustics," but the original nineteen plates remain. Gigot evidently had a strong sense of the importance of artifacts and the visual in studying the Word of God.

While writing and revising these volumes, Gigot was publishing articles in the *American Ecclesiastical Review* and, by 1903, had earned a DD from St Mary's University, Baltimore, where he had been teaching since 1899.[14] Clearly, he took full advantage of the opportunity that he saw offered by Leo's encyclical, to pursue critical studies of Scripture. This was in tune with the generally upbeat and expansive tone of the Sulpician seminaries in Baltimore, Boston and, after 1896, Dunwoodie in New York. By then, the expatriate Sulpicians had been joined by a number of talented and forward looking American-born members, including Charles Rex, Edward Dyer, and James Driscoll.[15] The Society was, however, part of the French province until 1903, when it became a vicariate with Dyer as vicar general.

Their connection with France became problematic. In 1880, the French Parliament, seeking to free scientific learning from ecclesiastical influence, had curtailed the rights of the *Institut Catholique*.[16] This did not deter the young Alfred Loisy, teacher of Hebrew from 1882 and a dynamic and influential lecturer in the Old Testament at the *Institut* from 1884. Although

---

12. The (undated) fourth edition in the Biblical Institute library includes the note that the second and subsequent editions, including the fourth, differed from the first only in a few verbal modifications and the promotion of "Inspiration" from an Appendix to "Part Fourth." The Institute has also a copy of the abridged edition of 1904.

13. Gigot, *General Introduction*, abridged, 5.

14. See Curtis, *The American Catholic Who's Who*, 241–42.

15. See Kauffman, *Tradition and Transformation in Catholic Culture*, 153, 179–80.

16. Hill, *The Politics of Modernism*, 51, 72.

supported by the rector, Mgr. Maurice d'Hulst, Loisy drew opposition by his attacks on traditional theological positions in the cause of advancing the "higher criticism," which took seriously the historical aspects of Scripture. Notable among his opponents was the Sulpician superior general, Henri-Joseph Icard, who in 1892 refused to allow his students to attend Loisy's lectures on exegesis and provoked d'Hulst to publish an ill-advised attempt at defending Loisy's views that led to the latter's resignation from the *Institut Catholique* in November of the following year.[17] Even so, Loisy continued to complicate ecclesial life, both theologically and politically.[18]

Icard died two days after Loisy resigned.[19] To Gigot's delight, the Sulpicians elected as his successor the moderately progressive Arthur Captier. During the more relaxed years of Captier's administration, from 1894 until 1901, Gigot could publish his books without difficulty, and the various American Sulpician projects flourished. This changed under Captier's successor, the more reactionary Jules Lebas, whose accession coincided with a deteriorating political situation in France that would lead to the closure of seminaries and, in 1905, the separation of church and state. Lebas's problem with Gigot was simply that he was not giving the common teaching: Thomas Shelley notes that Gigot "was no firebrand" but had definite views on the place of Scripture in seminary formation, having published an article of that title in the *American Ecclesiastical Review* of 1900, an article that reads well even today.[20]

In a key move for the Sulpicians in the United States, Lebas in 1901 removed the power of censorship of their work from their American superiors and relocated it in very safe hands in Paris. By this time, too, Americanism had been censured (1899), to some extent because of Roman concerns about the French church; theologically, the charge of semi-Pelagianism that was implied in the censure could be brought against those who used the "higher criticism" (which came to be known as the historical-critical method) to interpret Scripture.[21] In 1901 the American Sulpicians had established their

17. O'Connell, *Critics on Trial*, 128–31. A decade earlier, Icard had made a similar attack on the historian Louis Duchesne.

18. Loisy's influence was not restricted to Europe. Joseph Bruneau, a younger contemporary of Gigot who moved to the United States in 1894 after studying with Loisy at the *Institut Catholique* until Icard's ban, acted as his agent for articles that appeared in the *American Ecclesiastical Review* between 1896 and 1898. See Portier, *Divided Friends*, 212–13.

19. O'Connell, *Critics on Trial*, 213.

20. Shelley, *Dunwoodie*, 131. Gigot's article is "The Study of Sacred Scripture in Theological Seminaries."

21. See Fogarty, "American Catholic Biblical Scholarship: A Review."

own *Solitude* (house of formation), St. Austin's College, Washington, DC, on the campus of the Catholic University, and Gigot became part of this formation community, while continuing to teach in Baltimore.

The Move to Dunwoodie

In 1904 Gigot moved again, this time to the New York seminary at Dun-woodie. Archbishop Michael Corrigan had entrusted Dunwoodie to the Sulpicians at its foundation in 1896, much against the will of his auxiliary, John Farley, who would succeed him as archbishop in 1902. The seminary rector was James Driscoll, a talented and somewhat headstrong Sulpician who was not afraid to put pressure on his superiors to advance the cause of his many and varied projects. Those projects included assembling a simi-larly gifted and forward-looking set of colleagues; extending support to Lo-isy; forging ecumenical relations with Columbia University, Union College, and NYU; and, crucially as it turned out, working with New York diocesan priests Francis P. Duffy (1871–1932) and John F. Brady (1871–1940) to pro-duce the short-lived *New York Review* (*NYR*),[22] which in 1906 would be a major factor in the defection of four of the five Sulpicians on the seminary faculty, who at that point joined the Archdiocese of New York and took the seminary with them, so that Dunwoodie was no longer under the control of the Society of Saint Sulpice.

Gigot had not been happy in Washington: a letter of 1903 indicates that he was desperate to move out, even if that involved leaving the Sulpi-cians.[23] At this time, too, publication of the second volume of his Old Tes-tament *Special Introduction* was being held up by the Sulpician censors in Paris and, for reasons that are never stated but presumably relate to the anti-Modernist moves that came to a head in 1907, his projected New Testament *Special Introduction* never would appear, even though it was announced on the frontispiece of the 1906 Old Testament *Special Introduction*. Meanwhile, however, joining Driscoll and the others at Dunwoodie in 1904 provided the conditions in which Gigot could continue to be productive, at least for a few more years. The *NYR*, in particular, gave him a ready outlet for new

22. DeVito, *The New York Review (1905–1908)*. For a retrospective overview a cen-tury after the periodical's demise, see Shelley, "A Somber Anniversary."

23. Gigot wrote to James Driscoll on 7 March 1903 (Record Group 10, Box 9, Sulpician Archives, Baltimore), that he would go to St. Charles Borromeo seminary in Philadelphia if they would have him, and that the Paulist Fathers in DC would take him the following year if he left the Sulpicians.

articles and also for some that he had most likely already written[24] while, at the same time, enabling him to reach beyond the seminary, subscribers to the *American Ecclesiastical Review*, and the popular audience addressed in his *Biblical Lectures* (1901). The *NYR* gave as the first of its stated "objects in view": "To treat in a scholarly fashion, yet in a manner intelligible to the ordinary cultured mind, topics of interest bearing on Theology [and] Scripture."[25]

Gigot's articles certainly delivered on that objective throughout the three years of the periodical's existence, June 1905 to June 1908. For example, his pieces on the authorship of Isaiah, the historicity of Jonah, and the Book of Job engaged with some of the live biblical issues of the day. Indeed, so live were they that the Pontifical Biblical Commission found it necessary to issue decrees that would terminate further conversation involving Gigot, the Bible, and the "ordinary cultured mind."[26]

Gigot's six articles about "higher criticism" address the needs of such readers, as he explains what is involved, what is at stake, what can be gained from it, how it relates to Tradition, and the "objectivity" of the method. His precise and clear writing lacks any indication that he is not using his mother tongue. In the first two articles he acknowledges the problems that Catholics have with higher criticism because of its association with "doubt and infidelity" and because of meddlers who have rightly incurred the displeasure of theologians. By contrast, he himself is using the method, he says, "without anti-scientific and anti-religious bias" and counsels "earnestness,

24. In the first year of the *New York Review*, Gigot published there eleven articles on nine different topics, totaling about 165 pages. Overall, he contributed twenty-three articles and around the same number of book reviews. On this, see McDonald, "Biblical Brinkmanship."

25. From the announcement sheet, of which 25,000 were circulated prior to the first issue. See DeVito, *The New York Review*, 47–49 and Appendix A. The contributors were among the most avant-garde in Europe and North America, writing on a wide range of theological, ecclesial, and political matters. New books and periodicals were reviewed as they came out, matters of current interest were reported, and the regular "Notes" (probably written by Duffy) ensured that nobody could be in doubt about what the periodical stood for. Volume 3 even included Pius X's anti-Modernist decree *Lamentabili Sane Exitu* (in the original Latin and in English) and a translation of his encyclical *Pascendi Dominici Gregis*, along with editorial comment and reports of their reception. The text of Pius's third document, requiring adherence to the decisions of the Biblical Commission, the *New York Review* provided only in Latin. From January 1908 there were neither notes nor book reviews. The end was near.

26. The Pontifical Biblical Commission's decision of 1905 claimed historicity for such books as Jonah and Job; in 1908 it denied multiple authorship of the Book of Isaiah. Twelve more such decisions were issued between 1905 and 1915. See Béchard, *The Scripture Documents*, 187–211.

singleness of purpose and . . . modesty as is found with the textual critics."[27] Cautious and careful but never fearful or timid, he notes in the third article of this series that "[p]ure and simple appeals to the dictum of authority . . . will not weigh much against scientific theories."[28] Elsewhere in the same piece he quotes in Greek from 1 Thess 5:21, "test everything; hold fast to what is good"—excellent advice even to those of us who can learn from his diligence and fidelity whilst raising our own questions about the extent to which biblical interpretation can be "scientific" and "objective."

Gigot displays his skill as an exegete of the New Testament in his six articles on the synoptic gospels. As in his textbooks, he translates the Greek himself, here in three parallel columns. Each article considers a short pericope, e.g., the ministry of John the Baptist, or the Baptism or the Temptation of Jesus. Throughout, the focus is the gospel text, located in its New Testament and wider biblical context. Gigot is sensitive to each author's style and to the theological concerns that might have led an evangelist to alter what he found in his source(s). He assumes Marcan priority but without the hypothetical Q: like some more recent scholars, such as Austin Farrer, Michael Goulder, and Mark Goodacre, he thought that Luke used Matthew and Mark.

The Program and Anti-Modernism

Occasionally in these articles, Gigot leaves a topic unfinished, promising further studies to come on it. As things turned out, circumstances made that impossible: although after January 1906 he was no longer subject to the Sulpician censors, the mood of the church had changed radically. With his *motu proprio* of November 1907, *Praestantia Scripturae Sacrae*, Pius X put Scripture scholars on notice that the four decisions on biblical topics from the Pontifical Biblical Commission had to be accepted and would not be the last. Thus, the one of June 1911 insisted that, before Paul's arrival in Rome, Matthew wrote an Aramaic Gospel identical to the later Greek version. In June 1912, the first of two decisions on the Synoptics required assent to a variety of positions for which the available evidence was, at best, insufficient (e.g., about the precise identity of the evangelists), while the second allowed exegetes free rein in explaining the similarities and differences among the three gospels—provided that they agreed with all of the Biblical Commission's decisions and eschewed the Two-Source Theory.[29]

27. Gigot, "The Higher Criticism of the Bible: The Name and the Thing," 726.

28. Gigot, "The Higher Criticism of the Bible: Its General Principles," 161.

29. See Béchard, *The Scripture Documents*, 197–202.

All this struck at the heart of the work of scholars like Gigot, to whom it had seemed obvious that scholarly diligence and reason would help believers to come to a fuller understanding of God's word. Fear, academic and ecclesial power plays and, not least, complex political and social currents made for a fiercely protective response from those who had authority in the church. So the suppression of the *NYR* in 1908 did not, in the end, make much difference to Gigot, although the reasons for the suppression, combined with the dismissal of the charismatic Driscoll and his replacement as seminary rector by a former police chaplain, left no doubt that Archbishop Farley intended to regain the control of his seminary and its ethos. If Gigot wished to remain a seminary professor, he would have to fall into line. Indeed, the pages of the second and third volumes of the *NYR* provide evidence of his transition from careful-but-adventurous exegete to a much "safer" position. For in the issues between January–February 1907 and the final one of May–June 1908, which covered the months during which Pius X delivered his initial threefold response to Modernism, the *NYR* carried six articles by Gigot on "Divorce in the New Testament: An Exegetical Study."[30]

The choice of topic is significant. Like Dunwoodie itself, Gigot had belonged to the Archdiocese of New York only since January 1906, when he and the others had left the Sulpicians. He surely knew that Archbishop Farley had learned that the seminary he had finally wrested from the Society was in the care of several faculty members, including the rector, whose reputation regarding orthodoxy and safe practice was regarded as very dubious in the places that mattered.[31] For Gigot, who was a dyed-in-the-wool seminary professor, and would remain so until his death in 1920, prudence was in order. So there was practical wisdom in his writing exegetical articles about divorce, where the church's position was very clear and was, moreover, being challenged by impending civil legislation in the United States.[32] The project would show the archbishop that Gigot's expertise could be of practical use to the church because it moved the discussion about marriage into the scriptural arena, where it was possible to engage with a wider society that was largely Christian and disapproving of divorce, yet seemed prepared to tolerate it as a practical necessity.

The methodology of these articles is similar to that of Gigot's other *NYR* contributions, and in them he acknowledges that legal realities may

30. See Gigot, "Divorce in the New Testament."

31. The Apostolic Delegate, Diomede Falconio, had received complaints about the behavior of Dunwoodie graduate students in Europe. See Shelley, *Dunwoodie*, 166–70.

32. In November 1906, a national convention held in Philadelphia had agreed to a bill, to be sent to state lawmakers, which would make possible the establishment of uniform divorce laws across the United States. See "For Uniform Divorce Laws."

have to be at odds with those of religion and conscience. Yet the work has not stood the test of time, because of the complexity of the topic, the very different social context, its incompleteness (which Gigot admitted), and a more apologetic approach that at times sounds like special pleading. It is telling that these pieces required little editing to be transformed into a book, *Christ's Teaching Concerning Divorce in the New Testament: An Exegetical Study*, which Gigot published in 1912 and dedicated, in uncharacteristically extravagant language, to his archbishop, John Farley, who had been made a cardinal the previous year.[33]

Little else followed. A 1909 article about the Mosaic authorship of Deuteronomy in the *Irish Theological Quarterly* promised a follow-up which did not appear. In 1913 the same journal carried a two-part article on Luke 1:34–35 that uses the historical-critical method to demonstrate the Catholic Church's fidelity to biblical tradition and that the virginal conception was "a historical fact in the eyes of St. Luke."[34] A 1915 pamphlet argues for Moses as author of the Pentateuch. Gigot translated (with very unadventurous introductions) Revelation and the Pastoral Epistles, as part of an English series (1915 and, published posthumously, 1924). His *A Primer of Old Testament History*, published by Paulist Press in 1919, was far less detailed than his *Outlines of Jewish History* of 1897.

Gigot continued to teach Scripture at Dunwoodie until his death in 1920 but, along with his peers and successors, he was essentially shut down by the anti-Modernist legislation. Some seminaries continued to use his textbooks, although not always in ways that corresponded to their content:[35] with the exception of CUA's Department of Semitics and Egyptian Language and Literature, serious biblical scholarship could not be offered to priests trained in the United States.

The Program Today

The transition from this situation to our own, catalyzed by *Divino Afflante Spiritu*, began slowly and not without conflict. John L. McKenzie wrote a lively and unvarnished (though occasionally self-serving) account of the difficulties under which reputable and faithful American biblical scholars were laboring even in the early 1960s.[36]

33. See McDonald, "Biblical Brinkmanship," 33–35.

34. Gigot, "The Virgin Birth in St. Luke's Gospel."

35. For the example of Joseph P. Nelson, at Dunwoodie between 1913 and 1944, see Shelley, *Dunwoodie*, 192.

36. McKenzie, "American Catholic Biblical Scholarship, 1955–1980." According

Those initially involved in the renaissance were men who had received formation as priests[37] and undertook postgraduate studies at a range of institutions, including Johns Hopkins, CUA, the Biblical Institute, and the *École Biblique*. Gradually, women religious and lay people took up the challenge of *Divino Afflante Spiritu* and, after 1965, of *Dei Verbum*. The predominance of the historical-critical method enabled Catholic biblical studies to take its place alongside that of other denominations and the academy. Specialization ensued, and became ever greater as the range of methods employed grew wider. At the same time, those engaging in them were culturally and educationally more diverse and often lacked the theological grounding that their seminary-trained forebears (and the contemporary ecclesiastical establishment) had received.

Despite an impressive array of pastoral initiatives and resources developed over the decades, there arose a perception that the Bible had become the preserve of specialists whose methods were not providing what was needed for religious nourishment.[38] The Biblical Commission addressed the issue in its 1993 document, *The Interpretation of the Bible in the Church*, by reviewing the range of methods then current, exploring some hermeneutical questions, setting out some of the characteristics of Catholic interpretation of Scripture, and indicating practical ways in which biblical interpretation grounds the life of the church.[39] Benedict XVI's Exhortation *Verbum Domini* (2010), following the 2008 synod on the Word of God, addressed further ecclesial aspects of biblical interpretation, without any backtracking as regards the necessity of serious study on the part of biblical scholars.[40] Things had moved a very long way from the negativity of the

---

to McKenzie, Pius XII's 1950 encyclical, *Humani Generis*, was the root of the problem: "In the minds of many this encyclical was intended to bring to an abrupt halt the renascence of biblical studies initiated by the encyclical *Divino afflante Spiritu* issued by the same Pius XII in 1943" (212). In the United States, significant proponents of such a view were the Apostolic Delegate, Egidio Vagnozzi (in post 1958–68) and Joseph Clifford Fenton (1906–69), professor of dogmatic theology at CUA, editor of the *American Ecclesiastical Review* (1943–1963), *peritus* of Cardinal Ottaviani at Vatican II, and staunch defender of the mid-century ecclesiastical status quo against all comers, including the members of the Catholic Biblical Association of America.

37. A notable exception was Mother Kathryn Sullivan, RSCJ (1905–2006), the first woman member of the Catholic Biblical Association of America (1947) and the first woman to hold office in it (1958). See Osiek, *Kathryn Sullivan, RSCJ*.

38. See, e.g., Donahue, "A Journey Remembered."

39. Among the document's practical suggestions was a recommendation of *lectio divina*, for groups and individuals.

40. See, e.g., Pope Benedict XVI, *Verbum Domini* §29–30, 32–33, 45.

Biblical Commission's decrees with which Gigot had to contend, although the magisterium has ceded none of its teaching authority.

On the other hand, those Catholic Scripture scholars who are not members of the Biblical Commission (and perhaps even some who are) are not in a position to present an equivalent unitary view of their position when, for example, they wonder about the relatively slight impact that the scriptural renewal has had on the formulation of official church documents that are not directly concerned with the Bible itself, or when, as occasionally happens, parts of translations approved for liturgical use seem determined more by particular theological positions than by the best available reading of the biblical text. Yet such experiences bear no comparison with what Gigot and his contemporaries had to endure: they are, rather, an aspect of the ambiguity inherent in studying Scripture as members of a church that values the Bible as God's word and not simply as an object of academic study. Like Gigot, we faithfully do what we can with what we are given. This, too, I learned from Bill Portier.

Part 2

Inculturating the Catholic Tradition

The Lives We Read and the Life We Lead

Modern Sanctity, Modern Catholicity,
and the Case of Orestes Brownson

—————— ANDREW D. BLACK ——————

I n 1997 Robert Ellsberg produced *All Saints,* an annual cycle of readings featuring daily profiles of "Saints, Prophets, and Witnesses for Our Time." As the concluding phrase of its subtitle—"for our time"—makes clear it is not merely a repackaged book of traditional saints. Ellsberg sought to present diverse women and men who bring holiness to life as a real, attractive possibility for contemporary people. Though he gathered his subjects from all eras of church and biblical history, roughly a third of the men and women featured in *All Saints* lived during the past two centuries.

The selections reflect Ellsberg's own status as a Catholic (e.g., Dom Helder Camara [Feb. 7] and Henri Nouwen [Sept. 20] are the most recent figures narrated), and its pages are filled with canonized Roman Catholic saints. Yet more than half of Ellsberg's compelling portraits feature people that have not been canonized by any Christian communion, a good number were not Catholic,[1] and a handful were not professing Christians.[2] This ex-

---

1. A sampling of the non-Catholic Christians includes George Fox (Jan. 13), Martin Niemoeller (Jan. 14), Nikolai Berdyaev (March 23), J.S. Bach (March 21), Fannie Lou Hamer (March 14), Martin Luther King (April 4), Andre Trocmé (April 7), Dietrich Bonhoeffer (April 9), William Stringfellow (April 26), Karl Barth (May 10), John Wesley (June 17), Walter Rauschenbusch (July 25), Jonathan Edwards (Oct. 5), Clarence Jordan (Oct. 28), Fyodor Dostoyevsky (Oct. 30), and Sojourner Truth (Nov. 26).

2. Among the non-Christians are Mohandas Gandhi (Jan. 30), Martin Buber

pansive range, together with Ellsberg's appealing prose, has earned *All Saints* a broad readership. Now nearly two decades old, it can still be found in the Religion and Spirituality section of many booksellers and was reprinted in 2012. Given its character as a *vade mecum*, an aid to daily devotion, it no doubt rests today on many a nightstand and retreat center bookshelf.

The mere fact of its mass popularity, and its classification as devotional/spiritual literature, might lead some to overlook or even disregard *All Saints* as a work deserving of serious theological attention. Such a judgment would be unfortunate, because Ellsberg has provided not only a useful and engaging resource for reflection, but also an important work of constructive theology in its own right. Put simply, *All Saints* deserves to be read appreciatively, critically (i.e., carefully), and even more widely.

There is another obstacle likely preventing *All Saints* from garnering such widespread and considered appreciation, however. In short, its self-consciously modern and "prophetic" outlook raises the suspicion that this is a book of saints tailored to the sensibilities of *liberal* Catholics and their spiritual fellow travelers. In other words, is Ellsberg's a genuinely inclusive account of holiness (*all* saints), or simply an alternative take on sanctity?

The ecclesial and even religious diversity of the figures in *All Saints* confronts self-consciously orthodox readers, who may suspect that Ellsberg's selection criteria are not grounded in a specifically Christian conception of holiness/sainthood but, rather, in a general commitment to abstract principles like liberty, equality, and fraternity (or—more simply and broadly—"social justice"). In addition, many of his exemplary men and women were under suspicion by church authorities or in direct conflict with them. The table of contents is rife with confessors and martyrs honored by several disparate groups[3]—radical Protestants, secular critics, dissenting Catholics—united by a shared antipathy to traditional forms of ecclesiastical authority. *All Saints* could thus serve as a sourcebook for card-carrying progressives seeking to compose a litany of heroes who stood on the "right side of history."

One could, then, present evidence for concluding that *All Saints* is irredeemably partisan and heterodox. In a word, it fails the test of *catholicity*. Such a judgment, however, cannot be sustained. Rather than an uncritically

---

(Feb. 8), Abraham Joshua Heschel (Dec. 23), Dag Hammarskjöld (Sept. 18), Henry David Thoreau (May 6), Vinoba Bhave (Sept. 11), and Albert Camus (Nov. 7).

3. A full list of such figures would easily amount to a majority of the daily entries in *All Saints*. However, Ellsberg's treatments of Galileo Galilei (Jan. 8), Giordano Bruno (Feb. 17), Peter Waldo (May 8), Marguerite Porete (June 1), Jan Hus (July 6), Mechthild of Magdeburg (July 27), George Tyrrell (July 16), and Anne Hutchinson (Aug. 8), come particularly to mind in this regard.

ideological tract, the impressive achievement of *All Saints* is that Ellsberg's book displays a theological fecundity that generates important critical questions and a theological profundity that defies simple categorization.

A clue to this generativity can be found in Ellsberg's suggestion that it would be just as well to speak of his subjects as living illustrations of "wholeness" rather than "holiness."[4] Etymologically speaking, wholeness is synonymous with catholicity. An essentially contested theological concept, catholicity is notorious for being a quality sought and claimed by virtually everyone, even as particular judgments about catholicity quickly expose disagreements and divisions that call such claims to wholeness or universality into question. When college professors explain to undergraduates that part of the distinctive genius of Catholicism is its insistence on an inclusive "both-and" rather than a dialectical "either-or" approach, this is an appeal to catholicity. So too, however, is the claim that the Catholic "both-and" is specifically and dogmatically grounded in the church's traditional confession of the divine-human person of Jesus Christ (i.e., the catholic faith believed "always, everywhere, and by everyone," as in the famous formula provided by St. Vincent of Lérins). For now, let us simply take "catholicity" to refer to the proper relationship between substantive, normative identity (including "orthodoxy") and legitimate, substantial diversity among the people of God.

With *All Saints*, Ellsberg has provided a remarkably catholic presentation of living holiness for contemporary readers. To be sure, he made no claim to neutrality or balance. However, in the end, rather than reinforcing divisions, this motley crew of "saints, prophets, and witnesses for our time" can serve as a rough-yet-common ground upon which divided Catholics— not least, *American* Catholics—can meet, or at least come within hailing distance of each other.[5]

Because it has the potential to serve such an important role, there are stakes to dismissing *All Saints* as "mere" devotional literature, or, especially, as a party-line sermon preached to a self-consciously progressive choir. However, because catholicity is a contestable, ultimately aesthetic criterion of judgment, to assess this claim for its "wholeness" requires a special kind of critical engagement with Ellsberg and *All Saints*.

This way of reading the text, engaging its author, and testing its claims about holiness (all *saints*) and wholeness (*all* saints) can be enacted, I argue, by proposing an addition to Ellsberg's constellation of characters.

4. E.g., Hogan, "Quiet Gestures, Heroic Acts"

5. I have in mind here something like Karl Barth's oft-repeated statements that he and one of his theological opponents (e.g., Rudolf Bultmann, Emil Brunner, et al.) were like a whale and an elephant—both God's creatures, but—given their respective habitats—seemingly incapable of meeting.

Adjudicating this proposal, therefore, enables us to explicate the general character of *All Saints,* consider the arguments against its catholicity, and show that such an indictment cannot stand up to critical scrutiny. Because he is hardly a quintessential liberal, the candidate I have selected for this task can serve as a limit test case for the conception of catholicity just presented.

Underneath the Basilica of the Sacred Heart, on the campus of the University of Notre Dame, rest the earthly remains of Orestes Augustus Brownson (1804–1877). Unless they happen to be specialists in U.S. Catholic history or nineteenth-century American political and religious thought more generally, most of the people who pass by this site have little or no knowledge of who this man is. Those who are familiar with his biography would likely agree that it is both strange and yet, also, somehow appropriate that Brownson is now located here, so near the symbolic heart of American Catholicism.

By exploring briefly the "odd fittingness" of Brownson on the hallowed grounds at South Bend, we can gain an introduction to this complicated, compelling, and yet mostly little-known figure. Thus armed, we can assess whether Brownson possesses legitimate—even if surprising—qualifications for joining the ranks of the figures portrayed in *All Saints.* Not least because Brownson is most often today considered a conservative figure, this exercise provides a method for testing just how ideologically narrow—or not—*All Saints* really is, and therefore nudges us, imaginatively, into the question of catholicity "for our time."

"That Sturdy but Erratic Reformer"

Northwest Indiana is a surprising resting place for someone who was not a Midwesterner but, rather, a quintessential Yankee. Born in Vermont from Anglo-Saxon stock, Brownson came of age in upstate New York, was a pastor and public intellectual in Boston, and spent decades in the greater New York City area. As a consummate cultural insider in antebellum America who did not become a Catholic until he was 40, he had little in common with the "ethnic" Catholicism(s) that nurtured the university with which he was posthumously associated.

In 1939, Columbia historian and progressive stalwart Henry Steele Commager averred that "if Orestes Brownson is remembered at all today, it is as a convert who attempted unsuccessfully to liberalize and Americanize the Catholic Church."[6] In the nineteenth century, to call for the "liberalization" and, especially, the "Americanization" of the Catholic Church was to

6. Commager, "That Sturdy but Erratic Reformer," 88.

give aid and comfort to the organized forces of anti-Catholic "nativism." To speak in such terms was to reinforce the view that Catholics and Catholicism represented a foreign threat to the values and institutions of American democracy. In short, through much of his life Brownson openly expressed some of the prejudices and positions that inspired "fighting Irish."[7]

In multiple ways, then, Brownson was an outsider to the general ethos of the nineteenth-century "immigrant" U.S. Catholic Church. He was an outsider because he could, without hesitation, identify himself as the most authentic of "Americans" (as that term applied during his lifetime). But it is precisely because he *was* such an American insider-cum-Catholic that his eventual place of honor in South Bend also makes sense.

Brownson drank deeply from most of the social, political, and religious currents in the early republic. He grew up on the geographical outskirts and in the historical remnants of the "standing order" of Puritan New England. Amid the spiritual ferment of upstate New York, he had a conversion experience at an evangelical revival service as a young adult, later became a Universalist minister and, eventually, a declared "freethinker." After a new spiritual and intellectual awakening, he moved to the Boston area to serve as a Unitarian pastor and urban missionary. It was here, during the late 1830s, that he was invited to participate in the meetings of the later-famous Transcendentalist Club, alongside Ralph Waldo Emerson, Bronson Alcott, Margaret Fuller, and others.

Brownson became known throughout the country as a powerful orator, a skilled controversialist, and a radical thinker. He repeatedly cast his lot with what he called the "movement party" in human affairs, offering his voice in support of a variety of avant-garde social and religious agendas. Yet later, despite his antipathy toward Southern slavery, he came to esteem the political philosophy of South Carolina Democrat John C. Calhoun. During the Civil War, he became a staunch pro-Unionist and even ran for Congress on the Republican ticket. Poet James Russell Lowell immortalized him in American verse when, in his "Fable for Critics," he lampooned Brownson as a human weathervane, an unstable and unpredictable personality who, nonetheless, never lacked for confidence in his own judgments.

To the vast majority of his contemporaries Brownson's conversion to Catholicism in 1844 simply confirmed his mental and emotional instability. This undeniably clever-yet-troubled man had exhausted himself and collapsed into the authoritarian arms of an outdated, foreign superstition. To

---

7. See, for example, his 1856 essay, "The Mission of America," in which Brownson scolded the bulk of his fellow American Catholics (read: "Irish") for failing to embrace the particular genius of the American character and to identify their destiny with America's providentially prepared role in history.

his fellow American Catholics, especially in hindsight, Brownson's spiritual and intellectual pilgrimage seemed to provide incarnate evidence that the Catholic faith and Catholic Church represented the only ultimate satisfaction for the hearts and minds of restless Americans.

Indeed, Brownson's *magnum opus*, published near the end of his long and turbulent life, was an extended meditation on the "Constitution, Tendencies, and Destiny" of *The American Republic*.[8] To his mind there was no contradiction between loving "America"—especially, "America" as the embodiment of the spirit of "the age"—and being a staunch Catholic. Thus, it makes perfect sense that a later generation of American Catholics came to designate Brownson as a kind of unofficial patron of their preeminent intellectual institution in the United States.

A Witness or Prophet for "Our Time"?

Thus far we have not yet made the case that Brownson merits membership among Ellsberg's "saints, prophets, and witnesses for our time." We have simply established that Brownson was an interesting man immersed in the challenges of his times and substantially interested in the question of what it would mean to be a modern Christian. The case for his inclusion, however, must proceed on the basis of criteria internal to Ellsberg's own vision for contemporary "wholeness." A closer look at Ellsberg's account of what sanctity (or holiness) and catholicity (or "wholeness") look like in "our time" will not only prepare the way for this task but will clarify why adding Brownson to the roster of *All Saints* would help silence critics tempted to conclude that the book is, in the end, little more than progressive propaganda.

Modern Sanctity

All Saints can be helpfully read as a companion to Karl Rahner's reflections on "Christian Living Formerly and Today," written just a year after the close of the Second Vatican Council. This famous essay was a pastoral response to the "great unrest" then prevailing in the church—an unrest "pervading all 'classes' and groups."[9] Rahner described this dis-ease as an existential anxiety produced by uncertainty about what it would mean to be a Christian *now*—i.e., in a world (and church) conscious of existing on the far side of some kind of historical rupture. It was a world (and church) divided between

8. Brownson, *The American Republic*.
9. Rahner, "Christian Living Formerly and Today," 3.

those, on the one hand, who celebrated this sense of historical distanciation as liberation, and those, on the other, who lamented it as loss and alienation.

At the heart of the essay, Rahner identified three specific factors he believed would provide the contours of Christian living in the coming years. We will return later to these factors, using them as heuristics for assessing Brownson's candidacy as an exemplary modern Christian. For present purposes, what is most important to note is that Rahner inserted a substantial caveat before venturing his reading of the signs of the times. He warned that "abstract and theoretical postulates for this Christian living of the future are, and continue to be, something quite different from examples in the concrete, which are living and productive."[10] In other words, more than it needed to be conceptually described or prescribed, contemporary Christian living simply needed to be *seen*.

On this basis, we can describe *All Saints* as a report on the question: just who are some of the men and women who provide "living and productive" examples that should inform and inspire Christian living in the "world of today"? In his introduction Ellsberg cites Rahner's well-known description of a saint as one who shows how it is possible and desirable to be a Christian in "just *this* way."[11] Such lives enflesh Christian holiness, and they do so within the horizons of people living in particular times, places, and states of life.

Ellsberg quotes Rahner repeatedly as he explains his purposes in writing, and even includes Rahner among his saints, prophets, and witnesses (March 5). In light of our concern to discern the catholic character of *All Saints*, the relationship between *All Saints* and the "spirit" of Rahner's essay (especially as it has been popularly received) takes on a special importance.

"The Christian of the Future . . ."

It is now half-a-century since the publication of "Christian Existence Formerly and Today." The number of readers familiar with the essay's contents has, no doubt, declined markedly. Yet a much higher number can surely cite its most famous line—that is, Rahner's prediction that "the Christian of the future will either be a 'mystic' . . . or no Christian at all."[12]

At the level of a slogan, Rahner's claim strikes a harmonious chord with the progressive metanarrative of Western modernity. It maps easily

---

10. Ibid., 11.

11. Ellsberg, *All Saints*, 2.

12. Rahner, "Christian Living Formerly and Today," 15.

onto a diachronic axis with the coordinates arranged according to a "Weberian" contrast between spirit and institution.

More colloquially, of course, Rahner's prediction appears to lend authoritative support to the advocates of "spirituality" over against "religion." If we have already connected *All Saints* to the general themes of Rahner's essay, how much more, then, will it be possible to identify Ellsberg as a partisan in this struggle between past and future, institutional authority and charismatic freedom? Exploring this question will give us a clearer grasp of why Brownson can serve as a fitting test case for assessing the catholic character of *All Saints*.

All Saints?

It is not quite the case that Ellsberg draws his "saints, prophets, and witnesses *for* our time" exclusively *from* "our time." He acknowledges that "many traditional saints, precisely insofar as they responded to the demands of their own moment, remain a precious resource."[13] And so, alongside more and less familiar and more and less controversial contemporary figures—like Pedro Arrupe (Feb. 5), Thea Bowman (March 30), Oskar Schindler (April 28), Peter Maurin (May 9), Walker Percy (May 28), Anne Frank (June 12), John Howard Griffin (June 16), Walter Rauschenbusch (July 25), Simone Weil (Aug. 24), Maura O'Halloran (Oct. 22), and the El Salvadoran Martyrs of El Mozote (Dec. 11)—*All Saints* also includes sketches of nearly all the traditional doctors of the church, East and West.

There is nothing especially controversial about a book of exemplary lives that focuses especially on men and women of recent memory. However, as Ellsberg explains the need for new models of sanctity he begins to sound committed to a progressive, even supercessionist, hermeneutic of history. In a key passage, Ellsberg articulates his judgments about the kinds of holiness demanded by the present hour in the form of a series of antitheses between "traditional lists of saints" and the particular kinds of lives now most in need of emulation. For example, we could paraphrase a section of that thematic paragraph in this way: "You have heard it said, 'saints exhibit the virtue of charity.' But I say to you, '*today* we need saints who combine charity with a prophetic thirst for justice.'"

It is this self-conscious accent on the new and contemporary that creates the problem of how new and old are to be reconciled in a *catholic* whole. Just how new are these new models of holy living? How do they, how *can* they, coexist with the older ones? Do they presuppose the existence of a

13. Ellsberg, *All Saints*, 4.

new church altogether? Or does Ellsberg simply leave behind such churchly concerns, concluding that, in an age of enlightened and liberated human consciences, it would be both imprudent and small-minded to dwell on matters of structure and ("external") authority?[14]

As we would be led to expect by this point, Ellsberg's final category of contemporary sanctity consists of "the mystics, who see through the shade of everydayness and so remind us of the God who is ever-greater than our theologies or our imaginations."[15] Such mystics feature prominently throughout Ellsberg's year of readings.[16] To these formally designated mystics, we add the even more pervasive appearance in *All Saints* of martyrs or confessors whose consciences brought them into conflict with ecclesial authorities. All these examples share authoritative, "institutional" religion as a common foil.

On the Wrong Side of History?

With the preceding sketch of *All Saints* as a backdrop, we can now receive the report of an *advocatus diaboli*, in dutiful response to a campaign for Orestes Brownson's inclusion in Ellsberg's roster of saints, prophets, and witnesses. A single quotation from Brownson provides *prima facie* evidence that this man simply has no place among Ellsberg's exemplary figures. It comes from Brownson's 1842 review of a public lecture given by his fellow Transcendentalist, Theodore Parker. In "A Discourse on the Transient and the Permanent in Christianity," Parker urged his hearers to wean themselves from the contingent doctrines and institutions of traditional Christianity. These would eventually be eroded by the critical advances of modern historical inquiry. All that can and should remain, Parker argued, is the soul's fundamental trust in the ineffable mystery that grounds its existence.

Brownson used his review of Parker to make a public break from New England Transcendentalism. Though he had previously shared many of Parker's convictions, he was now convinced that there was, ironically, no

---

14. Similarly, it is certainly possible to argue that the historical outlook described above can also be broadly described as "biblical." The critical questions, then, are whether and how the components of the variegated biblical witness can be gathered under a single, catholic, heading.

15. Ellsberg, *All Saints*, 5.

16. Thus, among others, the portraits of C. F. Andrews (Feb. 12), Meister Eckhart (March 27), Hadewijch of Brabant (April 6), Teilhard de Chardin (April 10), the Baal Shem Tov (May 22), Sadhu Sundar Singh (June 25), Mechthild of Magdeburg (July 27), William Blake (Aug. 12), Richard Rolle (Sept. 29), Maura O'Halloran (Oct. 22), Dom Bede Griffiths (Dec. 17), and John Main (Dec. 30).

future in such thinking, and certainly no hope for progress. At the rhetorical apex of his critical response Brownson insisted that *"Humanity needs, and has a sacred right to an authoritative church . . . one catholic church, clothed with supreme authority over all matters pertaining to human life, whether spiritual or material."*[17] In the antebellum United States, one could hardly utter words more calculated to shock and bewilder.

When Brownson wrote that statement, the contemporary identity or existence of such an authoritative church remained for him an open question. He was received a few years later into the Roman Catholic Church, however, where he remained for his final three decades. He died a defender of the First Vatican Council's definition of papal infallibility and Pius IX's *Syllabus of Errors*. Put simply, Brownson stands rather opposed to Rahner (and, by extension, Ellsberg) with his decidedly unfashionable insistence that the *American* Christian of the future will either be a Catholic, or no Christian at all.

There is additional material evidence to support the view that Brownson simply would not make Ellsberg's cut. Brownson's absence from *All Saints*, even as Ellsberg included two of Brownson's contemporaries, is particularly noteworthy. Indeed, the substance of their included portraits strengthens the case against Brownson's proposed entry.

In 1836, a young Henry David Thoreau stayed as a guest in the Brownson home, at a time when Orestes was pastoring a small Unitarian congregation in Walpole, Massachusetts. We know little about that period other than the fact that Brownson's personality seems to have made a lasting impression on the young idealist.[18] Ellsberg commemorates Thoreau's memory (on May 6, the day of Thoreau's death) by highlighting the mystic of Walden Pond's ascetic nonconformity and by tracing the historical influence of Thoreau's writings on an influential modern tradition of conscientious civil disobedience.

Even more telling than Ellsberg's decision to include Thoreau and overlook Brownson is the fact that Ellsberg also wrote an entry for Brownson's friend and fellow Yankee Catholic convert, Isaac Hecker (Dec. 18). Brownson had played an instrumental role in Hecker's own conversion. Hecker went on to receive holy orders and, after much persistence, received approval from Rome to start the Paulists, with the goal of evangelizing spiritually earnest Americans, like his former self. Of primary concern for this investigation, Ellsberg's Hecker clearly strikes a quite different and much

---

17. Brownson, "Theodore Parker's Discourse," 383; my emphasis.

18. For a reflection on this encounter, see Walter, "Thoreau and Orestes Brownson."

more "mystical" note than Brownson's insistence that "humanity has a sacred right to an authoritative Church."

Ellsberg notes Hecker's desire to affirm, on Catholic grounds, all that was good about his country. It was thus a devastating blow when the 1870 definition of papal infallibility confirmed in the minds of virtually all his contemporaries that Catholicism and American democracy were simply incompatible. Ellsberg's sketch neglects the depths to which Hecker went in order to maintain both his fundamental faith in the church and his love of his country.[19] Ellsberg's necessarily limited treatment focuses instead on such things as Hecker's insistence that the Paulists should be guided by Spirit-led discernment rather than a comprehensive community rule. Ellsberg quotes Hecker's description of a "true Paulist" as one who "would prefer to suffer from the excesses of liberty rather than from the arbitrary actions of tyranny."[20]

There are, then, strong initial warrants for concluding that Brownson's life and thought are incompatible with both the spirit and the letter of *All Saints*. When juxtaposed with portraits of courageous nonconformists like Hecker and Thoreau, he appears to be little more than a reactionary. Having aired the potential objections to Brownson's inclusion in the text, we now change direction in order to discover the substantive reasons, internal to *All Saints,* for claiming that Brownson merits a place on this roster of notable contemporary prophets and witnesses.

Christian Living Formerly and Today

The argument for including Brownson in *All Saints* relies on the affinity already established between *All Saints* and Rahner's reflections on "Christian Existence Formerly and Today." As we have seen, Rahner and Brownson can be used to represent divergent poles on the contemporary Christian spectrum: on the one hand, the prophet who dares to imagine a future ("it's easy if you try"), in which mystics no longer suffer at the hands of benighted, fearful, and power-wielding souls; on the other, the quintessential "problem convert," an anti-modern reactionary who embraced Catholicism at midlife only after exchanging youthful idealism for cultural pessimism. Because it is possible to draw such a binary opposition between them, however crudely, it is all the more noteworthy if we can demonstrate that they both justifiably belong in the same collection of exemplars. The question then becomes a matter of the kind of "wholeness" and "holiness" on display in *All Saints*.

19. See Portier, *Isaac Hecker and the First Vatican Council.*
20. Quoted in Ellsberg, *All Saints,* 552.

Ellsberg insisted that the figures in his collection need not exhibit in themselves each of the specific forms of sanctity outlined in the introduction to *All Saints*. Nor must they necessarily be likable. Given Brownson's penchant for no-holds-barred polemics—and the fact that some of his views, which were quite mainstream at the time, are simply unacceptable by virtually all contemporary moral standards—this is important. More than anything, Ellsberg claimed, perhaps what all these women and men have most in common is "the uncompromising character of their commitment," and such steadfastness is often experienced by others as frustrating intransigence.[21]

Brownson was uncompromising in the service of truth and justice, and he certainly won more arguments than friends. So we can recognize him in this general description. But there are more specific reasons for concluding that he was genuinely the kind of Christian, immersed in "the joys and the hopes, the griefs and the anxieties"[22] of our times, that Ellsberg would have us ponder and emulate. There is no denying, however, that this is not immediately apparent.

In 1842, Brownson made his audacious claim that humanity has a "sacred right" to an authoritative church. He did so only after invoking "the sacred, the soul-stirring name of liberty," a name in which he believed he had earned a right to speak.[23] He was referring here to his reputation as a card-carrying member of the progressive "movement party" in American society. In other words, despite his strong criticisms, Brownson was claiming to know and even to share Parker's desire for the elevation and emancipation of humanity from all forms of spiritual tyranny and social injustice. And he presumed that none of his readers would doubt that he was speaking in good faith.

In what follows, we will look at Brownson's life and thought through the lenses of the three factors Rahner identified in the late 1960s as being particularly relevant for Christian living in the modern world. What emerges is not complete agreement. However, just as Brownson asserted to his readers, there is plenty of evidence that he shared enough with Ellsberg's saints, prophets, and witnesses for our time to deserve a hearing among them.

---

21. Ellsberg, *All Saints*, 5.

22. Second Vatican Council, *Gaudium et Spes* §1.

23. Brownson, "Theodore Parker's Discourse," 383.

"Life in the World and Service to the World Considered as Pertaining to Religion"

We begin with the second of Rahner's three factors. Rahner postulated that Christian living in the years ahead would be marked by a profound awareness of the fact that discipleship takes place in a world that has no exclusively "religious" sphere. The younger Brownson often resembles the nonconforming, prophetic, and progressive figures scattered throughout *All Saints* who demanded real-world justice for the oppressed, and often at great personal risk. For example, in one striking episode, Brownson wrote a poignant appeal on behalf of a convicted man whose hanging was about to be the occasion for a day of public spectacle.[24]

More famously, in the midst of the 1840 presidential election, he wrote a passionate and programmatic appeal on behalf of the interests of "The Laboring Classes."[25] In it, he called for the abolishment of a paid clergy (as they confer sanctity on the unjust status quo), the government takeover of banks (to break the link between money and political power), and an end to inheritance (in order to ensure something like an economic jubilee for each generation). Such willingness to put principle over party (enraged Democrats blamed their loss on the fact that Brownson associated them with such infidel notions) and to risk scandal by associating himself with unpopular persons and views remained his *modus operandi* throughout his life, even during his decades as a Catholic.

By 1842 Brownson claimed to have learned through difficult experience that "liberty must be organized or it is license, and ordained by authority or it has no basis, no safeguard, no guaranty."[26] He was convinced, contra Parker, that genuine social progress *for all* humanity required spiritual communion with a *higher* (i.e., supernatural) divine life, and that this divine life must be encountered via some actual, historical, real-world mediation. In no way, he insisted, did this embrace of a more traditional supernaturalism signal a retreat from politics into mere personal soul-craft. He demanded the "rehabilitation of the church" because only a church, properly understood, could rightfully assert such authority on behalf of the "poor and most numerous classes" and against the forces of plutocracy and demagoguery.

Such far-reaching claims on behalf of ecclesial authority sound very much like the Catholic integralism that Rahner was specifically rejecting as

24. Brownson, "An Address Prepared at the Request of Guy C. Clark."

25. Brownson, "The Laboring Classes." In *A Pilgrim's Progress*, Arthur Schlesinger, Jr. concluded that "The Laboring Classes" was "perhaps the best study of the workings of society written by an American before the Civil War" (96).

26. Brownson, "Theodore Parker's Discourse," 383.

a viable or salutary option for modern Christian living. Given Brownson's lengthy and winding pilgrimage through the landscape of nineteenth-century American religion and politics, it might seem possible to select from his voluminous writings a "Brownson" congruent with virtually any theological persuasion and cultural outlook. In reality, however, there is much greater continuity spanning Brownson's career—from heterodox free-thinker to ultramontane Catholic—than is immediately apparent.[27] One common thread is Brownson's desire to blend progressive social convictions with a populist mistrust of elite paternalism.

A serious analysis of the real differences between Brownson and Rahner on the question of the relationship between "church" and "world" is far beyond the scope of this essay. At a minimum, we can acknowledge that few modern Christians have devoted as much time and energy to these matters as Brownson.[28] As we have seen, his place of honor at Notre Dame bespeaks his status as a man of Catholic faith whose wide-ranging and rigorous thought never strayed far from the worldly struggles of his country.

"The Experience of God as Incomprehensible"

For Rahner, the Christian of the future "will either be a 'mystic' . . . or no Christian at all" simply because, for increasing numbers of people in the modern West, personal faith in God is no longer buttressed or formally compelled by social and cultural supports. Christian faith becomes simply one "take" on the meaning of existence among others. In such a situation, to be a Christian is by necessity to be a "mystic"—a term Rahner acknowledged would be open to a tremendous range of interpretation—in the basic sense of someone who has "experienced something" for themselves.[29]

What has Brownson, the ex-Transcendentalist advocate for churchly Christianity, to do with Rahner's transcendental Thomism and its focus on the believing subject? Much more than the allusion to Tertullian's rhetorical question implies, but an adequate analysis is not possible here. For present

---

27. This is a primary conclusion of Carey, *Orestes A. Brownson*. See also Carey's substantial introductions to the seven volumes of *The Early Works of Orestes A. Brownson*.

28. In "Vision and Praxis," John Coleman, SJ, includes Brownson among what he considers to be the handful of dead American theologians worth reading today for more than historical curiosity because, unlike most of their contemporaries, they zeroed in on the primary live questions in modern Catholic theology—i.e., the relation between "nature" and "grace," and the directly related matter of the connection between "secular" human history and salvation in Christ.

29. Rahner, "Christian Living Formerly and Today," 15.

purposes, we will focus on the steps leading Brownson the Transcendentalist philosopher, and anti-clerical radical of "The Laboring Classes," to an embrace of Catholicism.

Against some earlier scholars (e.g., Arthur Schlesinger, Jr.), Brownson's most recent biographer, Patrick Carey, contends that the decisive catalyst for Brownson's transformation was not despair over the prospect of American democracy, given that his essay on "The Laboring Classes" was met with "a universal scream of horror." Brownson's writings from the period indicate a kind of midlife religious conversion, Carey claims, rooted in a new, experiential grasp of what Brownson called the "freedom of God."[30]

In an 1843 essay, Brownson asserted that a truly religious understanding of progress in history is threatened by the reduction of God's providence to a one-time ontological intervention in creation that ultimately cancels out both human *and* divine freedom. We *live* and *move* and have our being in God, he granted. But "pantheist history" can only account for this third dimension. It can explain timeless truths, but it cannot account for all that is "exceptional, variable, individual, diverse."[31]

Brownson concluded that humanity needed a "mediatorial life" that could restore its now-lost communion with God. This was the ultimate basis for hope in human progress. With his new faith in a personal God able and willing to provide such a gift, Brownson eagerly embraced traditional Christian orthodoxy, but now with a decidedly Catholic, churchly accent. Because Jesus' mediatorial life was "literally, really, not by way of example, representation, or imputation, the life and salvation of the world,"[32] it enters into human history "by virtue of a communion between Jesus and his disciples, and to the rest of mankind in time and space only by communion with them."[33]

Brownson became a Catholic in 1845, essentially on the basis of this argument. Out of a new convert's sense of obedience, he began to engage the enemies of the American church using only the apologetic strategies his bishop and confessor deemed acceptable. Through a remarkable process of philosophical self-education, Brownson had developed a "synthetic" philosophy that he believed could hold together intuitive faith and reflective reason, "subject" and "object," individual freedom and the common good. Now he was employing the arguments of post-Cartesian scholastic philosophy

---

30. Carey, Introduction to vol. vi of *Early Works*, 3–4.

31. Brownson, "Remarks on Universal History," 399, 402.

32. Brownson, "Leroux on Humanity," 276.

33. Brownson, "The Mediatorial Life of Jesus," 210.

and theology, which sought epistemic confidence by foregrounding rational arguments for religious authority.

Brownson returned to his earlier, synthetic method in the 1850s, coming under some ecclesial suspicion in the process, as he had been prodded in this direction by the heterodox Italian philosopher Vicenzo Gioberti. Brownson's doctrine of "life by communion" represented a unique standpoint at the time, one that ranged beyond the boundaries of the neo-scholasticism that would become increasingly normative for Catholic thought. His method recognized no clean distinction between theology and philosophy, or the realms of grace and a hypothetically "pure" nature. In this way, as Carey notably concludes, Brownson anticipated both the twentieth-century *nouvelle théologie* of Henri de Lubac as well as Rahner's own transcendental Thomism.[34]

"A New Asceticism: Setting One's Own Limits"

Finally, Rahner proposed, in the world of the modern bourgeois, for whom moderation is, by and large, "no longer imposed from without" by the "natural" constraints of a pre-industrial, pre-consumerist world, that what is needed is a "new asceticism." Further, he claimed, because of the complex differentiation of modern life, this contemporary *askesis* would have a generally voluntary, self-imposed character.[35] Rahner's third factor fits very well with Isaac Hecker's vision for the Paulists' rule, as highlighted by Ellsberg.

It is hard to see how one might square Rahner's asceticism, characterized by personal discernment, with Brownson's hope for an authoritative church "that would make the hard, stony-hearted man of the world tremble before his ill-gotten wealth, and feel that he must disgorge his hoards."[36] There is certainly difference here. But the difference is instructive.

Brownson's voluntary acceptance of ecclesial authority can be understood as a kind of self-imposed asceticism. However ironic it may also be, there is something genuinely prophetic about making such a commitment in the context of the early United States, where the religious status quo was reinforced by something very much like Paul Tillich's iconoclastic "Protestant principle." In the midst of his reflections upon the task of Christian living in the modern world, Rahner himself makes an analogous claim:

---

34. Carey, *Orestes A. Brownson*, 388.

35. Rahner, "Christian Living Formerly and Today," 21–22.

36. Brownson, "Theodore Parker's Discourse," 383.

Perhaps we could go so far as to say that today the real non-conformists are to be found in the group of those who have a genuine, calm, and loving respect for the religious heritage of the past and the experience of past generations. . . . It is strange. The most complex techniques of Yoga are considered reasonable, yet the old Christian methods of prayer and meditation, as for example the rosary, are regarded as unmodern. But why precisely? Is this the result of experience or is it merely that the practitioners are all too eager to know better?[37]

This does not sound at all like the Rahner presented earlier as Brownson's foil.

Taking Stock

Brownson is not an immediately attractive figure. His prickly intellectualism will leave many readers cold when compared with the warm-hearted devotion and prophetic fire of, for example, Dorothy Day, who arguably came closest, of the contemporary members of *All Saints*, to embodying all of the aspects of holiness Ellsberg believes are needed "for the present moment."[38] In the end, according to Ellsberg, to call someone a saint is to say that his or her life "should be taken with the utmost seriousness."[39] The restless, thoroughly *American*, life of Orestes Brownson is not intrinsically compelling on the level of individual personality. Instead, it serves as a living witness to the desire for a communion characterized by both holiness and wholeness.

The task set out at the beginning was to show that Brownson merits inclusion among Ellsberg's *All Saints* on the basis of Ellsberg's own judgments about the kinds of holiness or wholeness demanded by the present hour. Reflecting upon Brownson's credentials, with Rahner's help, prods us to recognize that Ellsberg's depiction of holiness/wholeness is more elastic and more complex than it initially appears. Adding Brownson to the mix also provides a friendly-but-significant critique of *All Saints* by pressing—though not resolving—a critical question. That is: to what extent is a specific social structure necessary for preserving and promoting holiness and wholeness?

---

37. Rahner, "Christian Living Formerly and Today," 7, 9–10.

38. Ellsberg is a former Catholic Worker who has written extensively about Day and has recently promoted her cause for canonization.

39. Ellsberg, *All Saints*, 6.

Conclusion: Modern Catholicity

In 1966, Rahner addressed Catholics tempted to respond to recent changes in disjunctive ways. His response pointed to a possible, though less immediately satisfying, way beyond a standoff between partisans of the "church of history" and advocates of a "church of the future."

Rahner had already urged readers to remember that incarnate examples of Christian existence in the "world of today" were ultimately more important than abstract interpretations of this new world and its conditions. He concluded on a similar note, insisting that the task of providing an adequate account of contemporary catholicity also exceeded his capabilities. This is so, he claimed, because "the full synthesis of all these factors [i.e., the "old" and the "new"; the "mystical" and the "political"] in the concrete . . . is to be achieved only *in living practice*, and not by means of theological theorizing."[40]

Such "living and productive" models must be received as gifts from the Holy Spirit, Rahner insisted. That is, it is ultimately not for theologians to define the way forward simply on the basis of ideal commitments. The challenges of the days ahead would be met in the living. For this reason, he continued, a primary task in times of uncertainty is to cultivate patience and endurance. Otherwise, it would be nearly impossible to refrain from "indulging in self-will either by becoming reactionaries on the one hand, or by embarking upon destructive quests for novelty on the other."[41]

On these grounds, then, we can ask—and now answer—the critical question: is *All Saints* best understood as a presumptive "quest for novelty" in which a theo-political preference for progressive prophets overdetermines the contents? Or is this collection of saints, prophets, and witnesses a product of the patient discernment of the Spirit's work that Rahner recommended and, therefore, a quite valuable—catholic—resource indeed?

I submit that it is the latter. Precisely because of the tensions between Ellsberg's individually complex and compelling subjects, *when read together*, the remarkable women and men in *All Saints* serve as a powerful, *aesthetic* portrayal of not only holiness/wholeness, but also catholicity "for our time." Unfortunately, this aspect of the book can be eclipsed by Ellsberg's unmistakably "modern" and "prophetic" accent. Thus, a demonstration that Ellsberg could justifiably include Brownson among his exemplary figures makes the theological achievement of *All Saints*, as I have just described it, apparent to a wider set of readers.

40. Ibid., 22.
41. Ibid., 11.

Because he refuses to do violence to the integrity of his human sources, Ellsberg's subjects cannot be theoretically reconciled with each other, or to a single ideological template, in any simple or straightforward way. "Doubtless," he admits, "St. Augustine or St. Dominic would be alarmed to find themselves linked with the likes of Vincent van Gogh or Leo Tolstoy (The obverse is just as likely)."[42] He acknowledges that it is much easier to explain his reasoning for including traditional and nontraditional "saints" than to explain what exactly they all have in common.

The creative dissonance produced as one reads and reflects on Ellsberg's selections *together* is, in my judgment, the most theologically compelling characteristic of *All Saints*. Apologists for corporate "identity" (and "authority") on the one hand, and champions of "diversity" (and "conscience") on the other, should find themselves, by turns, discomforted and inspired by the lives they encounter while reading *All Saints*.

In the end, the issues and commitments that divide contemporary Christians matter too much for well-intentioned pleas for peace and unity to succeed. But where arguments fail, living witnesses can help us all to pause—and pray.

42. Ibid., 4.

6

Catholic Americanism

Past, Present, Future

DAVID J. O'BRIEN

American Catholics, who are they? Are they Catholics who happen to be American or Americans who happen to be Catholics? For much of their history most American Catholics have said both, but church leaders have always worried that national practices and civic loyalties might overwhelm religious obligations, a problem made acute by the minority status of Catholics. In the United States, from the start, church membership was voluntary, requiring church leaders to explain why people should devote time and treasure to religion, and to this religious group rather than another. And more than in most countries, national unity and stable and effective government also depended upon the voluntary civic commitment of citizens. So deciding how to be at once Catholic and American was, and remains, a challenging question.

Make no mistake: there are problems both ways. Love of country poses obvious dangers, all too evident in the last century as Catholics blessed soldiers and excused atrocities on both sides of brutal wars, looked the other way, or worse, took part as racism and anti-Semitism exacted their deadly toll, or adapted too easily to unjust economic practices and authoritarian political regimes. But neither have Catholics been exempt from excessive religious or, better, ecclesiastical, loyalties. Churchmen have their own questionable record in contemporary history, privileging Catholicism in practice as well as theory, assessing political, social, and cultural options in terms of the self-interest of the church and its institutions, at times embracing regimes which protected church institutions while crushing opponents and eliminating dissent.

The Second Vatican Council (1962–1965) arose, in part, from reflection on these tensions between religious and civic responsibilities, but it did not resolve them. In the immediate aftermath of the council, many reformers emphasized pastoral and strategic adaptation to the lived experience of Christians and their communities. The end of European empires and the emergence of non-western Catholic communities, along with emphasis on the "local church" and positive engagement with public problems of war and poverty, led to renewed consideration of the relationship between faith and diverse cultures. A "world church," composed of many and differing local churches, seemed to suggest the need to reconsider the relationship between the Catholic and American elements of American Catholic life. So did the pressing problems of race, poverty, and war that shook American society in the years following the Council.

Arguments for affirming the American side of American Catholicism, with a renewed sense of shared civic and social responsibility, found support in Catholic social teaching and in the Council's Pastoral Constitution on the Church and the Modern World. This led not only to emphasis on "the social mission of the church" but also to exploration of ways that American values might suggest changes in Catholic ideas and practices. In reaction, critics feared that by overemphasizing the church's historical experience and shared responsibility reformers put at risk Catholic identity and institutional integrity. They preferred to emphasize the carefully crafted theological compromises of the Dogmatic Constitution on the Church, where emphasis on the church as the "people of God" and the "universal call to holiness" were carefully blended with reaffirmation of Catholic exclusivism, papal primacy, and clerical authority. The world, including the American world, might matter, but the church matters even more. For years, Catholics vigorously debated how best to pursue "faithful citizenship" and "responsible discipleship," often in terms that suggested specifically Catholic differences about church teaching. But, in fact, there were also differences in how Catholics and other Christians should regard the country, what meaning they should assign to their own American experience. In 1975, as the country celebrated the bicentennial of the American Revolution, Protestant scholar Martin Marty offered a Christian commentary on American culture that reflected the growing debate among Catholics about the relative balance between American and Catholic responsibilities. After reading one half of Marty's book, entitled "America: Pro," the reader turned it over to read the other half, "America: Con."[1]

---

1. Marty, *The Pro and Con Book of Religious America.*

In this essay I to would like make three arguments about this Catholic-American relationship:

First, Americanization is a central theme of the American Catholic experience, and it requires serious consideration of Americanism, ideas about the religious meaning of American life—past, present, and future. Theologians and religious studies professionals naturally focus on what we all think of as religion—in this case Catholicism. America is simply the context for this branch of that religion. But it is also helpful to think harder about the American side of Catholics and their church, especially as both become, by choice as well as historical process, more comfortable and assured about their place in this particular society.

Second, the initial response of American Catholics to the Second Vatican Council, amid the conflicts of the country during "the long 1960s," was informed by a renewal of Americanism as theologians and pastoral leaders saw positive meaning in the American, as well as the Catholic, side of American Catholic life. This arose from the Council's historic affirmation of religious liberty, as well as ecumenical initiatives and long-developing endorsement of human rights and democratic practices. This "neo-Americanism" also gave meaning to the post-World-War-II movement of the children of immigrant, working-class families into the American middle class. Now fully accepted as Americans accessing the centers of American political, economic, and cultural life, Catholics, it was said, had "come of age" and would help renew the church and the country. Americanism, ideas about the importance of the nation and its people, gave positive meaning to the experience of Americanization.

Third, in the American Catholic culture wars that extended from the beginning of the pontificate of John Paul II in 1978 until the election of Pope Francis in 2013, critics of Americanization and Americanism claimed that many Catholics, and Catholic institutions, had over-adapted to American values and practices, putting at risk the identity, even the integrity, of the American church. They insisted that Catholic teaching, not American experience, should be the decisive factor in understanding American Catholics and directing the church. Here, attention was directed to those teachings and practices that most sharply distinguished Catholics, especially teachings on birth control, abortion, homosexuality, and the status of women. In this, they revived an older form of Catholic secularism, ratifying and extending theological and pastoral approaches that could not help but deprive public life, and daily experience, of religious meaning. This renewal of emphasis on distinctive Catholic identity, and Catholic interests, in the absence of even a hint of Catholic separatism, also brought with it the displacement among Catholics of American stories of liberation by declension narratives ending in calls for countercultural resistance to America. This declension narrative, and the pastoral and ecclesiastical policies that accompanied it, helped shape popular responses to changing patterns of religious practice, the decline of many Catholic institutions, and the crisis brought about by revelations of clerical sexual abuse.

The Making and Remaking
of Contemporary American Catholicism

I am an American Catholic and an historian interested in American politics and social movements, with particular interest in the history of American Catholicism. Starting out in the 1960s I became involved in various Catholic movements and I wanted to help the U.S. Catholic community situate itself historically. I argued that the dramatic changes taking place in the church in those years resulted from the intersection of three factors.[2]

First was Americanization, the changing social composition and location of the American Catholic population. To put it most simply, among the descendants of European immigrant Catholics a new middle-class, suburban Catholicism succeeded the ethnic-, family-, neighborhood-, and parish-centered Catholicism created by earlier generations. If earlier Catholics had, in religious terms at least, seemed "certain and set apart" in their rich Catholic subculture, postwar Catholics found religious, as well as social, boundaries more permeable, and identity less clear as that supportive subculture was transformed by social change.[3] Catholic doctrines and practices could no longer be taken for granted. Faith was becoming, for many, in the words of German theologian Karl Rahner, "a personal achievement constantly renewed amid perilous surroundings."[4] I was convinced that the changes in the social composition and location of Catholics were so profound that, even if there had been no Second Vatican Council, there would have been enormous pressures for change in the American church. Clues to the shape of those changes could be found in the long history of American Protestant Christianity.

The second factor was the Second Vatican Council, which solved some American Catholic problems, especially by affirming at last American principles of religious liberty and offering at least a provisional acceptance of religious pluralism. But these long-awaited changes also opened up new

2. I made this argument from the mid-1970s on. See my "American Catholicism after 200 Years."

3. Hennesey, *American Catholics*, 221, 307–32.

4. Rahner, "The Present Position of Christians," 34.

questions about personal faith and moral conscience, evident at first in the renewal of vowed religious life, then in the explosion of dissent that followed the 1968 reaffirmation of the church's opposition to artificial contraception. Less noticed but equally important was the turn toward a more critical stance on issues of race, war, and nuclear weapons, where Catholics were urged to make conscientious personal decisions about how they would carry out their social and political responsibilities. Most dramatic, in the context of the nuclear arms race and the Vietnam War, was the recognition of a legitimate Catholic tradition of nonviolence that made even war open to moral deliberation and conscientious choice. Here at least, life apart from the church, in communities shared with others, religious orientations and moral choices had profound, even religious, significance. And there were deeper questions posed by the Council about the very nature and mission, the what and the why, of the church itself. Older certainties about the church as "the ordinary means of salvation" were hard to sustain in the face of religious pluralism, ecumenism, and bottom-up renewal centered on persons, religious experience, and dialogue at a time of bewildering social change. Indeed, this second factor, the Council, made it extremely difficult for the pastoral and organizational leaders of the church, and Catholics themselves, to negotiate the changes arising from the first factor, Catholic arrival into the American mainstream.

The third factor was "the sixties," the explosive events in American society. While bishops and priests, sisters and families were inviting one another to religious renewal, the country seemed to be falling apart. It was this factor that gave the era its tone of crisis. It accounts for use of the word "disintegration" by the always-judicious historian Philip Gleason to describe what was happening to American Catholicism.[5] The combination of conciliar calls to conscience and American conflicts over race, war, and abortion accelerated the collapse of the American Catholic subculture—the well-established boundaries between American and Catholic ideas and practices—and with it (and here is the crucial point) the slow decline of Catholic Americanism.

There have been many excellent studies of the American experience of the Council and its aftermath, but I am convinced that the intersection of these three factors—Americanization, the Council, and the sixties—best explains the postconciliar experience of American Catholics. Some have credited or, more recently, blamed the Council for what they take to be a decline of Catholic identity. Others combine that revisionism with a critique of Americanization, as if the Council was interpreted in ways that

---

5. Gleason, "In Search of Unity."

lent legitimacy to the desire of Catholics for acceptance and belonging. This argument was dramatically present in widely publicized criticism of the University of Notre Dame when it honored President Barack Obama in 2009. For many committed and vocal Catholics, Notre Dame's success, like the success of so many American Catholics, came at the expense of their Catholic identity.

Critics were right to highlight the degree to which Catholic families and institutions actively sought a fuller role in their society, an historic quest that helped shape the American church throughout its history. Catholics were, and are, the agents of their own history. Immigrant Catholics—not all, but many—built parishes and other institutions to support their families, retain their heritage, and pursue a better life for their children. From that combination of "folk memories" and "new aspirations"[6] came a remarkable Catholic subculture. Theologian William Portier is close to the mark when he describes the collapse of that American Catholic subculture, the buffer between Catholics and American individualism and pluralism, as the single most important fact of recent U.S. Catholic history. In his essay "Here Come the Evangelical Catholics," Portier recognizes that the heart of the matter is the story of economic and educational changes after World War II that led to the multiplication of inter-ethnic and inter-religious relationships and the erosion of subcultural institutions and practices. In Portier's words, American Catholics then had to learn "how to be truly Catholic in American pluralism without a subculture."[7]

Portier also speaks of "the end of Americanism," ideas that gave meaning to the Americanization experience. For Americanizing Catholics—and other religious outsiders—the experience of assimilation found meaning in America's own religious meaning. As one important Jewish writer put it, one left behind one religious culture to enter another, larger one. Catholics, Portier believed, had long negotiated their dual role as Catholics and Americans with the help of natural law. Its argument was that the human values affirmed by the church corresponded with at least some of those affirmed by American culture. Natural law was useful for Catholic outsiders who wanted to be insiders—it made becoming American a good thing, fully confirmed by church teaching. It was less helpful for Catholics when they became insiders, with shared responsibility for the common life seen as, in

6. This combination of memory and aspiration was made by Timothy L. Smith. I have found that the aspiration side has often been overlooked, not only in historical work on immigrant Catholicism but in discussions of contemporary Catholicism in the United States, as well. It is closely related to the failure to understand Americanization and Americanism. See, in particular, Smith's "Religion and Ethnicity in America.

7. Portier, "Here Come the Evangelical Catholics," 51.

some respects, hostile to church teaching, because it allowed Catholics to minimize their specifically Catholic and Christian obligations. Even worse, the changes of the 1960s, in Portier's view, brought a "new pluralism," emphasizing differences and replacing the wartime emphasis on truths held in common. Now the wider culture valued "diversity over consensus" so that, for Catholics, identity required re-affirming the distinctive claims of Catholic faith. In the post-immigrant church, with its personalism and voluntarism, that helped explain the rise of what Portier called "evangelical Catholicism."

Evangelical Catholicism

Portier and John Allen have generously given me credit for introducing in this context the notion of "evangelical Catholics."[8] I used the term originally to describe the life and work of nineteenth-century convert evangelist Isaac Hecker. He hoped to convert other young Americans and inspire the zeal of young Catholics of immigrant stock who were but making their way in America. His insight into the situation of Americanized, post-ethnic Catholics and other Americans seemed to me particularly helpful to understanding middle-class Catholics of the Vatican-II era. Affirming democratic ideals of freedom, Hecker thought the keys to effective missionary work were appeals for personal commitments based on inner spiritual experiences, a Catholic and middle-class version of Christian revivalism. In addition, it would require openness to God's presence in history—divine providence—and shared responsibility among clergy, religious, and laity for the work of bringing about the Kingdom of God in the midst of history, American history.[9]

My argument has little to do with the assertive Catholicism that came to be associated with the leadership of Popes John Paul II and Benedict XVI. For official and unofficial neo-orthodox theologians, almost all working from an historical narrative of secularization, economic and social success for Catholics was achieved through accommodation to prevailing secular values and practices. This, they argue, has led to the decline of Catholic identity. In response they advocate pastoral strategies that emphasize Catholic distance from surrounding culture and differences with other-than-Catholic neighbors. In this context "evangelical" suggests assertive faith centered on Catholic versions of family values and gender and sexual ethics,

---

8. Allen, Portier, and I shared in a public discussion of evangelical Catholicism at the University of Dayton in 2008.

9. See my *Isaac Hecker*.

with less frequent reference to teachings on violence and economic justice, as components of "new evangelization."

I think that one needs to pay more attention to the American religious culture which, for many Catholics, is now their own. That is one consequence of Americanization. One can make the case that evangelical Christianity is usually the democratic form of Christianity. What this means is that, if you have a combination of religious freedom and religious pluralism in a single community, with promiscuous inter-religious mixing at work, school, marketplace, and city hall, even in families, then Christianity tends toward evangelical forms. These include personal, adult decisions of faith, emphasis on the Bible (especially on Jesus encountered in the Christian scriptures), and congregations focused on shared experiences of faith and the generational transmission of faith and culture. Many have argued that such evangelicalism, broadly understood, has been the default drive of American Protestant Christianity from Puritan beginnings through Great Awakenings, from Jonathan Edwards and Dwight Moody to the neo-evangelicalism spawned by Billy Graham. America's religious diversity and religious freedom, its individualism and mobility, consistently undercut European-based traditions and creeds, hierarchical authority, and theological and ministerial elitism. The same culture also produced religious seekers, intense-but-fragmented communities, armies of zealous preachers (some at revivals) bringing men and women to Jesus, others in lecture halls listening to Ralph Waldo Emerson and his disciples, urging the same men and women to listen to the Spirit within.

The marks of American evangelicalism were and are (a) the central place of the Bible (really, the New Testament), the people's book (modern American fundamentalism arose when scholars and mainstream ministers claimed one could not properly read the Bible except under the direction of better-educated teachers); (b) personal conversion, and periodic re-conversion, to Jesus—the born-again experience, often accompanied by moral reform of self and others; and (c) voluntary communities, congregations, to confirm the faith, share the experience, and, especially, pass faith on to the children. All the rest—traditions, rituals and creeds, sacraments, synods and bishops—had to adapt to this evangelical piety and democratic pastoral practice if they were to survive.

Some scholars would add the evangelizing impulse to announce conversion and seek to bring others to turn their lives over to Jesus. This marks many evangelical communities, of course, but American evangelicalism has usually tempered its evangelizing zeal and its Christian exclusivism, especially when it moved from marginalized subcultures to the pluralist mainstream. After all, evangelicalism arose from the heady experience of religious freedom; evangelicals almost always championed religious liberty and church-state separation, and they initiated many social reform movements, from anti-slavery through social gospels to anti-abortion. In today's headlines evangelicals include former President George W. Bush and former Governor Mike Huckabee, President Barack Obama and 2016 presidential candidate Hillary Clinton, suggesting once again that missionary evangelicalism takes many forms, almost all democratic in spirit and practice.

Among Catholics, immigration and ethnic solidarity amid widespread nativism and anti-Catholicism inspired well-organized Catholic communities and institutions that held American religious individualism/personalism at bay, at least for awhile. But, as Catholics moved out of old neighborhoods and up social and educational ladders, all the signs of American democratic religion—evangelicalism—appeared. Children learned biblical faith, many adults formed and talked about personal relationships with Jesus, and they thrived on intense but short-lived experiences of community. As sociologist Andrew Greeley argued, young Catholics of the baby-boom generations liked being Catholic, they went to church less than their parents but they respected the pope and most priests, and they liked saints and the Blessed Virgin Mary. Like other young Americans, they accepted the Christian creed, but within a biblical piety. They shrugged off complicated doctrines and moral claims that ignored their experience, and they tested priests and ministers (a new word for Catholics) by the quality of their personal faith and pastoral care.

Meanwhile, in a series of apostolic movements and renewal programs, their parents sat in living-room sessions listening to the word of God, sharing experiences of God's presence and absence, and renewing their commitment to the church that was now *their* church, the people of God. In church basements they shared experiences of faith with prospective converts, carried on sacramental preparation and religious education programs laced with scripture, and they discussed abortion, war, and poverty, asking "What would Jesus do?" more often than "What does the church teach?" A few decided that Catholicism had a theological, sacramental, and authoritative alternative to Protestant evangelical enthusiasm; these are Portier's evangelical Catholics. But, if the sociologists are right, the vast majority settled into more easygoing, open, and altogether American forms of evangelical Catholicism. A significant number of U.S. church leaders, encouraged by talk of "reforming the reform" from Rome, lamented what they saw as individualism, emotionalism, a-intellectualism, "cafeteria Catholicism," and recent versions of what the old pastors called "indifferentism." They were not wrong as the combination of Americanization and Vatican II, in the context of "the sixties," did indeed mean dramatic changes in Catholic belief and practice, along with the breakdown of subcultural boundaries. Catholics looked more and more like other American Christians.

So what happens to the American and/or Catholic question when the children of immigrants get the education and opportunity their parents fought for, and they confront the great religious questions in a setting of freedom, pluralism, and mutual respect? In the nineteenth century, Hecker, whose ideas were at the center of a version of "Americanism" condemned by Pope Leo XIII in 1899, wondered how Catholicism would fare in America when it confronted its own "earnest seekers." He believed that the ancient faith could not only handle the challenges of freedom and intelligence, but that it could find in the new experiences of freedom and democracy a God-given opportunity to take a giant step towards the Kingdom of God. Sadly, as many of his contemporaries noted, his church took another, countercultural route, confirmed in America by new waves of immigrants, revived anti-Catholicism, and that peculiarly Catholic form of secularization, confining religion to family values, ethnic solidarity, and clerically controlled sacraments and devotions.

But Hecker's church of earnest seekers never disappeared and found a new, mass base after World War II. Beyond the ethnic-based subculture, Catholicism, to flourish, has had to make its case, persuading free people that Catholicism best responds to everyone's questions and aspirations. In the democratic setting, the church depends on personal conviction, on conscience. The church has to support the inner spiritual life and inspire men and women to find God's will for them in the midst of daily activities. If Isaac Hecker came back to find that young millennial Catholics have a rich, if undisciplined, spiritual life, respected everyone's autonomy and freedom, and valued service to the poor as a Christian obligation, he would be delighted. The real challenge, as Hecker thought, is to welcome America's built-in evangelicalism and come up with robust movements of mission and ministry that will make the promise of the Kingdom of God visible and bring a sense of hope to shared life as Americans. For that to happen, Hecker believed that some Catholics would have to take up that work within the U.S. Catholic community. The condemnation of Americanism did not end that work, but it did locate the center of the church's attention away from the American nation as a whole and towards the church itself. The revival of Americanism after the council renewed attention to lay experience, social solidarity, and shared historical responsibility. But, as we have argued, Americanization came into disrepute, and Americanism—Catholic ideas lending positive meaning to American experience—all but disappeared from Catholic public discourse.

U.S. Catholicism Absent Americanism

In the absence of Americanism, readings of the trajectory of U.S. Catholic history—interpretations of past and present that point toward the future—have a passive and pessimistic spirit. There are divisions and problems in the American church, all acknowledge, but no one is at fault and not much can be done. To this reliance on the passive voice is added considerable pessimism about the subjects of study: American Catholics. Chester Gillis, for example, argued that "Catholics like their Christianity to fulfill their spiritual needs but not at the cost of severely disrupting their lifestyle."[10] Scott Appleby, attracted at times to Americanist themes, nevertheless speaks of younger Catholics in terms once used only by aggrieved conservatives: "Indoctrinated" by their parents with "the principle of religious choice," they now "lack a vocabulary that would help them form a Catholic identity or interpret their Catholic experiences, and they are situational in their ethical thinking."[11] Peter Steinfels, in the best recent survey of contemporary American Catholicism, failed to generate a centrist alternative to the countercultural vision.[12] For moderates like Steinfels, as for historian Philip Gleason earlier, Americanization without Americanism necessarily foregrounds issues of identity and integrity. Determined to be Catholic more than American, suspicious of partisanship and activism within the church, and seemingly convinced that Catholicism is about religion as distinct from secular life, they are unable to find solid ground for Catholic solidarity or awaken a sense of shared purpose: identity and mission are both detached from an historical setting. And thus the Americanist problem persists. Even when truly serious about Catholicism, as are these commentators and many others (feminist, Latino, and neoconservative), it is doubtful whether Catholics in the United States can renew their community without a richer and more positive reading of their shared American experience. Unfortunately many seem to think that the only alternative is to rebuild a Catholic subculture, "certain and set apart" from the rest of American culture. That is the strategy implicit in most theological and pastoral commentary on contemporary American Catholicism.

It is good to recall the theological and spiritual consequences of past subcultural strategies. Historians of popular religion notice how the reformed ultramontane church set out after Vatican Council I to systematically undercut popular devotions or incorporate them into the life of the

---

10. Gillis, *Roman Catholicism in America*, 279.

11. Appleby, "In Pursuit of Coherence," 12.

12. Steinfels, *A People Adrift*. See my lengthy review, "Moderate Manifesto."

institutional, clerically controlled church. God, and grace, could ultimately be contacted best through the church and its sacraments. There was another piece of that message: that religion is found in church and in those activities outside of church which it endows with religious significance, most notably sex and family life. Experiences outside the subculture, experiences of work, politics, encounter with non-Catholics and other-than-Catholic cultural symbols, were without religious significance—they were not sites of encounter with God. Thus Catholicism contributed to the very secularization it condemned. In the United States, the church could offer no religious meaning to its people's historic experiences of mobility and liberation.

One could also look at Philip Gleason's analysis of the history of Catholic higher education for evidence of the importance of Americanism and its absence.[13] Gleason says that Catholic colleges and universities found their purpose in offering an alternative to the chaos and confusion of modernity. Yet, to do so they first had to modernize their structures and programs to satisfy accrediting agencies (in which they participated) and meet the needs of aspiring students presumably less hostile to modernity than their teachers. While joining the rest of the American church in denouncing many aspects of modern society, from dirty movies to decadent materialism, priests and religious presidents and trustees proved quite adept at adapting to the changing needs of their constituents and to the changing opportunities provided by a generous public—as with the G.I. Bill and later student aid programs. Gleason believes that the anti-modern rationale of Catholic intellectual life and Catholic higher education collapsed in the 1960s. If he is right, perhaps the reason lay less in surrender to modernist currents, as many critics suggest, than in the fact that anti-modernism always masked powerful aspirations in the Catholic subculture. Gleason, however, sets the trap that Steinfels and Appleby cannot escape because he reduces immigrant aspirations to a matter of adaptation to American culture. He believes that classic Catholic Americanism, condemned in the 1890s, highlighted the "intimate connection that existed (and still exists) between higher education and the efforts of American Catholics to accommodate themselves to the modern world."[14] Rome was not ready for the supposed risks to faith in that accommodation in 1899, and its negative judgment closed off self-conscious reflection on the relationship between Catholic religion and national culture, and with it the possibility of endowing experience outside the subculture with religious meaning. Years later, after World War II, a recovery of Americanism preceded and helped set the stage for what

13. Gleason, *Contending with Modernity*.
14. Ibid., 12.

Gleason calls the post-Vatican-II "acceptance of modernity." And a similar counterculturual reaction followed, spurred by the Vatican under Pope John Paul II and eventually endorsed by leaders of the American church.[15]

But Americanism was not only, or even mainly, about accommodation. Indeed, neither was Americanization. There were certainly material hopes for jobs, secure incomes, homes, and other economic resources, and achieving those goals required a degree of accommodation, to be sure. But those were not always ends in themselves, but rather means to larger ends of dignity, freedom, social respect, and political participation. Peasants and industrial workers did not need lectures from their "betters" about the dangers of greed and materialism, for everything around them, including the church they were helping to build, testified to the intimate connection between freedom and successful accommodation. They knew from hard experience that the road to liberation from oppression might sometimes require the removal of roadblocks to equal access, and in the end it would always require a degree of acceptance of dominant economic, social, and cultural practices. But these were means: the ends were freedom, dignity, acceptance and, yes, power. How Catholics (or anyone else) uses that power consequent on freedom was the question that followed, and it is that challenge that makes the Catholic and/or American question so very important.

At its best, the Americanism pioneered by Isaac Hecker and revived by so many pastoral leaders of the Vatican-II era arose from experiences of God's presence outside the Catholic subculture, and it offered an ethic of responsibility as a counterweight to the isolation and occasional self-righteousness of official Catholicism. If its temptation was an emotional American nationalism—and it was—it was no more simply a rationale for middle-class belonging than Catholic culture talk was simply a rationale for Catholic institutional and clerical self-interest. No, there were some very good reasons, especially in the United States, why Catholic Christians might decide to contend with modernity from the inside, as a public work

15. Of course, the decline of Americanism and rise of the countercultural consensus reflects broader patterns in American life. In the sixties, progressive history and consensus history provided American stories within which people like me could tell our stories, in my case the story of American Catholics. But after the civil rights movement, the assassinations, the urban riots, and the Vietnam War, neither progress nor consensus could any longer sustain a common American narrative, even a contested one. By the end of the period, identity politics and identity history dominated: as Robert Novick wrote in *That Noble Dream*, every group became "its own historian" (469–521). That disappearance of American solidarity opened up a so-called postmodern cultural space for an American Catholic story for American Catholics, to be sure. But in the absence of shared commitments to American common life, that story can only be told around difference and distance from American culture itself. In short, the story becomes one about the Catholic piece of the American Catholic reality.

shared with others. For another thing, Americanism, like modernity, may have placed too high a value on freedom, but surely there is something to be said for it. Perhaps, as many believed, Vatican II brought a disruptive, often naively romantic "contagion for liberty." But once again, was that the whole story? At their best the Americanists linked liberty and justice, freedom and participation. And, most of all, they tried to find religious meaning in the experience of freedom and shared public responsibility.

Americanism was the crucial question, and it remains the missing page.[16] The agenda for scholars is to look at Americanization as an active process, to discern in recent experience the temptations of uncritical Americanism, and to take the next step toward the personal and political responsibility for church and society that was the outcome of this historic and liberating journey of immigrant, working-class American Catholics. That, not pessimistic subcultural restoration, would be most helpful to those Catholics still struggling to make that journey. A renewed Americanism might be composed of five elements: (1) a positive reading of U.S. Catholic history, anchored in family stories of desired and achieved liberation and consequent shared responsibility; (2) a pastoral theology that enables lay persons to read their lay experience through the eyes of faith and bring to their faith the wisdom gained through lay experience—this would anchor Catholic social and intellectual ministry within the framework of pastoral ministry; (3) an ethic of shared responsibility for American society and culture—an ethic informing work and politics, art and imagination; (4) a new commitment to shared responsibility for the life and ministry of the church at all levels, and organized efforts to translate that commitment into Catholic institutions and practices; and (5) a long-range vision of a single human family, grounded in the changing life of the universal church, but grounded as well in an understanding of Americanism that embraces the reflections of Lincoln, the dedication of democratic reformers, and the vision of Martin Luther King.

16. Many things can be explained by the preference for countercultural over engagement images: the inability to genuinely value the laity, their voice in church policy, their experience in church moral teaching (to the extent they are lay, they are part of the culture to which the church is counter); the collapse of the center in church politics as described by Peter Steinfels; the identity crisis of Catholic higher education, mirroring the identity crisis of educated and Americanized Catholic lay people; the failure to mount a counterattack against changes in liturgical rubrics, homosexuality pronouncements, or statements on women, all at odds with pastoral practice in middle-class American Catholicism; the decline of the power and resources of the national episcopal conference; the status of Catholic politicians today as compared with 1960; and much more.

A Personal Reflection

I did not have all this clear when I wrote *The Renewal of American Catholicism* in 1972, but what I did have was the conviction that America mattered and one could not renew the church without engaging the country and the larger Cold-War world.[17] *Renewal* was, in many ways, an unapologetic text of civil religion. Religion is "what matters," Robert Orsi once wrote.[18] In my book of forty-five years ago, America, and American Catholicism, both mattered. Years later, Mary Jo Weaver and Scott Appleby helped map American Catholicism in two books, *Being Right* and *What's Left?*, and Weaver quipped that the never-written third volume might have been called "*Who Cares?*"[19] That's exactly right. While Catholics have argued about whether Americanism is a good thing, they often forgot that Americanization means that the Catholic Church is now part of American religion. And American religion's default system features not unity, doctrine, liturgy, and priesthood—much less a shared sense of historic mission—but individualism, congregationalism, ministry, private over public faith, and pluralism with its constant companion, choice. In the United States, like it or not, religious experience usually trumps doctrinal orthodoxy, and populist hermeneutics always takes precedence over biblical scholarship. And the needed comforts of pastoral care will not always make room, nor should they, for the challenges of the social gospel. It isn't Americanism that causes all this, but Americanization. How Catholics respond to it depends, in part, on how much they care about Catholic doctrine and practices; that is obvious. But, as Weaver's question suggested, it also depends on how much they care about their country and their world. It is one thing to have a social ethic, as in Catholic social teaching. It is quite another to make that ethic the center of personal and community life. That requires genuine care for the world, and for our part of the world. The common good—of everybody—must truly matter. This is the Americanist question: what are Christians to make of, how are they to judge, America's amazing religious diversity, its bewildering popular spiritualities, its restless and ever-multiplying religious movements, sects, and independent congregations, its politics and its people? Is all this progress or decline? And when all this democratic messiness spills over into their own church, and seizes their people, when they become "cafeteria Catholics," or Pentecostals, or new-age prophets, or enthusiastic devotees of Pope "John Paul the Great"—or when they simply start to make up their

17. O'Brien, *The Renewal of American Catholicism.*
18. Orsi, *The Madonna of 115th Street,* xliii.
19. Appleby and Weaver, *Being Right*; and Weaver, *What's Left?*

own minds—then what are Catholic pastors and bishops and intellectuals to do? What do we think of all these people? That depends on our answer to the Americanist question.

One answer, I wrote in 1972, is to trust people and divine providence enough to "hang loose" and reserve judgment of others while trying as best we can to live by the light of the gospel. Pope Francis would say to avoid "rigidity" and live as best we can for others. Another answer, taken for granted in *Renewal*, is to acknowledge that the church makes choices and all are responsible for those choices: there is a Catholic politics. And those who do not take part in those politics nevertheless share responsibility for the outcome. And a third, I thought then and still think central to American Catholic life, is that those Catholic choices make a great American difference. In one of his last publications, a review of William Shea's book about Evangelicals and Catholics, the late Peter D'Agostino made a comment about contemporary religious politics that echoes what I was struggling to articulate in 1972: "Conservatives/traditionalists among Catholics, Protestants, Jews, and secularists have aligned themselves against their liberal/progressive Catholic, Protestant, Jewish, and secular counterparts in a struggle for America's soul."[20] The question in 2016, as it was in 1899 and 1972, is in what ways we Catholics will accept our responsibilities in that struggle.

20. D'Agostino, Review of *The Lion and Lamb*.

7

An Americanist in Paris

The Early Career of the Abbé Félix Klein

C. J. T. Talar

Through his involvement in the 1897 publication of the French translation of Walter Elliott's *Life of Father Hecker*[1] and the controversy it catalyzed, Abbé Félix Klein (1862–1953)[2] attained a certain notoriety in his own day. The enduring interest of the Americanist controversy and Klein's contribution to its historiography in the form of the fourth volume of his memoirs, rendered into English as *Americanism: A Phantom Heresy*, has given him a degree of familiarity to students of American Catholic history.[3]

Klein's identification with Americanist ideas antedated his editorial role in the Hecker biography and active propagandizing on its behalf. While it is clear that the controversy surrounding the book had enduring repercussions for Klein's reputation, his previous involvement with Americanist

1. Elliott, *The Life of Father Hecker*. Klein contributed a preface to the French translation, *Le Père Hecker: Fondateur des "Paulistes" américains, 1819–1888*, highlighting the originality of Hecker's thought and seeking to position him for a French readership.

2. Klein awaits a critical biography. See the entry on Klein in the *Dictionnaire du monde religieux dans la France contemporaine*, 359–60.

3. Klein, *La route d'un petit Morvandiau*. Volume 4 (*Une Hérésie fantome: L'Américanisme*) was translated as *Americanism: A Phantom Heresy*. Philip Gleason locates Klein's contribution within the trajectory of Americanist historiography in "The New Americanism in Catholic Historiography," 1–18. Phantom heresy historiography is discussed in Portier, *Divided Friends*, 26–28. See also Portier, "Isaac Hecker and *Testem Benevolentiae*."

The impact of the condemnation of Americanism on the American church is discussed in McAvoy, *The Great Crisis in American Catholic History, 1895–1900*, 303–43.

ideas helped to create a climate of reception for Hecker's biography. An examination of Klein's early career provides background to the controversial preface he contributed to *Le Père Hecker: Fondateur des "Paulistes" américains*, the hopes it embodied, the optimistic reading of the times it reflected.

Early Writings

After minor seminary at Meaux, Klein was sent to Saint-Sulpice where he was among those who showed intellectual promise and came under the influence of John Hogan.[4] While there, Klein heard a lecture by Archbishop James Gibbons on Catholicism in the United States, which he credits with stimulating his early interest in America.[5] Ordained to the priesthood in 1885, he subsequently obtained his licence ès lettres from the Sorbonne. Klein's health suffered under the regime of study, and he was sent to Algeria in 1889 for several months' stay to rest and recover. His acquaintance with Cardinal Lavigerie and the African missions resulted in his first published book, *Cardinal Lavigerie et ses oeuvres d'Afrique*. Klein later reflected that he found himself at several points in his life in the midst of controversy, sometimes by choice, sometimes by accident, on other occasions by association.[6] In this case it was a result of the timing of the book's publication. It was ready for press at the very time that the telegraph announced the famous Algiers Toast proposed by Lavigerie, in which he implicitly appealed to French Catholic conservatives to abandon their intransigent opposition to the country's republican regime. The cardinal intimated that he was expressing a view that was not merely his own, but hinted that it had Vatican backing.[7] Klein was able to print the text of the Toast at the end of the volume, just before the Table of Contents. Thus, what was intended as a laudatory account of Lavigerie and French missionaries in Africa appeared in the midst of the reaction to the cardinal's initiative, and classed its author

---

4. John Hogan (1829–1901) influenced a number of figures who actively worked for the renewal of Catholicism in France during the modernist period. Among those were Eudoxe-Irénée Mignot, Louis Birot, Pierre Batiffol, and Marcel Hébert. Klein's appreciation for Hogan's influence can be found in *La route d'un petit Morvandiau*, 1:70–82.

5. Klein, *La route d'un petit Morvandiau*, 1:87. Klein recalls this encounter as occurring in either 1883 or 1884. At Saint-Sulpice he learned to read English and thus followed up his interest by reading Gibbons's writings (1:100–101).

6. Ibid., 2:139.

7. James Ward traces Vatican initiatives for the *Ralliement*, and Lavigerie's role in those, in "The Algiers Toast."

"among the Republicans, Democrats, revolutionaries or simply, with greater benevolence, among the liberals and progressives."[8]

At the time of the book's publication Klein was teaching philosophy at Meaux. From there he was able to follow the strongly negative reactions from Catholics for whom an acceptance of the Republic was equated with a betrayal of their faith, and the eventual clarification of Rome's position with the encyclical *Au milieu des Sollicitudes* (February 1892), followed by a "Lettre aux cardinaux français" the following May.[9] Despite the opposition it received, the "esprit nouveau" played a part in the creation of an atmosphere of optimism, which sustained hopes that a reconciliation between the church and the age could be effected.

The *Ralliement* provided another stimulus to look to the situation of the church in the United States. In 1892 the Vicomte de Meaux published accounts of his travels in America. While acknowledging differences between democracy in the United States and in Europe, and admitting possible future conflicts between American Catholics' allegiance to Rome and to their church, he saw in the American church evidence that religion and democracy could come together without either of them relinquishing their respective rights. From this Catholics could derive "great hope" that accommodation could be reached in the situations particular to Europe.[10] De Meaux's book is credited with exerting a strong influence on Klein's desire to know the United States more profoundly.[11]

In the early 1890s Klein was able to find another source of optimism for the future of Catholicism in his area of academic specialization, literature. In "Le movement néo-chrétien dans la littérature contemporaine" Klein explored a rather diffuse set of tendencies oriented, in variable degrees, toward a positive appreciation of Christianity. Its origins were traced to a reaction against the excesses of a literary realism in naturalism or the claims of positivist philosophy. Its partisans, among whom were named Edouard Rod, Paul Bourget, Maurice Boucher, and Paul Desjardins, sought to move beyond positivism and scientism, stimulated by a need for something more. With the néo-chrétiens Klein saw a serious quest for truth. They were attracted to Christian morality and to the example of Jesus, but continued to view Christian dogma as incompatible with science, and the church as incompatible with scientific progress. Nonetheless, even here Klein detected

8. Klein, *La route d'un petit Morvandiau*, 2:139.

9. Dumont, *Le Saint-Siège et l'organisation politique des catholiques français aux lendemains du Ralliement, 1890–1902*.

10. The series of articles appeared later in book form. De Meaux, *L'Église catholique et la liberté aux États-Unis*, 408–9.

11. Klein, *La route d'un petit Morvandiau*, 7:18. Cf. 5:210.

grounds for hope in the possibility that they may go beyond an admiration for Christian moral teaching to appreciate its foundation in Christian belief and the role of the Church as guardian of both. In the néo-chrétiens Klein found another stimulus for serious engagement with science from the side of Catholicism. And there were signs of it. In 1888 the first Congrès scientifique international des Catholiques was held in Paris. Klein had followed its gestation and was able to attend, later recording the favorable impression the sessions had made on him.[12] The theme of overcoming ignorance and correcting misunderstandings, which runs like a thread through his writings of the period, makes an appearance here. He is able to find tangible signs of progress in this regard in those representatives of the neo-Christian movement who expressed not simply a dream but a firm hope in a reconciliation of science with faith. And of church with society. Klein is able to cite Melchior de Vogüé as an example of one who acknowledged the Christian Church, "transformed and adapted to the requirements of the new world" as "*alone* capable of giving effective direction to contemporary democracy."[13]

The year 1892 was something of a watershed for Klein. Vatican initiatives calling for Catholics to rally to the Republic held out promise for a brighter future for the French church, and put him on the side of papal policy. His assessment of the neo-Christian movement held promise of a different sort, and would shortly have implications for Klein's own future in the form of an invitation to join the faculty of the Paris *Institut Catholique*, largely on the basis of the article and the views it embodied. In mid-1892 there occurred two further events that would impact French Catholicism more largely and Klein more particularly. On his way back from Rome, Archbishop John Ireland delivered two lectures in Paris. Klein was able to attend the first of these, which made a notable impact on him. "The lecture of 18 June 1892 marks a date in my life. It confirmed my aspirations, stimulated my enthusiasm, made the examples I desired more accessible and more vibrant, not only to follow myself, but to spread energetically for the glory of God, for the good of the Church and humanity."[14] Klein could not attend the second lecture, which Ireland gave a week later, but was able to read the full text in *Le Monde*.[15] Together, these discourses inspired another article, "La Démocratie et l'Église," which appeared at the end of the year.[16]

12. Ibid., 1:271–72.

13. Klein, "Le movement néo-chrétien dans la littérature contemporaine," 42 (originally published in 1892).

14. Klein, *La route d'un petit Morvandiau*, 2:180–81.

15. *Le Monde*, a Catholic daily, was published between 1894 and 1896 by Paul Naudet (1859–1929), a priest who was active in Christian Democracy in France.

16. Klein, "La Démocratie et l'Église" (originally published in 1892).

Klein found in Ireland's words yet another reason to be confident regarding the church's future, within France and beyond it. The archbishop's portrayal of democracy in America is set within the context of Leo XIII's encyclical *Au milieu des Sollicitudes* promulgated but several months earlier. Klein is able to show that Ireland's position is in accord with papal teaching, and the upshot of both is that there exist "natural affinities between the Church and democracy."[17] To those who assert the contrary, arguing that the church emphasizes humans' eternal destiny to the neglect of their temporal wellbeing, Klein counters with *Rerum Novarum*, support for the Knights of Labor by the American hierarchy, and the successful coexistence of Catholicism and democracy in America. Ireland's words sustain his hopes for the future of church and society, the more so for being set against "unequivocal signs of democratic sympathy" manifest in Germany, Ireland, and—not least—France.[18]

Klein's *Nouvelles tendances en religion et en littérature*, which included the articles on the neo-Christian movement and democracy and the church, was published with a preface by Abbé Joinot which had "the effect almost of a manifesto of the young clergy."[19] The views expressed therein further identified Klein with those who saw much of the burden of resolving the current religious crisis as falling upon the church. The perceived antinomy between science and faith constituted the major obstacle. The movement toward Catholicism on the part of néo-chrétiens and efforts on the part of the church to address the social crisis provided major opportunities.

It was another book, however, that solidified Klein not only with reformist efforts in France, but with those of the Americanist party in the United States. Following his two lectures in Paris, Ireland enjoyed great prestige among French Catholics committed to the political and social ideas of the pope. A group that included Henri Lorin[20] desired to make these addresses, together with some others, available to a wider audience in France. Klein credits a letter published by Paul Bourget—then travelling in the United States, and, on the basis of his experience there, expressing optimism that Christianity appeared to be thoroughly reconcilable with the modern world—with catalyzing his decision to undertake the necessary translations and publication of Ireland's addresses.[21] The archbishop emerges from the

17. Ibid., 101.

18. Ibid., 122–23.

19. Klein, *La route d'un petit Morvandiau*, 2:206.

20. Together with René de La Tour du Pin and Albert de Mun, Henri Lorin was one of the principal proponents of social Catholicism in France. See Misner, *Social Catholicism in Europe*.

21. Klein, Preface to *L'Église et le siècle*, 1–3. Bourget later published an account of

pages of Klein's preface as a model for his French readers to follow: "Is it a question of freedom, progress, social justice, or democracy? The Archbishop of Saint Paul is more passionate than yourselves on these sacred issues."[22] What is asserted as true for the personal example of Ireland is held as also true for the collective example of the American church. While, admittedly, the situation of Catholicism in France is not identical with that of Catholicism in the United States, Klein invites his readers to take note of the church's success there, and, in comparing the two countries, "learn which attitude is best to destroy prejudices and to relate God to souls."[23] In his comments on the sermon, "The Church and the Age," which gives the volume its title, Klein notes that this sums up Ireland's fundamental thought and serves as the primary inspiration behind his words and actions: "Namely, that between the church and the present time there exists, despite reciprocal misunderstandings and prejudices, a secret and profound harmony that all intellectually gifted minds should undertake to make increasingly apparent to their contemporaries."[24]

The book accomplished its purposes of gaining greater recognition for Ireland's ideas and stimulating French Catholics to think along similar lines. *L'Église et le siècle* was widely, and favorably, reviewed, and a month after its initial publication had gone into a sixth edition. Klein received Ireland's commendation for accurately rendering his ideas in the preface.[25] More than with *Cardinal Lavigerie* and *Nouvelles tendances*, Klein's contributions to this volume put him in the forefront of the ranks of those who were (in the words of one reviewer) "completely dedicated . . . to reconciling, for the good of all, Catholicism and the modern world, religion and the contemporary soul, the Church and the Age."[26]

---

his American travels in *Outre-Mer: Impressions of America*. On Ireland see O'Connell, *John Ireland and the American Catholic Church*.

22. Klein, Preface to *L'Église et le siècle*, 11.

23. Ibid., 7.

24. Ireland, *L'Église et le siècle*, 21. In addition to "The Church and the Age," originally preached at the cathedral of Baltimore on 18 October 1893, the volume contained "The Future of Catholicism in the United States" (given at Baltimore, 10 November 1889 as "The Mission of Catholics in America"), the two addresses given in Paris in June of 1892: "The Situation of Catholicism in the United States" and "The Social Action of French Youth," and lastly, "Human Progress," pronounced at the Chicago Exposition on 21 October 1892. With the exception of the two Paris lectures, these texts may be found in Ireland, *The Church and Modern Society*.

25. Letter of Ireland to Klein, 20 April 1894. Text in Klein, *La route d'un petit Morvandiau*, 3:59–61. This letter was published in *Le Figaro*.

26. Cited in Klein, *La route d'un petit Morvandiau*, 3:171.

Autour du dilettantisme (1895)

His growing reputation in progressive circles opened the pages of several reviews to Klein, among those Abbé Paul Naudet's *Le Monde* and Paul Harel's
(later George Fonsegrive's) *La Quinzaine*. Articles that initially appeared in
these periodicals formed much of Klein's next book, *Autour du dilettantisme*
(1895). The *dilettantisme* of the title referred less to a doctrine than to a
disposition of mind that is open to experimenting with various forms of
life, but withholds commitment to any of them. Under the varied forms
that *dilettantisme* assumes there is a common denominator of skepticism,
a conscious relinquishment of the attainment of truth, engaging persons
or ideas solely to the degree that they can be transformed into instruments
of pleasure.[27] As examples of this mindset Klein identifies Ernest Renan,
Anatole France, Maurice Barrès, and Jules Lemaître. In contrast to the optimism and benevolence that he usually adopts toward his subject matter,
Klein is uncharacteristically severe toward these literary figures. In part
this stems from the influence they exercised, particularly in Renan's case,
on certain individuals that he encountered in the course of his work at the
Institut Catholique.[28] However, a critique of *dilettantisme* is only half the
story. Much of the book is devoted to figures who manifest "a desire for the
truth that is the exact contrary of dilettantisme"[29]—Paul Bourget and Henri
Bérenger (both of whom figured in the essay on the neo-Christian movement), Joris-Karl Huysmans, and Richard Wagner.

Bourget is styled "a Christian of desire."[30] Careful study of his works in
their chronological order reveals "a desire for truth that is the exact opposite of dilettantisme," "a battle between his pagan imagination and Christian
heart," an evolution from the "total uncertainty" of his early years to conclusions that border on orthodox Christianity.[31] In his exposition of Bourget,
Klein returns to the optimistic tone that dominates his writings, as he finds
in the development of his subject's ideas over the past decade "a new sign of
the movement that leads elite minds towards the respect, the desire, sometimes even the love and total acceptance of Christianity."[32] Klein credits the
work of the pope and the American bishops with having played a role in

---

27. Klein, *Autour du dilettantisme*, 19–27.

28. Klein, *La route d'un petit Morvandiau*, 3:190–96.

29. Klein, *Autour du dilettantisme*, 85.

30. Ibid., 126.

31. Ibid., 85, 87, 127.

32. Ibid., 136.

this evolution.[33] And he credits Bourget's work with providing a "motive for confidence" and "a reason for hope," as the convictions of the intellectual elite leaven the mass of society.[34]

The writings of Henri Bérenger likewise show movement toward a more just appreciation of Christianity, as the examples of Leo XIII, Lavigerie, Gibbons, and Ireland challenged his former view that the church was in principle opposed to democracy, and the apologetic efforts of Paul de Broglie and Alphonse Gratry have shown that Christian dogma is not incompatible with the findings of science. While Bérenger has not embraced Catholicism, he is one of the admirers of its moral teaching. Klein classes him among the "neighbors of the Church" and is able to enlist him in the ranks of those who resist *dilettantisme*, in Bérenger's case taking the form of a criticism of "*intellectualisme*."[35]

En Route (1895) was Huysmans's first "Catholic" novel, bearing traces of his literary evolution from naturalism through decadence, and personal conversion to the faith he had abandoned in his youth. Here was no mere admirer of the church, or at best an ally, but one who had gone beyond appreciation of Christian moral teaching to acknowledge the truth of dogma and the role of the church in transmitting and preserving it. True, the Catholicism represented in the novel and by its author's personal convictions was poles apart from the progressive vision espoused by Klein. Nonetheless, the title given to this chapter, "Aux antipodes du dilettantisme," indicates that Huysmans exemplified not only the rejection of secular ideologies but the successful completion of a journey toward the Catholic faith.

In the book's final chapter Klein took notice of another publication that had appeared in 1895: Marcel Hébert's *Le sentiment religieux dans l'oeuvre de Richard Wagner*. In a departure from his writings on philosophy Hébert traced Wagner's development through successive phases represented by his major operas and prose writings to a Christianity, albeit of an unorthodox sort. In this Klein sees Wagner as a precursor of the neo-Christian movement, anticipating in his own development—from belief in indefinite

33. Ibid., 138. Bourget had seen American Catholicism firsthand during his travels in the United States and met some of its prominent representatives. In his account of his experiences there he remarked upon "the vitality of Catholicism in the United States" and noted that "'The names of the three great authors of this renascence—Cardinal Gibbons, Archbishop Ireland, and Monsignor Keane—are as familiar to us as to Americans themselves." See Bourget, *Outre-Mer*, 22–23. Bourget acknowledges the role played by Klein's translation of *L'Église et le siècle* in making Ireland better known in France (162).

34. Klein, *Autour du dilettantisme*, 136.

35. Ibid., 234, 219–20. *Intellectualisme* refers to the monopolization of life by the intellect, to the neglect of willing and loving, ending in a skeptical attitude toward reason itself.

progress through science and freedom, to a disappointed pessimism by their failure to deliver on their promises, then in a slow return to the wisdom, the love, the divine purity embodied in the gospels—the movement of the literary figures singled out by Klein.[36]

During the summers of 1894 and 1895 Klein was able to spend time in England and Scotland, and managed a stay at Oxford in the spring of 1895. This widened the scope of his networks and, apparently, of his interests, for in 1896 he took up the subject of possible union between the Anglican and Roman communions. While well aware of the obstacles to union, including the delicate question of Anglican ordinations then under study at Rome, Klein could point to the *Revue Anglo-Romaine* as a symptom of hopes from both sides of the confessional divide that a collective union could be possible. He is convinced that better mutual understanding weakens hostility and reunion thus "becomes both more desired and less impossible."[37]

It is difficult to communicate the atmosphere of a time. Nonetheless, this rapid survey of Klein's involvements and writings may suggest something of the tenor of this half decade of the 1890s. It was a period which seemed to hold out great promise for the future of Catholicism, one of intellectual ferment, political realignment, social engagement. It was a time of overt change within Catholicism, which resonated with changes in the perception of the church on the part of secular intellectuals. These were years of great excitement, of enthusiasm on the part of Catholics who were open to these changes and were able to make a contribution to them in whatever forms. The *Ralliement*, new initiatives in apologetics, International Congresses of Catholic Scholars, the growth of Catholicism in the United States and the impact of forceful prelates such as Ireland were cumulative in their effect and created expectations that further change was desirable, possible, and indeed forthcoming.

Of course, not all Catholics were as optimistic as Klein nor as favorable to what was occurring in France. The resistance to Lavigerie's appeal to French Catholics to relinquish their dreams of a restored monarchy aroused sharp opposition, and cost the cardinal's missionary efforts severely with loss of benefactors. Even after Lavigerie's initiative was vindicated by the papal encyclical of 1892, intransigent Catholics like Charles Maignen

---

36. Ibid., especially 291–92. Hébert, *Religious Experience in the Work of Richard Wagner.*

37. Klein, "Anglicans et romans," 400. The *Revue Anglo-Romaine* was short-lived, appearing in three volumes over 1895–1896. In its brief existence a number of Catholics who were working toward renewal in the church appeared in its pages; among those were Pierre Batiffol, Henri Brémond, Louis Duchesne, Vincent Ermoni, and Alfred Loisy.

continued to argue that the church and the republic, such as it existed in France, were radically incompatible. Maignen's *La souveraineté du peuple est une hérésie* not only represented a principled opposition to democracy but served as a reference point for those who shared its conviction.[38] In those same circles Ireland's addresses, either as originally given in Paris or as published in *L'Église et le Siècle*, garnered more resistance than resonance. Maignen would later avow that the thought of the Americanist school was contained in the two words of the volume's title and in the conjunction that brought them together.[39] One of Ireland's addresses that Klein included in the book was originally given at the Chicago Parliament of Religions held in 1893 at the Universal Exposition in Chicago. Klein figured among a number of progressives who became interested in the idea of replicating the event at the Paris Exposition in 1900. Their proposal aroused controversy, and it became clear that the French hierarchy was generally opposed. A directive from Rome in November of 1895 stipulated that, in the future, Catholics would hold their congresses separately from all others.[40] Hopes for corporative reunion with the Anglican Communion were dashed with the promulgation of Rome's negative decision on the validity of Anglican orders, in September of 1896. Despite such counterfactuals, Catholic progressives could still regard the future with optimism.

Catalyst of Controversy: The Hecker Biography

All of this provides the context for Klein's involvement with the French translation and adaptation of Isaac Hecker's life. The initiative for undertaking a French edition of Elliott's biography originally came from Comte Guillaume de Chabrol, who had a translation made and sent the manuscript to a publisher. Klein was selected as a referee and suggested that the text be cut and some expressions toned down for a more conservative French readership. His help was enlisted in making the desired changes and further extended to writing a preface to introduce Hecker to French readers. Originally, de Chabrol was to have contributed the preface.[41] The decision to

38. Maignen, *La souveraineté du peuple est une hérésie*. See Dumont, *Le Saint-Siège et l'organisation politique des catholiques français aux lendemains du Ralliement*, 143–54.

39. Maignen, *Le Père Hecker*, 223.

40. At that point Klein and several others withdrew their support from the project. Victor Charbonnel, who eventually took the lead in the project, has left a detailed account in his *Congrès universal des religions en 1900*.

41. De Chabrol had actually done so, but withdrew his own in favor of Klein's. De Chabrol's preface appeared as "Un Prêtre américain, le Révérend Père Hecker." Klein, *La route d'un petit Morvandiau*, 4:13. Klein, *Americanism*, 4.

substitute Klein's would prove consequential. As Klein was to judge in retrospect, "It seems safe to say that my Preface was chiefly responsible for the
unusual history of the book—for its amazing initial success, for the heated
controversy between its friends and its foes, and finally for the extraordinary
action by which in 1899 Pope Leo XIII gave a quietus to the whole affair."[42]
In his critique of the biography, *Le Père Hecker: Est-il un saint?*, Maignen
relied on the book before him; he had not read any of Hecker's own writings.
It is apparent that Klein's preface figured heavily in shaping his perception
of the founder of the Paulists. It is also apparent from the condemnation of
Americanist errors in *Testem Benevolentiae* that Maignen's critique figured
heavily in shaping Vatican perception of Americanism.[43]

As part of a campaign to stir up interest in the Hecker biography,
Klein's preface had been independently, and widely, circulated prior to the
book's publication. The preface was printed as a pamphlet and sent to "many
prominent people, especially to members of the hierarchy," and reprinted
in the *Revue du clergé français*, preceded by a two-page note.[44] In August
of 1897, not long after the publication of *Le Père Hecker*, Klein attended
the International Congress of Catholic Scholars in Fribourg, Switzerland.
In one of the sessions Denis O'Connell, closely identified with Ireland and
other notables of progressive Catholicism in America, gave a paper entitled
"A New Idea in the Life of Father Hecker." Although he had not been present
for the reading of O'Connell's paper, Bishop Turinaz followed with a speech
in which he made several criticisms of Hecker, obviously based on the biography.[45] On the advice of friends Klein undertook to refute the attack made
upon Hecker at the next session, drawing from his preface and from the text
of the biography. As further criticism of Hecker's Americanism mounted in

42. Klein, *Americanism*, 4. Cf. Klein, *La route d'un petit Morvandiau*, 4:14. More
specifically, the concentration of new and original ideas in the relatively short compass
of a preface could deeply impress—positively or negatively—much more so than when
these same ideas were scattered over four hundred pages. Klein, *Americanism*, 120;
Klein, *La route d'un petit Morvandiau*, 4:196.

43. Portier, "Isaac Hecker and *Testem Benevolentiae*," 19–23.

44. Klein, *Americanism*, 18. Klein, *La route d'un petit Morvandiau*, 4:29. Klein's
preface appeared as "Un grand mystique aux États-Unis," 5–20. As part of his initiatives to make Hecker and the Catholicism he represented more widely known, Klein
wrote "Catholicisme américain." It attracted the criticism of the Orientalist Alphonse
Delattre who critiqued it in *Un Catholicisme américain*. Delattre had earlier published
Un Congrès d'intellectuels à Gand en fevrier, 1897, which contained a sustained criticism of Klein's presentation at the Congress on the subject of the literary ideal, relating
that—negatively—to its author's Americanist sympathies.

45. Charles-François Turinaz (1838–1918) became bishop of Tarentaise in 1873
and of Nancy in 1882. He vigorously intervened in the controversies of the day in a
series of polemical works. See Hogard, *Quarante-cinq ans d'episcopat*.

subsequent months Klein continued to intervene, especially on those occasions where he was named in the critique. The campaign against the book and the larger tendencies it represented continued into 1898. The English translation of Maignen's polemic as *Father Hecker: Is He a Saint?* made the French controversy accessible to an American public.

Klein's book on Lavigerie had landed him in the midst of controversy, and his articles on the neo-Christians and on democracy had attracted accusations of doctrinal minimalism in a spirit of accommodation to those who admired Christianity's moral teaching in the former case and comparisons with Léon Grégoire in the latter. Nonetheless, those attacks had left him relatively unscathed. With the controversy over Hecker and Americanism, however, matters were different: "On me, perhaps more than anyone else in Europe, the fury of the tempest had broken."[46] Although no one was named explicitly in *Testem Benevolentiae*, it did make reference to "the book on the life of Isaac Thomas Hecker" which, "owing chiefly to the efforts of those who undertook to publish and interpret it in a foreign tongue, has excited serious controversies by introducing certain opinions on a Christian manner of life."[47]

Klein and Americanism's Aftermath

Klein "laudably submitted" to *Testem Benevolentiae* and voluntarily withdrew *Le Père Hecker* from sale—which, in retrospect, he later regretted, as in some quarters it was taken as an admission of guilt.[48] It soon became clear, however, that, if chastened, Klein had not changed his fundamental commitments. Klein's interest in education was manifested in his involvement with *L'Enseignement chrétien*, a periodical devoted to Christian education at the secondary level. He served as its director over the years 1895–1896.[49] It is understandable that the discourses on education by Bishop John Lancaster Spalding attracted Klein's attention, and that he undertook their translation and publication, first in periodical form,[50] then in a volume entitled *Opportunité*.[51] The volume offered Maignen an opportunity to return to the

46. Klein, *Americanism*, 180. Klein, *La route d'un petit Morvandiau*, 4:313.

47. Text reproduced as an appendix in Klein, *Americanism*, 314.

48. Klein, *Americanism*, 228–33. Klein, *La route d'un petit Morvandiau*, 4:379–85.

49. Klein, *La route d'un petit Morvandiau*, 3:167–85.

50. "Mission vitale de l'Université" appeared in the *Revue du clergé français* in February of 1900; "L'Education et l'avenir religieux" in *Annales de philosophie chrétien* in October 1900.

51. Spalding, *Opportunité*. In addition to the two discourses already mentioned

lists against Americanism, alleging that, in his latest publication, Klein was merely serving up "the same idea, the same thesis, less the enthusiasm of Mgr Ireland, and the naïve originality of P. Hecker"—"the Church and the age, the alliance between Catholicism and modern progress, liberty, initiative . . . etc."[52] Whatever the expression, the same fundamental errors of Americanism were present. Maignen professed to find Klein's introduction to Spalding's discourses more interesting than the discourses themselves, as he finds that "the condemnation of Americanism has changed nothing in the opinions of the translator of the *Vie du P. Hecker*."[53]

In 1903 Klein was able to travel to the United States, and published an account of his travels which gives further evidence that his admiration for American Catholicism and for many of its principal figures continued undiminished.[54]

By that point Klein's optimistic hopes for reconciliation between the church and the age had received a series of setbacks. The *Ralliement* had not only failed to gain much traction among French Catholics; in the aftermath of the Dreyfus Affair it was deemed a failure.[55] The anti-Dreyfusard stance of Catholics, combined with the condemnation of Americanism, had disillusioned many of the neo-Christians, who turned away from the church. Klein's association with Alfred Loisy would lead to renewed accusations of heterodoxy after the publication of the latter's *Autour d'un petit livre* in 1903. In 1908, under pretext of a reorganization of its programs, which

---

the volume included "Opportunité," "L'Education supérieure du prêtre," "Le faux patriotisme et le véritable," and "Dieu et le Christ." The English texts of these discourses may be found in Spalding's *Opportunity and Other Essays, Means and Ends of Education,* and *Lectures and Discourses.* Between 1894 and 1900 John Hogan's articles on clerical studies, originally published in the *American Ecclesiastical Review* over 1891–1898 and in book form in 1900, were appearing in French translation in *Le Canoniste contemporain.* See Talar, "Seminary Reform and Theological Method on the Eve of the Modernist Crisis." In *Vérité française* Maignen attacked the series as a "course in ecclesiastical skepticism" (Klein, *La route d'un petit Morvandiau,* 5:48). In the charged atmosphere of the time, education could be a volatile subject.

52. Maignen, *Nouveau catholicisme, nouveau clergé,* 164–65.

53. Ibid., 167. As noted earlier, Klein was not the primary translator of the biography, but adapted an existing translation to render it more accessible to a French readership.

54. Klein, *Au pays de la vie intense.* See also Klein, *In the Land of the Strenuous Life.*

55. Accused of selling military secrets to the Germans, Captain Alfred Dreyfus was—wrongly—convicted of treason in 1894. The question of his innocence or guilt attracted widespread public attention and brought to the surface deep-seated divisions in French society. The Dreyfus Affair heightened antagonisms between the political right and left, split France into Dreyfusards and anti-Dreyfusards, and intensified French anti-Semitism. See Bredin, *The Affair* and Brown, *For the Soul of France.*

rendered Klein's course superfluous, he lost his position at the Paris *Institut Catholique*. Klein continued to publish but Americanism remained a volatile issue, to the extent that, when attempts were made to find a publisher for an English translation and adaptation of the volume of his memoirs devoted to Americanism, it had to be privately published.

Conclusion

Klein's close identification with the Americanist controversy and the stigma of its condemnation gave him a vested interest in disassociating the "Americanist heresy" from the "synthesis of all heresies" that was Modernism.[56] In his memoirs he maintained that "The teachings of Hecker, Ireland or Keane were mistaken for those heretical tendencies which a few years later were to be assembled and condemned by Pius X under the name of Modernism."[57] Phantom heresy historiography emphasized the practical nature of the errors that were identified as Americanism, and contrasted those with the more intellectual issues that were condemned in Modernism. In the decades following Vatican II revisionist historians have challenged this separation, arguing for greater continuity between Americanism and Modernism. William Portier has made significant contributions to this revisionist perspective, both in his earlier work and in the recent *Divided Friends*. On a micro level of individual figures, Portier's strategy of paired biographies sheds light on the elusive Denis O'Connell by examining his relationship to John Slattery through the latter's writings. A convincing case is made for O'Connell's sharing a symbolic approach to dogma held by Slattery and, in their various ways, by other figures identified with Modernism, such as Alfred Loisy and Marcel Hébert. Continuity between Americanism and Modernism is also detectable along a whole range of ideas. The rejection of Hecker's ideas by Maignen and, by extension, *Testem Benevolentiae*, may be termed a "clash of worldviews," a collision of a Romantic-inspired theology with neo-scholasticism.[58] That clash involved very different ways of understanding the role of history in theology, of the relationship between nature and grace, between state and church, of appreciation of religious experience, issues that also came to the fore in the modernist crisis. Moreover, Roman authorities who opposed theological Modernism were well aware of connections between freedom in politics and freedom in intellectual life,

---

56. Pope Pius X, *Pascendi Dominici Gregis* §39.
57. Klein, *Americanism*, 167.
58. Portier, "Isaac Hecker and *Testem Benevolentiae*," 28–36.

providing yet another point of continuity.[59] Framing these movements in this way not only alters perceptions of relations between them, but reveals that Modernism made a deeper imprint on the United States than has been appreciated.

An interval of some four decades separates the Roman condemnation of Modernism in 1907 from the publication of the fourth volume of Klein's memoirs in 1949. It may be argued that the four short years of the Second Vatican Council did more to provide perspective and refocus assessments of both Americanism and Modernism than all of Klein's forty-plus years. In the half-century that separates us from Vatican II there has been a great deal of retrieval and reassessment of both of these controversies. William Portier's writings have signally contributed to this work, and those of us who share his interests in these people, their ideas, and the events that shaped their church and their world remain indebted to him.

59. Portier, *Divided Friends*, 10, 15.

8

The Italian Problem

Immigration and Inculturation in the
American Catholic Context

MICHAEL F. LOMBARDO

B etween 1880 and 1920, more than four million Italian immigrants
landed on the shores of the United States, making Italians one of the
largest ethnic groups to arrive during a period historically known for mass
immigration. The overwhelming majority of these immigrants were Roman
Catholics from an area in the south of the newly formed Kingdom of Italy
known as the *Mezzogiorno*.[1] The impoverished economic, social, and educational condition of immigrants from the *Mezzogiorno*, combined with
their pious form of faith that was left largely untouched by the internecine
squabbles of the Reformation and the rationalism of the Enlightenment,
presented unique challenges that made inculturation into American society
in general, and the American Catholic Church in particular, one of the foremost challenges of its day.[2] In 1883, the U.S. bishops were already discussing

1. The *Mezzogiorno* includes the modern regions of Abruzzi, Campania, Molise,
Basilicata, Puglia, and Calabria, as well as the islands of Sardinia and Sicily.

2. The literature on inculturation is extensive. For an overview of the ways in which
theologians have used the term, see Doyle, "Concept of Inculturation." In the present
work I have drawn upon the thought of Roberto Goizueta, who argues that Latino/a
Catholicism in the United States relies on a liturgical and devotional worldview that
remains largely untouched by the rationalism that came to dominate Northern Europe
and, by extension, the English colonies in America after the Reformation ("Symbolic
Realism," 256–65). There is an historical warrant for extending Goizueta's argument to
Southern Italy, where a similar intellectual climate prevailed (see for example Ginzburg,

the best way to address the needs of the immigrant Italian community.[3] By 1888, the situation became so desperate that Pope Leo XIII issued an encyclical, *On Italian Immigrants*, to discuss the plight of his compatriots.[4] Leo and the bishops were not alone. American social reformers such as Jacob Riis and Edward Steiner, authors like Henry James and Mark Twain, secular newspapers like the *New York Times*, Catholic journals like *America*, and politicians like Theodore Roosevelt,[5] all sought to understand and address what eventually came to be known as the "Italian Problem."[6]

Despite the prominence of the Italian Problem, studies of Italian immigration have been marginal among scholars of American Catholicism. In fact, Italian immigration to the United States in the late-nineteenth and early-twentieth centuries represents a lacuna in American Catholic history.[7] Most existing studies have been conducted by sociologists and secular

---

Cheese and Worms) and where Spanish political domination of the southern portion of the Italian peninsula continued, in one form or another, through the eighteenth century.

3. For an overview of the U.S. bishops' response to Italian immigration, see Stibili, *What Can Be Done to Help Them?*, 9–39. The "Italian Problem" was not unique to American Catholicism, which had only recently struggled over questions related to the "German Problem." See, for example, Carey, *Catholics in America*, 56–58. For local responses to Italian immigration, see Brown, *Churches, Communities, and Children*, esp. 27–47. See also Juliani, *Priest, Parish, and People*, which pays particular attention to St. Mary Magdalen de Pazzi, the first Italian national parish in the United States.

4. Pope Leo XIII, *Quam Aerumnosa*.

5. Riis, Steiner, James, and Twain are each the subject of a chapter in Cosco, *Imagining Italians*. Riis's most famous work is *How the Other Half Lives*. For a brief overview of Riis's and Roosevelt's thought, see Brown, *Great Debate*. For representative examples in the media, see "Italian Problem," *New York Times*; Sorrentino, "The Italian Question."

6. Though the expression "The Italian Problem" has roots in the early debate surrounding Italian immigration to the United States, the phrase did not become widespread until the Irish American priest Henry J. Browne used the phrase as the title of his 1946 work on Italian immigration, "The 'Italian Problem' in the Catholic Church of the United States, 1880–1900," the first history of Italian immigration in the United States (Brown, *Churches, Communities, and Children*, 27–28). For an annotated bibliography on religion and Italian Americans see Tomasi and Stibili, *Italian Americans and Religion*, which offers an invaluable catalogue of primary and secondary source materials in both English and Italian dating back to the colonial period. The Center For Migration Studies in New York, founded by the Scalabrinians in 1964, contains another important collection of primary and secondary source materials related to Italian American immigration (www.cmsny.org).

7. One exception is Jay Dolan's frequent discussion of issues affecting Italian Americans in *The American Catholic Experience*. The absence of Italian immigration is particularly noteworthy since Rudolph J. Vecoli noted as early as 1969 that "we lack studies of the interaction between the American Church and many of the Catholic ethnic groups" ("Prelates and Peasants," 219).

historians, and have treated theological questions about Italian American Catholicism only peripherally.

This chapter seeks to make a modest contribution to the study of American Catholic history by presenting a general overview of the Italian Problem. The essay does not intend to be exhaustive, but rather seeks to introduce the reader to some of the key issues in the debate surrounding Italian immigration and then to use two methodological concepts drawn from the thought of William L. Portier to shed light on the implicit ways in which scholars have treated the "problem" of Italian American immigration. It is my hope that these two concepts will provide new resources for thinking about immigration and also for exploring the relationship between Catholicism and American culture.

The Italian Problem

The crisis facing Italian immigrants in the late-nineteenth and early-twentieth centuries was not a single problem, but in fact a series of interrelated problems, a complex web of challenges that emerged from the particularities of Italian history, ignorance of which served to complicate the immigrants' reception in America. The Italians—poor, illiterate, uneducated, and uncatechized—desperately needed pastoral attention and yet were famously difficult to reach.

Poverty

If the hardscrabble existence of life in Italy was difficult, unskilled and semi-skilled southern Italians were in for a shock once they arrived in the United States: they were utterly unprepared for life in industrial America. Some attempts were made to transfer the immigrants to rural settings in the United States more complementary of their agricultural skills; however, these largely proved failures, even with government support, for a number of reasons, including an Italian aversion to the isolation typical of American rural life, the gulf between Italian and rural American cultures, and the lack of opportunity for financial advancement.[8] Instead, Italian immigrants

8. Nelli, "Italians in Urban America," 81–87. Nelli discusses one attempt to establish "an Italian agricultural colony at Daphne, Alabama, in 1892" that "received counsel and financial aid from Jane Addams and the residents of Hull House" (82). The venture failed because it received "little support" from Italian Americans living in Chicago (82). However, the failure of Italian immigrants to establish themselves in rural settings was by no means universal. For more on Italians in rural America see Vecoli, ed., *Italian*

gravitated to major industrial centers on the coasts, where community life flourished and where unskilled labor was in demand.

Even when they were employed, life in America was not easy for the first generation of Italian immigrants. Poverty and tenement conditions in the cities made life difficult, and economic survival was the immigrants' primary concern. Not surprisingly, primary sources from the period attest that initiating ministry to Italian immigrants usually involved social service rather than direct evangelization or catechesis.[9] Italian return migration complicated efforts at outreach. By some estimates half of all Italian immigrants eventually returned to Italy.[10] The transient outlook of many Italian immigrants contributed to instability vis-à-vis established American institutions like the Catholic Church, which made outreach all the more difficult to achieve.

Language

Language also presented a formidable barrier to outreach. Due to the idiosyncrasies of history, Italy presented a challenging linguistic situation. When the nation was finally unified in 1861, there was yet no single language spoken on the peninsula. The regionalism that prevailed in Italian politics prior to unification meant that most of the newly christened "Italians" spoke only a local or regional dialect and displayed only local loyalties. From the beginning, Italians were an isolated demographic group, even among themselves.[11]

The prevalence of regional dialects prevented generic recruitment of clergy from Italy, or even of American clergy who had studied in Rome, to serve as ministers. Since few immigrants spoke the standardized version of Italian that developed from the Florentine dialect,[12] the clergy assigned

Immigrants.

9. Juliani, *Priest, Parish, and People*, 181; Sullivan, *Mother Cabrini*, 270.

10. Nelli, "Italians," 547. However, not all scholars accept these numbers. For a counter view, see Gallo, *Old Bread*, 83. For an interpretation of Italian return migration see Cerase, "Nostalgia or Disenchantment," 217–39.

11. In the United States, Italian Americans developed a form of pidgin Italian in order to communicate. "This new Anglicized Italian was almost solely the language of the immigrant generation. The American-born did not bother to learn it, and Italians in the homeland would not have understood it" (Nelli, "Italians," 555–56).

12. Even northern Italians and educated elites would have been more likely to speak their local dialects rather than standard Italian during this period. "Standard" Italian initially developed as a literary language directly out of the Florentine dialect through the influence of the Tuscan poet Dante Alighieri; over the centuries it became the language of the educated elite on the Italian peninsula. Hence, its use was by no means

to each community had to hail from the same region as the immigrants in order to effectively communicate.[13] Since dialects could vary considerably over even short geographical distances, communication was a constant problem.[14]

Education & the Family

Compounding the communication problem, more than half of the Italians who arrived in America between 1899 and 1910 were illiterate, one of the highest rates among all European immigrants.[15] At the start of World War I, an astonishing 99 percent of Italian American children failed to attend high school.[16] In the golden age of the American press, when muckraking journalists like Upton Sinclair exposed injustice and Progressive Era reformers sought to remedy social ills with pamphlets and pickets, illiteracy only served to further isolate the immigrant Italian community. In 1910, G.E. di Palma Castiglione, manager of the Labor Information Bureau for Italians in New York, complained to the *New York Times*: "It is difficult to reach the Italians, especially by literature, even if it is in their own tongue, for it must not be forgotten that 50 per cent. [sic] of the Italian immigrants are illiterate. Much information must be given by word of mouth. It is a tedious process, but an inevitable one. We send out bulletins to the parish houses of Italian priests and to Italian newspapers. We trust that those who can read will spread the news among those who cannot."[17]

Illiteracy could be dangerous. The inability to read instructions or communicate effectively in English caused many fatal accidents on the

---

delineated by strict north-south geography, but rather by educational attainment. Only mass migration, the implementation of compulsory education in the late-nineteenth century, and the rise of popular media in the twentieth gradually facilitated widespread use of what we now call "Italian," although contemporary colloquial Italian still reflects distinct regional variations (Tosi, *Language And Society*, 7–12).

13. For an overview of the attitudes of the clergy towards Italian immigrants in the United States, see Stibili, "St. Raphael Society." See also, McKevitt, *Brokers of Culture*, 249–55.

14. Brown, *Churches, Communities, and Children*, 104, 129–30. The First World War famously exposed many of the communication difficulties facing Italians, as soldiers and their commanding officers from different regions of Italy could not understand each other in the conduct of the war. The confusion did not abate until after the Second World War (Tosi, *Language And Society*, 7, 11–12).

15. Nelli, "Italians," 554.

16. Ibid.

17. Quoted in "Making American Farmers of Italian Immigrants."

industrial worksites that Italian immigrants populated.[18] It is not surprising then that schools were one of the primary ways that relief societies attempted to serve the immigrant Italian population.

The family was the primary impediment to education. Suspicious of outsiders, Italians considered the American education system a threat to family sovereignty and to the maintenance of Italian culture. Moreover, although literacy and schooling may have been the main avenues of integration and economic advancement, the practical needs of everyday life prohibited most Italians from seeing the value of educating their children. In most cases, abject poverty made work a necessity even for very young children.[19] When parents did send their children to school, the cost of the Catholic school system, Italian anticlericalism, and the prejudice that Italians encountered among American Catholics often meant that Italian American children received a public, rather than parochial, education.[20]

The American Catholic Church

Saving the faith of Italians, however, depended on more than just providing them with social services and teaching them how to read. It also meant accommodating their particular style of worship. In fact, one of the biggest obstacles preventing Italian integration into the American Catholic Church was the American Catholic Church itself.

The religious beliefs and practices of southern Italian immigrants were complex, rooted in the particularities of Italian history, and incorporated folk practices and traditions—including a particular style of patronizing the saints, which emphasized elaborately staged public rituals accentuating physical embodiment—that stood in tension with the staid variety of religious expression that prevailed in the United States.[21] Italian devotion to the saints gave rise to elaborate street festivals, community-wide events that marked the high point of the liturgical year in Italian villages and

18. "Italian Society Uplifts Immigrants," in the *New York Times*. The most poignant piece of literature written on Southern Italian labor is surely *Christ in Concrete*, a 1939 story written by Pietro di Donato. For an extended study of di Donato's story, see Ferraro, *Feeling Italian*, 51–71.

19. "Characteristics of Italian Immigrants."

20. Vecoli, "Prelates and Peasants," 249–51; Sullivan, *Mother Cabrini*, 271; Dolan, *American Catholic Experience*, 280–82.

21. Primeggia, "La Via Vecchia," 15; Primeggia and Varacalli, "Sacred and Profane"; Vecoli, "Prelates and Peasants," 227–235. The similarities between Italian Catholicism and Latino/a Catholicism in the American Catholic context are striking. Cf. Goizueta, "Symbolic Realism," 256–65.

cities in the Old World. In *The Madonna of 115th Street*, Robert A. Orsi chronicles one such religious festival—the Feast of Our Lady of Mount Carmel—which was transferred from Italy to New York in the late-nineteenth century. A popular, public, and days-long communal event featuring food, family, dancing, and a public procession of the reverenced statue of Our Lady through the streets of East Harlem,[22] Orsi calls the *festa* a "very complex religious drama"[23] that "completely subverted" the "sanitized, carefully bounded and contained notions of spirituality" that predominated in the American context.[24] Most Americans frowned upon these public displays of Italian religiosity and considered them superstitious, pagan, and primitive.[25] Italian street festivals remained, for the most part, incomprehensible among Americans, where privatized, rationalized, and disembodied religious faith prevailed,[26] and where overt displays of "popish" Catholicism were frowned upon as anti-American.

Among fellow American Catholics, Italian immigrants received no greater welcome. For a variety of reasons, Irish antagonism towards Italian immigrants could be particularly harsh, which only served to exacerbate Italian anticlericalism.[27] Distrust of the clergy was particularly rife among Italian men, who rarely attended Mass and who typically left religious obligations to the women of the family. Of course, Italians could be equally fierce in their denunciation of the typical Irish-led Catholic parish, which they condemned as "a cold, remote, puritanical institution" akin to a Protestant church.[28]

22. Orsi, *Madonna*, xlv.

23. Ibid., xxxix.

24. Ibid., xviii.

25. Vecoli, "Prelates and Peasants," 233.

26. Goizueta, "Symbolic Realism," 256–57, 269–71. See also Orsi, *Madonna*, xvi–xvii.

27. Vecoli chronicles the source and nature of this antagonism, along with Italian anticlericalism, in "Prelates and Peasants." See also Linkh, "Catholic Attitudes"; Gesualdi, "Comparison," 40–46, especially 43–44.

28. Nelli, "Italians," 553. Vecoli writes, "The coldly rational atmosphere, the discipline, the attentive congregation, were foreign to the Italians who were used to behaving in church as they would in their own house" ("Prelates and Peasants," 230). It is interesting that the Gothic style is (with a few notable exceptions) relatively unknown in Italy. It is possible that Italian American immigrants, unable to distinguish between Protestant and Catholic expressions of Gothic Revival upon arrival in the Protestant-dominated U.S., lumped all northern European ethnic groups together when they considered Irish and German Catholic churches in the United States "as cold and as foreign as Protestant chapels" (McKevitt, *Brokers of Culture*, 254).

Ambivalence towards liturgical celebrations was not absolute, though, since Italians did attend sacramental rites such as baptisms, weddings, and funerals, and did participate enthusiastically in the feast days associated with their local saints.[29] However, limited participation, combined with the historical experience of state-supported churches in Italy, meant that Italian immigrants, already impoverished, contributed little financial support to their local parishes, a fact that chafed the community of more strictly observant Irish Catholics. It also meant that Italians typically lacked knowledge of even the most basic Catholic doctrines.

Despite their ambivalent attitude towards parish ritual and administration, Italian immigrants still considered themselves "good" Catholics and resented any suggestion to the contrary. Notwithstanding historical caricatures of Italian immigrants as "little better than pagans and idolators" by Protestants and even fellow Catholics in the United States, recent scholarship has demonstrated that Italian immigrants did have a vibrant Catholic faith. In fact, it is impossible to dismiss the central role Catholicism played in the life of the Italian American community.

Racism

Conflict with the Irish-dominated clergy exposed racist sentiment toward Italian immigrants.[30] The Italian-born Mother Cabrini—a naturalized U.S. citizen and the first American saint—experienced this kind of reaction herself, noting in one of her earliest letters from the United States that Italian missionary sisters were liable to be called "guinea pigs"[31] if not dressed well, and that the English-speaking public "cannot bear the sight of the Italians."[32]

Racism towards southern Italians was not unique. Like many other forms of xenophobia during the period, attitudes towards southern Italians were infected by the pseudo-science of racial theory and reached the highest levels of American society.[33] In the racial scheme most often presented,

29. Femminella, "Impact of Italian Migration," 234–35.

30. LaGumina, "Anti-Italian Discrimination," 16; Cosco, *Imagining Italians*, 12. For an extended treatment of Irish and Italian relations in New York see Moses, *Unlikely Union*.

31. Cabrini to "Mie figlie carissime," 11 April 1889, cited in Sullivan, *Mother Cabrini*, 267 n. 10.

32. Cabrini to "Reverendissimo Signore," 12 June 1889, cited in Sullivan, *Mother Cabrini*, 267 n. 11.

33. Lears, *Rebirth of a Nation*, 10–11, 110. For example, in 1891 New Orleans, a mob lynched eleven Italians. Theodore Roosevelt "referred to the lynching as 'a rather good thing' and boasted that he had said so publicly in the presence of 'various dago

southern Italians were classified as African in origin, while northern Italians were classified as Teutonic and/or Scandinavian. Irish American Catholics were not beyond resorting to this type of racial denigration of Italians, with the result that Italian immigrants were often racially discriminated against and treated as second-class citizens by the Irish clergy.[34]

The Italian Problem

In spite of the long list of challenges, the Italian Problem did not become a crisis in the church until it was linked to the fear of an Italian exodus from Catholicism. Throughout the late-nineteenth and early-twentieth centuries, as Protestant churches in the United States made a concerted effort to turn the Italian Problem into an advantage by converting Italian immigrants, a sense of urgency developed around the question of Italian American Catholicism. Though Protestant efforts resulted in few conversions, they did not escape the attention of the Catholic clergy, who were particularly concerned about maintaining the faith of the second generation of Italian Americans (those born in the United States).[35] Alarmed by continued Italian indifference and by the attempts of Protestant denominations to proselytize, the U.S. bishops debated how best to remedy the situation, but could not agree among themselves on a course of action.[36]

Monsignor Gennaro De Concilio helped breach the impasse. De Concilio, an Italian-born professor of theology at Seton Hall University, wrote the *Baltimore Catechism*. It was De Concilio's 1886 tract on the sorry state of Italian immigrants, *Sullo stato religioso degli italiani negli Stati Uniti d'America* (On the Religious State of Italians in the United States of America), that inspired Pope Leo XIII's 1888 encyclical to the bishops of America, *Quam Aerumnosa*.[37] In the encyclical, Leo noted that he had accepted the request of Giovanni Battista Scalabrini, Bishop of Piacenza, to establish a seminary for the training of missionary priests destined to work among Italian emigrants. The Scalabrinian order, which still exists today, was the first organized ecclesial attempt to address the Italian Problem in the Americas,

---

diplomats'" (Cosco, *Imagining Italians*, 12). For an extended examination of the question of race and Italian American identity in the United States, see Guglielmo and Salerno, *Are Italians White?* and LaGumina, *WOP!*.

34. Cosco, *Imagining Italians*, 47. See also Fisher, *Communion of Immigrants*, 73.

35. Vecoli, "Prelates and Peasants," 247.

36. Tomasi, "Scalabrinians," 257. Tomasi notes that the bishops made an appeal to future saint Don Giovanni Bosco, who was unable to provide assistance.

37. Vecoli, "Prelates and Peasants," 233. See also De Concilio, *Sullo stato*, 1886. For De Concilio's role in the Italian Problem see Rocha, "De Concilio's Catechism," 126–34.

and it was Scalabrini himself who encouraged Mother Cabrini to direct the work of her own order, the Missionary Sisters of the Sacred Heart, towards the relief of Italian immigrants in the United States.[38] The two new religious orders were part of a coordinated attempt to meet the needs of the Italian American community, which included the erection of Italian national parishes, the establishment of mutual aid societies and sodalities, social outreach programs, catechesis and parochial education, and support for Italian religious festivals.[39] Catholic outreach programs were particularly creative, and included opportunities such as debate teams, choral groups, drama clubs, sports programs for youth, and popular daycare facilities for working mothers.[40] By most estimates, these efforts were a resounding success. By the late-twentieth century, Italian Americans seemed to be fully assimilated into the American mainstream.

The Problem of Italian American Historiography

In his 1993 discussion of the ways in which both liberal and conservative American Catholic scholars have claimed the mantle of John Courtney Murray, William L. Portier warns of the dangers associated with a certain kind of shallow Americanist historiography in which "appeals to the past" attempt to "evoke a narrative in which contemporary American Catholics can find themselves at home." The problem, as Portier notes, is that "Historians upon whom contemporary commentators must rely for their knowledge of the past have tended to see their own reflections in the Americanists as paradigmatic American Catholics." Contemporary scholars, in other words, are "victims" of a superficial historiography in which accommodation to American norms is implicitly and uncritically presented as the ideal. Though he does not deny the truth of accommodationist attempts to "adapt Catholicism to the forms of modernity we find in American political institutions," Portier labels such one-sided approaches "woefully incomplete" for their failure "to do justice" to the other, transformative, critical and "incarnational," side of the Americanist tradition.[41]

38. Vecoli, "Prelates and Peasants," 260. For a history of the founding of the Scalabrinians see Brown, *The Scalabrinians*.

39. For an overview of the creative ways the church met the needs of the Italian immigrants see Brown, *Churches, Communities, and Children*, 48–116.

40. Ibid., 78–86. Brown writes that the nursery at Saint Anthony of Padua on Sullivan Street in Manhattan offered comprehensive child care—including three meals a day and weekly doctor visits—for up to sixty children "from age of two until they entered school" (85).

41. Portier, "Inculturation as Transformation," 111. On appeals to Murray from

Discussion of the Italian Problem suffers from a similar methodological limitation. In her history of Italian immigration in the Archdiocese of New York, Mary Elizabeth Brown asks the fundamental theological question that finally emerges from any historical consideration of the Italian Problem, "But Is It Catholicism?"[42] In other words, did (or does) Italian American Catholicism qualify as a legitimate expression of the Catholic faith? Of course, the very need to ask the question indicates that not everyone thinks that it does. Although Brown concedes that one's ability to answer the question depends in large part on one's ability to understand the historical context from which Italian immigrants emerged, she concludes that the question is ultimately "an issue on which the historian must yield to the theologian."[43] Fair enough. However, Portier would be quick to respond that theologians "are at the mercy of the historians upon whom they rely" for an understanding of the past.[44]

Unfortunately, among the various historical treatments that catalogue the symptoms of the Italian Problem in its myriad forms, few provide the kind of detailed and extended historiographical analysis required to properly situate Italian immigration within the broader context of late-nineteenth- and early-twentieth-century Italian and American cultures. As a result, much of the scholarship on the Italian Problem is superficial. This is particularly true of scholarship in American Catholicism.

The dearth of historiographical analysis has had a delimiting effect on the ways in which American Catholics have discussed Italian immigration. For example, the peak years of Italian immigration to the United States occurred during the Progressive Era (1890 to 1920). Though the Progressive Era provides the historical context within which Italian American identity first took shape, the period remains a virtually unknown subject in American Catholic historiography, despite the fact that Progressive Era notions of citizenship, education, race, and national identity acutely influenced both the American and Catholic responses to Italian immigration.[45]

Nor does the impact of the Italian *Risorgimento*, the unification of the Italian peninsula as one nation under the Piemontese King Vittorio Emanuele II in 1861, regularly figure into considerations of Italian American

---

both the left and right, see also Derek Hatch's essay, chapter 12 in this volume.

42. Brown, *Churches, Communities, and Children*, 47.

43. Ibid.

44. Portier, "Inculturation as Transformation," 111

45. Brown discusses the intersection of Progressive thought and responses to Italian immigration in *Churches, Communities, and Children*, 71–90. For an extended treatment of the intersection of Progressive Era thought and American Catholicism, see Lombardo, *Founding Father*, chapters 1 and 2.

identity, even though the *Risorgimento* provided the primary catalyst for the mass emigration from Italy that began around 1880.

Equally important, when attempts are made to contextualize the challenges posed by Italian immigration, the interpretive model on which American Catholic scholars have typically relied tends towards an Americanist narrative.[46] Nowhere is this more apparent than in the way the word "problem" has become permanently affixed to the Italian American experience.

Of course, Italians were undeniably a problem when judged by the standards of the dominant American culture. They were a problem first because they arrived in what Jay Dolan calls a "tidal wave" that effectively overwhelmed the limited resources of existing social service institutions,[47] and then, more importantly, because they defied the expected trajectory of assimilation into the American mainstream. Absent a thick historical framework to interpret their behavior, observers quickly reduced Italians to crude stereotypes. Countless examples can be offered to demonstrate the ways in which a limited historiographical treatment of the period restricts our understanding of the Italian Problem. For the sake of brevity, I offer one example which suggests, in part, an explanation for Italian resistance to the process of assimilation: the *Risorgimento*.[48]

Though Italians have been in the Americas in one form or another since the age of the great explorers, Italian immigration to the United States began *en masse* only after the *Risorgimento*.[49] Prior to unification, "Italy" was in fact a conglomeration of regions and kingdoms, the historic legacy of a series of invasions dating all the way back to the fall of the Roman Empire in 476.

While scholars are quick to note the trouble Italian regionalism caused those attempting to aid the immigrant community in the United States, treatment of the immigrants' self-understanding rarely transcends the historical boundary set by the unification of Italy in 1861, even though the

46. In 1969, Vecoli noted this "apologetic perspective" ("Prelates and Peasants," 219).

47. Dolan, *American Catholic Experience*, 131.

48. It is impossible to overstate the importance of the *Risorgimento* when discussing Italian-American immigration or Italian attitudes towards the Roman Catholic Church during the late-nineteenth and early-twentieth centuries. As John C. Rao argues, "the difficulties of Church-State relations accompanying the movement for Italian unification provided the framework and much of the explanation for the great migration of the population of the *Mezzogiorno* to the New World . . ." ("Secular Italy," 195).

49. For a brief history of the ways in which Italian Americans used Columbus as a rhetorical trope in their plea for American citizenship, see Applebaum, "Columbus Day."

fragmentation and stratification of Italy into regional factions has ancient roots.[50]

The Italian *Risorgimento* was more than a period of patriotism and national unification. It was an era of intense church-state conflict.[51] Unlike Ireland or Poland, where the Roman Catholic Church historically served as a bulwark against foreign oppressors and played an integral role in aiding the nationalist causes, the church in Italy opposed national unification and politically aligned itself with the foreign (ostensibly Catholic) monarchs who controlled both the government and the land, particularly in the southern regions from which most Italian immigrants came.[52]

Due to the close association between church and state, the Italian church was rarely supported by charitable giving, but rather by some combination of state financing, taxation, and noble patronage. Southern Italian peasants—desperately poor and accustomed to economic exploitation—looked upon the wealth generated by this arrangement with cynicism.[53] The *Risorgimento*, which was virulently anticlerical, promised liberation from a system that had prevailed in Italy for centuries.

Unification, however, did not ameliorate conditions in southern Italy. Although foreign domination ended, economic exploitation of the rural south persisted and even worsened under northern Italian rule in the form of "uneven land distribution, heavy taxes, ruthless deforestation," and "military conscription."[54] Continued exploitation at the hands of northern rulers gave southern Italians little choice.[55] "The mass migration of the period 1880–1924 was largely made up of southern peasants driven to emigrate by the poverty of their region and attracted by the economic possibilities of an expanding and industrializing America."[56]

Northern domination was aided by a particularly virulent strain of north-south racial rhetoric that was consistently used to legitimate northern

50. Indeed, by the early 1300s Italian regional identity was so firmly entrenched that Dante Alighieri bemoaned the tendency in the sixth canto of the *Purgatorio*. See Alighieri, *Purgatorio* 6, 76–87.

51. Ciani, "Across the Wide Ocean," 10. For accounts of the ways in which the *Risorgimento* was received in the United States, see Vecoli, "Prelates and Peasants"; Yocum Mize, "Defending Roman Loyalties"; and Juliani, *Priest, Parish, and People*, 33–45.

52. Nelli, "Italians," 554. It was therefore difficult to be both a Catholic and a patriot in Italy (Vecoli, "Prelates and Peasants," 222, 229).

53. Italian immigrants were equally scandalized by the common practice of paying an admission price to attend church in the United States (Vecoli, "Prelates and Peasants," 237).

54. Gauthreaux, *Italian Louisiana*, 21–22.

55. Ibid.

56. Stibili, "The Italian St. Raphael Society," 301.

hegemony. The seminal piece in this regard was the work of Italian social anthropologist Alfredo Niceforo, whose 1898 publication *L'Italia barbara contemporanea* (*Contemporary Barbarian Italy*) aggregated a number of prevalent racial theories and gave them the stamp of scientific authority. Niceforo's work, filled with all of the familiar stereotypes of southern Italians (superstitious, sensuous, criminal) became a handbook for early-twentieth-century discussions of Italians and race.[57] Americans drew heavily on these racial stereotypes to substantiate their own racial prejudices, and to rationalize the gap that existed between their own romantic notions of Italy as the land of Tuscan villas and Renaissance art and the squalor that confronted them on the streets of cities like New York, Philadelphia, and Boston.[58]

The *Risorgimento* helps to explain some of the characteristics associated with Italian immigrant culture that so baffled American observers. First, it explains the timing and sheer number of immigrants; it is no accident of history that the largest exodus from Italy happened shortly after unification.[59] After unity the economic situation in southern Italy only became worse as the new rulers in the north used their political hegemony to further exploit an already desperate southern population. Second, the *Risorgimento* explains the Italian American immigrants' ambivalence towards both church and state, neither of which created an economic system that ameliorated the poverty that plagued the south. Third, the experience of state-supported churches and the wealth generated by the church's temporal landholdings prior to the *Risorgimento* clarifies the immigrants' lack of financial support for their local parishes and parochial schools.[60] Fourth, the *Risorgimento* offers a rationalization for the tension that existed between Italian and Irish Catholics in the United States, where the ambivalent, embodied, decentralized, and devotional Italian approach to faith contrasted sharply with the committed, doctrinal, ecclesial, and nationalistic approach favored by the Irish.[61] Finally, the *Risorgimento* explains the origin of some

57. Cosco, *Imagining Italians*, 10, 64, 176. Remarkably, Niceforo was Sicilian.

58. Ibid., 178. The legacy of this bipolar racial approach to all things Italian, neatly divided into northern and southern categories, can be seen in popular American culture, which waxes poetic about Tuscan villas and the banal romantic stereotypes of Frances Maye's *Under the Tuscan Sun* while simultaneously gawking in pleasant horror at the philistine antics of the southern Italian *mafiosi* on *The Sopranos* and the guidos on MTV's *Jersey Shore*.

59. Stibili, "The Italian St. Raphael Society," 301.

60. For an exploration of the relationship between the *Risorgimento* and Italian attitudes towards parochial education see Walch, "Ethnic Dimension," 144–46.

61. On the importance of distinguishing religious identity from national identity in countries dominated by a single religious tradition, see Swierenga, "Religious Factor."

of the prevailing racial theories that have haunted Italian Americans into the present day. However, for all of its explanatory power, the *Risorgimento* is only part of the reason for Italian intransigence.

Inculturation as a Model for Understanding Italian American Catholicism

Italian intransigence in the face of pressure to assimilate may not have been atypical at all. In fact, it may have been the norm. David L. Salvaterra presents an overview of three dominant perspectives that have shaped the ways in which American scholars have thought about immigration. The first perspective, assimilation, dominated American thought in the late-nineteenth and early-twentieth centuries, reached its zenith in the 1920s, and lingered into the 1960s. It stressed the "unidirectional, inescapable, and salutary" process of the American melting pot.[62] The second perspective, pluralism, began in the 1960s. Proponents of this perspective criticized linear models of assimilation for their cultural coercion and their destruction of difference, noted the failure of assimilation models in the face of ethnic unrest, and highlighted the need for cultural continuity and coexistence. The pluralist perspective culminated in the ethnic revival of the 1970s.[63] In the midst of the ethnic revival, a third perspective emerged that stressed ethnic identity. It attempted to understand the "multifaceted, dynamic phenomenon" of ethnicity, broadly construed.[64] One of the most interesting findings of this third line of research, and the one most relevant to the current argument, involves the persistence of ethnic identity (despite the dissolution of ethnic subcultures) in populations of European descent "to the fourth and fifth generations and beyond, albeit in greatly altered form."[65]

Salvaterra catalogues many of the attempts scholars have made to account for this persistence of ethnic identity beyond assimilation. He concludes that "Americanization" is not always an "eagerly and indiscriminately" accepted process, but that it often involves resistance, bargaining, concession, cajoling and the balancing of "a more complicated multiple-element identity."[66] It therefore must necessarily take into account both personal agency and the various ways in which immigrants transformed American culture, even as they were transformed by it.

62. Salvaterra, "Becoming American," 31.

63. Ibid., 35–37.

64. Ibid., 39.

65. Ibid., see also 50 n. 45.

66. Ibid., 47.

The process described by Salvaterra bears striking resemblance to the process of inculturation. In the same 1993 essay in which he bemoans the inadequacy of Americanist historiography, Portier suggests inculturation as a more appropriate model for understanding Americanist thought.[67] I would like to suggest it as an equally appropriate model for understanding the Italian Problem.

Pedro Arrupe defines inculturation as the "incarnation of Christian life and of the Christian message in a particular cultural context, in such a way that this experience not only finds expression through elements proper to the culture in question, but becomes a principle that animates, directs and unifies the culture, transforming and remaking it so as to bring about a 'new creation.'"[68] As a dialectical process, inculturation necessarily comprises two moments, "one of accommodation or adaptation" to the host culture "and one of transformation or critique" of that culture.[69] Portier calls these two moments "inseparable aspects of any genuine attempt to live one's faith in a particular cultural setting."[70] He also argues that by portraying "the relationship between Catholicism and American civilization as dynamic," inculturation leaves "little danger that the Catholicism pole of the relationship will be swallowed up or subordinated to the American civilization pole," as so often happens in narratives with an Americanist trajectory.[71]

Several obvious points of contact with the perspective of cultural identity suggest why inculturation is a more appropriate model for understanding the Italian Problem, particularly in its religious form. First, as an incarnational process, inculturation avoids the cultural chauvinism associated with assimilationist models and leaves room for personal and communal agency.[72] Second, as a dialectical process, inculturation leaves room for the kind of authentic cultural exchange that can only occur when resistance (Portier and Salvaterra's "transformation") is permitted the freedom to express itself without being labeled obstructionist or un-American. Third, inculturation is more conducive to a pluralistic context, insofar as it allows for the possibility of a "multiple-element identity."[73] In this sense, it is more sympathetic to the kinds of "multifaceted, dynamic relation-

67. Portier, "Inculturation as Transformation," 113.

68. Arrupe, "Letter to the Whole Society on Inculturation," 2. See also Portier, "Inculturation as Transformation," 112–13.

69. Portier, "Inculturation as Transformation," 113.

70. Ibid.

71. Ibid., 114–15.

72. Schineller, *Handbook*, 68.

73. Salvaterra, "Becoming American," 47.

ships" that inevitably form in a globalized context permeated by cultural mobility,[74] and will by consequence be more receptive to the kind of cultural cross-pollination suggested in works like Thomas J. Ferraro's *Feeling Italian*. Fourth, as a creative process, inculturation allows for the kind of transnational Catholic religious expression explored in Robert Orsi's *Madonna of 115th Street*.[75]

Finally, and perhaps most importantly, inculturation offers what Portier calls "an incarnational path for negotiating the distance between historical description or reconstruction and theological significance."[76] In other words, it helps bridge the gap between history and theology, thus promising the possibility that scholars might finally propose an answer to the question posed by Mary Brown: "But Is It Catholicism?"

Implications

In closing, I would like to briefly suggest three implications that seem to follow naturally from what has been said above. My hope is that these examples will provide new resources for thinking about immigration, but also that they will broaden the conversation about the relationship between Catholicism and American culture.

First, evidence that cultural identity lingers long after assimilation has occurred must necessarily nuance any discussion about the dissolution of the American Catholic subculture.[77] This statement is not intended to deny that the subculture has dissolved. Rather, it is intended to highlight the fact that relics of the not-so-distant cultural past can still haunt the cultural present, even in a post-religious climate.[78]

Cultural "memory" might explain any number of the seemingly odd examples of the Italian American subculture that continue to exert influence, including Italian American religious street festivals, which continue to flourish in places like Harlem, New York's Little Italy, and Boston's North

---

74. Ibid., 39.

75. Orsi's account of the way New York's Mt. Carmel festival went through a period of tension with the local Puerto Rican community before being successfully transformed into a hybrid Italian-Haitian event demonstrates the complex ways in which religion, ethnicity, and cultural agency interact (albeit sometimes in negative ways), but also how the Italian American experience can serve as a creative tool for inculturating more recent immigrant groups, especially those who emphasize similar devotional styles and practices (Orsi, *Madonna*, xxxiii).

76. Portier, "Americanism and Inculturation," 154.

77. Portier, "Here Come the Evangelical Catholics," 45–48.

78. Salvaterra, "Becoming American," 40–47.

End.[79] It may also be a useful tool for understanding some of the contemporary religious trends found among American Catholics of Italian descent, including the different worship styles found between social classes,[80] the lackluster representation of those of Italian descent in the American hierarchy,[81] and the seeming ambivalence towards theology displayed by Italian Americans in academia.[82]

Beyond the Italian American community, cultural memory might also help scholars clarify the genealogy of other American Catholic cultural remnants—what Portier calls the obscured "religious boundary markers" that lay fragmented about the horizon after the subculture's collapse—and to give some account for their persistence.[83] Lastly, it might serve as a resource for thinking about the sometimes-revived/sometimes-hybridized religious practices of evangelical Catholics "who have never known a subculture they want to be freed from," but for whom "identity formation and maintenance" are key issues.[84]

Second, inculturation forces one to reframe the relationship between religion and American culture in a way that avoids dualistically reducing the integrative process to either cultural engagement or cultural resistance.[85]

79. Gesualdi raises precisely this possibility in "Comparison," 47. Alba and Orsi also note the presence of Italian traits in the fourth generation in "Passages in Piety," 53. For more on Boston's Italian festivals see Ferraiuolo, *Boston's North End*.

80. Gesualdi, "Comparison," 48–49.

81. The first Italian American made archbishop of a large American diocese was Joseph Bernardin in 1983, over 100 years after mass Italian immigration began. The Archdiocese of New York, which welcomed the highest total number of Italian immigrants in the United States, has never had an archbishop of Italian descent; nearly every single one of the thirteen bishops, archbishops, and cardinals of the archdiocese have been of Irish descent. Rhode Island, with one of the highest per capita percentages of Italians of any state in the country, has also never had an Italian bishop.

82. For Italian Americans in academia see Alba and Abdel-Hady, "Galileo's Children." An interesting phenomenon, and something worth considering, is the absence of advanced *theological* scholarship on Italian American Catholicism by Italian Americans. Most of the scholarship on Catholicism done by Italian Americans comes from sociologists who study Italian religious practices, not theologians. In other words, it seems that Italian Americans have structurally transferred their practice-oriented (one is tempted to say functional) approach to religion into the academic world. Taken collectively, what emerges is an ethnic group that still exhibits a certain fondness for devotional practices (Orsi's "lived religion" in *Madonna*, xix) and a certain indifference to doctrinal questions (Mary Brown's "But Is It Catholicism?" in *Churches, Communities, and Children*, 47).

83. Portier, "Here Come the Evangelical Catholics," 47.

84. Ibid., 48.

85. O'Brien Steinfels, "Is the Papacy Obsolete?," 12–14. Though I am sympathetic to some aspects of O'Brien Steinfels's argument, I fear that her categorization—particularly

Obviously, this point has broader implications for theology than just the debate surrounding Catholic immigration. In a pluralistic world (and one would think even in a non-pluralistic world), human beings have mixed loyalties and, therefore, mixed motivations that modern nationalism obfuscates. Inculturation allows individuals and communities to work out the implications of these often-transnational loyalties—whether American and Catholic, Italian and American, or even Italian American Catholic—without essentializing to the point where something like Americanization becomes inevitable. In other words, one need not imagine immigration as a process of either mutual exclusion or of linear assimilation, but rather as a "dynamic" and "incarnational" process of transformative exchange.[86]

Finally, due to the fact that Italian immigration is sometimes considered "paradigmatic for the model of generational progression into the mainstream,"[87] there is warrant for arguing that the Italian American experience might serve as a resource for thinking more broadly about contemporary Catholic immigration itself, with the caveat that any use of the Italian experience for comparative purposes be mindful of the historiographical and transformative aspects unique to the Italian Problem. This is especially true when discussing Mexican immigration, which is "tantalizingly similar in some respects" with the Italian experience, "but quite distinctive in others."[88]

The enduring legacy of Italian street festivals is, I think, the most poignant point of contact between contemporary Latino/a American

---

her dismissal as obstructionist those "conservatives" and self-described "radical orthodox" who try to resist some of the more degrading aspects of contemporary culture—is guilty of precisely the kind of simplistic reduction that Portier and Salvaterra are trying to avoid. For an argument contra O'Brien Steinfels, see Douthat, *Bad Religion*, 83–145.

86. Portier, "Inculturation as Transformation," 114–15. Portier's point is that inculturation as a category alleviates the temptation to dualistically reduce the tension between conflicting identities by either (1) leaving the two poles of identity externally juxtaposed and therefore in unresolved tension, or (2) swallowing one up into the other, as happens in the case of Americanization. Instead, inculturation allows—even demands—that accommodation and transformation happen in a dialectical process of exchange (112). The need for exchange and nuance should be obvious, since not all accommodation is transformative (e.g., accepting Italian street festivals without challenging some of their more unorthodox practices and beliefs), and not all transformation is accommodating (e.g., forcing newly arrived Italian Catholic immigrants to worship exclusively in an American idiom). It is worth noting that this very process of exchange stands at the heart of Pope Francis's call for dialogue. See, for example, his address to the U.S. Bishops on 23 September 2015.

87. Alba and Orsi, "Passages in Piety," 54.

88. Ibid. For a complete comparison of the Italian and Mexican experiences, see the first part of Alba et al., *Immigration and Religion*.

Catholicism and the Italian Problem, and therefore perhaps the best place to end the essay. With the rise of Pentecostalism evoking new fears of an exodus to Protestantism among Latino Catholics in the U.S. and beyond, many scholars are asking why Latinos are leaving Catholicism in such reportedly high numbers. One of the most prevalent answers given—that the affective spirituality of Pentecostalism is appealing for those who crave a personal encounter with God—is both an indictment and an invitation. It is an indictment, ironically enough, of contemporary American Catholicism for its failure to create and sustain the very types of embodied religious practices that so many non-Western Catholics—and so many evangelical Catholics—find appealing. But it is also an invitation to rediscover, and perhaps to finally understand, the enduring appeal of Italian American religious festivals. When John Allen surveyed the landscape of Pentecostalism in his 2009 book *The Future Church*, he noted several other factors that accounted for Pentecostalism's attractiveness, including the desire for community, the desire for "spectacle" to overcome the "ecstasy deficit" of post-Enlightenment religion, the desire for healings and miracles, the empowerment of women, and the ease with which inculturation occurs.[89] He may as well have been describing the Madonna of 115th Street.

---

89. Allen, *Future Church*, 389–98.

9

"Voices to Be Silenced or Ignored"

World War II and the Flattening Out
of American Catholicism

BENJAMIN T. PETERS

I n February 1943, *The Ecclesiastical Review* published an article by Joseph J. Connor, a Jesuit at the theologate in Weston, Massachusetts, titled "The Catholic Conscientious Objector." The article was intended to offer advice to Catholic clergy on what to do if asked to sign a military questionnaire attesting to the sincerity of belief held by a Catholic applying for conscientious objector status (CO). Connor began his article by summing up what he saw as the present state of the question concerning American Catholic COs in World War II. He noted that in the First World War there was little movement to foster or support Catholic COs, but he did highlight the case of Benjamin Salmon, one of the four American Catholic COs in the war.[1] Following the "Great War," though, Connor noted that revulsion to the horrors of the trenches and the seeming futility of the conflict itself had led many Catholics to question whether such a war met the traditional criteria of a "just war." And as a result, a much more organized movement in support of Catholic COs emerged between the wars, with many carefully

---

1. Connor noted that Salmon was sentenced to 25 years in federal prison in 1917 after he was told that his Catholic religion could not have forbade him from participating, since the Catholic hierarchy was actively supporting the war (Connor, "The Catholic Conscientious Objector," 127). For more on Salmon, see Finney, *Unsung Hero* and Catholic Peace Fellowship, "The Life and Witness of Ben Salmon."

articulated theological positions published by "prominent and authoritative theologians" in pages of Catholic periodicals.[2]

All of these discussions came to an abrupt end with the entrance of the United States into World War II, followed by the American Catholic hierarchy's quick endorsement of the war effort. As Connor explained, the argument in support of American Catholic conscientious objection seemed to have been "lost by default." That is, it did not suffer official disapproval, but it was also not simply accepted as "the specifically Catholic attitude to the present war."[3]

But despite this loss of popular and hierarchical support, some American Catholics continued to object to World War II and had turned to the prewar literature for theological justification of their CO positions. And since the theological arguments presented in this literature had never been "officially repudiated by the Church," Connor wrote that the use of such arguments to support American Catholic COs had caused something of a "controversy" for the church in the United States: could a Catholic be a conscientious objector?[4]

Connor's article is enlightening for several reasons. Not only does it lay out some of the different stances toward war taken by various American Catholics during the interwar period, but it also points to something of the significance World War II had on American Catholics. Indeed, one of the arguments running through much of William Portier's work is that, following the war, a kind of "flattening out" occurred within American Catholicism. Many voices—such as several of those involved in the interwar debates Connor described—suddenly became marginalized.

In addressing this, I have divided this essay into three parts. The first will highlight some of the now-often-overlooked Catholic voices that existed before World War II, voices that made up a discourse marked by a certain creative energy and enthusiasm that was critical of not only U.S. war-making, but of other American economic and political institutions as well. Part two will examine the flattening out of this discourse that abruptly occurs with World War II—a process that was greatly facilitated by John Courtney Murray, SJ. And finally, I will highlight the legacy of this postwar flattening out and its effect on American Catholics, particularly on contemporary "Catholic radicals"—theological descendants of those Catholic

2. Connor, "The Catholic Conscientious Objector," 127.

3. Connor argues that, while any such movement in support of American Catholic COs would have been very difficult in the face of "modern society's high-pressure salesmanship of war," American Catholics had "not even wished to combat society on this issue" (ibid., 126).

4. Ibid.

voices from the 1930s—whose critique of various aspects of American society and culture continues to be marginalized today. In all this, I hope to show not only something of the profound shift that occurred in American Catholicism as a result of the "Good War," but also to suggest that some of the silenced and ignored prewar Catholic voices, whose historical context of war and economic instability is not all that unlike our own context today, continue to be relevant to Catholics in the United States.

"The New Social Catholicism"

There certainly was much critical discussion of Catholic participation in war taking place in America during the 1930s. Connor referred to these debates as "a potpourri of asceticism, moral theology and sociology,"[5] and he divided the various arguments into a few distinct positions, the most popular of which held that Catholic conscripts could presume that the nation's cause was just and, therefore, should—and in "legal justice" must—enlist. This was the position advocated by some of the most prominent European moral theologians, such as Dominic Prümmer, OP, Arthur Vermeersch, SJ, Edward Genicot, SJ, and Benoît Merkelbach, OP.[6] And, not insignificantly, Connor pointed out that this was also the stance articulated by the U.S. bishops in a November 1942 statement, "Victory and Peace," which was published in the *New York Times* following the American entry into the war. "At times it is the positive duty of a nation to wage war in the defense of life and right. Our country now finds itself in such circumstances," the bishops declared. "From the moment that our country declared war we have called upon our people to make the sacrifices which, in Catholic doctrine, the virtues of patriotism, justice, and charity impose."[7] Connor explained—apparently missing the irony—that this was also the stance taken by the Catholic bishops in *all* the various countries fighting on both sides of the war in Europe.[8]

---

5. Ibid., 127.

6. For instance, Connor cites a March 1935 *Modern Schoolman* article in which Vermeersch had written that conscience objectors "take their stand upon a principle which is socially untenable, a principle which would give private persons the right to pass judgment upon public measures, a right which belongs to the sovereign power. At that rate there could be neither peace nor order in the internal affairs of the state. Everyone would manufacture his own opinions, whereas in things which are not evident, the presumption is in favor of the authorities" (quoted in Connor, "The Catholic Conscientious Objector," 137).

7. The bishops' statement appeared in the *New York Times* on 15 November 1942. For the full text, see "Victory and Peace."

8. Connor, "The Catholic Conscientious Objector," 135–37.

Nevertheless, other arguments more critical of Catholic participation in the American war effort also existed. For instance, there was the position, which Connor noted was held by "the greater majority of the prewar Catholic pacifist intellectuals," that argued that modern warfare no longer met the criteria of a just war.[9] Proponents of this argument turned to the writings of prominent Europeans, such as the English artist Eric Gill and the Italian exile Father Luigi Sturzo, as well as Dominicans Franziscus Stratmann, Gerald Vann, Victor White, and Vincent McNabb.[10] While in the United States, the work of clerics George Barry O'Toole and John K. Ryan, both faculty at the Catholic University of America, as well as James Gillis, CSP, of the *Catholic World* supported this stance.[11]

Connor also highlighted a less-commonly held antiwar position whose advocates he labeled as "Perfectionists."[12] He summed up their stance toward the war as follows: "I have an inalienable right to practice the counsels. Practice of the counsels includes non-resistance to an unjust aggressor. Therefore, even in a just war, I can, out of supernatural love of the enemy, refuse to resort to violence against him. Therefore I am exempt from military service, on the same grounds as the religious who practice Christian perfection."[13] Connor pointed out that adherents of this stance often cited "ecclesiastical supporters," such as Stratmann, Vann, O'Toole, Ryan, as well as the British theologian Father W.E. Orchard and the American Jesuit Daniel Lord, author of the pamphlet *So You Won't Fight, Eh?*.[14] Connor noted that, while some of these cited theologians, like Ryan, had publicly

9. Ibid., 130. Another position argued that the Allied cause, in particular, did not meet the standards of a just war. But this was not a widely held stance, for, Connor noted, "government suppression" of publications that questioned the justice of the Allied cause was "sufficient testimony to the futility of trying to propagate this opinion" (ibid., 135).

10 See Stratmann, *Church and War*; and Vann, *Morality and the War*.

11 See O'Toole, *War and Conscription at the Bar of Christian Morals*; and Ryan, *Modern War and Basic Ethics*.

12. Connor, "The Catholic Conscientious Objector," 127.

13. Ibid., 129.

14. Despite having an impressive list of significant Catholic supporters, Connor argued that these three positions in support of Catholic COs did not include a sufficient number of "outstanding moral theologians" to warrant this position the technical note of "extrinsic probability"—a term associated with "Probabilism," describing a position which was outside the consensus of moral theologians, but still held by at least five or six "outstanding moral theologians." He concluded that such arguments seemed to suggest "an air of exhilarating aloofness and detachment" and implied a desire to "dissociate" the church from American life. But such detachment, which he likened to "Albigensian purism and Calvinist theocracy," was as foreign to Catholic dogma as was Communist secularism (ibid., 136).

come out in support of the U.S. entry into the war, this perfectionist argument was still being made in the pages of *The Catholic Worker*.

Indeed, Dorothy Day's very public declaration following the Japanese attack on Pearl Harbor that the Catholic Worker was a pacifist movement is perhaps the most remembered articulation of this argument, but other examples existed as well.[15] For instance, Father John Hugo, the Pittsburgh priest who was Day's spiritual director for most of the 1940s, wrote several important articles in *The Catholic Worker* theologically defending this position, including a two-part piece titled "Catholics Can Be Conscientious Objectors," which Day had asked him to write in response to Connor's article.[16] In fact, Patricia McNeal has described Hugo as providing a theological justification to the more historically-based pacifist arguments that were being employed by Day and *The Catholic Worker*.[17] Hugo's wartime articles were later collected into a booklet titled *The Gospel of Peace*, which was published by the Catholic Worker Press in 1944. Three years prior, the Catholic Worker Press had also published several of Barry O'Toole's articles defending American Catholic COs in a pamphlet titled *War and Conscription at the Bar of Christian Morals*. Helpful here, for historical context, is Gordon Zahn's account of Camp Simon, the work camp for Catholic COs organized by the Catholic Worker in New Hampshire during the war. Zahn—himself a CO at Camp Simon—recalled that of the very few American clergy to publically support Catholic COs, O'Toole, Hugo, and Father Paul Hanly Furfey, a sociologist and Zahn's teacher at The Catholic University of America, were the most prominent.[18] In addition, there were the "Good Friday" editorials written by Father Joachim Benson, MSSsT in *Preservation of the Faith*, during the war, which also advocated something of this "perfectionist" stance.[19] All of this points to the often-overlooked fact that there were Catholics—members of the so-called "Greatest Generation"—who were critical of American involvement in the "Good War" and who advocated, in both word and deed, for Catholic nonparticipation in it.[20]

15. See Day, "Our Country," 1.

16. See Hugo, "Catholics Can Be Conscientious Objectors," 6–8.

17. McNeal, *Harder Than War*, 41.

18. Zahn, *Another Part of the War*, 32. Zahn also pointed out that some 6,000 Americans who were denied CO status went to prison for refusing to enlist (ibid., 28). While unable to determine the number of Catholics in this group, Zahn guessed it was significant. Included in this group were the future National Book Award winner J.F. Powers and the poet and Catholic convert Robert Lowell (Piehl, *Breaking Bread*, 199).

19. Portier, "Good Friday in December."

20. Zahn distinguished the various types of Catholic COs at Camp Simon: those who embraced a "Thomistic pacifism" that argued that the war did not meet the

What is important to recognize in all this is that many of these American Catholics were also part of a loosely identified movement that emerged in response to the Great Depression. This economic catastrophe "had opened the cultural fault lines of the 1920s and created new possibilities for cultural reconfiguration"—possibilities which these American Catholics wanted to grasp in response to the economic and political issues at the fore in the 1930s.[21] But, as Portier has argued, this movement was not "political" in the Right Reverend New Dealer John A. Ryan (1869–1945) sense of working to reform the existing U.S. political and economic structures. For such political reform was not seen as addressing the true causes of the society's problem. The economic depression and approaching war were not seen as historical aberrations, but rather were understood as the result, not only of sin, but of a lack of saints in the world.[22] And so, instead of more superficial political and economic reform that did not go to the *root* of the problem, these Catholic "radicals"—who, themselves, often pointed out that the term "radical" was derived from the Latin word for "root" (*radix*)—offered a more "personalist alternative for the reform of society, and to the policies that had brought on the Great Depression and then the Second World War."[23] These personalist methods were termed "weapons of the spirit" and included prayer, fasting, and the works of mercy.

In fact, Furfey articulated something of this kind of personalist alternative in a 1936 letter inviting various American Catholics to a colloquium on the "New Social Catholicism," though he noted that it was "new" only in the sense that it represented "a return—with new loyalty—to the traditional social doctrines and methods of the Catholic Church."[24] All of this pointed

---

requirements of a "just" war, "Catholic liberals" who believed that any war was incompatible with the Gospels, Catholic Workers who sought "nothing less than spiritual perfection," followers of Father Charles Coughlin who opposed any collaboration with Communist Russia, Irish Catholics who did not want to support Great Britain, and even some Catholics of German or Italian descent (Zahn, *Another Part of the War*, 13–14, 34–35).

21. Portier, "Paul Hanly Furfey," 35.

22. Elsewhere, Furfey had called for "the extreme Catholic ideal" of the saints. (Furfey, *Fire on the Earth*, 17).

23. Portier, "Paul Hanly Furfey," 35.

24. Furfey noted that the title "Revised Social Catholicism" would have also worked (Furfey, "The New Social Catholicism," 184). Portier summarized this "New Social Catholicism" as: "(1) the priority of faith over social science data in approaching social theory, (2) a preference for spiritual means (prayer, sacraments, liturgy) over political methods, necessary as they might be, in attempting to reform society . . . (3) personalism or the personal practice of Christian social virtues summed up in the word charity, (4) living the doctrine of the mystical body by charity to all" (Portier, "Paul Hanly Furfey," 34).

to a Catholic movement for social *reconstruction*, rather than one of simple reform of the existing political and economic structures. Peter Maurin (1877–1949), co-founder of the Catholic Worker—borrowing from the Industrial Workers of the World—described such reconstruction as "building a new society in the shell of old," where it would be easier for people to be good.[25] And so this social reconstruction involved a discernment of which aspects of society and culture could be embraced and even made more perfect, and which had to be rejected and resisted. Such discernment led to what Furfey described as the selective "technique of non-participation" from various aspects of American society and culture, such as not voting, refusing to work in certain occupations, not making certain types of financial investments, in addition to objecting to military service.[26]

This "new spirit" of Catholic social thought became more and more apparent within American Catholicism in the 1930s, from the Catholic Worker movement started by Day and Maurin, to Friendship House begun by Catherine de Hueck Doherty (1896–1985), to the Campion houses organized by Furfey's former graduate students such as Mary Elizabeth Walsh. Furfey noted that this New Social Catholicism was also being articulated in periodicals such as *The Catholic Worker*, *Liturgy and Sociology*, *Christian Front*, and *Social Reform*. The Catholics Furfey hoped would attend this gathering included not only Day, Doherty, Walsh, and Benson, but also the Benedictine liturgist and social critic Virgil Michel, Richard Deverall of *The Christian Front*, the activist John LaFarge, SJ, Gerald B. Phelan, CSB, from the Pontifical Institute of Medieval Studies in Toronto, Gillis at *The Catholic World*, and Father William Howard Bishop, founder of the Glenmary Home Missioners.[27]

Beyond Furfey's mailing list, other examples of this kind of social Catholicism were also emerging in the United States during the Depression. For instance, in addition to his influential anti-conscription writings in *The Catholic Worker*, Monsignor George Barry O'Toole also helped form the Catholic Radical Alliance in Pittsburgh in 1937, along with the labor priests Charles Owen Rice and Carl Hensler.[28] The Catholic Radical Alli-

25. Maurin, "What the Catholic Worker Believes."

26. Furfey, *Fire on the Earth*, 117–36.

27. Furfey, "The New Social Catholicism," 184.

28. "Labor priests" appeared in the early-twentieth century, offering both material and spiritual support to strikers, preaching the benefits of union membership, and often mediating between labor and employers. O'Toole is a particularly fascinating, but overlooked, figure who taught philosophy at St. Vincent College and Seton Hill College in Pennsylvania and the Catholic University of America. He was also the first president of the Catholic University of Peking in China.

ance (CRA), an offshoot of Pittsburgh's St. Joseph Catholic Worker house, sought "a changed and reformed social order" that would be "Christian and just in every sense of the word."[29] To this end, the three Pittsburgh priests set up an educational program to train workers in what labor historian Kenneth Heineman referred to as a new catechism of "Catholic social action."[30] Such training included a pamphlet that began: "Is the present economic and social system a good one? Is it Christian? . . . Emphatically no! It is materialistic and Godless."[31] Rice, Hensler, and O'Toole were some of only a handful of American clergy at the time to publically participate in labor strikes against companies owned by very prominent Catholics, such as the Heinz family.

And it is important to remember that this "New Social Catholicism" popping up in America was part of a broader flourish of creative activity that was occurring in Catholicism in general during the interwar years. Something of this intellectual energy is what Stephen Schloesser, SJ, described as the "Jazz Age Catholicism" that emerged in response to the horrors of the First World War.[32] This energy also blossomed into a "Catholic revival" in art and literature, which Peter Huff has depicted as taking place in America as well as Europe.[33] After the "Great War," many Catholics sought to articulate a more intrinsic account of their faith in contrast to both the suffocating positivism that dominated the secular world and the overly rationalistic "Strict-Observance Thomism" that prevailed in Catholicism at the time.[34] And it was this creative energy that spurred a reinvigorated notion of the social nature of Catholicism over and against modernity's more individualistic emphasis. Peter Bernardi, SJ, highlights this "social Catholicism" at work in the *Semaines Sociales* and the *Le Sillon* (of which Maurin was briefly connected) taking place in France at the time, pointing out its similarities with Furfey's new social Catholicism in the United States.[35] And as Portier explains, all these various proponents of this social Catholicism sought to offer a more integrated faith and, thereby, become a leavening presence in

---

29. CRA, leaflet, 1937, cited in Heineman, *A Catholic New Deal*, 122.

30. Heineman, *A Catholic New Deal*, 122.

31. *Pittsburgh Catholic*, 29 April 1937, cited in ibid.

32. Schloesser, *Jazz Age Catholicism*, 18–45.

33. Huff, *Allen Tate and the Catholic Revival*, 18–24.

34. For more on this form of Thomism, see John, *Thomist Spectrum*, 3–15; Nichols, *Reason with Piety*, 1–16.

35. Bernardi, *Maurice Blondel, Social Catholicism, and Action Française*, 264.

the modern world—not rejecting or embracing society and culture whole cloth, but rather seeking holiness within it.[36]

It is worth acknowledging this interwar activity since it challenges the still-common perception that American Catholicism during this period was uniform and unimaginative.[37] Clearly there was much discussion and disagreement in Catholicism, and many Catholic voices critical of American society and culture existed. And more important for our purposes here, it also helps to highlight the moment when much of this activity ended somewhat abruptly, and when whatever critical Catholic voices remained were effectively silenced.

"A Vast American *Unum*"

As Connor pointed out, so much of the interwar years' creative debates and possibilities were largely extinguished with the U.S. entry into World War II. Patriotic fervor of the American war effort caused many involved in the new social Catholicism to lose their more critical stance toward American society and culture.[38] This was vividly seen within the Catholic Worker movement. Several Workers left the movement to enlist, some houses of hospitality closed, subscriptions waned, and donations dried up in response to Day's continued pacifism—though it should be remembered that tension over the war began to emerge within the Catholic Worker even prior to the attack on Pearl Harbor.[39]

But perhaps more pivotal than the American entry into the war was the postwar period of prosperity and consensus which Portier has described as having quickly "flattened out" and "re-directed" much of the energies produced by the political and economic pressures of the 1930s.[40] While the New Deal did address some of the extreme need to which Day, Furfey, and others were responding, nevertheless, "something was lost" during the war years.[41] Indeed, the war's end brought "a consolidation" that turned the

36. Portier, "Twentieth-Century Catholic Theology and the Triumph of Maurice Blondel," 115.

37. For example, Leslie Woodcock Tentler has depicted this as a time of "complacent anti-intellectualism, reflexive anti-communism, and a repressive sexual ethic" (Tentler, "On the Margins," 113).

38. Portier, "Paul Hanly Furfey," 35.

39. For more on this, especially John Cogley's criticism of Day's August 1940 letter to all Catholic Workers that the movement was pacifist, see Piehl, *Breaking Bread*, 155–59. For a copy of Day's letter, see Ellsberg, *All the Way to Heaven*, 117–19.

40. Portier, "Theology of Manners as Theology of Containment," 95.

41. Portier, "Paul Hanly Furfey," 35.

movements of the 1930s, with their personalist approaches to social issues, toward more "conventional directions."[42] Joachim Benson, for instance, left his post as editor of the *Preservation of the Faith*, then the "publishing arm" for the new social Catholics, to become a mission pastor in Farmville, North Carolina—a move that can be seen as "emblematic" of this postwar shift.[43] So, too, was the redirection in focus of the Catholic Radical Alliance. Not only did much of the CRA's more critical pro-labor "agitating" activities cease, but the group itself split over the war. While O'Toole sided with Day and the Catholic Worker in opposing the U.S. war effort, Rice and Hensler supported the fight against the Nazis, arguing that "Loyalty to our country comes first."[44] After the war, the CRA focused almost exclusively on fighting Communism in American unions, leaving behind its prewar mission of teaching Catholic social action and supporting labor strikes.[45]

The Harvard sociologist Daniel Bell shed light on this postwar "consolidation" in his 1960 book, *The End of Ideology*, where he announced that World War II had forged "a rough consensus among intellectuals on political issues."[46] The war had not only ended Depression-era struggles between capital and labor, but it had also melted religious and ethnic groups into "a vast American *unum*."[47] In fact, five years earlier, Will Herberg unveiled "The American Way of Life," which was comprised of three narrowly defined possibilities of "Protestant," "Catholic" or "Jew."[48] The creative energies that emerged from the 1930s—and which had fueled the criticisms and alternatives of the "New Social Catholicism"—had become, by the 1950s, ideological, passionate, non-pragmatic religious commitments. As a result, they were seen as impediments to the postwar consensus, and it was the task of proponents of this consensus, Bell's "cultural arbiters," to remove such impediments.

At the center of the Catholic third of Herberg's troika was John Courtney Murray, SJ, the Woodstock theologian who made a strong-but-qualified embrace of this postwar consensus in *We Hold These Truths*, published the same year as Bell's book. For, despite Murray's disdain for "the barbarian in the Brooks Brothers suit," Portier suggested that "Bell's consensus mood and the 'gray flannelled stoicism' of his cultural arbiters (Murray's *sapientes*)"

---

42. Ibid., 35.
43. Portier, "Good Friday in December," 43.
44. Heineman, *A Catholic New Deal*, 195.
45. Ibid.
46. Bell, *The End of Ideology*, 373.
47. Portier, "Theology of Manners as Theology of Containment," 90.
48. Herberg, *Protestant-Catholic-Jew*.

pervaded the American Jesuit's widely read book.[49] So it was Murray, along with fellow Catholic "cultural arbiters" like the Catholic University of America historian John Tracy Ellis, who "constructed a covenant of containment, a "public theology" or "civil religion," for the New Deal-Cold War order."[50] And it was this "covenant of containment" that Eugene McCarraher declared as not only having "ratified the managerial authority of Bell's cultural arbiters," but also—and more importantly for our discussion—as having "stigmatized the indecorous enthusiasms of radical politics."[51]

[handwritten margin note: "disciplined imagination"]

For Murray and his fellow Cold War cultural arbiters, like Reinhold Niebuhr, America in the 1950s was "an imperialism, like it or not" run by the "best and the brightest," and those Catholic voices who did not also take this postwar American empire for granted had to be discredited.[52] Any Catholic embrace of the "end of ideology" required the suppression of Catholic voices that critiqued this postwar consensus. Chief among these voices that needed to be suppressed were the "indecorous" Catholic radicals, such as Day, Furfey, Hugo, and others who continued to advocate the new social Catholicism of the 1930s. As Portier notes, such voices "had to be silenced or ignored."[53]

[handwritten margin note: This is the beginning of "America first!"]

In *We Hold These Truths*, Murray carried out this task through the use of an eschatological-incarnational humanism paradigm, a paradigm Murray took up in the aftermath of his debates with Furfey over inter-creedal cooperation in the 1940s.[54] And so Murray's discussion of these two "humanisms" should be read, at least in part, as a critique of Catholic radicals like Furfey. In his discussion of mid-century Catholics, Murray noted that there was a temptation to make a "spiritual withdrawal" from some American political and economic institutions.[55] He argued that the desire to make such a withdrawal was rooted in the view that human nature and history were completely corrupted, and so their withdrawal should be seen as an "utter prophetic condemnation" of the *res humana* which American society

49. Portier, "Theology of Manners as Theology of Containment," 90. For instance, Murray argued, "Order is, by definition, the work of the wise man: *sapientis est ordinare*. It is the work of men and peoples who are able to say: There are truths and we hold them" (Murray, *We Hold These Truths*, 53).

50. McCarraher, *Christian Critics*, 91.

51. Ibid.

52. Murray, *We Hold These Truths*, 254.

53. Portier, "Theology of Manners as Theology of Containment," 95.

54. Komonchak, "John Courtney Murray," 74. For more on these debates, see Baxter, "In Service to the Nation," 435–43.

55. Murray, *We Hold These Truths*, 173.

and culture represented.[56] Murray declared that these Catholics tended toward an "eschatological humanism" which emphasized a final transcendent end of human nature "radically discontinuous with history, the arena of human effort and achievement"—an emphasis that led to a "contempt of the world."[57] American social conditions, institutions, and ideals were seen as necessary evils, and participation in them was regarded as, at best, irrelevant—like the basket-weaving of the Desert Fathers.[58] Murray, who was borrowing terms from earlier European debates, contrasted this "eschatological" humanism with a more "incarnational" form, which he clearly preferred—a humanism that took a more affirming approach to human nature and the world, and likewise a more positive stance toward the structures and institutions in America.

In all this, Murray seemed to argue that any critique of American society and culture, such as the one leveled by Catholic radicals, was rooted in the assumption that such American institutions were sinful, that is, in violation of the natural law. Underlying this assumption was a "two-tiered" understanding of nature and grace, with its view of the supernatural building a kind of superstructure on a largely self-contained nature. This was the account, dominant in early-twentieth-century Catholic theology, that the French theologian Henri de Lubac, SJ (1896–1991), argued had exiled Christianity from the modern world.[59] And it was through this theological lens that Murray saw Catholics like Day and Furfey—for if human nature was self-contained and largely self-sufficient, only that which was sinful or in violation of the natural law would need to be renounced. In short, if American institutions were not corrupted by sin, why withdraw from them?

From such a theological perspective, non-participation in certain aspects of American society and culture that were discerned to be impediments to fully living out one's faith—a desire at the heart of what Day called "a supernatural life"—appeared extreme.[60] For Furfey, Hugo, and Day, a Christian life entailed something more than simply following the natural law and avoiding sin; it also included selective detachment—not only from that which is sinful, but from anything that distracts or impedes one's desire for

56. Ibid., 172.

57. Murray titled his section on eschatological humanism: "Contempt of the World." See ibid., 173–76.

58. Murray, *We Hold These Truths*, 174–75.

59. This is the central assertion in de Lubac's *Surnaturel*. It should be noted that a growing number of scholars are attempting to nuance claims of the degree to which this dualism existed in Catholic theology. See Portier, "Thomist Resurgence."

60. Day, *Long Loneliness*, 256.

God.[61] This was the life of "supernatural happiness" which Day poignantly detailed in the third part of *The Long Loneliness*. It was also, Hugo pointed out, the image of the Christian life articulated by many of the great spiritual writers within the Christian tradition, such as John of the Cross, Francis de Sales, and Ignatius of Loyola.[62] For Murray, though, such a life not only seemed to undergird Catholic critiques of American "imperialism," but it also would have looked excessively eschatological in its focus and, therefore, too ideological to fit into the postwar consensus.

It should be noted that in all this Murray can be seen as highlighting the political implications of the form of neo-Thomism that, while clearly beginning to wane, still very much prevailed in Catholic theology in the mid-twentieth century.[63] Starting from an account of human nature as largely autonomous, the life of a Catholic in America, with his or her responsibilities to family and nation, was also affirmed as largely self-sufficient. Granted, Murray and other American neo-Thomists were critical of certain aspects of American life, but such criticism was always in line with the binding precepts of the natural law.[64] So long as one held to these precepts, he or she could remain morally upright and comfortable within American life—or, in Murray's terms, he or she could live "civilly" and "respectably" within the American consensus.[65]

The problem with this approach to Catholic social engagement in the U.S. was the difficulty it had in identifying how and where the Christian life was something more than simply following the natural law—a life Hugo sarcastically summed up as: "Eat, drink, be merry, and avoid mortal sin."[66] And it points to Murray's theologically deficient understanding of the natural law as something separated from faith—a separate philosophy he described as having "no Roman Catholic presuppositions."[67] As Portier recommended,

61. For instance, this was one of the main themes of Hugo's retreat. See Peters, "Nature and Grace."

62. Hugo, *A Sign of Contradiction*, 140–64.

63. For a broader discussion of the political implications of this two-tiered theology and its critics, see Bernardi, *Maurice Blondel, Social Catholicism, and Action Française*, 231–68.

64. For instance, Murray critiqued the policy of not using public funds to support U.S. Catholic schools (Murray, *We Hold These Truths*, 139–48). And, in an address given at Western Maryland College on 4 June 1967, Murray publically opposed the prohibition on selective conscientious objection in the U.S. military (Murray, "War and Conscience"). That these two issues typically fall on opposing sides of the contemporary political spectrum in the U.S. reveals something of the expanse of Murray's project.

65. Cuddihy, *No Offense*, 64–100.

66. Hugo, *Applied Christianity*, 123.

67. Murray, *We Hold These Truths*, 111.

"If ever anything needed 're-theologizing,' it is Murray's doctrine of the natural law."[68] Such a "re-theologized" account would not regard the natural law as isolated from revelation in some kind of two-storied sense, but rather it would recognize human nature's inherent insufficiency and need for grace.

"Voices Silenced or Ignored"

These and other such weaknesses have led to much critique of Murray's postwar consensus-building "project."[69] Nevertheless, the American Jesuit's legacy clearly lingers on, particularly in the way Catholic voices critical of American society and culture continue to be placed on the margins of Catholic discourse. Indeed, for all their celebrated importance and significance in American Catholicism, at the same time Day and other Catholic radicals are often placed on such margins, even by those who do the celebrating. For instance, historian David O'Brien praised Day and her fellow Catholic Workers for their work with the poor and their opposition to the arms race, but he also concluded that they embodied a certain "perfectionism" in which they devalued citizenship and reduced the moral significance of politics and the broader society.[70] As a result, Day and the Catholic Worker lacked a sense of "responsible citizenship" and became "marginalized" from larger public-policy debates. All of this led O'Brien to conclude that Day and the Catholic Worker movement ultimately tended toward what he called an "apocalyptic sectarianism."[71] It is interesting that, in Tranquillitas Ordinis, George Weigel describes Day in terms not all that different from O'Brien's, arguing that Day's theological perspective, especially evident in her pacifist stance in World War II, was rooted in "a radically eschatological view of history" which was heavy with "apocalyptic overtones."[72] That Catholic intellectuals as different as O'Brien and Weigel appear to be in agreement on this point

68. Portier, "Theology of Manners as Theology of Containment," 96.

69. For instance, see Weithman, "John Courtney Murray." Portier referred to We Hold These Truths as more of "a period piece than an enduring work of scholarship" (Portier, "Theology of Manners as Theology of Containment," 96).

70. O'Brien, Public Catholicism, 246.

71. Ibid., 246. Likewise, James Fisher followed up his praise of Day by arguing that her "aesthetic Jansenism" and embrace of "a downward path to salvation" reflected an elitism that alienated her from the materialist aspirations of most working-class American Catholics at the time (Fisher, Catholic Counterculture in America, 60, 69). And working from Fisher's depiction, Eugene McCarraher argued that this self-alienation of Day and other Catholic radicals from the vast majority of their fellow Catholics led to their becoming largely "irrelevant" in American Catholicism (McCarraher, "The Church Irrelevant," 186).

72. Weigel, Tranquillitas Ordinis, 150.

reveals something of the often-overlooked commonality that exists between so-called "liberal" and "conservative" thinking among American Catholics still influenced by Murray. For while particular policy issues are hotly debated, a deeper, more probing critique of U.S. institutions themselves—like the one offered by Day and the Catholic Worker—is dismissed.[73]

Likewise, Charles Curran's initial praise for the Catholic Worker in *American Catholic Social Ethics* quickly turned critical as he portrayed Day and the Catholic Worker as espousing a "radical type of social ethics" emerging from a "gospel radicalism" which insisted that all Catholics were called to a life of holiness.[74] And Kristen Heyer provided an even more recent instance of such a reading in *Prophetic & Public: The Social Witness of U.S. Catholicism*, a book which relied heavily on the work of both O'Brien and Curran.[75] For Heyer, more contemporary Catholic radicals, such as Michael Baxter—like Day and Furfey two generations earlier—represent a "prophetic sect type" and "a rigorist, evangelical social ethic" which corresponds to O'Brien's "evangelical style" of Catholicism.[76] All of which informs their nonparticipation in particular American institutions, including their refusal to support American war-making, to vote, to pay federal income tax, or to engage in public-policy debates.[77] Their advocacy of this kind of selective nonparticipation led Heyer—no doubt unknowingly—to borrow Joseph Connor's term and label such Catholics as "perfectionists."[78]

Heyer contrasted this approach to Catholic social engagement with the more "public" approach taken by theologians such as Curran, J. Bryan Hehir, David Hollenbach, and Kenneth and Michael Himes—an approach

---

73. Peter Maurin's "three-pronged plan" for the Catholic Worker: roundtable discussions, houses of hospitality, and agronomic universities can be understood as the heart of this critique, for Maurin clearly was proposing a non-state-centered form of social reconstruction or the building of a society where it is easier for people to be good (Maurin, "Purpose," 36). And his plan spawned other Catholic Worker practices that rejected state-centered politics and market-driven economics, such as living in voluntary poverty, not paying federal income tax, not voting, or not claiming tax-exempt status.

74. Curran, *American Catholic Social Ethics*, 137, 142, 158–59. Though he describes this as the "radical" Catholic approach—one that ultimately views grace as "radically incompatible" with nature—Curran does admit that Furfey is anticipating the universal call to holiness at Vatican II (see Second Vatican Council, *Lumen Gentium* §39–42). For more on the theology operative in such criticism of American Catholic radicals, see Peters, "Apocalyptic Sectarianism."

75. Heyer, *Prophetic & Public*, 90.

76. Ibid., 70.

77. Ibid., 76.

78. Ibid.

Heyer also embraces.[79] And in much the same way, Richard Gaillardetz contrasted Curran, Hehir, Hollenbach, and the Himeses with Baxter, Michael Budde, David Schindler, and William Cavanaugh.[80] Gaillardetz preferred the more "Thomistic" approach toward social engagement embodied in the former grouping in contrast to the "Augustinian" theological framework operative in what he called the "radical cultural engagement" of the latter group.[81] Gaillardetz suggested that such American Catholic radical cultural engagement is rooted in the "counterculturalism" and "commitment to fundamental gospel values" found in Day and other "sources of Catholic radicalism" in the United States.[82] In short, for O'Brien, Weigel, Heyer, Gaillardetz, and other stewards of Murray's project today, such perfectionism and commitment to fundamental gospel values is too uncompromising and critical of American society and culture—too "ideological" for the American consensus—and so those who embrace it must be relegated to the fringe of American Catholicism.

Conclusion

A few other significant points can be gleaned from this discussion. One is that while the Second Vatican Council continues to be generally regarded as *the* pivotal event in twentieth-century Catholicism, in fact World War II—not Vatican II—may have been more determinative for American Catholics in the second half of the century. Indeed, Portier has convincingly argued that the war and its aftermath provided the lens through which Vatican II was understood by Catholics in America.[83] And so perhaps, at the very least, the helpfulness of the somewhat ubiquitous historical markers "preconciliar" and "postconciliar" needs to be reconsidered.

Interesting, as well, is the possible connection that can be made between the Catholics associated with Furfey's "New Social Catholicism" and other voices that were similarly silenced or ignored for refusing to embrace the postwar consensus. For instance, while J. Leon Hooper, SJ, has argued that a link should be made between Murray and Day since both had "common enemies" in the eminent American theologians Francis J. Connell, CSsR (1888–1967), and Joseph Clifford Fenton (1906–1969), the counter-argument could also be made that it was Fenton and Connell who shared a kind

---

79. Ibid., 59.

80. Gaillardetz, "Ecclesiological Foundations," 77.

81. Ibid., 78.

82. Ibid., 77–78.

83. Portier, "Here Come the Evangelical Catholics," 39.

of synchronicity with Day.[84] Indeed, as R. Scott Appleby and Jay Haas have pointed out, the two Catholic University of America theologians fiercely resisted Catholic entry into the postwar consensus that Murray was helping to facilitate. Keenly alert to such "changes in emphasis" in the Catholic mind, Fenton and Connell, "raised their voices against the powerful Americanizing forces at work in postwar society and culture, forces which they believed were working to revive Americanism within the Catholic community."[85] Murray's call for an "end of ideology" and its replacement with "civility" was a call for American Catholics to become "respectable" and fit into the postwar consensus.[86] But, as John Murray Cuddihy has pointed out, Fenton and Connell read this desire to be respectable as simply a desire to put social ambitions—to be what they termed a "respecter of persons"—over theological truths (i.e., "ideology").[87] While Hooper is certainly correct that Fenton and Connell had many differences with Day, nevertheless, they all saw the "Americanizing" effect of the postwar consensus as something to be resisted by Catholics, a resistance Murray worked to silence.[88]

Of course, both Fenton and Connell worked out of the same two-storied account of nature and the supernatural that was operative in Murray's thinking. Such a theological perspective is evident in the critiques that Fenton and Connell made of John Hugo and "the retreat" he was offering in the 1940s, a retreat Day claimed had brought about her "second conversion."[89] For Fenton and Connell, Hugo was blurring nature and grace—a criticism very similar to the one leveled against de Lubac at the same time.[90]

While beyond the scope of this article, I would suggest that underlying these distinctions and similarities are the various ways these Catholics understood the relationship between nature and the supernatural.[91] For Day, Furfey, Hugo, and other Catholic radicals, the supernatural is more than simply that which is not sinful, it is also distinct from nature. And so the Christian life entails something more than simply avoiding sin and

---

84. Hooper, "Day and Murray," 46.

85. Appleby and Haas, "Last Supernaturalists," 40.

86. Cuddihy stated that for Murray the central question was of "civility *versus* ideology (in this case, theology)." Cuddihy, *No Offense*, 95.

87. Ibid., 80.

88. Portier, "Theology of Manners as Theology of Containment," 89. The success of Murray in this regard can be measured by the fact that Fenton and Connell were two of the most prominent and influential American Catholic theologians from the 1940s to the 1960s, while today they are largely forgotten.

89. Connell, "Review"; Fenton, "Nature and the Supernatural."

90. See Peters, "Nature and Grace."

91. For a fuller discussion, see Peters, "Apocalyptic Sectarianism."

following the tenets of the natural law. It involves an ongoing discernment of what is encountered daily in American life, embracing that which can be a pathway to holiness while rejecting what is not. This was Hugo's argument in defense of American Catholics who were conscientious objectors to a war that many regarded as "just" according the natural law.

These reflections lead to a final point that Portier has emphasized in many of his more recent articles. In this time of the "great recession" and seemingly never-ending American wars—as I write this, U.S. warplanes and drones have once again begun to bomb targets in Iraq—there is clearly a need to recover the voices and arguments of those American Catholics from the 1930s whose more radical critique of American "imperialism" has been silenced or ignored.[92] For such voices offered a vision of the Christian life that is neither a wholesale embrace nor blanket rejection of American society and culture. Instead, it presents a means of selective nonparticipation in certain aspects of American life that is rooted in the belief that grace does not simply *build on* nature, but rather *perfects* it.

92. Portier writes: "Though the differences are many, the relation of the war to our economic situation, for example, our own time recalls the 1930s and the beginning of World War II in many ways. . . . Perhaps it's time to dip into the 1930s again and take another look at Furfey's personalism and Catholic extremism" (Portier, "Paul Hanly Furfey," 96).

10

1960s America and the Christic Vision of Teilhard

Susan K. Sack

Pierre Teilhard de Chardin, SJ, 1888–1955, visionary priest, paleontologist, and writer, is an important landmark figure in twentieth-century Catholicism. Teilhard strove to place humanity's desire for unity with the divine within the context of both religion and science. The period of 1959–1968 was the crucial age during which Teilhard's writing was first available in North America; over five hundred primary and secondary works concerning him were published in the U.S. during these years. His thought inspired a "phenomenon" that significantly impacted the Catholicism of the United States at that time, and continues to do so today.

This essay examines the U.S. reception of Teilhard's work, particularly in terms of his Christological vision, during this era. This reception occurred as it did at this particular point in the history of both the United States and the Catholic Church because of a confluence of religious, social, and political factors. Various aspects of Teilhard's thought were deemed of value, including progress, energy, hope, as well as his teleological understanding of suffering and exile. This essay will show that Teilhard's optimism and belief in progress were not rooted solely in humanitarian activism in the world, but instead in a Christian hope that all the matter of the world, all the effort expended on a daily basis, and all our own suffering are redeemed through the power of the Paschal Mystery.

We will first briefly introduce some key points of Teilhard's Christology and then examine the reception of his thought in the United States during three different time periods: 1959–1964, 1965–1967, and 1968. Although space does not permit an extensive consideration of the political or social developments of these years, a brief review of the pertinent historical context is provided.

Teilhard's Christology

A reductive understanding of Teilhard's thought and spirituality often drove the fascination of diverse populations, Catholic and beyond, with his writing. Often overlooked was a lifelong devotion to Christ's life, especially to his Sacred Heart and Passion, which was first foundational to his devout mother's spirituality, and later became the basis of his own. Indeed, at one point he wrote to a friend: "Exalting Christ over everything: this is all I can be accused of."[1] Additionally, the Jesuits taught him to see God at work in the world, even when pain and suffering were the norm, and were formational to his kenotic spirituality.[2]

Teilhard's Christocentric cosmology was not entirely his own theological invention. He is, however, perhaps the only modern Catholic thinker who makes the Pauline Cosmic Christ thematic in his work.[3] In his interpretation of Christ the divine and human not only are genuinely blended into one entity via the Incarnation, but Christ is the foundation of a new evolutionary theology. He understood humanity and the whole of nature as combining incarnationally in an historical progression guided and drawn forth by the Pauline Cosmic Christ, who gives guidance to the cosmos via evolution.[4] His religious formation suggested to him that evolution was not simply random mutations and struggles for survival, but something beyond Darwinism in that it consisted of a convergent progression of life towards

1. Bravo, *Christ in the Thought of Teilhard de Chardin*, 84. Although Bravo does not provide a reference for this quote, Teilhard wrote in the same vein in 1916 to his cousin Marguerite: "I want to love Christ with all my strength in the very act of loving the universe. Can this be absurdity, blasphemy?" (Letter to Marguerite Teilhard-Chambon, 15 March 1916).

2. Teilhard de Chardin (hereafter Teilhard), *The Divine Milieu*, 89. God, he wrote, "must, in some way or other, make room for himself, hollowing us out and emptying us, if he is finally to penetrate into us."

3. This Christology is found in Pauline passages such as Rom 8:19–23, 1 Cor 15:28, Eph 1:9–10, and Col 1:15–20.

4. "To create, to fulfill, to purify the world is for God to unify it by uniting it organically with himself. How does he unify it? By immersing himself in things, by becoming 'element' and then from this vantage in the heart of matter, assuming the control and leadership of what we now call evolution" (Teilhard, *The Phenomenon of Man*, 149).

an even greater unity in Christ. As he put it, "The answer to the riddle of the universe is: Christ Jesus."[5]

In Teilhard's "Christogenesis," God first Christifies himself through the Incarnation and then Christ, the "all in all," is fully formed by drawing the entirety of earthly life into mystical consummation. This is the heart of Teilhard's theology and his evolutionary theory. Teilhard claims that just as each person is in a continual process of growth, so too is the entire cosmos a growing and developing whole. It is the responsibility and the privilege of each created being to develop the Christ-element within so as to add to the fullness that Christ the divine being already is. This transformative activity originating in the Incarnation therefore extends to each of us, and requires human cooperation with God's own creative action. For Teilhard all the activities of our lives help to complete Christ's achievement and move the cosmos toward Christogenesis. This is not a solitary, individual achievement, but that of a community united in the spiritualized love which is the primary unifying force.[6] The role of the church is as an agent of Christogenesis: nurturing and furthering the crucial phylum of love, building the Mystical Body of Christ, and assisting Christians in learning how to "see" the divine milieu, as well as becoming aware of Christ's presence in the world.

The Early Years, 1959–1964

During these early years Teilhard's thought was received favorably by numerous people in the Catholic population in the U.S. who, even if they struggled with some of his theology, grasped the importance of his Christological vision. Many were attracted to him at this time due to the synchronicity of the publication of his first books in the U.S. and massive changes underway in American society. It was, one might say, a perfect storm of coincidence.

During this Cold War era the political, religious and social consensus of the United States began to crack due to a number of factors.[7] These included increasing education and prosperity, and the resultant changes in family structure, the workplace, and Americans' religious understanding of

5. Quoted in Corbishley, *The Spirituality of Teilhard de Chardin*, 71.

6. As he wrote: "God who is as immense and all-embracing as matter . . . is the center who spreads through all things. . . . [S]ouls are irresistibly drawn . . . towards a common center of beatitude. . . . [T]he multitude is bound together into one solid whole. . . . [T]he Communion of Saints is held together in the hallowed unity of a physically organized whole; and this whole . . . is the body of Christ" (Teilhard, "Cosmic Life," in *Writings in Time of War*, 48).

7. See Ellwood, *The Sixties Spiritual Awakening*.

themselves. Inklings of the change that would dominate the later 1960s were already in the air; almost tangibly the question was "where are we headed?" Concerns also existed, particularly in light of the nuclear bomb and the space race, over the trajectory of science. Additionally, Pope John XXIII's actions were drawing the attention of the entire world, and were already shaking the "unchanging" Catholic Church. The paradigm was indeed shifting, but its future direction was not yet clear.

Teilhard's optimistic teleology held a possible answer many American Catholics easily embraced. It stated that, despite omnipresent difficulties, we are indeed moving in a positive direction; we are progressing, and this is good.[8] The need existed, though, to synthesize the evolving political, religious, scientific, and social changes into the American and Catholic worldview. Here Teilhard's integrated, organic view of the world served as an exemplar for many.

In addition, as United States' society became increasingly middle-class and prosperous, progressively more secular and materialist, and as the immigrant Catholic "ghettoes" dissolved into suburbia and educational opportunities expanded, questions over how to continue to live a spiritual life abounded.[9] The struggle became, in a changing world, to discern how the spiritual could inform the secular, and the material world the sacred. In response to these issues, Teilhard, the mystical Jesuit scientist who "loved the world," exemplified a contemplative form of life that saw God in potentially all aspects of the everyday.[10] Even in the early years of the sixties, his spiritual thought attracted many who agreed: "There is neither spirit nor matter in the world; the stuff of the universe is *spirit-matter*."[11]

A *Time* article in 1959 was one of the first published in the U.S. suggesting that much of U.S. society was eager to listen to a scientific visionary who looked at the world through spiritual eyes, bridging the gap between God and material existence.[12] This piece appeared shortly after the publication of Teilhard's *The Phenomenon of Man* in the U.S., the first of his work

---

8. Consider this quote from Teilhard on the eve of World War II, in a Letter from Peking (Summer 1940), as quoted in Lukacs, *The Last European War*, 515: "Personally, I stick to my idea that we are watching the birth, more than the death, of a World."

9. William Portier later wrote: "This dissolution of the subculture is the single most important fact in U.S. Catholic history in the second half of the twentieth century" (Portier, "Here Come the Evangelical Catholics," 46).

10. Teilhard, *The Making of a Mind*, 241: "My strength and my joy derive from seeing in some way made real for me the fusion of God and the world, the latter giving 'immediacy' to the divine, and the divine spiritualizing the tangible."

11. Teilhard, *Human Energy*, 58.

12. "Toward Omega," 62.

to be made available in English.[13] The unexpectedly high sales figures for *Phenomenon* point to its tremendous popularity, first in Europe, then later in the United States.[14]

The early publications about Teilhard in U.S. journals point to several themes that continually reappear in discussions of his work. Predominant is an inability to adequately classify Teilhard's thought. It does not neatly fit into any category, whether philosophy, theology, or science. As Wilfred Sheed reflected in a 1959 article in *Jubilee*, those who do not deal well with speculation and hypothesis would be uneasy with what Teilhard is attempting.[15] Indeed, the aforementioned *Time* article notes that the Pontifical Roman Theological Academy devoted an entire issue of its quarterly *Divinitas* to attacks on Teilhard's ideas, calling them "a maximum of seduction coinciding with a maximum of aberration."[16] This inability to classify Teilhard's work or comprehend his vision caused his thought not only to be often misinterpreted, but condemned as heretical.

In his article "A Call to Greatness," Robert Francoeur asserts that the complexity and depth of Teilhard's work ensures that it will take quite some time for the world to understand his real vision.[17] Francoeur believed Teilhard was: "One of those rare men who combined the attitude of the scientist with the visionary qualities of a mystic and the warmth of a great humanness. . . . [T]o study man and his place in the evolving universe and then to synthesize the findings of modern science with the light of supernatural revelation is the whole purpose of Teilhard's vision."[18] What is especially noteworthy, Francoeur writes, is that Teilhard's discoveries explicate the ultra-sacramental nature of that same universe, and situate it in a Christology that has as its foundation the Mystical Body of Christ.[19]

One of the best-known Catholic authors of the mid-twentieth century, Thomas Merton, wrote a review of Teilhard's *Divine Milieu* in the fall of

---

13. Teilhard, *The Phenomenon of Man*.

14. Within six months of its first publication in English, *Phenomenon* had already sold 17,000 copies, unheard of at the time for its genre (Hugh Van Dusen to "Friends of Father Teilhard," 7 April 1960).

15. Sheed, "Père Teilhard's View of Evolution."

16. "Toward Omega," 62.

17. Francoeur, "A Call to Greatness," 441.

18. Ibid.

19. Francoeur's edited volume, *The World of Teilhard*, was the first concerning Teilhard written and published in the U.S. This book is representative of many subsequent Teilhardian publications, the essays exhibiting the synthetic worldview exemplified by Teilhard himself.

1960.[20] That Merton, living in a monastery hermitage hidden deep in the American Midwest had Teilhard's *Divine Milieu* suggested to him as a "good read," and that he was so taken with the author and the book's content to write a positive review points to the appeal of Teilhard at the time.

Merton asserted that at the heart of Teilhard's spirituality is his incarnational Christology. As a result, Merton wrote, for Teilhard his love for the material world leads to his understanding that, rather than being an obstacle, material reality "is indispensable for our service and knowledge of Christ."[21] He noted that Teilhard's writing overflowed with an optimism that declared that somehow this world was progressing toward something far better, and that even though Teilhard's thought is supremely Christocentric, in a country built on the myth of hard work and love of the material, these themes are tantalizing. It is no surprise, then, that Catholic Americans especially were enthralled by this message.

One sign of this early Teilhardian interest was a well-received television program on Teilhard's thought sponsored by the Knights of Columbus in Baltimore in early spring of 1960. Four well-known Catholic scholars from the New York area were panelists, and the transcript of the show "Evolution, Science and Religion" was later published in *Jubilee* magazine.[22] An expressed summary of the discussion was that Teilhard gives people hope that "one can be a modern man, one can be an evolutionist, and one can be a Christian."[23] Already in 1960, a few people grasped and were disseminating the Christ-centered focus of Teilhard's thought.

In his article of the same year Bernard Gilligan notes that *Phenomenon* was widely acclaimed as "THE publishing event" of 1959. . . . [R]eviewers predict it will remain a classic and be read assiduously for decades to come."[24] Gilligan lavishly praises the book, commenting that it contains "a brilliant synoptic vision of total cosmic and human evolution," one that

---

20. Merton, "The Universe as Epiphany," in *Love and Living*, 176. When the review was completed, Merton as usual sent it on to the censors for perusal, who, given the controversy surrounding Teilhard, passed it on to the Abbot General. In response the Abbot demanded that Merton read a critical attack on Teilhard, one penned, in Merton's words, "by a rather second rate theologian." Merton would neither read the other book nor alter his own review, and as a result his work was only published posthumously in 1979 (Merton, *The Road to Joy*, 237).

21. Merton, "The Universe as Epiphany," in *Love and Living*, 176.

22. "Evolution, Science and Religion," 48–51.

23. J. Franklin Ewing, SJ, quoted in "Evolution, Science and Religion," 51.

24. Gilligan, review of *The Phenomenon of Man*.

is quite consistent with traditional Christianity.[25] This vision is completed only by what "the doctrine of the Mystical Body of Christ" supplies.[26]

Despite these glowing comments, many Catholics insisted that Teilhard's thought was close to heretical. The controversy reached its apex on June 30, 1962 when a *monitum* was issued by the Sacred Congregation of the Holy Office of the Vatican.[27] The admonition warns that Teilhard's posthumously published works contain numerous ambiguities and errors. As a result, the Holy Office exhorted rectors of seminaries and university presidents to protect minds from the "dangers presented by the works of Father Teilhard."[28] But, as the transformation in American society gained momentum, so too did public interest increase in Teilhard; the hype surrounding the *monitum* only amplified this.

Those Catholics seeking change similarly rejoiced in January 1961, when John F. Kennedy took the presidential oath of office. He spoke of a new frontier, of the necessity of sacrifice for the good of the country, and of the strength of America. He stirred up the idealism of the young people who especially appreciated his vision, intelligence, and wit. Kennedy did not hesitate to tackle the religious issue head on, stating that he would operate as president within the parameters of separation of church and state.[29] Although Kennedy won the election by the slimmest of margins, he put to rest the notion that a Catholic could not be elected to high office. Additionally, his obvious education, poise, wealth, and admired wife were all signs, according to some, that Catholics truly had come of age and were now well integrated into American society.[30]

Teilhard's evolutionary understanding of change as intrinsic to ongoing life is easily envisioned as foundational to "Americanism." At this time of the two "Johns," the other being Pope John XXIII, American Catholics found the "shining city on the hill" image of the earlier Americanist controversy

25. Ibid.

26. Ibid.

27. Sacred Congregation of the Holy Office, *Warning Considering the Writings of Father Teilhard de Chardin*. This *monitum* was recently addressed in an article in the December 28, 2013 issue of the Italian edition of *L'Osservatore Romano* which eulogized Teilhard and his thought. See "Studio la materia e trovo lo spirito: Nel pensiero di Pierre Teilhard de Chardin."

28. Sacred Congregation of the Holy Office, *Warning Considering the Writings of Father Teilhard de Chardin*.

29. Kennedy's Address to the Houston Ministerial Association in Houston, Texas in September 1960 can be found in Avella and McKeown, *Public Voices*, 361–64.

30. Dolan, *The American Catholic Experience*, 422.

again quite apt.[31] The understanding of at least some United States Catholics that they had been given a special mission to point American society toward Christ and the church arose again now. After all, the Kennedy administration reaffirmed the American sense of possibility, progress, and promise implicit in the Americanist assumptions.[32] Still, in an era when a new historical consciousness was rocking the church and the nation, this awareness was both vital and threatening.[33] Then suddenly Kennedy was dead; the country's hope for the future was severely shaken. Perhaps even more than his election, Kennedy's assassination in 1963 was a decisive watershed for many.[34] This event was just the first in a series that would ravage, at least for a while, Americanist optimism about historic destiny.

31. Thanks to William Portier for the suggestion to examine the ties between Americanism and Teilhard's reception, as well as the comment that, in many ways, Teilhard's reception in America is the reversal of Isaac Hecker's reception in France. Teilhard was a firm believer in progress and evolution, yet in a resolutely Christian manner, similar to that of the Americanists of the late-nineteenth century. One might recall the writings of Walter Elliott, friend and disciple of Isaac Hecker, himself founder of the Paulists, who consistently claimed Christ as the culmination of the providential workings of history. Christ's activity was centered not above and beyond time, but in, through, and at the final end of it. The links that Elliott made between creation, humanism, and the unifying aspects of Christ's love was common among the Americanists. For a more thorough look at Americanism see Reher, "Phantom Heresy." The "two Johns" reference is from Garry Wills, *Bare Ruined Choirs*, 79–100.

32. Lytle, *America's Uncivil Wars*, 139. The Americanist assumptions referenced here were that the world is in an era of radical change, that America is at the cutting edge of change, and that America is indeed the very embodiment of the future. Additionally, the Catholic Church is obliged to change with the times; and the Catholic Church in America has been given a divine mission to point American society toward Christ and the church. See Russell Shaw, "Americanism: Then and Now." As an example of Teilhard's influence upon the Kennedys, consider that Robert McNamara was recruited as Secretary of Defense by John F. Kennedy's brother-in-law, Sargent Shriver. Although he initially had his doubts about McNamara, then newly hired chair of Ford Motor, when Shriver heard that McNamara was reading Teilhard's *Phenomenon*, he exclaimed: "How many other automobile executives or cabinet members read Teilhard de Chardin?" McNamara had the job (Stossel, *Sarge*, 183). Shriver and McNamara found Teilhard's thought so amenable to Kennedy's "Camelot" politics that they later put Teilhard's name on a list of most-valued authors for the administration. See Wills, *Bare Ruined Choirs*, 98. In recognition of the ready reception of Teilhard's thought by the Kennedy administration Wills notes later in his book that "This strange priest in the French army [Teilhard] was preparing the rationale for a weird American optimism, voiced . . . a decade after Teilhard's own death. He became the posthumous theologian to Camelot" (117). Wills's purpose in writing on Teilhard was certainly not to justify his thought, but instead to note his proclivity to the Kennedy administration, the Americanists, and the Vatican-II era.

33. An excellent study of this is found in Lonergan, "The Transition from a Classicist World-View to Historical Mindedness."

34. Ellwood, *The Sixties Spiritual Awakening*, 102. See also Jenkins, *Decades of*

For many, the dominant religious figure in the world at this time was Pope John XXIII. His calls for *aggiornamento,* or updating, the life of the Catholic Church caused rejoicing; suddenly the emphasis became love over legalism, grace over gravity.[35] Hopes were high that the Second Vatican Council would bring a new manner of the church's presence in the world, something more than "the dead inertia of merely conventional Christianity" against which Teilhard protested.[36] It is no surprise that Teilhard, who had eagerly pursued the integration of modern science with Catholicism, the secular with the sacred, and who had especially intended his book *The Divine Milieu* for modern people who "loved the world," would be caught up in this Catholic revolution.

Indeed, some would claim that Vatican II was the "vindication of Teilhard" and that he was "its absent but presiding genius," for they believed it was he who made this kind of progressive worldview unavoidable for those of intelligence within the Catholic Church.[37] Teilhard's evolutionary consciousness and unifying, optimistic vision are qualities that several commentators on the Council point to as his greatest impact. His contribution to the Council primarily appeared to occur through the efforts of his own great Jesuit friend and supporter, Father Henri de Lubac.[38]

Nightmares.

35. Ellwood, *The Sixties Spiritual Awakening,* 66.

36. Merton, "Teilhard's Gamble," in *Love and Living,* 185.

37. Wills, *Bare Ruined Choirs,* 99. On this topic see also Donovan, "Was Vatican II Evolutionary?," 493–502. Donovan notes, "Protestant and Catholic alike have commented on [Teilhard's] influence at the Council" (494). He argues that, although Teilhard's name was never explicitly mentioned in the conciliar documents or the official proceedings, it was well known how *Gaudium et spes* was shaped by theologians from the University of Louvain, as well as the French bishops and *periti* who were especially familiar with Teilhard's work (494). Henri de Lubac later agreed, with some reservations, that Teilhard's impact amounted to "a certain influence, at least indirect and diffuse, on some orientations of the Council" (496). Cyril Vollert has no reservations in asserting that Teilhard's influence was immense and significant. Vollert includes a quote here from Paul VI: "Teilhard is an indispensable man for our times: his expression of the faith is necessary for us" (Vollert, "Teilhard in the Light of Vatican II," 147).

38. In the years surrounding Vatican II de Lubac intervened on Teilhard's behalf numerous times, providing both written and verbal explications of his works at various gatherings. See especially de Lubac, *Theology in History,* 505–40, 565–66. In particular, *Gaudium et spes* expressed "precisely what Père Teilhard sought to do" (quoted in Haught, "More Being," 17). In an article written in 1968, de Lubac extensively examined issues concerning the "goodness of the world," the separation between the natural and supernatural, and the Christian vocation in the world, quoting Teilhard several times in his explanation of how the Christian anthropology of *Gaudium et spes* evolved. Already at this time, only a few years after the closing of the Council, however, de Lubac expressed his concerns that the Christological heart of *Gaudium et spes* was being

The Years of Hope, 1965–1967

The mid-1960s were the years of secular theology, countercultural movements, serious dissatisfactions with traditional religious expressions, and widespread questioning of long-accepted views on the university, the state, and societal expectations.[39] These were also the years during which Teilhard exploded onto the American scene. In this timeframe immediately following Vatican II, interest in his thought, and publications concerning it, was at its peak.

Table 1. Published manuscripts about Teilhard worldwide, 1959–1972

Year	Number of Books
1959	47
1960	77
1961	50
1962	108
1963	153
1964	265
1965	250
1966	245
1967	399
1968	202
1969	150
1970	136
1971	109
1972	94

Dall'Olio, "Teilhard de Chardin: Thinker Wedded to Wisdom," 82.

---

subsumed within a secularism concerned solely with the urgent problems of the world and with human progress. See de Lubac, "The Total Meaning of Man and the World," cited in Portier, "What Kind of a World of Grace," 145–48.

39. See, for example, Ahlstrom, "The Radical Turn in Theology and Ethics," 1.

Yet it is also at this point, at the height of his popularity, that a reductive interpretation of Teilhard's thought and the Christology that underpinned it begins to regularly appear. During this period much of American society was transfixed by the possibilities inherent in the Civil Rights Act, in new forms of interpersonal relationships and sexual mores, in the spiritual effects of psychedelic drugs, and in a church opening to the world. The counterculture was rising, and the counterculture adored Teilhard, but at the same time it often chose to ignore his Christocentric focus.

Consider the Civil Rights movement, certainly a sign of progress and unity as it introduced nonviolent resistance to new populations in the nation and emphasized the importance of community. By the sixties, civil rights became imperative for many who saw the years of nonviolent sit-ins and the Freedom Rides of 1960–1961, the March on Washington under Martin Luther King Jr., the Civil Rights Act, and the Voting Rights Act as its greatest glories. As the Civil Rights movement grew, what became clear was the necessity of building and holding together a community of activists if any hope of lasting progress was to be had.[40] The movement speaks to several Teilhardian themes, particularly building the earth and the unification of peoples. Teilhard very much discerned that it was the work of all people, even those far beyond the Catholic Church, to create progress in the world, prioritizing a deep appreciation of the dignity of every person and the unity of all the races.[41]

Teilhard had also written, however, that a generalized desire for progress and unity, for movement toward convergence, is not in itself sufficient. Instead, what is needed is to develop a relationship with others in terms of Christ, the heart of the universe.[42] This center of the universe, this Omega Point, also implies for Teilhard that in loving Christ we love those with whom we live and strive. In working to build the earth and to progress, the Christian then sees "that he can love by his activity, in other words he can be directly united to the divine center and to others by his every action, no matter what form it might take."[43] Without that center, convergence and love cannot survive. One wonders how many of those Americans reading Teilhard while striving at the time for racial equality, or in antiwar

40. Ellwood, *The Sixties Spiritual Awakening*, 80.

41. See, for example, Teilhard, *Human Energy*, 137: "Socially the mingling and melting of races are directly leading to the establishment of an equally common form . . . of morality and ideology. . . . [T]he community of interest and struggle for common objectives is *ipso facto* accompanied by a comradeship in battle, the natural prototype of *love* or *sense of human dignity* exemplified in the Incarnation."

42. Teilhard, *Science and Christ*, 68.

43. Ibid., 170.

protests, understood this about his thought. In any case, the race riots that occurred later in the decade rapidly decelerated the pace of the Civil Rights movement. The unity that had existed around the issue deteriorated in the midst of the violence, and never fully recovered. At least in part, however, the cessation of activism in this area occurred because energies aroused by civil rights were shifting instead toward the Vietnam War situation.[44] An antiwar protest movement developed concurrently in the U.S., consisting of student protesters, countercultural hippies, and concerned middle-class people. The movement gained national prominence in 1965, peaked in 1968, and remained powerful throughout the duration of the conflict.

Both the Civil Rights and the antiwar protest movements contributed to the growth of the counterculture; however, the counterculture was also a phenomenon that simultaneously developed and existed on its own. From about 1965 onward a variety of esoteric religious ideas began to reach a much wider audience, cutting across the traditional religious communities, including Catholicism. Sociologists saw a strong correlation between counterculture involvement and a rejection of Christianity.[45] The counterculture included the nonreligious and "mystics" interested in astrology, extrasensory perception, and Native American religions. Countercultural spirituality emphasized the need for personal exploration, highlighting the subjective, the emotions, and the intuition rather than rational argument or traditional devotions.

The mystical, ecumenical qualities of Teilhard's thought were quite appealing to those in the counterculture.[46] For those seeking union not only with each other, but with the cosmos, someone who wrote of his own mystical experiences was alluring. In addition, those who advocated love for all would have been quick to embrace someone like Teilhard who spoke of love as the ultimate force of life. Consider, though, that for Teilhard, "love" was

44. In 1962, President Kennedy sent American "military advisors" to Vietnam to help train the South Vietnamese army. A year later a U.S.-backed coup overthrew the government. Kennedy's successor, Lyndon B. Johnson, pledged to honor Kennedy's commitments, but hoped to keep U.S. involvement in Vietnam to a minimum. However, after the Gulf of Tonkin incident in 1964, Johnson began to send U.S. troops to Vietnam. Within a week of Martin Luther King Jr.'s initial protests in Selma, Alabama, and only a month after President Johnson's "Great Society" State of the Union speech in January, 1965, the war in Vietnam suddenly escalated with the regular bombing of North Vietnam by the United States—Operation "Rolling Thunder." By the end of 1966, Johnson's "Americanization" of the war led to a presence of nearly 400,000 U.S. troops in Vietnam.

45. McLeod, *The Religious Crisis of the 1960s*, 134.

46. In another fifteen years their practices would be labeled "New Age," and some would place Teilhard in their midst. See, for example, Lane, *The Phenomenon of Teilhard*.

first found in a love of Christ. Repeatedly he noted that "it is impossible to love Christ without loving others. . . . [I]t is impossible to love others without moving nearer to Christ."[47] It would seem, then, that those in the counterculture who rejected Christ, Christianity, and the church were also rejecting Teilhard, even as they supposedly embraced his work. In addition, at least in Teilhard's view, they were rejecting the very community of love they claimed they most desired.

Harvey Cox's *The Secular City* was another indicator of the national mood during this timeframe. His comment, "Man, seen as the steersman of the cosmos, is the only starting point we have for a viable doctrine of God," strongly parallels Teilhard's own conviction that humanity is the apex of God's creation.[48] With his incarnational center, however, Teilhard never loses sight of Christ as the focal point for all the created world, a thought that does not appear so readily in Cox's work. Still, scholars noted the correspondences between Teilhard's work and some aspects of *The Secular City* and similar offerings focused on the growing secular world. This was a theological topic that "grew legs," so to speak, giving momentum and agency to the ongoing efforts of those actively involved in the various social and racial justice movements of the time.[49]

Cox, in particular, discusses how religion, especially Christianity, has encouraged a secular response to change throughout the ages. Teilhard is one who has especially plumbed these ideas, Cox argues, calling him one of the most important teachers of the future because of his emphasis on "man as 'that point where the cosmos begins to think and to steer itself.'"[50] What Cox discerns as key is his understanding of humans as "creatures who can hope."[51] As Cox recognizes, hope is certainly essential to Teilhard's discussion of transcendence. Cox believes that for Teilhard, hope is, at least in part, discovered in humanity's growing capacity to apply science in the shaping of that future; the future then becomes not just that for which humankind is responsible, but that for which we now *know* we are responsible.

47. Teilhard, *Divine Milieu*, 125.

48. Cox, *The Secular City*, 199.

49. On those writing in the manner of Cox, see Niebuhr, *Radical Monotheism and Western Culture*, and Vahanian, *The Death of God*. On those using Teilhard in parallel, see Faricy, *Teilhard de Chardin's Theology of the Christian in the World*; Martin, *The Spirituality of Teilhard de Chardin*; and Hefner, *The Promise of Teilhard*.

50. Wills, *Bare Ruined Choirs*, 98. In the afterword to *The Secular City Debate*, Cox refers to Teilhard as a "pariah" whose efforts to transcend metaphysical dualism with a secular theology, or more than that a Christian cosmology, are poetic and only accidentally scientific. This is a cosmology, Cox notes, that is "the first in some time to truly engage the imagination of modern man" (Cox, "Afterword," 197).

51. Cox, "Afterword," 198.

Donald Gray reaffirms that Teilhard's spirituality is decidedly secular in that it is directed to finding God in and through the "evolving world" and in "building the earth."[52] According to Gray, no dichotomizing tendency between sacred and secular exists for Teilhard. The future of the world is humanity's responsibility; left solely to scientific evolution, the world would devolve into chaos and multiplicity from what order and unity presently exists.

Gray believes, however, that Teilhard's hope becomes for him a way of seeing. Teilhard, he argues, is writing against pessimists, those overly individualistic Christians unwilling to build the earth, as well as humanists whose hope ceases at instances of death and suffering.[53] Gray contends that, for Teilhard, neither our present Christianity nor secular humanism focused on science is sufficiently optimistic; instead, true optimists draw their sustenance from a hope that embraces all of cosmic evolution, matter and spirit, nature and grace, through the power of the Paschal Mystery and especially the Resurrection of Christ. This is an explanation of Teilhard's hope that those who later shunned him for too facile an optimism would have done well to make note of. His optimism was not one rooted solely in humanitarian activism in the world. Teilhard's "optimism" was, instead, a hopeful understanding that all of humanity, all the matter of the world, all the effort expended on a daily basis, and all our own suffering is redeemed through the power of the Paschal Mystery. We have no reason, therefore, not to hope. Whereas for Cox hope can be found in the secular world of science and technology, driven by humankind's innate capacity for further knowledge, for Teilhard hope is found in Christ.

The Bitter Year of 1968

Of course, 1967 was not yet the end of the sixties, and the popular optimism of this time would not last. In the difficult years yet to come, the accusations that Teilhard was merely a facile optimist who neglected to account for the inevitability of human failing would increase. How was it, though, that just when it was so very much needed, so many of those he inspired failed to catch the importance of his cosmic Christology?

Robert Ellwood contends that 1968–1970 were bitter years in the United States, as many desired social and cultural changes did not occur. Instead, society found itself further polarized by war, assassinations, riots,

52. Gray, "The Phenomenon of Teilhard." Gray writes that "Teilhard hopes in order to understand" (48).

53. Ibid., 49.

and overall violence. The murders of Dr. Martin Luther King and Robert Kennedy in 1968 obliterated the budding promise of reconciliation and hope for many young activists.[54] By mid-1968 the Vietnam War, and particularly the aftereffects of the Tet offensive, would also destroy President Johnson and his administration. Voices of protest would become even louder and yet more violent over the next few years.[55] Robert Kennedy's assassination only two months after King's reemphasized the shift in the social, cultural, and political wind of the 1960s, as well as in the reception of Teilhard. Along with his older brother John and Dr. King, Robert Kennedy exemplified progress toward racial and economic justice. With his violent death not only did the age of Camelot come to an end, but in a sense so too did the era of Teilhard, the "theologian" of that age.[56]

A comment Edward Kennedy made during the eulogy he gave for his brother very much personified not only Bobby Kennedy, but the Camelot years in general: "As he said many times, to those he touched and who sought to touch him: 'Some men see things as they are, and say why. I dream things that never were and say why not.'"[57] Additionally, several commented that Robert Kennedy's greatest asset was his capacity for growth, for "he was always in the process of becoming."[58] Both of these statements are quite Teilhardian in nature. For those who turned to Teilhard in these times of sorrow, the answer discerned was that, in the end, the question of why evil happens must be transmuted into some very different questions. It is no longer important to know why something happened, but to ask, now that it has, how we plan to respond.[59]

For many at that time, the response was the defeat of hope. The counterculture, founded on the budding optimism of the mid-1960s, lost its sheen.[60] Particularly after the deaths discussed above, the patience that originally existed for Dr. King's path of nonviolence, with its associated 'teach-ins,' was growing thin not only among mainstream youth, and giving way to the methods of the increasingly radical Black Panthers. It appeared that, rather than working in harmony with others toward the evolution of the world, some were determined to force an evolutionary path of their own

54. Lytle, *America's Uncivil Wars*, 256.

55. Ibid., 269.

56. See Murphy, "'A Time of Shame and Sorrow,'" 402.

57. The quote is a paraphrase of a line spoken by the devil (The Serpent) to Eve in George Bernard Shaw's *Back to Methuselah*, written during the years 1918–1920.

58. O'Neill, *Coming Apart*, 374.

59. Teilhard, *Divine Milieu*, 83–86.

60. See Ellwood, *The Sixties Spiritual Awakening*, 249–325.

choosing.[61] For Teilhard and those who fully understood his vision, the unity the counterculture supposedly craved was not only necessary, but was also possible only through participation in the Paschal Mystery of Christ, and hence also inherently involved suffering.

Mid-1960s theology, as exemplified in Harvey Cox' *Secular City*, had expressed an increasing interest in the secular, as did the documents of Vatican II. The waning years of the decade, however, exemplified the concerns that an ongoing cheerful secularism rooted in the Incarnation and God's immanence was improbable.[62] These were years in which there simply was less about which to be jovial. The last months of 1968 saw poverty declining as real income went up; so, too, did educational levels, as the work force shifted toward skilled or white-collar occupations. Still, many blacks felt cheated by the supposed wars on poverty, as their own lives did not reflect much growth. Additionally, for the first time on a large scale, environmental preservation became a priority. The unity that had seemed such a sure thing in 1963 was not coalescing. Convergence appeared to be dead and many wondered why. Surely those who had given their lives to the work of social progress could expect to see movement in a positive direction by now? From the viewpoint of Teilhard's evolutionary Christology, though, the roadblocks were temporary; what was needed was simply ongoing faith and perseverance.

Instead, society further turned against both secularism and institutional churches during these years. The Catholic Church Teilhard loved, that which he believed would lead the world's populations through Christification, was in upheaval. The promulgation of *Humanae Vitae* tore the U.S. Catholic Church apart, as for the first time many adult Catholics turned their backs on church teaching. No wonder so many found it difficult to believe convergence toward Omega would happen through the church. "Seekers"—those searching for their spiritual path—had been born. Rather than the previous emphasis on orthodoxy and orthopraxy, the emphasis now was on the right and duty of all to follow their own "path," which many did— right out of the church. The need for personal exploration was consistent with the societal stress on individual freedom.[63] This subjective spirituality

---

61. One could claim that, unfortunately, they did not truly perceive, as did Teilhard, that "driven by the forces of love, the fragments of the world seek each other so that the world may come into being. Love alone is capable of uniting living beings in such a way as to complete and fulfill them, for it alone takes them and joins them by what is deepest in themselves" (Teilhard, *The Phenomenon of Man,* 264).

62. O'Neill, *Coming Apart,* 314–15.

63. See, for example, Roof, *A Generation of Seekers.*

highlighted experience rather than doctrine, feeling and intuition rather than rational argument or tradition.

Nothing was working anymore. Concomitantly, for many these were the years in which doubt about the optimistic Teilhardian vision grew stronger; after reaching their pinnacle in 1967, the numbers of Teilhardian books published dropped by almost half in 1968, and then continued to fall.[64] The movement toward progress and unity which Teilhard saw as inevitable appeared increasingly elusive. Yet all too often, rather than the patient, persevering faith rooted in a deep relationship with Christ which Teilhard himself exemplified, for U.S. Catholics and non-Christians both, what dominated was an expectation of progress centered on the efforts of humanity itself. This was a progress certain to be waylaid, if not destroyed, by the political and cultural upheavals currently taking place. For Teilhard's brand of evolutionary progress to occur, willingness for a personal, as well as societal, Christ-focused transformation was critical. As he wrote in 1946: "Faith in humankind does not appear capable of being satisfied without a fully explicit Christ. . . . Any other method would only lead to confusion or to syncretism without any vigour or originality."[65]

It became obvious during this time that the mystical Christology that grounded Teilhard and strengthened his perseverance and fortitude did not do the same for everyone. Most likely many of the sixties radicals and flower children would argue that they did indeed wish to see as Teilhard did. However, Teilhard's sight was focused on Christ and his Paschal Mystery. Everything in his life, including his mystical experiences and his scientific work, pointed toward and was derived from seeing the diaphany of Christ in the world, and in living that Mystery.[66] They, however, whether Catholic or not, did not appear to understand this vision, nor had the desire to do so.

Conclusion

This essay explored the reception of Teilhard's Christological vision in the United States between the years of 1959 and 1968. The primary argument of this work is that this reception occurred as it did because of the confluence of the then-developing social, religious, and political milieu, which included the Kennedys, the counterculture, the Second Vatican Council, the Civil

64. See Table 1.

65. Teilhard, "Ecumenism," 197–98.

66. The word "diaphany," for Teilhard, means seeing the inner presence of God behind the outer layers of the "stuff" of the everyday. See, for example, Savary, *The Divine Milieu Explained*, 218.

Rights movement, and the Vietnam War. Additionally, as these social and historical events unfolded within U.S. culture during these years, the manner in which Teilhard was read, as well as the aspects of his thought which were especially deemed of value, changed. In the end, it was an inability by many to truly understand and live his unique Christological vision at this time that led, at least for a while, to a precipitous decrease in interest in his work.

In regard to the reception of Teilhard by the end of the 1960s, an editorial in *America* in 1975, on the twentieth anniversary of Teilhard's death, noted:

> Teilhard dealt in millennia; two decades therefore seems a pitifully short time in which to judge the success of so sweeping a venture. Indeed, his falling stock in the popular marketplace of ideas over the past 10 years tells us as much about ourselves as about him. Our buoyant optimism ran aground in the sands of a war we could not win abroad and of a peace we could not keep at home. Military debacles, political assassinations, race riots, government scandals, double-digit inflation and unemployment—such have been the dolorous milestones on the journey we began so bravely with Teilhard 15 years ago. We can be excused for feeling that Point Omega looks much further away now than it did then. But a sustaining vision is still necessary.[67]

Two years later de Lubac wrote "a little book" on Teilhard in which his essential goal was to show the dissimilarity of what he calls a certain "Teilhardism" to Teilhard's actual thought. Even many of the serious authors, de Lubac believed, did not seem to grasp Teilhard's underlying synthetic Christocentric character. This foundational Christology he believed is the reason "Teilhard found scarcely any hearing anymore."[68] Instead, de Lubac argued, a "pan-critical, pulverizing mentality," an "anti-intellectualism," and excessive individualism reigned, "crushing" everything else potentially possible.[69] Teilhard was instead, de Lubac argued, "hyper-Catholic." Very few,

---

67. "The Teilhard Phenomenon after 20 Years," 2.

68. de Lubac, *At the Service of the Church*, 153. The "little book," *Teilhard Posthume: Réflexions et Souvenirs*, was published by Fayard in 1977 in France.

69. de Lubac, *At the Service of the Church*, 153. De Lubac notes that the quoted phrases are from von Balthasar, and it appears that both here refer to the critical theory of the Frankfurt School. A while after this de Lubac also wrote that, having published so many works on Teilhard explicating his work, not to mention his participation in conferences and dissertations directed on the same subject, he felt he had well contributed to the recognition that Teilhard was "a true religious and a faithful Catholic." Perhaps as a result of this, however, de Lubac lamented, people have lost interest in Teilhard. He was no longer either "a scandal or one who could easily be derided for heretical notions."

he believed, have perceived the historical importance of Teilhard's effort to create a "spiritual interpretation of universal evolution that featured the 'transcendence of man, the value of the personal being, freedom, openness to God, and most importantly, consummation in Christ.'"[70]

With the dawning of the 1970s some previously under the Teilhardian influence were undoubtedly dismayed by the havoc of the preceding few years, particularly those who had not "caught" his particular brand of persevering faith. Still, Teilhard's thought had already so become part of the foundation of Catholic religious thought and U.S. culture as a whole that it could neither be ignored nor wholesale rejected. Instead it would go underground for much of the next decade. It would yet emerge at various times in the work of politicians, artists, writers, theologians, and social theorists, yet too often remain unnamed, as if in fear that to claim a Teilhardian influence was to elicit immediate categorical rejection.[71]

Resurrection of Teilhard's thought, however, would occur repeatedly and cyclically during the next forty years up until today, as those optimistic about the future of the world were willing to take it up and reconsider it. As Pope Benedict XVI noted in a homily in 2009: "This is the great vision of Teilhard de Chardin: in the end we shall achieve a true cosmic liturgy, where the cosmos becomes a living host."[72] Although Teilhard's vision was not always well understood or appreciated in 1960s U.S. Catholicism, its impact remains substantial. His hopeful Christology still today points those who know how to "see" toward the future Christification of the universe.

70. de Lubac, *At the Service of the Church*, 110.

71. These would include, among others, the writers Flannery O'Connor, Morris West, Dan Simmons, and Annie Dillard; composer Edmund Rubbra; architect Paolo Soleri; artists Henry Setter and Frederick Hart; politician Robert Muller of the United Nations; and the first U.S. Catholic environmentalist, Thomas Berry, CP.

72. Pope Benedict XVI, "Homily for Vespers at the Cathedral of Aosta."

Part 3

Exploring
Faith and Reason
in the Body Politic

11

Revisiting the *Requerimiento*

Fealty, Unsacred Monarchy,
and Political Legitimacy

DAMIAN COSTELLO

I magine the scene: somewhere in sixteenth-century Central or South America, an Indian community conducts the work of everyday life. Suddenly, a Spanish war party bursts on the scene. They are in possession of things that you have never seen: horses, beards, swords, and armor. Despite their seemingly magical belongings, the strange-looking foreigners smell badly and are in various levels of malnutrition. But it is their first act that is the most puzzling. One Spaniard, who appears to be a leader, unfurls a document and issues a long speech in a foreign tongue, describing new gods, kings across the great water, and threats of war. Meanwhile, a translator struggles to keep up and another high-ranking member carefully records the ceremony.

This ceremony, what is known as the *Requerimiento* (henceforth the Requirement), is an iconic feature of the Spanish conquest of the Americas. It required Indian societies to recognize Castilian sovereignty, willingly serve the crown and its delegates as vassals, as well as allow the uninhibited presence of missionaries. The document begins with a genealogy of the crown's sovereignty over the Americas. God created the world and gave jurisdiction over it to St. Peter. One of St. Peter's successors "made a donation of these said islands and mainland of the Ocean Sea to the Catholic kings of Spain." The Requirement then explained the choices available to the Indian listeners and their respective consequences. On the one hand, the

a holder of land by feudal tenure on conditions of allegiance

acceptance of vassalage preserved Indian political structures without any
new forms of servitude, granted the freedom from forced conversion, and
offered the possibility of further "privileges and exemptions." Although un-
stated in the document, Indians would presumably pay the tribute inherent
in the suzerain relationship. On the other hand, the Requirement detailed
the severe consequences of rejecting allegiance to the crown. "With the
help of God we shall forcefully enter into your country and shall make war
against you in all ways and manners that we can," the Requirement reads,
"and shall subject you to the yoke and obedience of the Church and of their
highnesses; and we shall take away your goods and shall do to you all the
harm and damage that we can." According to the logic of the document, the
violence is seen not as war against a competing foreign power, but against
"vassals who do not obey and refuse to receive their lord." Thus, "the deaths
and losses which shall accrue from this are your fault, and not that of their
highnesses, or ours, or of these soldiers who come with us."[1]

Understandably, Indians often found this ceremony incomprehensible.
Yet there were even stranger readings of the document: to empty beaches, to
the trees, and to already-conquered Indians marching in slave gangs, often
without translators. Even Spaniards reacted to such incidents with disbelief.
The author of the Requirement, Juan López de Palacios Rubios, was unable
to stop laughing when he was told the above stories.[2] Bartolomé de las
Casas, called the defender of the Indians, voiced the modern reader's emo-
tion almost 500 years in the past with the lamentation that he did not know
whether to laugh or cry.[3]

Even today, the Requirement remains bizarre and often misunder-
stood by commentators. This essay will revisit the Requirement and clarify
its meaning, employment, and origin. In the first half, I will clearly define
the Requirement, explain the many and often strange ways it was employed,
and argue that the demand of the Requirement and those agents who used it
was fealty to the Castilian crown. In the second half, I will contextualize the
composition of the Requirement historically within the Castilian crown's
ongoing construction of political legitimacy. I will argue that the Requirement played an important role in deflecting theological critique of Spanish
colonial practices, and that it was one of the crown's various and sometimes
contradictory theological positions in its ongoing construction of political
legitimacy.

why a gov't has the right impose and enforce laws

1. Quoted in Seed, *Ceremonies of Possession*, 69.

2. Oviedo y Valdes, *Historia general y natural de las Indias*, 297.

3. Las Casas, *Historia de las Indias*, 31.

Definition of the Requirement and
Context of Its Application

In the first case, many modern-day readers are unfamiliar with the roots and meaning of the Requirement. Many may be surprised to learn that the name *requerimiento* was not initially a proper name but stemmed from a legal instrument of the same name, which was—and still is—a standard legal practice in Iberian law. A recent dictionary of legal terms reads "[f]or good order's sake, 'requerimiento' can be, as per the context, 'demand, summons, injunction, writ of summons, subpoena, notification.'"[4] In the early-modern era the requirement was read aloud as a public notification of legally required action and, according to historian Hugh Thomas, "[t]he procedure had a firm peninsular basis: a town council in a dispute with a lord might read aloud a 'Requirement' against a magnate in respect of a disputed boundary."[5] One such example was the requirement of Seville's *jurados* to the council of *veinticuatro* in 1454 to address crime and gangsterism.[6] Thus, the concept of the Requirement was not inherently related to military conquest but the standard manner of demanding a precise legal response in the civil judicial system.

In the case of the Requirement of lasting fame, the specific legal demand was fealty to the Castilian crown. Like any good legal procedure or treaty of the day, the Requirement was to be issued in the presence of a public notary, who recorded the proper reading of the document and the response of the Indians.

Spaniards, interestingly enough, had already employed both options in the Indies—tributary vassalage and war, with enslavement of those who rejected fealty—long before the Requirement and without crown permission. The crown originally planned to establish Portuguese-style *factorías*, or fortified trading posts, where royal employees would trade for expected high-value Asian commodities.[7] When the lack of sufficient goods became apparent, Columbus turned to two alternatives: traffic in slaves of Indians who resisted Spanish dominion and the imposition of a tribute system in

---

4. Alcaraz Varó and Hughes, *Diccionario de términos jurídicos*, "Requerimiento."

5. Thomas, *Rivers of Gold*, 301.

6. Edwards, *The Spain of the Catholic Monarchs*, 53. Even in the Indies *requerimientos* were employed for other reasons than conquest of the native peoples and lands. When Hernán Cortés paused his conquest of Mexico to battle rival Pánfilio de Narváez both leaders fired *requerimientos* at each other ordering immediate surrender. See Thomas, *Conquest*, 366, 372.

7. Deagan and Cruxent, *Columbus's Outpost among the Tainos*, 18–19.

1495.[8] In early 1497, Columbus's brother Bartolomé negotiated tributary vassalage with the largest and most developed polity in Hispaniola, Xaragua.[9] Such political arrangements were apparently readily understood even by the comparatively unstratified Taino (natives of the island of Hispaniola) as the head *cacique* (chief), Beheccio, managed to bargain down the tribute requirement from gold to foodstuffs and cotton.

Whether intended by the crown or not, conquistadors used the flexibility of the Requirement according to local conditions and their immediate concerns. Booty and slaves often better served the conquistadors' needs than tribute-paying vassals. As a result, many conquistadors preferred the rejection of fealty, and thus shaped their performance of the document accordingly, such as reading it without a translator or to empty beaches and deserted villages. Having fulfilled their part, conquistadors were now legally justified in reducing the Indians to slavery. Rodrigo de Albornoz, accountant of New Spain, described this tendency in a letter to Charles V in 1525, writing that it was not uncommon for Spaniards to reject Indian overtures for fealty and to make war instead since the Spaniards "did not wish the Indians to offer them obedience, so that they might rob them and make them slaves."[10] Perhaps it was this unexpected-yet-expedient conquistador innovation, and the resulting absurdity of reading the Requirement to trees and already-chained Indians, that caused Palacios Rubios's uncontrollable laughter.

The preceding facetious readings, however, are not inherent to the Requirement itself. There are many examples of conquistadors successfully communicating the Requirement when they deemed ongoing Indian tribute to be more desirous than booty and slaves, especially as conquistadors encountered larger, more-developed societies starting in the 1520s. According to Robert Chamberlain, at the founding of Merida in the Yucatan, the Spanish leader Francisco de Montejo summoned the surrounding Maya lords to "accept the dominion of the sovereign of Castile and acknowledge Christianity." Chamberlain explains that "the caciques of at least the greater part of Canpech seem to have given fealty on this first summons. At about the same time, a number of caciques of the province of Ah Canul, just north of Canpech, also gave allegiance in the same peaceful manner. Montejo had, therefore, no immediate need to resort to warfare."[11] In a later expedition, a

---

8. He also saw Indian slaves as the most valuable commodity available in Hispaniola. See Wilson, *Hispaniola*, 90–95.

9. Ibid., 125.

10. From Simpson, *The Encomienda in New Spain*, 208. Vasco de Quiroga made the same argument. See Rivera Pagán, *A Violent Evangelism*, 37.

11. Chamberlain, *The Conquest and Colonization of Yucatan*, 97–98.

Mayan lord responded to the same demand to accept Spanish lordship with the threat of war, saying that the Maya would give tribute of "fowls in the form of their lances and maize in the form of their arrows."[12] Likewise, Aztec emissaries offered to become tributary vassals of Castile even before Hernán Cortés arrived in Tenochtitlan, an offer that was later formalized during the uneasy Spanish occupation.[13] Upon hearing of the fall of Tenochtitlan several other groups sent emissaries to offer fealty to the new imperial power.[14]

Indian understanding of the Requirement's demand for fealty should not be surprising as analogous political relationships of tributary vassalage existed in much of pre-contact Central and South America.[15] But the fact that Indians generally understood the demand for allegiance to the Castilian crown did not mean that the Requirement was entirely intelligible, even when Spaniards sincerely attempted to communicate its content. The first section of the Requirement justified Castilian lordship by papal donation, explaining that one eternal God created heaven and earth and the first man and woman. All peoples came from this couple in the 5,000 years since their creation. God gave St. Peter dominion over all peoples, who obeyed him as Lord, King, and Superior of the universe. In turn, a recent heir to St. Peter's throne gave jurisdiction over the Americas to the Spanish crown.

It was precisely this theological defense of Castilian lordship—and not the demand for fealty—which seemed to have mystified Indian hearers. One Indian said he understood the political demands of the document, but as for the pope, he must have been drunk when he made the donation, and that his people had no need of a new lord.[16] One version of the infamous events at Cajamarca, where approximately 167 Spaniards massacred thousands of unarmed Incan soldiers in a surprise attack, recorded the Inca emperor Atahualpa apparently misunderstanding the Requirement's theology, thinking that the Christians believed in four gods and also demanded conversion. But he clearly understood the demand for submission, responding "I will be no man's tributary. I am greater than any prince upon earth."[17]

fealty = allegiance to another.

12. Ibid., 102.

13. Thomas, *Rivers of Gold*, 273, 322–25.

14. Sherman, *Forced Native Labor in Sixteenth-Century Central America*, 21.

15. See Chamberlain, *The Pre-Conquest Tribute and Service System of the Maya*.

16. See Rivera Pagán, *A Violent Evangelism*, 36.

17. Prescott, *History of the Conquest of Peru*, 115–16. There is some question whether the Requirement was read at Cajamarca or merely a speech summarizing its essential points. While of historical value, this question is irrelevant for this essay as the conquistadors succeeded in making the essential point of the document. See Restall, *Seven Myths of the Spanish Conquest*, 95.

While many modern commentators interpret the Requirement as if it declares "convert or die," it actually had nothing directly to do with conversion.[18] The only time the document refers to conversion is to reassure the hearer that conversion, unlike the demand for fealty, will be optional. The Requirement was not, as Silvio Zavala points out, a call to conversion but to fealty, a point reflected by the new name given to the document in 1573, "Instrument of Obedience and Vassalage."[19] Optional conversion in the context of forced vassalage was nothing new in Iberian practice, perhaps best illustrated by the various capitulations made between the crown and Muslim kingdoms in Iberia. The capitulation of 1491 between the Catholic Monarchs and Granada contained sixty-seven articles that included numerous provisions for the toleration of Islam and Islamic law, including the article that no Christian that embraced Islam should be compelled to return to Christianity.[20]

Not only was conversion subordinate [*lower in rank*] to political allegiance in the text of the Requirement, it was also subordinate in conquistador practice. During the conquest of Mexico, a priest restrained Cortés from pushing acceptance of Catholicism, telling him not to make Christians by force, a practice that repeated itself throughout the course of Spanish colonialism.[21] The only consistent pressure to convert that conquistadors applied was on Indian women taken as concubines [*mistresses*], and even this was not a universal practice.[22] Conquistadors routinely executed Indians, but like the many Spanish executed by conquistadors, Indians were put to death either for rebellion or to extort wealth. While a second wave of missionaries would make conversion a priority in imperial administration, John E. Kicza categorically states that the "zeal to convert did not drive Spain's expansion across the Atlantic."[23]

The subordinate importance, or even irrelevance, of conversion to the Requirement should be seen in light of numerous examples of Indians and

18. For a good example of this reading, James J. Miller writes that the Requirement "ordered all Indians who encountered a Spanish expedition to agree to become Christian or else be killed or enslaved" (Miller, *An Environmental History of Northeast Florida*, 90).

19. Seed, *Ceremonies of Possession*, 95.

20. Gibson, "Conquest, Capitulation, and Indian Treaties," 6. Later policy decisions produced the order of conversion or expulsion from Spain.

21. Thomas, *Conquest*, 24.

22. Cortés had the women given to this expedition by a vassal cacique baptized. Rodrigo Rangel, a member of the De Soto expedition to Florida and Mississippi Valley (1539–1540), observed that expedition members took women for service and "their lewdness and lust," baptizing them "more for their carnal intercourse than to instruct them in the faith" (Socolow, *The Women of Colonial Latin America*, 33).

23. Kicza, "Patterns In Early Spanish Overseas Expansion," 250.

Africans who continued to practice Catholicism while rejecting Castilian lordship. The Taino cacique Enrique maintained a fifteen-year rebellion while remaining a practicing Catholic, reportedly saying the rosary while he guarded his camp at night and requesting a church bell, religious images, and a Franciscan priest to conduct religious duties during negotiations with colonial authorities.[24] There are numerous African parallels, including the Cimarron community in Central Mexico, led by fugitive slave Yanga, which maintained its own chapel, and in peace negotiations included the demand that only Franciscans minister to their community.[25] Needless to say, neither the crown nor the colonial elite found Indian or African political independence acceptable, despite the rebels' Christian practice.

Reduced to its essence, then, the Requirement was a legal demand for submission to the Castilian crown with the option of tributary vassalage or armed conflict with slave status for the defeated. Why then, one may ask, was the Requirement composed? The demand for fealty had already been successfully employed from early Spanish colonial presence in the Americas. Why formalize a relatively simple, easily translatable demand into a long, convoluted ceremony?

Part of the answer is that there is a long tradition, in both Western and non-Western contexts, of ceremonial demands for fealty. Indeed, modern readers may imagine the Requirement to be primarily the product of a fanatical crusading violence unique to Iberia. Yet similar dramatic demands and symbolic declarations of wars fill the historical record.[26] The Roman Empire, to which Spanish colonial apologists appealed, proclaimed grievances and declared war through heralds and symbolic acts. Yvon Garlan describes one such practice recorded by the Roman historian Livy. First, an ambassador bound his head in a woolen fillet and journeyed to the rival nation. On the frontier, the ambassador proclaimed, "'Hear O Jupiter! Hear, ye confines,' naming the particular nation whose they are, 'Hear O Justice! I am public herald of the Roman people. Rightly and duly authorised do I come; let confidence be placed in my words.'" The ambassador then recited Rome's demands and called the god Jupiter as witness: "If I am demanding the surrender of those men or those goods contrary to justice and religion, suffer me never more to enjoy my native land." He crossed the frontier and repeated his declaration to the first person he met, as he entered the gates, and then as he entered the forum. If, after thirty-three days, the demand

24. See Altman, "The Revolt of Enriquillo and the Historiography of Early Spanish America."

25. See Davidson, "Negro Slave Control and Resistance in Colonial Mexico, 1519–1650," 94–97.

26. Seed, *Ceremonies of Possession*, 181–85.

is refused, the ambassador declares war: "'Hear, O Jupiter, and thou, Janus Quirinus, and all ye heavenly gods, and ye gods of earth and the lower world, hear me! I call you to witness that this people'—mentioning it by name—'is unjust and does not fulfill its sacred obligations.'"[27] After the ambassador returned to Rome and confirmed the case for war with the senate, a blood-smeared spear was hurled into enemy territory with the declaration of war.

The Roman Requirement-like declaration of terms and war formed a tradition of warfare that both Christianity and Castilian culture inherited. Similar examples are found outside of Western tradition, including tribal cultures, such as the Mongol empire. An important component of Mongol imperial negotiation and expansion were practices that followed the same dynamics of the Requirement. During their three-year campaign in modern-day Russia and Ukraine, the Mongols "followed the same protocols in every case." In the words of Jack Weatherford, the Mongols "began the campaign in each territory by sending official envoys to request the capital city to surrender, join the Mongol family, and become vassals of the Great Kahn." In return for becoming vassals of the Mongols, "the envoy offered protection to the new vassals from their enemies and allowed them to keep their ruling family and religion. In return for such protections, the people had to agree to commit tribute of 10 percent of all wealth and goods to the Mongols."[28] Like the Requirement, the Mongols viewed the rejection of their offer of fealty as rebellion and responded with total war.[29]

That the Spanish crown made the demand for fealty into a standardized ceremony is not strange. That it transformed a simple ultimatum into a long, convoluted theological argument is. After all, it was precisely the religious language that confused Atahualpa and other Indian leaders. In the next section, I will argue that the theological argument of the Requirement—papal donation of the Indies to Castile—was an important technique in the crown's ongoing construction of legitimacy. The evidence will show, perhaps counterintuitively, that the Requirement was written not for Indians, but for Spaniards.[30]

27. Quoted in Garlan, *War in the Ancient World*, 49.

28. Weatherford, *Genghis Khan and the Making of the Modern World*, 49. See also Voegelin, "The Mongol Orders of Submission to European Powers."

29. Hartog, *Genghis Khan*, 146.

30. For an examination of this possibility from a linguistic perspective see Faudree, "How to Say Things with Wars."

Origins of the Requirement: Unsacred Monarchy

At first glance, those familiar with Castilian history should be, like the Indians, confused by the Requirement's theological argument. Castilian monarchs were uncomfortable with the principle behind papal donation, namely, that royal legitimacy was related to the church. In fact, for centuries Castilian monarchs emphasized the crown's independence from any ecclesial authority, a characteristic that historian Teofilo F. Ruiz refers to as "unsacred monarchy." Unlike other European monarchs, Castilians consciously rejected most of the religious trappings of royal power.[31] The few coronation ceremonies that monarchs conducted in Castile embodied this royal claim. According to Ruiz, King Alfonso XI intentionally minimized the role of the ecclesiastics in his coronation ceremony of 1332. After being knighted by a mechanical arm of a statue of St. James, Alfonso deliberately crowned himself in the presence of the nobility and high clergy. Such liturgies, according to Ruiz, boldly underscored their claim that royal power "was not mediated by the Church or its representatives."[32]

While not dependent on the church for its power, the crown did not reject religious authority. The famous medieval codification of Castilian law, the *Siete Partidas*, proclaimed that kings are "vicars of God" that are "put upon the earth in place of God to render justice and to give each one his right."[33] In this statement we see a claim to unmediated—and thus unquestionable—divine sanction of royal legitimacy. In this Castilian version of divine right, religious symbolism and discourse became a means of reinforcing and extending royal power. As a part of the self-coronation described above, Alfonso knighted the great nobles in the cathedral, who in turn knighted the members of their warrior bands. The ritual chain from monarch to noble to knight, according to Carlos Estepa, was designed to renew the nobility's loyalty to the crown and "secur[e] their recognition of the king as their 'natural lord.'"[34]

"Natural lord" (*señor natural*), a term used by Castilian temporal elites to refer to themselves, was the keystone of royal ideology. Its sources are

31. Ruiz, "Unsacred Monarchy," 110.

32. Ruiz, *From Heaven to Earth*, 135. The unsacred character of the Castilian monarchy was demonstrated by the "martial and secular" symbols and ceremonies which marked their authority: popular acclamation, the German tribal tradition of raising the monarch on a shield or chair, and the exchange of oaths between the sovereign and representatives of the nobility, clergy, and towns.

33. Composed under Alfonso X in 1265. Quoted in O'Callaghan, *A History of Medieval Spain*, 430.

34. Estepa, "The Strengthening of Royal Power in Castile under Alfonso XI," 197.

multiple—Castilian political philosophy, Roman and Germanic law, biblical and theological texts, feudal practice—but its meaning is singular: nature itself made the sovereign. The natural lord ruled "by inherent nature of superior qualities, goodness, and virtue, and by birth of superior station."[35] By natural and divine law, subjects are bound to serve and obey their lord, and the king is to administer justice and protect his subjects, a pact usually formalized by public oath.

Thus, Castilian monarchs understood themselves ordained by the natural order, and not by the church, to hold dominion. Nor was one merely ordained by the accident of birth. In war-torn medieval and early-modern Castile, arms often created natural lords: whether through conquest, usurpation of vacant offices, or civil conflict between rival claimants to the throne. Military force was so much at the heart of legitimate dominion that "[a] monarch's ability to succeed at competitive politics—in effect, his capacity to win—was sufficient justification for his rule, both personally and as part of an ongoing institution."[36] Unsacred monarchy, in other words, justified itself primarily through the power to enforce its claims.

It would be a mistake to reduce the Castilian monarch's self-understanding and operating horizons solely to blatant Machiavellian cynicism. However, the basic core of royal unsacred ideology is clear: the monarch was established and/or maintained by force, legitimized by nature and God. While not dependent on the church for its legitimacy, the crown nevertheless utilized religious channels to strengthen its rule. This unsacred Castilian monarchy is perhaps no better illustrated than by the sovereign behind the composition of the Requirement: King Ferdinand of Aragon, eventual Regent of Castile.[37]

While Ferdinand was occupied on many fronts during his decades of rule—with a rebellious nobility, the Portuguese crown, Granada, Italy, and North Africa—it was his campaign in Navarre that best illustrates his political savvy as an unsacred monarch. Ferdinand invaded the small independent Pyrenean kingdom on July 18, 1512, with approximately 17,000 troops. Navarre was caught off guard and surrendered in only a few weeks.[38]

---

35. Chamberlain, "The Concept of the Señor Natural as Revealed by Castilian Law and Administrative Documents," 132, 130. "Relatively frequent appearance of the term in the *Siete Partidas* of Alfonso el Sabio indicates that by the mid-thirteenth century the concept was fully formed and generally comprehended" (ibid., 130).

36. Cohen, "Secular Pragmatism and the Thinking of Pere III," 25.

37. He ruled Castile with his wife, Queen Isabel, since her ascension to the throne in 1474. When she died in 1504, he had no legitimate claim to the crown. But he was fortunate; the heir was unfit to rule, and he was called back as regent in 1507.

38. Edwards, *The Spain of the Catholic Monarchs*, 289.

A year later, he secured public recognition of his rule in the *cortes* (the legislative body) of Navarre, where the representatives swore to obey and serve Ferdinand as *rey y señor natural* (king and natural lord).[39]

More important for our purposes is the much longer, two-pronged ideological conquest that accompanied the military campaign. The first prong consisted of the production of theological justification for his seizure of Navarre. On April 17, Ferdinand wrote to Pope Julius II "for a papal bull excommunicating all those in Navarre supporting France."[40] A few weeks later, on June 5, he requested a new bull to justify action against the Navarrese crown. A bull was issued three days after the invasion, on July 21. A second appeared on February 18, 1513, but according to the historian J.N. Hillgarth, "its authenticity is dubious."[41]

Regardless of the bull's authenticity, it is clear that Ferdinand was not asking for permission to pursue his campaign. Rather, he understood the utility of ideological defense of conquest, which he also pursued in his court, commissioning two apologies of the conquest. Among other things, the first apology portrayed Ferdinand as a "great Constantine."[42] The second work was authored by Juan Lopez de Palacios Rubios, who also served as the author of the Requirement. As a member of the Council of the Realm and President of the Council of the Mesta (the governing council of the large Castilian sheep-herding industry) he was sympathetic to the crown's agenda, and as a jurist he often lent his services for its defense. He produced a juridical defense of Ferdinand's "very holy, very just war" in Navarre, which depicted the conquest as the culmination of the re-unification of the Peninsula.[43] But more importantly for our purposes, Palacios Rubios rendered the conquest a holy crusade against "the allies of the impious Louis XII."[44] "The argument of Palacios Rubios boils down to establishing that the rulers of Navarre favored the schism against the pope," Silvio Zavala explains, "who in turn could punish and even depose those rulers that committed a crime against the unity of the Church; the Roman Pontiff was lord of the world in the spiritual and the temporal."[45]

Thus, Ferdinand, through the papal bulls and royally sponsored apologies, constructed a type of divine sanction for a campaign won by military

39. Fernández, *Fernándo el católico y Navarra*, 272.

40. Hillgarth, *The Spanish Kingdoms*, 567.

41. Ibid.

42. Quoted in ibid., 568.

43. Thomas, *Rivers of Gold*, 299.

44. Hillgarth, *The Spanish Kingdoms*, 568.

45. Zavala, *Las doctrinas de Palacios Rubios y Matías de Paz*, xxiii–xxiv.

force. Ferdinand embodied his ideological conquest with a second, more public prong: a royal entry into the Castilian royal city of Valladolid on January 5, 1513. According to Tess Knighton and Carmen Morte García, the event was a standard ritual of sixteenth-century Europe and one of five during his regency, all of which were designed to reestablish "royal charisma" and "intended to create an effective public image for the king at the most critical moments of the last years of his reign."[46] In particular, the entry into Valladolid was designed to quell criticism of Ferdinand's invasion of Navarre.

The details of the entry, though not given here in their entirety, portray the multifaceted techniques employed to bolster Ferdinand's image. The entry itself was modeled after the triumphs of the Roman emperors. As singers sang the newly introduced polyphonic song, Ferdinand passed under the specially constructed arches adorned with symbols from classical antiquity, Catholic tradition, and classical and Spanish heroes, such as Julius Caesar, Alexander, and El Cid. Like a coronation ceremony, Ferdinand was crowned; in this case with seven crowns, which harkened back to the Roman tradition of crowning different warriors. In an effort to publicize the event throughout Spain a description was published in a popular pamphlet.[47]

Stepping back to look at the entirety of the Navarre campaign, then, we see a multifaceted package of conquest. Ferdinand utilized military action and a simultaneous construction of legitimacy consisting of papal bulls, sponsored academic work, and public display. This pattern of Ferdinand's "unsacred monarchy"—state expansion and construction of legitimacy—is key to understanding his involvement in the Indies and interpreting the Requirement. The Requirement, much like the ideological conquest of Navarre, was an intentional part of the construction of royal legitimacy in the Americas.

Unsacred Monarchy and the Requirement

Unlike Navarre, Ferdinand inherited rather secure control of the Indies and its revenue when he returned to Castile as regent in 1507. The administrative stability allowed Ferdinand to expand his revenue stream as he entered American mining directly, reserving the best mines and grants of Indians for himself, including 10–15 percent of the Indians on the four largest islands.[48]

---

46. Knighton and García, "Ferdinand of Aragon's Entry into Valladolid in 1513," 157.

47. Ibid., 119, 136, 141, 142.

48. Floyd, *The Columbus Dynasty in the Caribbean*, 126–27. Ferdinand also

According to John Edwards, Ferdinand channeled the increased resources into more difficult European campaigns, such as Italy.[49] Ferdinand was not beyond questions of morality, commenting that the high mortality rate of the Indians enslaved from the "useless" non-gold-bearing Lucayos islands "is somewhat burdensome to our conscience" but was also "not very profitable for business."[50] Unlike other Castilian sovereigns, he promoted territorial expansion in the Indies, and as he moved into Navarre, he planned a new American campaign of unprecedented scope. After hearing that there were certain caciques in the area of modern-day Panama with "gold that grows like maize in their huts," Ferdinand renamed the colony "Castilla de Oro" and began planning a new expedition, the first financed by the crown since 1493: an armada of 23 ships and 2,000 hidalgos and veterans of Italy.[51]

In short, Ferdinand enjoyed legitimacy in the Americas which, in turn, provided important revenue and opportunities for territorial expansion. In the midst of preparing the expedition to Panama, and a little more than a year before the composition of the Requirement, the crown experienced an unexpected setback in its perceived legitimacy. A group of reforming Dominicans had established a friary in Hispaniola in 1510. Learning of the brutality of Spanish colonists and the demographic collapse of the Indian population, they issued their theological opposition during a Catholic Mass, asking "by what right do you hold these Indians in such cruel and horrible servitude? By what authority did you make unprovoked war on these people . . . ?"[52] War and servitude, it will be remembered, were the consequences of rejecting fealty to the crown detailed by the Requirement. The colonists complained to the king, reporting that the Dominicans challenged not their own behavior but the crown's authority, designed "to deprive him [the king] of the lordship and the rents he has in these parts"—in effect, an ideological revolt.[53]

Ferdinand first attempted to silence the island Dominicans' ideological revolt against the conquest and servitude which undergirded royal dominion and revenue. When this failed, Ferdinand called a *junta* to investigate the validity of the Castilian claim to the Indies. The *junta* was a gathering of scholars from the three branches of morality: civil law, canon law,

---

distributed grants of Indian laborers to absentee holders in Castile, paying off political debts accumulated during his return to power, with the added benefit of not disturbing the "seigniorial status quo in Castile" (ibid., 92).

49. Edwards, *The Spain of the Catholic Monarchs*, 287.

50. Simpson, *The Encomienda in New Spain*, 26.

51. Thomas, *Rivers of Gold*, 327, 334.

52. Parry and Keith, *The Caribbean*, 310.

53. Las Casas quoted in Anthony Pagden, *The Fall of Natural Man*, 31.

and theology. Participants gave formal speeches and, at the end, submitted a written "opinion." According to Anthony Pagden, whether they had any effect on royal policy, or were even read, is difficult to judge. "[I]t would certainly be unwise to assume . . . that they had much direct bearing on major policy decision. Their function was to legitimate, not to judge. If a junta challenged the royal will, it was usually ignored or silenced."[54]

In this particular case, the *junta* served the desired royal purpose, as all participants supported the broad contours of the colonial system. Not surprisingly, one of the participants was Palacios Rubios. Like in Navarre, he defended Ferdinand's lordship of the Indies, arguing that Indian resistance to the gospel and authority of the crown allowed Christians to declare war, and as a result the Indians will have to serve the Spaniards "as subjects their lords."[55] The *junta* resulted in a set of laws designed to improve the administration of the Indian vassals.[56] The Dominicans found this response inadequate and carried their opposition to the royal court. The Dominican opposition began a half-century-long debate over the morality of the wars in the Indies and the legitimacy of the empire, something well beyond the scope of this essay. The immediate outcome, however, is directly relevant: at Ferdinand's request, Palacios Rubios put his theological defense into the legal form of a Requirement, and the document was sent with Ferdinand's armada to Panama.

At this point, it is possible to draw a number of clear parallels between events and royal response to events in Navarre and the Indies. The papal bulls for Navarre, Palacios Rubios's defense of the conquest, and the Requirement were sought by Ferdinand and clearly designed to bolster royal legitimacy. The core argument of defense of the conquest of Navarre and the Requirement—the authority of the pope to depose temporal sovereigns and grant their territory to the Castilian crown—needs little analysis; it is sufficient to note that the conquered rulers in one case were Christian and in the other were not.

It is the public delivery of the Requirement and its similarity to other royal liturgies that need a bit more explication. Like Alfonso's coronation, the Requirement appeals to religious justification for its dominion. Yet there is no actual ecclesial agency. The Requirement conjures the pope to support the royal claim, yet does not allow him to arbitrate the Dominican argument against war and servitude or revoke Castilian dominion. The pope's voice becomes much like the arm of the mechanical St. James, authorizing

54. Ibid., 28.
55. Quoted in Gutiérrez, *Las Casas*, 283.
56. Pagden, *The Fall of Natural Man*, 28.

the designs of the crown. The ceremony—its legal trappings, its official recitation regardless of translation, and the careful notation of the royal notary—reproduces the royal presence in a similar, if less-extensive manner as Ferdinand's royal entrances. In a sense, the Requirement served as a portable coronation ceremony and royal entrance which the conquistadors re-enacted with each new encounter with Indians or their territories.

Seen in light of other royal ceremonies, then, the Requirement's intended audience was not primarily the Indians. Rather, it was for Ferdinand's own subjects. Those Spaniards present at its readings had the imagined justness of their cause reinforced and heard the royal answer to the Dominican's theological scruples to conquest and servitude. The pope gave the crown dominion and the expedition is merely enforcing a legitimate claim. The Requirement reassures the soldiers that the violence is the fault of the Indians "and not that of their highnesses, or ours, or of these soldiers who come with us." When asked, Palacios Rubios himself confirmed that the Requirement "calm[ed] the conscience of the Christians."[57]

Not only did the Requirement justify conquest for Spanish listeners, it had the practical effect of reinforcing the crown's claim to dominion over the expedition itself. Historically, the warrior class in Castile was always ready to assert itself at the expense of royal prerogatives. The broad expanse of the Atlantic Ocean had only encouraged Castilian independence, especially in the early years of the Spanish presence in the Americas. The ceremony reminded the soldiers of the very persistent royal power, which slowly but surely followed in the wake of colonial expansion.

Thus, the Requirement was a very useful document for the crown. Perhaps Ferdinand and his supporters were not entirely cynical, yet as we have seen there is ample historical evidence that political expediency was the primary concern. There is also compelling theological evidence as well. A contextual reading of Ferdinand's royal ideology and Palacios Rubios's royally sponsored work reveals a fundamental inconsistency. On the one hand, Palacios Rubios based both his apologies for the conquest of Navarre and Castilian dominion in the Indies on a heightened portrayal of papal power. On the other, only a few years earlier Ferdinand commissioned Palacios Rubios to write a defense of the spiritual power of the crown in the *Patronato Real*, maintaining that royal power was supreme in matters of

---

57. Thomas, *Conquest*, 72. Gonzalo Fernández de Oviedo, who went on Pedrarias's Panama expedition, wrote in his *Historia General*, "Later in the year 1516, I asked Doctor Palacios Rubios (since he had ordered the Notification) whether the conscience of Christians was satisfied by the Notification, and he told me yes, if used as it says it ought to be" (bk. 29, ch. 7, in Gutiérrez, *Las Casas*, 501 n. 35.).

church patronage.[58] Palacios Rubios had the rare distinction, then, of being perhaps the only theologian in the long history of the church to simultaneously advocate the full temporal authority of the papacy and a minimalist understanding of its governance of the church, a contradiction unthinkable outside of the pragmatic needs of the crown.

The author's theology was not merely inconsistent; indeed, it has also been argued that it was not even Christian in origin. Patricia Seed has shown the remarkable parallel between the Requirement and Islamic tradition, pointing to the Islamic practice of the Mālikī school of jurisprudence whereby a messenger of the Islamic state summoned the enemy to conversion to Islam before attacking.[59] Palacios Rubios's key justification for the Requirement was Deuteronomy 20:10–16, the most important passage in Islamic tradition on warfare. This Christian use of Deuteronomy, according to Seed, was an Iberian innovation, as "Christian theologians and canon lawyers did not use the Old Testament to justify Christian methods or aims of warfare."[60] Rather, this use of Deuteronomy was absorbed from Islamic scholars who made similar use of this passage to defend warfare in ecumenical debates. There had long been cultural, economic, and genetic cross-pollination between Christian and Islamic Iberians and apparently, Islamic tradition offered a rather convenient theological package for the needs of Ferdinand's unsacred monarchy.

Conclusion

Our examination of the Requirement revealed it to be at once simple and complex. On the one hand, it made a rather simple demand for fealty and threat of war and slavery for those who refused. Conquistadors used this option depending on their particular needs, sometimes for tribute and other times for slaves and booty. We also saw that the Requirement did not demand conversion but, in fact, stated that it was optional.

On the other hand, we saw that the Requirement's complexity lay in its theological justification designed to overcome criticism of conquest and servitude. The document, like the ideological conquest of Navarre, built on the long Castilian tradition of unsacred monarchy. Overall, the public nature of the document's performance was a type of portable coronation ceremony, designed to build legitimacy among its Spanish listeners. The Requirement's ability to overcome critique was based not on theological

58. See Hillgarth, *The Spanish Kingdoms*, 568.

59. Seed, *Ceremonies of Possession*, 76.

60. Ibid., 91.

coherency but on the authority of the crown. The author's simultaneous exposition of contradictory theological positions—full temporal authority of the pope and the crown's spiritual authority over the church—reflected the multiple, seemingly self-contradictory, ideological needs of the crown. But the Requirement is only contradictory if seen in the abstract, a luxury which seldom concerned early-modern sovereigns in general and Ferdinand in particular, chief *encomendero*, chief miner, and "chief architect" of expansion.[61] Overall, the Requirement was an act that would have impressed Machiavelli, who praised Ferdinand in *The Prince* for never failing to utilize "religion as a pretext" in his campaigns.[62]

use

a reason given in justification of a course of action that is NOT the real reason.

61. Floyd, *The Columbus Dynasty in the Caribbean*, 122.
62. Macchiavelli, *The Prince*, 98–99.

12

"Builded Better Than They Knew"?

A Blondelian Reading of John Courtney Murray's Legacy

DEREK C. HATCH

I n the story of twentieth-century American Catholicism, the figure of John Courtney Murray, SJ (1904–1967) looms large. Indeed, the Jesuit theologian became something of a public intellectual in the United States during the middle part of the century as broader openness to Catholic life and thought emerged. Within American Catholicism, Murray's story is well known. Whether as the editor of the Jesuit journal, *Theological Studies* (1941–1967), or as associate editor for the Jesuit periodical *America* (1945– 1946), Murray became the central figure for U.S. Catholics, especially when opposed by secular lawyer Paul Blanshard and the organization Protestants and Other Americans United for the Separation of Church and State. Donald Pelotte, SSS, has situated Murray's thought within the Americanist tradition, extending from the work of nineteenth-century figures such as Isaac Hecker (founder of the Paulists), Archbishop John Ireland, Archbishop John Keane, and James Cardinal Gibbons.[1] Like these coreligionists, Murray argued that the United States' founders built "better than they knew," indicating that the nation's philosophical underpinnings cohered with the Catholic natural-law tradition.[2] In the middle of the twentieth century, Murray was the public

---

1. See Pelotte, *John Courtney Murray: Theologian in Conflict.*

2. Murray, *We Hold These Truths*, 77. This phrase and its variants have a significant role in American Catholic history, though this trajectory begins with Ralph Waldo Emerson's 1839 poem, "The Problem." American Catholic convert Orestes Brownson invoked the phrase in his 1856 essay, "The Mission of America," stating that the founders

Catholic voice in the United States, often associated with American ideals, which earned him suspicion from Rome. Yet to many observers, his appearance as a *peritus* at the Second Vatican Council and his participation in conversations surrounding the Council's Declaration on Religious Freedom, *Dignitatis Humanae*, seemed to offer Murray much deserved vindication.

Despite this deep American appreciation of Murray, both in his own context and currently, contemporary scholars of Murray have discerned a rift between various inheritors of Murray's thought. In his book, *John Courtney Murray and the Dilemma of Religious Toleration*, Keith Pavlischek argues that the legacy of the eminent twentieth-century Jesuit, who stands at the center of discussions concerning being American and being Catholic, is a fragmented one, dividing a "conservative Murray" over against a "progressive Murray." In many ways, this description seems compelling when surveying the spectrum of Murray's descendants within American Catholicism, especially when public policy advocacy is the main issue in view. This chapter will treat these two trajectories emerging from Murray's thought, but it will ultimately center on a different set of "Murrays." To make these explicit, this essay will contend that reading Murray through the lens provided by French philosopher Maurice Blondel (1861–1949) offers crucial insight not only for understanding and evaluating Murray's legacy, but also for charting a path forward and appreciating the presence of Maurice Blondel's thought within American Catholicism.

The "Two Murrays"

Pavlischek's claim that Murray's legacy is a divided one indicates that those American Catholics who claim his influence share at least several characteristics in common. For instance, Matthew Shadle notes that one marked similarity is "a belief in the value of public reason, expressed in terms of the natural law."[3] This much is clear, yet marked differences remain. On the one hand, the "progressive Murray" champions rights and democratic processes as worthy of being upheld in order to pursue the common good

---

of the United States "did not follow their Protestantism. They were bravely inconsequent, and 'builded better than they knew'" (Brownson, "The Mission of America," 569). In the pastoral letter of the Third Plenary Council of Baltimore in 1884 (which was presided over by Gibbons), a variant of the phrase was used, again emphasizing a providential fit between the United States and the Catholic Church: "We consider the establishment of our country's independence, the shaping of its liberties and laws as a work of special Providence, its framers 'building wiser than they knew,' the Almighty's hand guiding them" ("Pastoral Letter of the Third Plenary Council of Baltimore," 20).

3. Shadle, *The Origins of War*, 181.

within American society. On the other hand, the "conservative Murray" emphasizes ordered liberty and church loyalty over the perceived libertinism of liberal Protestantism.[4]

J. Bryan Hehir is one prominent representative of the "progressive Murray."[5] Hehir, who served as a policy advisor for the United States Catholic Conference (1973–1992) and as the principal author of the U.S. bishops' 1983 pastoral concerning nuclear weapons, "The Challenge of Peace: God's Promise and Our Response," portrayed Murray as a symbol of freedom not only within the world, but also within Catholic thought. Hehir notes that Murray was "an eloquent voice in support of freedom as the necessary condition of theological progress in service of the church."[6] Particularly insightful for Hehir was what he called Murray's theological asceticism—his desire for the church to speak to the world regarding public issues in a language it can understand. This privileges a philosophical, natural law approach to the public square rather than one consisting of theological arguments.[7] Because of the growing emergence of pluralism within the global society, Hehir has, however, seen Murray's work as unfinished, echoing some of the Jesuit's own words near the end of his life. Taking up this cause, Hehir argued for the extension of freedom from the civil sphere established at the Second Vatican Council (notably in *Dignitatis Humanae*) to include the ecclesial realm as well. In particular, Hehir sees Murray pushing against an institutional model of church, interpreting *Lumen Gentium* as presenting a more communal mode—"a charismatic community directed toward service of the larger human community."[8] In other words, what Murray began at Vatican II needed to be carried forward by a new generation of Catholics. To Hehir, Murray's legacy is indispensable when discussing American Catholicism, yet insufficient due to contemporary developments that outstrip the scope of Murray's vision.[9]

In contrast to the "progressive Murray" is a conservative version exemplified by the work of George Weigel, the Distinguished Senior Fellow of the Ethics and Public Policy Center. Weigel appeals to Murray's use of the *duo sunt* ("two [powers] there are") of Pope Gelasius I, which established

4. See Pavlischek, *John Courtney Murray*, 4.

5. Kristin Heyer notes that Murray is "the single most important analytical influence on Hehir, theologically or philosophically" (*Prophetic & Public*, 65).

6. Hehir, "The Unfinished Agenda," 392.

7. Heyer, *Prophetic & Public*, 66.

8. Hehir, "The Unfinished Agenda," 392. As a comparison, one might invoke Avery Dulles's ecclesiological models to see Hehir articulating a shift from the church as institution to the church as servant (cf. Dulles, *Models of the Church*, 26–38, 81–94).

9. Hehir, "Murray's Contribution," 5.

both royal and ecclesiastical power as sovereign in contrast to various monistic alternatives (such as that put forth by Paul Blanshard).[10] Instead of situating being Catholic and being American at odds with one another, Weigel, arguing with proponents of human rights, sets up Murray as the fountainhead for a "nascent Catholic theology of democracy."[11] The result is that liberation theologians and progressive scholars do not determine what counts as defense of human rights.

In the end, Weigel invokes Murray in order to praise democracy, but not as uninhibited freedom. Instead, Weigel argues that what democracy offers to the world is an "ordered liberty" that gives rise to a provisional yet proper shape of society.[12] Weigel writes, "America is *intrinsically* a nation locked into an ongoing, public moral argument about the right-ordering of our lives, loves, and loyalties."[13] Centering this order within the nonestablishmentarian American context transformed the United States from the exception (or "hypothesis") to the norm for relations between the papacy and various political authorities (or "thesis") into the new norm,[14] investing the American nation with a responsibility for the fate of freedom in the world.[15] The present task is infusing the American form of life with the content of Catholic culture and values. Contrasting with the "progressive Murray's" prioritizing of the common good and public peace, the primary culture that Catholicism offers, according to Weigel, centers on life issues and the manner in which they order American life.[16]

Clear differences exist between these two trajectories emerging from John Courtney Murray's legacy. In fact, one could also see this as a fairly

---

10. Pope Gelasius I (d. 496) stated in a letter to Emperor Anastasius, "Two there are, august emperor, by which this world is ruled on title of original and sovereign right—the consecrated authority of the priesthood and the royal power." Cf. Murray, *We Hold These Truths*, 190–191; Weigel, *Catholicism and the Renewal of American Democracy*, 86.

11. Weigel, *Catholicism and the Renewal of American Democracy*, 94.

12. Ibid., 212.

13. Weigel, "Catholicism and the American Proposition," 39. Weigel borrows the phrase "American proposition" from Murray.

14. The thesis/hypothesis distinction originated with Félix Dupanloup (1802–1878), a French bishop, in response to the *Syllabus of Errors*, an interpretation that was commended by Pope Pius IX. See Portier, "Theology of Manners as Theology of Containment," 85.

15. Weigel writes, "The issue is whether the United States of America remains 'this home of freedom' in the sense of a truly human and liberating freedom" (Weigel, *Catholicism and the Renewal of American Democracy*, 214).

16. "[L]ife issues are not only genuine social-justice issues; they are the *priority* social-justice issues" (Weigel, "The Evangelical Reform of Catholic Advocacy," 28).

accurate description of the most prominent voices within American Catholicism. It is also clear that these Murrays align quite easily with the
American political spectrum, leaving the impression that supporting one
perspective involves voting with a particular political ideology. Moreover,
the exposition of these two Murrays leaves American Catholics in a tenuous
place. Can Murray's synthesis hold in the present or does it crumble when
the circumstances become too difficult? What, if anything, might serve as
an alternative for Catholicism to understand itself within the United States?

Maurice Blondel on Historicism and Extrinsicism

The author of *L'Action* (1893) and *The Letter on Apologetics* (1896), Maurice
Blondel's influence within Catholic thought has only recently received ap-
propriate attention. To be sure, John Courtney Murray never met Maurice
Blondel, nor is there an intellectual genealogy that connects the French lay
Catholic philosopher with the American Jesuit theologian. Nonetheless,
Blondel offers a significant lens for reading the reception of Murray in the
American context. To properly deploy this lens, attention to Blondel's phi-
losophy, especially his work in *History and Dogma* (1904), is needed.

Returning to an Augustinian impulse that understood God to be
"more intimate to me than I am to myself," Blondel adopted a "method of
immanence" that focused on the phenomenon of action. This consisted in
"trying to equate, in our own consciousness, what we appear to think and
to will and to do with what we do and will and think in actual fact—so that
behind factitious negations and ends which are not genuinely willed may
be discovered our innermost affirmations and the implacable needs which
they imply."[17] Thus, these reflections on action should not be understood
as immediate experience itself; rather, the focus is on what could be called
a "logic of life," where philosophy is not simply an abstract science, but the
"progress of the soul."[18]

In his 1893 *L'Action*, Blondel made a distinction between the "willing will" (*volonté voulante*) and the "willed will" (*volonté voulue*), where the
former involves human action as it tends (even unbeknownst to it) toward
the universal and the latter marks human action as it wills a particular finite
point. In the relationship between these two lies Blondel's philosophy of
action. In short, he argued that philosophy (consisting of human doings and

17. Blondel, "The Letter on Apologetics," in *The Letter on Apologetics & History
and Dogma*, 157.

18. Dru and Trethowan, "Introduction," in *The Letter on Apologetics & History and
Dogma*, 84.

makings) "poses questions it cannot answer and solutions it cannot verify," leading it to the limits of human rationality.[19] Blondel calls this the "super-natural insufficiency of human nature."[20] However, contrary to the claims of his opponents, Blondel did not base such an argument on religious or theological grounds (which would have amounted to apologetics), but rather on philosophical grounds. In other words, while granting to philosophy the autonomy to pursue its own ends, Blondel did not see this field as a closed one—in his words, a "separate philosophy" (*philosophie séparée*). Instead, he posited that philosophy was an open system that would be faced with an inevitable decision for or against the transcendent, thereby highlighting the necessity of the supernatural: "Only God can fill the abyss between a finite willed action and the infinite power of willing we have found running through the entire phenomenon of action, so that we have to say that what we will ultimately, in everything we will in the immanent order of the universe, is to be God, the One Thing Necessary, who wills the very being of our willing and of all that is contained in the phenomenon of action."[21] Thus, philosophy and faith do not find themselves at odds or even on separate juxtaposed tracks. Instead, they are distinct from one another, yet converge at philosophy's limits.

In *History and Dogma*, which was written in 1903 at the urging of two of his friends (Fernand Mourret & Jean Wehrlé), Blondel addresses the relationship between Christian facts and Christian convictions. According to Blondel, both were necessary for the proper understanding of Christianity, yet each were distinct from the other. Thus, the relationship (and even the use) of historical data and dogmatic ideas confronted Blondel with an important investigation. He saw each as positioned toward the other, "a sort of coming and going passing over two obscure intervals."[22] This "double movement," as he called it, had two serious dangers (i.e., by setting history over dogma or dogma over history) that could potentially distort both and make synthesis nearly impossible. To make this clear, Blondel sought to describe the two "incomplete, but equally dangerous" approaches to this relation, doing so with neologisms: extrinisicism and historicism.[23]

19. Kerlin, "Maurice Blondel," 77.

20. Blondel, "The Letter on Apologetics," in *The Letter on Apologetics & History and Dogma*, 141. One can see the later resonances with the writings of Henri de Lubac, SJ, whose work rests heavily on the *desiderium naturale vivendi Deum* (natural desire to see God).

21. Blanchette, *Maurice Blondel*, 148.

22. Blondel, "History and Dogma," in *The Letter on Apologetics & History and Dogma*, 223.

23. Ibid., 225.

Extrinsicism subordinates historical facts to truth convictions. For the less-educated or less-enlightened, they "serve as signs to the senses and as commonsense proofs."[24] In other words, history helps point to the truth of dogma, but need not offer anything original to that conclusion. This is, of course, if history genuinely appears at all, since the main function of historical facts, for extrinicists, is authentication and confirmation of the dogmatic statement one (or one's community) has already affirmed. For instance, one would find in a miraculous healing evidence of God's activity in the world, with little to no attention given to the circumstances and context of the healing itself. Or the incarnation of the Word of God as a poor first-century Palestinian Jewish man safeguards some other doctrine (e.g., salvation) rather than revealing anything new about the world as God's creation, human beings as God's creatures, or the nature of the church as followers of Jesus.[25] As Blondel describes this perspective, "the historical facts are merely a vehicle, the interest of which is limited to the apologetic use which can be made of them; for, whether *this* or *that* miracle is involved, provided it is *a* miracle, the argument remains the same."[26] Therefore, once the historical authentication is complete, history is removed from the conversation. The external character of the relationship between history and dogma is summed up by Blondel: "[T]he relation of the sign to the thing signified is extrinsic, the relation of the facts to the theology superimposed upon them is extrinsic, and extrinsic too is the link between our thought and our life and the truths proposed to us from outside."[27]

In Blondel's context, the main site for discussing this relationship was biblical criticism. Yet extrinsicism's apologetic perspective leaves very little with which to embrace the historicity of the biblical text. As Oliva Blanchette observes, "It separates facts and dogmas in such a way that they can only remain at odds with one another, whence the defensive and ultimately defeatist attitude it takes in the face of modern historical studies."[28] In response to this perceived accommodation, extrinsicists aver that the historicity of the text is significant, but only to confirm the veracity of its contents, which were then read in a literalistic manner in order to preserve the absolute

---

24. Ibid., 226.

25. Blondel underscores that extrinsicism views as extraneous "the link which may exist between that miraculous character and the particular historical event invested with it, or the essential relationship which may exist between the facts and the ideas" (ibid., 227).

26. Ibid.

27. Ibid., 228.

28. Blanchette, *Maurice Blondel*, 195.

conclusions that have been predesignated as divinely revealed.[29] As Blondel writes of the extrinsicists, they "imagined they knew everything without having examined anything."[30] In the end, Blondel sees not only an ignorance of historical facts, but their ultimate demise: "The ageless facts are without local colour, vanish, as the result of a sort of perpetual Docetism, into a light that casts no shadow, and disappear beneath the weight of the absolute by which they are crushed."[31]

While Blondel shows no preference for extrinsicism, he writes that his treatment of it is meant to set the stage for making sense of the other danger: historicism.[32] In relation to biblical criticism, this approach displayed an "insistence on studying Christian facts only according to the canons of strict historical observation."[33] For example, according to historicism, the significance of Jesus Christ can be apprehended solely by means of historical study. Thus, while historicism, with its emphasis on exercising relative autonomy in order to take facts seriously, should initially appear to manifest a legitimate alternative to extrinsicism, Blondel notes that pure history cannot provide a bridge to Christian dogma, leaving unanswered the question of whether "the tissue of critical history [is] strong enough to bear the infinite weight of the ancient faith and the whole richness of catholic dogma."[34]

Much of Blondel's discussion of history centers on the nature of the discipline's relative autonomy. While he affirms history's competence, he is clear that this does not indicate self-sufficiency, since that would mean that history would see itself as "a sort of total metaphysics, a universal vision, a *Weltenschauung* [sic]."[35] Instead, arguing that "real history is composed of human lives; and human life is metaphysics in act," Blondel notes that the historian, because he or she is always embedded in the complex exigencies of human experience, must always be open to other vantage points and horizons. Moreover, the externalities that are open to observation do not exhaust all of reality. As Blondel writes, "What the historian does not

---

29. "All that counts in the Bible for extrinsicism is some external seal of the divine" (ibid., 196).

30. Blondel, "History and Dogma," in *The Letter on Apologetics & History and Dogma*, 230. Blanchette notes that this phrase is one that Blondel borrowed from French Catholic Alfred Loisy (Blanchette, *Maurice Blondel*, 196).

31. Blondel, "History and Dogma," in *The Letter on Apologetics & History and Dogma*, 229.

32. Ibid., 231.

33. Blanchette, *Maurice Blondel*, 196–97.

34. Blondel, "History and Dogma," in *The Letter on Apologetics & History and Dogma*, 232, 233.

35. Ibid., 234.

see, and what he must recognize as escaping him, is the spiritual reality, the activity of which is not wholly represented or exhausted by the historical phenomena."[36] Thus, even though historians make seemingly totalizing claims on reality, they must always remain open to a depth that is not available for historical observation. To fail to do so, to claim that critical scientific history can offer an all-encompassing sense of reality is to make history into an abstract doctrine. Here Blondel notes that history's observational method merges with abstract determinism to form a phenomenological ontology that edges out other metaphysical claims (e.g., the final end of human beings or of creation as a whole).[37] This is the heart of the "historicism" against which Blondel warns: "The alternation between 'real history' and 'scientific history' or the substitution of one for the other."[38] The results of historicism are several: historical phenomena are accepted as reality itself, the external and concrete is understood to be the sum total of any given object, effects take precedence over causality, and historical moments are tied together in an organic (perhaps even evolutionary) development stripped of any final determination.[39]

Extrinsicism and Historicism among the Two Murrays

Even though Blondel's discussion of extrinsicism and historicism arises with regard to reading and interpreting Scripture in light of the early-twentieth-century Modernist crisis, his reading of his situation offers tremendous insight for understanding Murray's legacy. Indeed, William Portier describes the contours of the history of Catholic theology in the twentieth century as "the triumph of Blondel."[40] In short, through the interpretive lens provided by Blondel, each trajectory of Murray's legacy displays elements of both extrinsicism and historicism.

Conservatives evidence extrinsicism through their reliance on Murray's use of a Gelasian distinction between church and state. While both Weigel and Richard John Neuhaus are clear that these are "provisional spheres of sovereignty," nonetheless they give rise to a dualistic understanding of the church-world relationship.[41] The divide between spiritual

36. Ibid., 237.

37. Ibid., 240.

38. Ibid., 239.

39. Ibid., 240–41.

40. Portier, "Twentieth-Century Catholic Theology and the Triumph of Maurice Blondel."

41. Neuhaus, *The Catholic Moment*, 192. Neuhaus, in fact, accepts this

and temporal realities produces realms of competence in a manner similar to Martin Luther's "two kingdoms."[42] Thus, at particular junctures, Weigel and Neuhaus argue that the church is not competent to speak in particular areas of discourse. The church is active in the public square, but offers no economic or political models.[43] As for the church's doctrine, Weigel states that it is unchanging through time as the "settled understanding of the truth of things" and that the pope is the "guardian of an authoritative tradition."[44]

Weigel asks the bishops to empower the laity "to bring the Gospel and the social doctrine of the Church into the culture, the economy, and the political community."[45] With this in mind, he states that the church's competence in public discourse involves first principles, but not the prudential reasoning deployed to discern how to apply those principles. For instance, Weigel notes that the church has no competence to declare one political system better than another. Further, while the church is competent to state that taxation is just and that the poor, the elderly, and the sick should be cared for, the church does not have the competence to discuss how those goals might be achieved (e.g., what makes for a just tax rate and which tax rates are, in fact, just).[46] Such tasks are reserved for lay Catholics and not the church's hierarchy.[47] Once again, their advocacy is one of cultural and moral formation, not legislative lobbying. More specifically, both Weigel and Neuhaus argued in defense of military action in Iraq in 2003 (even the use of preemptive strikes), noting that the church was incompetent to make the tactical judgments necessary, even as they deployed the logic of just war tra-

---

characterization but writes that it accurately describes the present state of pluralism (ibid., 194).

42. H. Richard Niebuhr describes Luther as exemplary of the "Christ and Culture in Paradox" type, with which Neuhaus identifies (Niebuhr, *Christ and Culture*, 170–85). Neuhaus was a Lutheran when he wrote *The Catholic Moment*, converting to Catholicism in 1990.

43. Weigel, "The Evangelical Reform of Catholic Advocacy," 29–30. At this point, Weigel invokes John Paul II's words in *Centesimus Annus* (1991): "'The Church's 'contribution to the political order is her vision of the dignity of the person revealed in all its fullness in the mystery of the Incarnate Word'" (ibid., 29).

44. Weigel, "What Popes Can and Can't Do."

45. Weigel, *Evangelical Catholicism*, 226.

46. Ibid., 227. What is lost on Weigel in this distinction (and exacerbates his extrinsicism) is that pursuit of certain first principles does exercise some measure of discernment about application since the principles at times necessitate certain methods and prohibit others.

47. Weigel clarifies that by "lay Catholics at work in the world" he is excluding those who work for state and national Catholic conferences, viewing their work as an extension of the bishops in their collective pastoral role. Cf. Weigel, "The Evangelical Reform of Catholic Advocacy," 30.

dition (including *jus in bello* principles related to military tactics) to support U.S. intervention. In other words, the Catholic just war tradition provided first principles to nations (e.g., just cause), but the discernment of how those principles are interpreted, and what means are justified in pursuit of those ends, are "beyond the competence of religious authority."[48]

By invoking the separation of church and state as an avenue to dissent from the church's teachings, the progressive inheritors of Murray also manifest extrinsicism. That is, the church has a voice in matters of belief, but conscience operates beyond ecclesial boundaries. Thus, when *Humanae Vitae* (1968) reaffirmed the church's case against artificial means of contraception, progressive Catholics were quick to dissent, led by Charles Curran, invoking freedom of conscience. This limiting of the church's sphere of influence shifted the focus of Catholic social thought to the common good.[49] However, following Murray, this is understood to be a broad and nontheological concept.[50] What Hehir calls theological asceticism, or a desire to use nontheological language to speak to the state, reflects the notion that theological language has a circumscribed realm of activity. In fact, Hehir's contrast of a natural-law approach to a theological approach indicates that theological arguments that operate outside their appropriate boundaries are impotent. Here, Hehir and other progressive Catholic interpreters of Murray follow from his statement that "the doctrine of natural law has no Roman Catholic presuppositions."[51] What matters most in these conversations, especially when "the coercive power of the state" is involved, is that these arguments be "cast in terms of a public philosophy."[52]

Representatives of the "conservative Murray" also demonstrate historicist tendencies, though not in the manner of the historicists of Blondel's era. In the early-twentieth-century, historicism was displayed by biblical critics who equated the history of the biblical text with the whole of history itself. In other words, there was no sacred history beneath the development of the text. By contrast, the late-twentieth-century conservatives evidence historicism primarily in their affirmation of the providential character of the United States and American-style freedom. Neuhaus argues that the United States retains significant responsibility for the fate of freedom in the world.

48. "Father Richard John Neuhaus on the Iraqi Crisis," *ZENIT* interview, 10 March 2003.

49. Progressive Catholics rarely numbered *Humanae Vitae* among the church's social tradition.

50. Murray also describes the common good as "public peace" (Murray, *We Hold These Truths*, 73).

51. Ibid., 111.

52. Hehir, "A Catholic Troeltsch?," 203.

That is, more hangs on the U.S., its actions, its past, and its future than is readily apparent. Weigel accomplishes this aim by invoking what he calls "the classic story line of American Catholicism," exemplified in Catholic historians such as Thomas McAvoy and John Tracy Ellis.[53] This story centers on the triumphs of the Americanists (e.g., Ireland, Gibbons) in defending the fit between America and Catholicism.[54]

While clearly different than the biblical critics of Blondel's day (i.e., those he viewed as embodying historicist tendencies), the strong providentialism found in the conservative story declares that a certain kind of history (i.e., one centered on the virtues of the United States) can deliver the truth of reality and chart a course for the future, and it is here that both Neuhaus's and Weigel's historicism is most fully on display. Despite Weigel's qualifications that the actors in the Americanist controversy (both so-called conservatives and liberals) are not easily labeled, his defense of the Ellis/ McAvoy narrative identifies the historical phenomenon of democracy in the United States with reality itself. In fact, the heroes of Weigel's story were driven by precisely this impulse. For instance, John Ireland and Cardinal Gibbons countered the thesis/hypothesis distinction by arguing that the historical emergence of democracy in the United States did not simply offer the church another viable option to consider; rather, they viewed it as a providential development that represented the entire movement of history: "With our hopes are bound up the hopes of the millions of the earth. The Church triumphing in America, Catholic truth will travel on the wings of

53. Weigel, "Telling the American Catholic Story," 43.

54. McAvoy, *The Great Crisis in American Catholic History*; Ellis, *American Catholicism*. Weigel's real interest in the classic story is its contrast to what he calls the "revisionist" narrative in the work of Jay P. Dolan, which emphasizes discontinuity between American Catholics and the church in Rome (Weigel, "Telling the American Catholic Story," 45). Weigel opens *Catholicism and the Renewal of American Democracy* with a prologue entitled "John Ireland's Dream," where he concludes that this dream remains "an essential task for the Church in America" (5). This dream hit an unexpected snag when confronted by *Testem Benevolentiae* (1899), which censured the opinions known as "Americanism," and *Pascendi Dominici Gregis* (1907), which condemned Modernism by describing it as the "synthesis of all heresies" (§39).

American influence and encircle the universe."[55] Thus, the United States, when properly ordered, becomes the site of the church's true reality.[56]

The providential fit between the United States and Catholicism extends beyond political structures to include economics as well. While Neuhaus and Weigel are clear that the church's teaching only supplies first principles for specific economic policies, they are confident that one of those principles working in concert with the American experiment is the centrality of free-market capitalism. For example, in John Paul II's *Centesimus Annus* (1991), a social encyclical on the occasion of the hundredth anniversary of Leo XIII's *Rerum Novarum*, both Weigel and Neuhaus find a "strong endorsement of democratic capitalism, or, as [John Paul II] prefers, 'the free economy,'" despite prominent alternative readings of the papal statement.[57]

The "progressive Murray" also displays historicism, though in a different manner. Rather than trumpeting the accomplishments of the United States, the focus rests on the progress of freedom in the world at large, represented by the growth of global pluralism. Hehir and David Hollenbach refer to this as the "unfinished work" of Murray's legacy. Grounded in Murray's understanding of the common good, the historical movement of progress encapsulates even the church, prompting Hehir to direct his aim at the ecclesial expansion of freedom after the Second Vatican Council. The culmination of such expansion is the development of a new international order of human rights and justice.

With this view of a new global community, Hehir describes the deliberations of the Vatican during the Cold War and in the wake of the Second Vatican Council as one of embracing "a changing church and a changing

55. Ireland, "The Mission of Catholics in America," in *The Church and Modern Society*, 1:76. In another address, Ireland proclaims Leo XIII as "The Pontiff of the Age," stating, "He sees in the United States the country in which the aspirations of the age are to-day best realized, the country in which the world of the future will soonest [sic] take shape, and in which the grandest field opens for the Church of Christ" (Ireland, "The Pontiff of the Age," in *The Church and Modern Society*, 1:424). The irony is that seven years later, Leo would pen *Testem Benevolentiae*, which cut against the grain of this statement.

56. Weigel displays such providential conviction by concluding one essay as follows: "[I]t is not to be regarded as merely an accident of chronology that the Feast of the Chair of St. Peter and Washington's (real) Birthday both fall on February 22" (Weigel, "Catholicism and the American Proposition," 44).

57. Fellow conservative Michael Novak declared, "We are all capitalist now, even the Pope" (Novak, *The Catholic Ethic and the Spirit of Capitalism*, 101). This determination is in contrast to an affirmation of socialism or the proposal of a "third way" between the two economic ideologies. Cf. "Editorial: That Encyclical," 11. For an example of a reading of the encyclical that is less supportive of free-market capitalism, see Hollenbach, "Christian Social Ethics after the Cold War"; and Hehir, "Reordering the World."

world order."[58] Beginning with John XXIII's and Paul VI's implementation of *Ostpolitik*—a strategy of conversation with communist regimes—and moving through John Paul II's more "revisionist" approach (depicted primarily in the 1987 encyclical *Sollicitudo Rei Socialis*), Hehir understands the papacy to have embraced a broader pluralism that minimizes the importance of ideologues and superpowers.[59] Drawing on Murray's embrace of a need for an international political authority, Hehir argues for interdependence between state actors and international institutions. This perspective relativizes the role of nation-states such as the United States and places more weight on international actors like the United Nations Security Council in service of a broader movement of peace and justice, with Hehir even stating that "a renewal and revival of the U.N. system in all its possible forms—political, security, economic and human rights—is clearly the idea which most closely approximates the papal teaching of the last five decades."[60] In other words, the United Nations represents more than simply another historical actor, but functions as a symbol of the pluralism and freedom within the global human community and new world order.

As is clear from the discussion above, those labeled as conservative or progressive using Pavlischek's rubric exhibit characteristics of both extrinsicism and historicism. Each in their own way, conservatives and progressives set the church over against a more important public sphere (extrinsicism) yet also identify the progress of a certain aspect of history with the movement of reality itself (historicism). This casts doubt upon the depth of terms like conservative and progressive, and also further underscores the divided legacy of Murray's thought, perhaps stretching it to the breaking point (where it has no purchase on the present and future of American Catholicism). Moreover, while initially this may seem to invalidate the significance of Blondel's categories, it actually legitimates them further. Indeed, Blondel understands historicism and extrinsicism, while distinct from one another, to be two sides of the same coin. As he states, they are "opposite extremes, but of the same kind, based upon similar habits of mind, suffering from analogous philosophical lacunae."[61] In other words, in pathological terms, the conservative and progressive Murrays suffer from a similar affliction internally, but display different symptoms outwardly. For Blondel, this is a

58. Hehir, "Papal Foreign Policy," 33.

59. Ibid. Weigel strongly refutes any claims of continuity between the political stance towards communism of Paul VI and John Paul II; cf. Weigel, "An Eminent Distortion of History."

60. Hehir, "The Social Role of the Church, 48.

61. Blondel, "History and Dogma," in *The Letter on Apologetics & History and Dogma*, 225.

crucial point because it underscores that any alternative will need to reconceive of both history and dogma in order to offer a genuine way forward (perhaps one beyond Murray himself).

Conclusion: Reading Blondel, Reading the Two Murrays

Blondel is clear that both historicism and extrinsicism are deficient approaches to the relation between history and dogma. Each maintains relative autonomy, but cannot be granted total explanatory power over reality. Yet, as he notes, separating them from each other creates deeper problems: "Truth is invoked on either hand, but the fragmentary aspects which each thesis displays are so presented that the fragmented truths, instead of being joined together and completed, seem to be exclusive of one another."[62] The challenge, then, is as follows: "The need for an intermediary between history and dogma, the necessity for a link between them which would bring about the synthesis and maintain solidarity without compromising their relative independence."[63] As an alternative to the twin ditches of extrinsicism and historicism, Blondel offers a robust sense of Tradition. However, he is clear that Tradition should not be understood to be a static object that is merely passed, without effect, from one generation to another, nor is it simply a code word for theological development over time. Rather, Blondel writes that Tradition is "linked . . . to historical facts without being absorbed into history" and "bound up . . . with speculative doctrines though . . . not completely absorbed in them."[64]

Blondel's notion of Tradition aims to refocus the questions surrounding the relationship between history and dogma by highlighting the importance of action. Indeed, the extrinsicist perspective, whether in its conservative or progressive form, fails to account for the historical embeddedness and development of first principles, while the historicist identifies the contours of the historical drama as reality itself without accounting for the philosophical. In short, the problem with each is a stone-like stasis that betrays the dynamism inherent within doctrinal development.[65]

62. Ibid., 265.

63. Ibid., 264.

64. Ibid., 264–65.

65. "So far is 'development' from being heterodox, as so many believers fear, that it is the static idea of tradition, *fixism*, which is the virtual heresy—whether the static conception is that of the historian who claims to seize the truth of Revelation in its earliest version, or that of the speculative theologian, ready to confine infinite reality in a completed synthesis, as though at some given moment in history the spirit of man had exhausted God's spirit" (ibid., 275).

Consequently, the historicism and extrinsicism of the two Murrays fails to embody this sense of Tradition. Instead, each Murray offered an oscillation from one problematic conception of history and dogma to the other (often rhetorically patterned against the opposite position). This false binary does not present genuine reconciliation between history and dogma; instead, it only recreates the same oppositional dichotomy.

For Blondel, the fullness of the necessary reconciliation is found in the incarnation as the Word made flesh in history. Not only was the historical character of Christ displayed in his human existence, but even the description of his life came from other historical sources than Jesus himself: "The divine and human Word of Christ did not fix itself in immobility. Jesus wrote only in the sand and impressed his words only on the air: his living teaching comes to mobile and inconstant minds."[66] Dogma must be open to the vicissitudes of historical development while not losing its philosophical depth. The historicity of Christ does not reduce him to what can be confirmed by historical or scientific examination, but it also guards against reifying Christ as an extrahistorical entity or principle.

Moreover, an emphasis on the incarnation brings the church, the guardian of the faith and the historical pilgrimage of the people of God, to the fore: "The active principle of the synthesis lies neither in the facts alone, nor in the ideas alone, but in the Tradition which embraces within it the facts of history, the effort of reason and the accumulated experiences of the faithful."[67] The church, then, becomes the locus of the act of Tradition, including but not limited to ecclesial practices. This is omitted by both Murrays since each retained the church in a minimized capacity (as either the speaker of parochial theological language or an institution with a limited competency regarding sociopolitical issues). In fact, rather than the linear conception of ideas influencing actions proffered by the extrinsicism of the two Murrays, Blondel notes that the dynamic actions of the church also generate ideas: "Nothing is more reliable than the light shed by the orderly and repeated performances of Christian practices."[68] These practices do not merely form thoughts or beliefs, they lead to genuine encounters with historically situated dogmas within reality itself.[69] Thus, it is no surprise

66. Ibid.

67. Ibid., 269.

68. Ibid., 277.

69. Along these lines, Blondel writes, "the essential truth of Catholicism is the incarnation of dogmatic ideas in historical facts" (ibid., 274).

that French Jesuit Henri de Lubac, who was heavily influenced by Blondel's work, states that "the Eucharist makes the Church."[70]

Going forward, Murray's well-known pursuit of a public philosophy, while perhaps helpful in the consensus period of mid-twentieth-century America, closes in on itself, as the fragmentation of Murray's thought after his death demonstrates. As William Portier has noted, he is a "1950s period piece."[71] Ironically, then, in spite of Murray's declaration that the U.S. founders "builded better than they knew" in incorporating Catholic doctrine into the American constitutional system, his own legacy has crumbled under the weight of history. By contrast, Blondel's appeal to the incarnation, which views Tradition as the extension of Christ's hypostatic union of the dogmatic and the historical, holds history and dogma as distinct, yet never divorced from one another. In the end, the final turn in a Blondelian reading of Murray is toward the church, the body of Christ in the world. Both the conservative and progressive Murrays emphasized the public role of the church insofar as it participated in the cultural affairs of civil society or in the machinations of the *polis*, yet neglected the nature of church as church. American Catholicism, when using Blondel's distinct Augustinian key, grounds its future in the church as the vital public reality for Christians, ever on a pilgrimage of dogmatic discovery within the web of history.[72]

70. de Lubac, *Corpus Mysticum*, 88.

71. Portier, "Theology of Manners as Theology of Containment," 105.

72. I would like to thank Ethan Smith for offering invaluable feedback on an earlier version of this essay.

Public Reason as Historical Reason

Post-Conciliar Social Teaching in the United States

————— MATTHEW A. SHADLE —————

T wo days before the visit of U.S. Representative Paul Ryan to Georgetown University on April 26, 2012, ninety faculty of the university sent Ryan a letter, along with a copy of the *Compendium of the Social Doctrine of the Church*, a summary of Catholic social teaching published by the Pontifical Council for Justice and Peace in 2004. The faculty faulted Ryan for his "misuse of Catholic teaching" and for "profoundly misreading Catholic teaching." The *Compendium* was included "to help deepen your understanding of Catholic social teaching."[1]

Ryan had come to prominence through his role as chair of the House Budget Committee and his budget proposals designed to drastically cut federal spending and encourage economic growth. Only four months later, in August, Ryan was named the vice-presidential running mate of Republican presidential candidate Mitt Romney in his ultimately unsuccessful campaign. Ryan's proposals had drawn the attention of Catholic critics, including the U.S. Catholic bishops themselves, who, in four letters released in the week prior to Ryan's address, challenged the proposed cuts to programs serving the poor.[2] Ryan, himself a Catholic, had attempted to defend his proposals in terms of Catholic social teaching, in particular with the

---

1. Reese, et al., "Georgetown Letter to Rep. Paul Ryan."

2. United States Conference of Catholic Bishops, "Federal Budget Choices Must Protect Poor, Vulnerable People, Says U.S. Bishops' Conference."

principle of subsidiarity, and in fact his speech at Georgetown was his most comprehensive attempt to do so.[3]

Although the Georgetown faculty's gesture had a relatively small political impact, it is nevertheless ecclesially significant because it was paradigmatic of the current state of discourse within Catholic circles about the role of the Catholic faith in public affairs. Why send Ryan a text compiled by Roman ecclesiastics nearly a decade earlier? Why hinge the criticism on an interpretation of an abstract principle, subsidiarity? Why address Catholic teaching to a politician at the highest levels of power? The answers to these questions were self-evident to the Georgetown faculty, but the purpose of this essay is to argue that the apparently self-evident understanding of the "public reason" of the Catholic Church embodied in the Georgetown faculty's gesture is in fact historically contingent, dependent on a mixture of ecclesial and sociopolitical contexts that are rapidly disappearing.

The Context of the *Compendium*

Before addressing the historical background for Ryan's Georgetown address and its response, it is worth exploring the *Compendium* itself. As its title suggests, the *Compendium* was intended as a summary of over a century of the Catholic Church's social teaching. The first chapter of the *Compendium* roots that teaching in salvation history, and the second chapter provides a theological justification of the church's authority to speak on social issues. The remaining chapters are the heart of the text, first organizing Catholic social teaching around four core principles—the dignity of the person, the common good (with the associated sub-principle of the universal destination of goods), subsidiarity (with the associated sub-principle of participation), and solidarity—and then applying those principles to a number of issue areas: the family, human work, economic life, the political community, and the international community.

By rooting Catholic social teaching in the scriptural witness and presenting it in terms of abstract principles, the *Compendium* gives it a timeless air. The *Compendium* masks the historical contingency of Catholic social teaching and the manner in which it is conceptualized and lived out. Kenneth Himes has indirectly noted this contingency, pointing out that, in the *Compendium*, "There are more citations of John Paul II than of all previous popes combined, more than all conciliar references combined, more than all patristic and medieval authors combined," and that there are even

---

3. Ryan, "Full Text of Paul Ryan's Remarks at Georgetown University."

more citations of John Paul II than of the Bible.[4] This editorial decision demonstrates that the *Compendium*'s presentation of Catholic social teaching reflects the ecclesial and theological context of John Paul II's pontificate. That context helps explain the structure of the *Compendium*. It may seem strange, considering how easily we speak of Catholic social teaching in terms of principles, but the *Compendium* is the first Vatican-level text to explicitly organize that teaching around abstract principles. Of course the concepts themselves—the dignity of the person, subsidiarity, solidarity—have long been found in the documents of Catholic social teaching, but making them the architectonic structure of the teaching is a relatively recent phenomenon.

Despite its newness, the decision to structure Catholic social teaching in this way was a long time coming. In his 1987 encyclical *Sollicitudo Rei Socialis*, John Paul affirmed the constancy of the church's social doctrine, which remains unchanging "in its 'principles of reflection,' in its 'criteria of judgment,' in its basic 'directives for action.'"[5] These terms are, in turn, drawn from Pope Paul VI's 1971 apostolic letter *Octogesima Adveniens*, where their timeless quality is more ambiguous, as these "principles of reflection," "norms of judgment," and "directives for action" are drawn by local Christian communities from the church's social teaching, which itself "has been worked out in the course of history."[6] John Paul's reworking of Paul's statement is in response to the French theologian Marie-Dominique Chenu's 1979 book *La 'Doctrine sociale' de l'Église comme idéologie*, which argued that Catholic social teaching's tendency to present an ideal, static vision of society based on timeless principles downplays the role of social change in liberating the oppressed and neglects the role of Christians in the ongoing formulation of the church's social teaching. John Paul's formulation also must be understood in the context of the debates over liberation theology and the relationship between truth and praxis. John Paul's purpose is to assert that the church's doctrine, including its social teaching, as defined by the official magisterium, in a sense exists prior to Christians' engagement with the world, an assertion supported by his clear and repeated reference to the church's social *doctrine*.[7] The *Compendium*, then, is the codification of this affirmation of centralized magisterial authority.

---

4. Himes, "To Inspire and Inform."

5. Pope John Paul II, *Sollicitudo Rei Socialis* §3.

6. Pope Paul VI, *Octogesima Adveniens* §4.

7. Elsbernd, "What Ever Happened to *Octogesima adveniens*?"

Principles Amidst Partisanship

The *Compendium* was not the earliest official source to conceptualize Catholic social teaching through a framework of timeless, abstract principles, however. In the relatively little-known document *A Century of Catholic Social Teaching: A Common Heritage, A Continuing Challenge*, published in 1990, the United States Catholic Conference for the first time introduced six principles—the life and dignity of the human person, human rights and responsibilities, the call to family and community, the dignity of work and the rights of workers, the option for the poor, and solidarity—summarizing the ongoing concerns of the Catholic social teaching tradition.[8] Soon after, in 1991, these six principles reappeared in *Political Responsibility: Revitalizing American Democracy*, the bishops' quadrennial voting guide.[9] The list of principles precedes the bishops' analyses of the issues facing the nation, such as abortion, housing, and the transition to democracy in Eastern Europe, and serves as a summary of what the Catholic social teaching tradition brings to bear on those problems. Henceforth these principles became the U.S. bishops' central pedagogical tool in communicating Catholic social teaching, primarily through the voting guides. A seventh theme focused on the environment, care for God's creation, later appeared in the 1998 document *Sharing Catholic Social Teaching: Challenges and Directions*,[10] and then in subsequent voting guides.

Just as the *Compendium*'s resort to abstract principles has a history, so does the U.S. bishops' document. In the latter case, the conceptualization of Catholic social teaching as a set of principles is one facet of the bishops' efforts to keep the church publicly engaged in the midst of the increasing partisan divide among American Catholics. For most of American history, Catholics were reliably Democratic voters. In the nineteenth century, the Democratic Party successfully established patronage networks among the masses of immigrants arriving on American shores, many of whom were Catholic. Although there were exceptions, including among the episcopal leadership, the Democratic loyalties of most Catholics remained firm and were reinforced by immigrant Catholics' role as part of President Franklin

---

8. United States Catholic Conference, *A Century of Catholic Social Teaching.*

9. United States Catholic Conference, *Political Responsibility* (1991). The U.S. bishops have produced these voting guides in the years of presidential elections since 1976, although at times the guides were published in the year prior to the election: 1976, 1979, 1984, 1987, 1991, 1996, 1999, 2003, 2007, and 2011. Since the bishops' statements use the same title over several years, I will include the year of publication in every citation.

10. United States Catholic Conference, *Sharing Catholic Social Teaching.*

D. Roosevelt's New Deal coalition in the 1930s. In the decades after the Second World War, however, Catholic partisan allegiances slowly began to change, primarily as a result of two factors. First, Catholic demographics began to change as the socioeconomic status of many Catholics improved; the end of mass immigration in the 1920s facilitated Catholic immigrants' cultural assimilation, and Catholics shared in the increased prosperity of the postwar years through the access to higher education provided by the G.I. Bill, the affordable housing found in the suburbs, etc.

The second factor contributing to the increasing partisan divide among Catholics was the shifting focus of American politics in general to issues of identity and lifestyle in the 1970s. In particular, the increasing acceptance of legal abortion, culminating in the Supreme Court's *Roe v. Wade* decision in 1973, proved politically significant for Catholics. By the 1980s, the Democratic Party had become the party of abortion rights, leading to a conflict of conscience for Catholics. A sizeable number of Catholic voters began voting for the Republican Party, a transition accelerated by the increasing prominence of sexual politics, and in particular the issues of homosexuality and same-sex marriage, in the 1990s and 2000s. By the 2000s, American Catholics were no longer a reliably Democratic voting bloc, but rather a bellwether, voting with the majority, whether Democratic or Republican, in each presidential election.

It is no coincidence, then, that the U.S. bishops published their first guide for Catholic voters, *Political Responsibility: Statement of the U.S. Catholic Conference Administrative Board*, in 1976, marking the bicentennial of America, but also a critical moment in the transition of Catholic political allegiances. In previous decades Catholic voters could be reliably mobilized for the Democratic Party through a network of party offices, labor unions, neighborhood associations, and church organizations. With Catholic political allegiances in flux and, in many cases, these social networks in decline,[11] the bishops decided that the church must engage in a new educative effort to encourage the participation of the Catholic faithful in the political process.[12] Unlike the past, however, this participation must be based on a thorough understanding of the Catholic faith and its implications for the public policy

11. Although many factors were involved in this decline, it is worth noting that it was in 1972, during the previous presidential election, that the Democratic Party modified its nomination rules, diminishing the role of local party bosses, the traditional vehicles of white ethnic Catholic political power.

12. Indeed, in the 1976, 1979, and 1984 iterations of their voting guide, the bishops begin their reflections by lamenting post-Vietnam and post-Watergate political disillusionment, evident in decreasing voter registration and participation, and they insist that political participation is a responsibility of all faithful adult Catholics.

issues facing the nation. Even as early as 1976, however, the bishops were conscientious to avoid partisanship—insisting, "We specifically do not seek the formation of a religious voting bloc; nor do we wish to instruct persons on how they should vote by endorsing candidates"—and they were careful to introduce their treatment of major issues "without reference to political candidates, parties, or platforms."[13] In a sense, the bishops here recognized the reality of Catholics' divided political loyalties, instead hoping that a shared process of reflection on Catholic teaching and analysis of public policy could produce unity amidst diversity.

The Consistent Ethic of Life

In these early voting guides, however, the U.S. bishops did not present an appealing vision of how the gospel message could illuminate the nation's public policy issues, a task which was taken up by Joseph Bernardin, Archbishop of Cincinnati and later Cardinal Archbishop of Chicago. In his 1983 Gannon Lecture at Fordham University, Bernardin first proposed what he called the "consistent ethic of life,"[14] an ethic which he also referred to as the "seamless garment,"[15] a reference to the Gospel of John's comment that, as Jesus' tunic was seamless, the Roman guards at his crucifixion refused to tear it (19:23). As chair of the bishops' Ad Hoc Committee on War and Peace, Bernardin had overseen the drafting of the U.S. bishops' pastoral letter on war and peace, *The Challenge of Peace: God's Promise and Our Response*, published earlier that year, which, along with the 1986 pastoral letter *Economic Justice for All*, well embodied the church's public mission outlined in the 1976 document. Noting that *The Challenge of Peace* not only contributed to the debate over nuclear policy, but in fact helped make possible new thinking on the issue, Bernardin added that it "provides a starting point for developing a consistent ethic of life but it does not provide a fully articulated framework."[16] He insisted that the sacredness of human life, including more specific norms such as that prohibiting the direct taking of innocent human life, demands a consistent ethic of life that "cuts across the issues of genetics, abortion, capital punishment, modern warfare and the care of the

---

13. United States Catholic Conference Administrative Board, *Political Responsibility* (1976) §16, 19.

14. Bernardin, "A Consistent Ethic of Life."

15. Bernardin, "Religion and Politics," 44.

16. Bernardin, "Consistent Ethic of Life," 10.

terminally ill."[17] He believed that such an ethic is both authentically Catholic and publicly relevant.

According to Bernardin, the consistent ethic of life could serve as a basis of consensus among Catholics while at the same time presenting a persuasive message to the non-Catholic residents of the United States. He noted that the consistent ethic cut across partisan boundaries, challenging cherished positions of both the left and the right.[18] Implying that Catholics themselves were divided amongst themselves as a result of their political loyalties, he maintained that "We should begin with the honest recognition that the shaping of a consensus among Catholics on the spectrum of life issues is far from finished," and that the consistent ethic of life provided the ground for that consensus.[19] Although potentially serving as a basis for Catholic unity, the consistent ethic of life was not a sectarian ethic, but rather one that non-Catholics could likewise find morally compelling if Catholics adopted the right substance and style in sharing their vision.[20]

The language of the "consistent ethic of life" was first incorporated into the bishops' voting guides in 1987's *Political Responsibility: Choices for the Future*, in which the bishops state, "We are convinced that a consistent ethic of life should be the moral framework from which we address all issues in the political arena."[21] In both Bernardin's writings and the bishops' statements of the period, however, it is not clear what the political vehicle for the consistent ethic is to be. Bernardin himself claimed that the consistent ethic "must be linked to a community—a constituency—which holds and embodies this vision. A vision without a community is not capable of influence. A vision tied to a committed community is the first prerequisite of serious social impact."[22] Bernardin proposed that the church is the ethic's most basic constituency,[23] but as we have seen, he believed its effectiveness also depended on reaching a broader non-Catholic audience. Bernardin avoided discussion of political mobilization in support of the consistent ethic, instead focusing on its potential for changing political discourse. In their 1987 guide, the bishops as a whole also disavowed seeking "the formation of a religious bloc" and eschewed any partisan loyalty, as they had in their previous statements. There is little indication, however,

17. Ibid., 12.
18. Ibid., 13.
19. Ibid., 15.
20. Ibid., 15–16.
21. United States Catholic Conference, *Political Responsibility* (1987).
22. Bernardin, "The Consistent Ethic of Life and Public Policy," 55.
23. Lysaught, "From *The Challenge of Peace* to *The Gift of Peace.*"

of how Catholics and their allies committed to the consistent ethic were to exercise concerted political power to influence public policy. This failure to adequately grapple with the reality of partisan politics would contribute to the declining influence of the consistent ethic of life.

The consistent ethic was unable to counteract the hardening of partisan loyalties and a growing recognition of how this phenomenon was dividing the Catholic Church itself. A revived conservative impulse in American politics, embodied in the Republican Revolution of 1994, closed the door on efforts to reform the health care system in 1993 and led to the reform of the welfare system, as a budget-cutting measure, in 1996. Meanwhile, the Supreme Court's 1992 *Planned Parenthood v. Casey* case demolished any hopes of overturning *Roe v. Wade*, and the failure to ban partial-birth abortion and efforts to legalize euthanasia and physician-assisted suicide confirmed that vulnerable human life was under threat as never before. In a 1996 address, Bernardin recognized that hardening attitudes on both the left and the right posed a serious challenge to the ethic.[24] The bishops as a whole, in their 1996 voting guide, expressed similar concerns about the political culture, warning that at the root of cynicism and frustration are self-interest, fear, division and polarization, and a lack of compassion.[25]

The 1990s also saw an increased awareness of how the ecclesial disagreements that had divided the Catholic Church since the Second Vatican Council in the 1960s were increasingly aligning with the partisan political divide, to the detriment of the church. Disagreements over the liturgy or Catholic teaching on sexual morality were treated as political disputes, while political battles over abortion or welfare increasingly became markers of authentic Catholic identity. Again perceiving this problem, in 1996, just before his death, Bernardin established the Catholic Common Ground Project as a way for Catholics of different ecclesial and political stripes to discuss their disagreements respectfully.[26] As Margaret O'Brien Steinfels notes, however, because the project touched on thorny issues like doctrine and Catholic identity, "The effort became another source of polarization mirroring the fractured state of the church rather than healing it."[27] The shift in the U.S. bishops' social strategy after 1996 was a response to this impasse.

24. Bernardin, "The Catholic Moral Vision in the United States," 151, 156.
25. United States Catholic Conference, *Political Responsibility* (1996).
26. Bernardin, "Faithful and Hopeful."
27. Steinfels, "Defenders of the Faith!"

"Simply Catholicism" in the Public Square

A marker of this shift was a speech given by Cardinal Francis George, who succeeded Bernardin as Archbishop of Chicago in 1997, at a forum held by the liberal Catholic magazine *Commonweal* in 1999. After controversially claiming that liberal Catholicism was an "exhausted project," George proposed what he called "simply Catholicism" as the antidote to both liberal and conservative Catholicisms.[28] George was, in effect, seeking to move beyond the rancorous political and ecclesial divides within Catholicism by appealing to the authentic gospel of Jesus Christ proclaimed in Scripture and passed on in the church's tradition. He diagnosed the liberal culture of the United States as suffering from a "crisis of truth," as liberal skepticism of authority led to relativism and individualism. George feared that liberal Catholicism imported the same skepticism into the church, challenging the authority of the bishops and therefore undermining the very gospel they are tasked with teaching. He therefore very strongly affirmed the role of the bishops as teachers of immutable doctrine. George criticized conservative Catholics, however, for believing that the bishops could enforce orthodoxy through the exercise of disciplinary power; he countered, "The church does have power given her by Christ, the power to proclaim the gospel and celebrate the sacraments and pastor his people."[29] George therefore proposed the proclamation of the gospel of Jesus Christ by the bishops as an antidote to Catholic divisions, and this "simply Catholicism" found its way into the U.S. bishops' social engagement through the more detailed articulation of the key doctrines of Catholic social teaching, a greater emphasis on the teaching role of the bishops, and a greater focus on Catholic identity rather than cooperation with non-Catholics.

As we have already seen, it was only in their 1991 voting guide that the bishops proposed six (and later seven) key themes, or principles, as a summary of Catholic social teaching, and as the decade of the 1990s progressed, the themes came to be seen as the key to understanding that teaching. In the 1991 document, the six principles are listed in an introduction to the larger section presenting the bishops' analyses of the major issues facing the nation; they are intended to summarize the church's century-long tradition of addressing these and similar issues.[30] By 1999, the function of the principles in the larger document had shifted. Most obviously, the descriptions of the themes are lengthier. More importantly, the seven principles

28. George, "How Liberalism Fails the Church."

29. Ibid., 29.

30. United States Catholic Conference, *Political Responsibility* (1991). The wording in the 1996 document is identical.

are listed in a separate section prior to that analyzing issues of concern. The bishops justified this ordering by claiming, "The Catholic approach to faithful citizenship begins with moral principles, not party platforms."[31] These changes suggest that the principles had become the starting point for the bishops' understanding of the church's social mission; the church's stance on issues such as abortion and the social safety net are applications of the principles. Whereas in 1991 the bishops wrote that these basic principles "are at the heart of these issues,"[32] referring to the issues of concern discussed in the document, by 1999 the themes were described as "at the heart of our Catholic social tradition."[33] Although a subtle change, again it represents a shift from thinking about the principles as arising out of engagement with social problems to thinking of them as the starting point for engagement with those problems. The bishops' 1998 document *Sharing Catholic Social Teaching*, comprising both a statement by the U.S. bishops and a summary report by the Task Force on Catholic Social Teaching and Catholic Education, was a full-fledged effort by the U.S. bishops to promote these seven key themes of Catholic social teaching as part of catechesis and Catholic education, therefore representing the wholesale adoption of the seven themes as central to their social strategy.[34]

Although given increasing prominence throughout the 1990s, the seven themes were not intended to replace the consistent ethic of life, but rather to elaborate upon its contents. In the 1991 document the bishops continue to appeal to the consistent ethic, echoing earlier voting guides in claiming that "a consistent ethic of life should be the moral framework from which to address all issues in the political arena."[35] The principles were understood as an elaboration of this framework.

Despite this continuity, however, the elaboration of the seven themes represented something new. For one, it allowed the bishops to more clearly articulate the reasons for traditional positions of Catholic social teaching—for example, the just wage or the rights of the family—only vaguely suggested by the consistent ethic of life. Furthermore, the seven themes presented a more robust and clearly articulated vision of Catholic social teaching. In Bernardin's own mind, the consistent ethic was meant to be the beginning of a discussion, a "catalyst" setting in motion a process in pursuit

31. United States Catholic Conference, *Faithful Citizenship* (1999).

32. United States Catholic Conference, *Political Responsibility* (1991). Again, the wording in the 1996 document is identical.

33. United States Catholic Conference, *Faithful Citizenship* (1999).

34. United States Catholic Conference, *Sharing Catholic Social Teaching*.

35. United States Catholic Conference, *Political Responsibility* (1991).

of consensus, not a set of well-defined doctrines;[36] while still requiring a process of discernment and application, the seven key themes presented a more thorough and definite starting point than the consistent ethic, mirroring George's emphasis on the clear proclamation of the gospel in a world in search of truth, and John Paul II's insistence that doctrine precedes praxis.

Beginning in 1999, the bishops' voting guides also put a much greater emphasis on the role of the bishops as teachers who guide the Catholic faithful in forming their political consciences. Going back to 1976, the statements had always discussed the right of religious groups to proclaim the relevance of their teachings for public life in America in light of First Amendment freedoms. In 1999, however, the document teaches that it is *"the leaders of the Church"* who "have the right and duty to share the Church's teaching and to educate Catholics on the moral dimensions of public life, so that they may form their consciences in light of their faith."[37] This language is repeated in the 2003 statement,[38] although the more recent statements of 2007 and 2011 returned to the older language of speaking of "the right of individual believers and religious bodies to participate and speak out without government interference, favoritism, or discrimination."[39] These later documents do, nevertheless, strongly affirm the bishops' teaching role, stating, "Together with priests and deacons, assisted by religious and lay leaders of the Church, we are to teach fundamental moral principles that help Catholics form their consciences correctly, to provide guidance on the moral dimensions of public decisions, and to encourage the faithful to carry out their responsibilities in political life."[40] Although also proposing a teaching role for the bishops, the statements from 1984 through 1996 defined this role less emphatically: "As teachers and pastors, they must provide norms for the formation of conscience of the faithful, support efforts to gain greater peace and justice, and provide guidance and even leadership when human rights are in jeopardy."[41] The later documents' emphasis on forming Catholics' consciences *correctly* and on the guiding role of the bishops demonstrates the greater importance put on the clear teaching of doctrine, as does the exclusive focus on the

36. Bernardin, "Consistent Ethic of Life and Public Policy," 55.

37. United States Catholic Conference, *Faithful Citizenship* (1999); emphasis mine.

38. United States Conference of Catholic Bishops, *Faithful Citizenship* (2003).

39. United States Conference of Catholic Bishops, *Forming Consciences for Faithful Citizenship* (2007) §11; United States Conference of Catholic Bishops, *Forming Consciences for Faithful Citizenship* (2011) §11.

40. United States Conference of Catholic Bishops, *Forming Consciences for Faithful Citizenship* (2011) §15.

41. United States Catholic Conference, *Political Responsibility* (1996). The statements from 1984, 1987, and 1991 contain identical wording.

teaching role, in contrast to the other roles given to the bishops in the earlier documents.

Finally, the greater emphasis on the teaching role of the bishops is demonstrated by the fact that, from 1976 to 1996, each voting guide cited Paul VI's statement from *Octogesima Adveniens* that the Catholic faithful should "draw principles of reflection, norms of judgment and directives for action from the social teaching of the Church,"[42] but beginning in 1999 this passage is absent. This editorial decision shows that the bishops' statements reflected developments in the universal church, following Pope John Paul II's lead in avoiding any suggestion that Catholic doctrine emerges out of the lived faith of the people, instead proposing that the magisterium teaches clearly defined doctrines which are received and lived out by the faithful.

From the bishops' 1976 statement to that produced in 2011, all focus on outlining the implications of Catholic faith for public policy, and each statement is a reflection on the complex relationship between religious faith and public life. Nevertheless, despite the shared focus on that relationship, the moral dilemma garnering the bishops' attention shifted. From 1976 to 1991, the statements focused on the public relevance of the faith and insisted that Catholics must continue their ongoing collaboration with non-Catholics in pursuit of their shared goals. For example, the 1976 document introduces the bishops' positions on the issues facing the nation by stating, "We wish to point out that these issues are not the concerns of Catholics alone; in every case we have joined with others to advocate these concerns."[43] In 1996 the wording of this line was changed to "The issues that follow are not the concerns of Catholics alone; in every case we are joined with others in advocating these concerns."[44] Although this passage could be interpreted as meaning the same thing as the earlier one, the shift from the active to the passive voice diminishes the role of collaboration on the part of Catholics and suggests that all that is intended here is that non-Catholics are involved in advocacy on the same issues. Beginning with the 2003 statement the line is dropped entirely.

In fact, from 2003 on, the bishops' statements contain no explicit mention of collaboration between Catholics and non-Catholics. By 2003 the concern of the bishops had shifted from the public relevance of their faith to maintaining the purity of the Catholic voter in the midst of pluralism. This concern was reflected in public controversies over the denial of communion

---

42. Pope Paul VI, *Octogesima Adveniens* §4.

43. United States Catholic Conference Administrative Board, *Political Responsibility* (1976) §19.

44. United States Catholic Conference, *Political Responsibility* (1996).

to pro-choice Catholic politicians, supporters of same-sex marriage, and so forth from the 2004 elections onward. The bishops developed a moral casuistry of voting, expounding upon themes such as the role of prudence in political decision making and the relative weight of "intrinsic evils." Although clearly the bishops did not eschew cooperation with non-Catholics, this change in emphasis reflected the broader shift toward a greater emphasis on Catholic identity and the clarity of Catholic teaching we have already seen in the more-detailed elaboration of Catholic social teaching and the stronger emphasis on the teaching role of the bishops. Responding to what Cardinal George called the "crisis of truth" in American culture, the bishops attempted to provide sure guidance to Catholics through the murky waters of partisan politics.

While the social strategy of the U.S. bishops in the late 1990s and 2000s was an attempt to counteract the influence of ideology and partisanship, to proclaim "simply Catholicism," compared to the strategy of the 1980s and early 1990s the bishops had become more comfortable with working through partisan politics. Their 1991 statement was the first to admit what was already obvious in 1976: "We [Catholics] are Democrats, Republicans, and Independents."[45] Although the statement insisted that Catholic teaching does not fit easily into either party's platform, neither did it protest Catholics' diverse political identifications. Beginning in 2007, the bishops provided a more concrete idea of how Catholics should work through partisan politics: "When necessary, our participation should help transform the party to which we belong; we should not let the party transform us in such a way that we neglect or deny fundamental moral truths."[46] The bishops envisaged Catholics as a transformative force within each party, striving to move their party's positions closer to those compatible with Catholic social teaching. The bishops, however, admitted that the key principles of Catholic social teaching could be applied in diverse ways, allowing Catholics to pursue different partisan loyalties. Even so, it is clear that the "fundamental moral truths" taught by the bishops should be a unifying force for Catholics, regardless of party affiliation.

Public Reason after the Dissolution of the Subculture

The 2012 presidential election, with vice-presidential candidates Paul Ryan and Joe Biden clearly advertising the important role their Catholic

45. United States Catholic Conference, *Political Responsibility* (1991).

46. United States Conference of Catholic Bishops, *Forming Consciences for Faithful Citizenship* (2007).

faith played in their public lives, was a significant moment for evaluating the public role of Catholicism in American politics. Although the election campaign did generate significant discussion among theologians and the Catholic intelligentsia, have the U.S. bishops been successful in encouraging faithful citizenship among Catholics? The evidence is discouraging. A survey looking back on the 2010 midterm elections, conducted by Fordham's Center on Religion and Culture and the Center for Applied Research in the Apostolate, showed that only 16 percent of U.S. Catholics were even aware of the bishops' *Forming Consciences for Faithful Citizenship* voting guide, and only 3 percent had read it. Of those who were aware of it, three quarters said that it had no influence on their vote in the 2010 elections, and a similar percentage of those who were not aware of it claimed that even if they had been, it would not have impacted their vote.[47] Clearly there is a wide chasm between the bishops' view of their role as teachers of Catholic social teaching and the reality of their influence on the typical Catholic voter. So what does shape the decisions of Catholic voters? Since 2000, the Catholic vote in U.S. presidential elections has closely tracked with the national vote; when a Democrat wins the presidency, a small majority of Catholics vote Democratic, and when a Republican wins, a small majority of Catholics vote Republican.[48] In essence, there is no discernible "Catholic vote," and whatever is shaping the partisan identities of Americans is having a greater influence on Catholics than the teaching of the bishops. In the digital age we can surround ourselves with cable news shows, web sites, and radio stations catered to our own worldview, reinforcing and radicalizing the polarization of American culture. Arguably, the individualism and materialism of late-modern consumer culture also form us in mindsets that reinforce political partisanship, making the dichotomies and polarizations we are presented seem obvious and inevitable.

What accounts for the failure of the U.S. bishops to provide a credible alternative to polarization and, as Cardinal Bernardin recognized almost a decade ago, the increasing disregard for vulnerable human life? Why have the bishops been unable to form a sizeable counter-witness within the Catholic Church, instead shepherding over a church itself increasingly polarized and partisan? The bishops have failed to develop a social strategy that successfully addresses the roots of the problem and that sufficiently draws on the resources of the Catholic tradition in the formation of a response. One reason for this is that by presenting Catholic social teaching as a set

47. Center for Applied Research in the Apostolate, "CARA Catholic Poll 2011," 6–7.

48. Silk and Walsh, "A Past Without a Future?"; Wisniewski, "Most Catholics Vote for Obama."

of seven key themes that unify Catholics but that can be interpreted or applied in divergent ways, the bishops failed to consider the extent to which this approach enabled party and ideological identities to shape the faithful's understanding of the church's public witness. The Georgetown faculty rightly protested Rep. Paul Ryan's misuse of the principle of subsidiarity, yet the same year only nine faculty (only one of whom had signed the letter to Ryan) could be mustered to protest the selection of then Secretary of Health and Human Services Kathleen Sebelius as the commencement speaker, despite her radical views on abortion, not to mention her role in denying funding to the U.S. bishops' Migration and Refugee Services and in the contraceptive mandate controversy associated with the Affordable Care Act. Catholics pick and choose elements of Catholic social teaching that fit their partisan agenda, leaving the rest to "prudential judgment."

Behind this weakness lies the failure of the bishops to adequately respond to the cultural sources of polarization and to grasp how their own self-understanding of the church's public role has contributed to that failure. This failure stems from a lack of full awareness of the changing sociological status of the Catholic Church in America. As William L. Portier has argued, the "dissolution of the subculture is the single most important fact in U.S. Catholic history in the second half of the twentieth century."[49] The "subculture" refers to the network of parishes, schools, hospitals, social agencies, labor unions, and religious groups that formed U.S. Catholic identity from the nineteenth century to the middle of the twentieth, and which by the end of that period was gradually dissolving as Catholics moved to the suburbs and increasingly participated in the same social institutions as their non-Catholic neighbors. In light of this dissolution, Catholics coming of age in the immediate aftermath of the Second Vatican Council have since come to view the subculture as parochial, unthinking, and authoritarian. As Portier argues, the dissolution of the subculture has decisively shaped the reception of the council in the United States, with most Catholics in the postconciliar years interpreting the council as liberating Catholics from the perceived limitations of the Catholic subculture.[50] Catholic public advocacy, understood as a fulfillment of the council's call for the church to engage the modern world, must be interpreted in the same light. Moving beyond the party machine politics, based on parochial and tribal loyalties, associated with the Catholic subculture, the U.S. bishops' quest to encourage political responsibility and to rally Catholics around a set of intellectualized ethical principles which they, the laity, have responsibility for implementing,

49. Portier, "Here Come the Evangelical Catholics," 46.
50. Ibid., 46–48.

is of a piece with the "full and active participation by all the people" in the liturgy,[51] the removal of statues and other visual accoutrements of worship for a more cerebral, barren style, and the encouragement of "mature," "adult" faith through the development of the Rite of Christian Initiation for Adults (RCIA) and the proliferation of faith formation programs, all associated with postconciliar Catholic life.

As Portier suggests, however, the dissolution of the Catholic subculture has left American Catholics exposed to the full force of American pluralism, and what at first seemed like a liberating opening to the wider culture now threatens to dissolve Catholic identity entirely. Beginning in 1976, the bishops rightly began to encourage the Catholic faithful to actively participate in the political process by reflecting on the abstract principles of Catholic teaching and exercising political responsibility in their voting decisions. While maintaining the political involvement that had long characterized Catholic life in America, this represented a shift away from the parochial and authoritarian patterns of the subculture. The bishops wanted Catholics to embrace the belief that their faith was publicly relevant, that it could be translated into a form of public reason, and that they could participate in the political life of the nation alongside their neighbors and make an impact in the name of justice. What the bishops neglected was that the Catholic social teaching guiding their own pastoral initiatives and which they wished to pass on to the faithful had, in many ways, been worked out in the lived practice of labor unions, neighborhood organizations, and advocacy groups that were part of the Catholic subculture gradually passing away. The church's public reason is also historical reason. The abstract principles only gained life within the ecosystem of the subculture, and without some analogous environment, the principles of Catholic social teaching cannot compete with the formative role that contemporary consumerism plays in American culture.

Portier's work is a study of a subgroup of American Catholics he classifies as "evangelical Catholics," those for whom American pluralism is their natural environment and who have adapted the practice of their faith to pluralism in a powerful way. Although I am not necessarily proposing an "evangelical Catholic" social strategy for U.S. Catholics, I do believe that, like evangelical Catholics, a renewed Catholic social strategy must embrace pluralism while at the same time recognizing the importance of the formation of identity in community. It must also heed Portier's warning against the potentially negative impact pluralism can have on religiosity, namely the dangers of privatization and consumerist faith. Therefore, learning from

---

51. Second Vatican Council, *Sacrosanctum Concilium* §14.

both Portier's work and nearly thirty years of social engagement by the U.S. bishops, I propose the following as an outline for a renewed social strategy:

Focus first on rebuilding civil society, and only then on engaging the state.

Despite the changes in strategy over time, the U.S. bishops' social engagement has consistently focused on transforming public policy through influencing the state. Although important and necessary, this strategy has failed to mobilize a constituency needed to advocate for the policies recommended by the bishops. Instead, the bishops should put a greater priority on encouraging Catholics to create and participate in civil society organizations, including new forms of labor organizing, advocacy groups, and charities, as well as associations with primarily social or religious purposes. These associations can be either Catholic-inspired, interconfessional, or non-confessional. While these associations promote social goods valuable in their own right, it is also true that only by engaging in face-to-face practices that demand solidarity and respect for the dignity of the person will Catholics come to approach larger political issues with the attitudes encouraged by the bishops.

Focus on the imagination, not just the intellect.

By making abstract principles central to their proclamation of Catholic social teaching, the bishops have emphasized the intellectual dimension of faith at the expense of the affective and imaginative. Admittedly the U.S. bishops have successfully integrated their social teaching with biblical themes in a way that does evoke the imagination, but more should be done. Pastors should be encouraged to use the liturgy as a way of shaping the faithful's imagination in ways that extend beyond the church sanctuary. Catholics should be taught how to interpret their work and family lives as part of a larger narrative of faith.

Trust the laity to work out what the Catholic faith means in public life.

Pope John Paul II's decision to envision Catholic social teaching as taught by the bishops and then applied by the laity, although understandable when faced with the dangers of distortions to Catholic doctrine, was a pastoral mistake. Faith is more than doctrine. The bishops should encourage the laity to reflect on what their faith means when lived out in the midst of pluralism, increasingly digital social interaction, and the increasing inequality of twenty-first-century capitalism. The bishops should be open to drawing on the experience of the laity in formulating their teaching.

These three proposals are underdeveloped and merely suggestive, but I believe they possess the potential to revitalize the public presence of Catholicism in American society.

Writing History with the End in Sight

Notes for a Catholic Radical Historiography

———————— MICHAEL J. BAXTER ————————

"When the history of America and Catholicism in the 1950s is written, Francis Cardinal Spellman will be a footnote and Dorothy Day will be a chapter."[1] This is what Michael Harrington quipped to William F. Buckley at a party in the 1950s as a way to suggest that Day's Catholic radicalism would endure the test of time, while Spellman's and Buckley's Cold War Catholicism would eventually wind up where it belongs—in the dustbin of history.

Harrington recalled his exchange with Buckley in an interview with Catholic Worker oral historian Rosalie Riegle in 1988. By that time, Buckley was the nation's leading articulator of conservative politics and free-market economics, while Harrington had become the elder statesman of democratic socialism—not exactly a potent political force in U.S. politics. It therefore must have gratified Harrington to note how the twists and turns of history had brought to Day an honorable mention from the U.S. Catholic bishops in *The Challenge of Peace* (1983). As Harrington explained to Riegle: "When I was at the Worker in the fifties we appeared a small band of nuts. Catholic puritans. Totally marginal nuts. Who would have predicted, at that point, that the bishops of the United States would write a pastoral letter on nuclear weapons and quote Dorothy Day? It turns out that Day in 1952 was closer to

1. Riegle, *Dorothy Day*, 58.

what became the official position of the hierarchy than Spellman. Spellman is nowhere in there 'cause he was simply a cold warrior."[2]

Harrington died a year after his interview with Riegle, but had he lived longer, he would have witnessed an even more remarkable turn of events. In 2000, Cardinal John J. O'Connor, Spellman's successor in New York and former head of the military vicariate, initiated Day's cause for canonization. In 2012, the U.S. Catholic bishops unanimously approved Day's cause and forwarded it to Rome. And in 2015, while addressing the U.S. Congress, Pope Francis extolled Day for her social activism rooted in the gospel, her faith, and her devotion to the saints. Even if Harrington's prediction to Buckley has not literally come to pass,[3] it has certainly become more true over time—evidence of what Harrington, a subscriber to the historiography of Marx, might call the cunning of history, or what Day, a devout Catholic convert, might rather call the work of providence in history. In either case, the idea here is that history unfolds according to an appointed end.

In this essay, I take up the idea that history can be written in light of its end. Here I use the word "end" in two senses: in the sense of its culmination and conclusion, and in the sense of the goal or purpose of the actions of agents within history. Both senses come together in the historical figure of Dorothy Day, for as she saw it, her life and work could not be understood apart from the working of divine providence, and the same is true of all history, she would insist. In other words, for Day, history is governed by a logic that reveals God's purposes for humanity, and it was according to this logic and purpose that Day lived. Everything she believed and practiced— her practice of hospitality, her call for justice for workers and the poor, her unswerving pacifist stance, and her devotion to Christ, to the sacraments, to the saints—was generated out of an understanding of how history has a purpose or goal or end. What I want to suggest is that we can write history in the way Day envisioned and wrote history: with the end in sight.

But here we run into a problem. This is not (to put it mildly) an approach endorsed by academic historians. "History," as an academic profession, was founded in the late-nineteenth century to move beyond the amateurish confessional, theologically shaped accounts of the past. As a result, even now, in spite of a remarkable variety of approaches and perspectives in the writing of history (sociological, psychological, Marxist, feminist, and so on), historians are trained and encouraged to steer clear of theological explanations of historical events. Thus even among Catholic historians,

---

2. Ibid.

3. For instance, Spellman is only mentioned once in the body of McGreevy's *Catholicism and American Freedom* (174).

it is rare to find those whose research and writing reflect the traditional Catholic vision of the unity of knowledge and the interrelation among theology, philosophy, and the writing of history.

With this in mind, I argued in a previous essay that three histories of Catholicism in the United States—John Tracy Ellis's *American Catholicism*, Jay Dolan's *The American Catholic Experience*, and David J. O'Brien's *Public Catholicism*—are, in fact, informed by the theology and philosophy of John Courtney Murray who argued, and who emerges in these narratives as a hero for arguing, that a fundamental harmony exists between Catholicism and public life in the United States.[4] My strategy was to show how Murray's Americanist theology and philosophy (as I called it) is embedded into these historical narratives so as to envision politics as a sphere of activity that deals with means rather than ends, and also to suggest that these narratives can, therefore, be challenged on the basis of a theology and philosophy that sees final ends as essential to politics—that is, a theology and philosophy like that of the Catholic Worker. In concluding that essay, I noted (citing Hayden White) that the partisan perspective of academic history prohibits theological explanations in historical writing and, thereby, disciplines our imaginations, against narrating events as godly or divinely inspired. "What would it be like," I asked, "to narrate the emergence of the Catholic Worker as a godly event, as a divinely inaugurated interruption in the history of the *imperium* we call the United States of America?"[5]

This is the question I address in this essay, not in a fully developed way, which would require a comprehensive re-narration of Catholicism in the United States, but in a preliminary way, by offering a set of theological, philosophical, and historiographical notes on how to think about such a re-narration. For the second note (this concludes the first note), I want to return to Michael Harrington's recollection of Dorothy Day and the Catholic Worker in the early fifties.

Note II: Center or Periphery?

"Totally marginal nuts" is how Michael Harrington described people at the Catholic Worker at the time he was at the New York house, from January 1951 until December 1952. But a good historian could dispute Harrington's description by making several points. She could point out, for example, that in October 1952 *The New Yorker* published a two-part, strikingly

4. Baxter, "Writing History in a World without Ends."
5. Ibid., 469.

sympathetic profile of Dorothy Day by Dwight Macdonald.[6] Totally marginal nuts don't draw attention and adulation on the pages of highbrow magazines with a national audience. She might further point to Macdonald's article itself, which reported that, soon after the Catholic Worker started in 1933, Day's cause "struck fire in certain Catholic circles, especially among young priests. Catholic Worker groups started up all over the place—often by spontaneous combustion, without any help from headquarters."[7] It also noted that this "headquarters" in New York had been visited by Catholic notables such as Fr. John LaFarge, an editor of *America*; Msgr. John A. Ryan, a director at the National Catholic Welfare Conference; Carlton J.H. Hayes, a history professor at Columbia; and Jacques Maritain, a world-renowned French philosopher.[8] Macdonald also noted that *The Catholic Worker* paper had a circulation of 58,000, which equaled the circulations of *The Nation* and *The New Republic* combined.[9] As a result, he observed, "by now Catholic Worker alumni and alumnae are numerous, and their ideas have acted as a leaven on the American Catholic community. There are not many nuns and priests who have not heard of Dorothy Day."[10] All of these points, drawn from Macdonald's 1952 article, indicate that Day and the Worker were *not* "totally marginal nuts," as Harrington says in 1988; they were interesting, compelling Catholics whose life and witness was on the rise.

But another historian could counter this argument by contending that any influence of Day and the Catholic Worker in the 1950s was undercut by their anarchism and pacifism. In defending this contention, he might rebut the points made above with the following counterpoints: that the fast-paced, early growth of the Catholic Worker did not continue into the 1940s and 1950s because its anarchism and pacifism was seen as irresponsible in the face of fascist and communist aggression; that LaFarge, Ryan, Hayes, and Maritain were drawn to visit and support Day and the Worker, but in no way endorsed its absolute pacifism or anarchism; that the circulation of *The Catholic Worker* dropped precipitously during World War II, due to its anarcho-pacifist stand, and that the number 58,000 was, in any case, inflated because many copies were bundled and sent to parishes, schools, and lay groups; that most nuns and priests had indeed heard of Dorothy Day, but the majority did not agree with her radical stance against war and the state; that the image of Day and the Worker as a "leaven" is misleading, because

6. Macdonald, "Profiles."

7. Ibid., part 2, 37.

8. Ibid., part 1, 42.

9. Ibid., part 2, 46.

10. Ibid., part 1, 37.

relatively few people in the American Catholic community actually lived a Catholic Worker life with the poor, in voluntary poverty, and resisting war; and finally, that Macdonald wrote sympathetically about Day because he, too, was an anarcho-pacifist and was also a rather marginal figure (albeit a well-placed one) in the cultural and intellectual ethos of the United States in the 1950s. Taken together, these counterpoints lend credence to the description of Day and the Worker as "totally marginal nuts."

So were Dorothy Day and the Catholic Worker of the 1950s marginal or not? This is the kind of question that absorbs historians striving to portray Day and her coworkers accurately and fairly on the basis of the available evidence. In doing so, other questions are sure to come up as well, such as: Didn't the editors of *Commonweal* chide Day for her harsh, judgmental, pacifist stance during the Cold War?[11] And wasn't *Commonweal* a balanced, liberal periodical, not a hardline, right-wing publication? Doesn't that point to Day being marginal? Moreover, wasn't Fr. John Hugo a mentor and spiritual advisor to Day? And wasn't Hugo on the margins of the Catholic theological world? Doesn't Day admit that he was in trouble with church authorities for denigrating nature?[12] But then again, on the other hand, didn't *The Long Loneliness,* published in 1952, sell numerous copies and always remain in print?[13] And wasn't Hugo extolled in that book as the articulator of the spirituality and theology of the movement?[14] Moreover, didn't Day and others at the Catholic Worker draw hundreds into their annual protest against New York's civil defense drills in the late fifties, so that the city eventually stopped the drills altogether?[15] Historians pursue and answer such questions by examining evidence, testing its reliability, judging its significance, and comparing it with other evidence, and so on, in order to come up with an accurate, reliable, reasoned account of "history"—in this case, the history of Dorothy Day and the Catholic Worker, and whether or not she and the movement were marginal.

But at some point a more probing set of questions can and should be addressed by historians: What do we mean by "marginal"? If there is a "margin," there must also be a center, so where is this "center"? With what framework should we define the "margin" and "center"? And on what basis do we decide who is "marginal" and who is "central"? In pursuing these questions, another question also can and should arise: What did Dorothy Day view as

11. Day, *Dorothy Day,* 101–2.

12. Day, *The Long Loneliness,* 253–58.

13. Forest, *All is Grace,* 192–94.

14. Day, *The Long Loneliness,* 254–60.

15. Ibid., 202–10.

"marginal" and "central"? This question is the crucial one for our purposes, because it opens up the possibility of not simply writing a history *of* Day and the Catholic Worker—there are plenty of those—but writing a history of Day and the Catholic Worker *from the perspective of Day and the Catholic Worker*. I want to entertain this possibility by turning to the work of R.G. Collingwood.

Note III: What Is History?

In *The Idea of History*, Collingwood explains what history is and what it is not. History is *not* what he calls "medieval historiography"; that is, it is not an account of past events centering so much on God's plan and purposes in history that "the human agent finds himself caught up in the stream of divine purpose, and carried along in it with or without his consent."[16] The problem with medieval historiography is that God is portrayed as a transcendent force acting on history from the outside, intruding on human events. For Collingwood, this is not really history at all, for it looks at the past as a series of spectacular occurrences to be observed, whereas genuine history, as it has emerged over the past two centuries, has to do with human agency and action.[17] For Collingwood, interestingly, this same problem is found in modern scientific approaches to history, what he calls "positivist historiography."[18] Here, human agency and action is given short shrift in favor of establishing the facts, and then determining the causal connections among facts, so as to offer general explanations as to how historical events occurred. On this view, understanding history is analogous to the way scientists understand nature, by means of the empirical method of detached observation. But history and nature, Collingwood argues, are not the same and do not allow for the same method and analysis. While nature can be grasped externally, so to speak, as a series of events understandable from the outside, history must be understood internally, in light of human actions, and it is precisely these that are not considered in scientific or naturalistic conceptions of history.[19] Both medieval Christian historiography and modern positivist historiography thus suffer from the same fundamental flaw: they lack a conception of human agency.

So then, what is history? For Collingwood, history is the study of human agents, activities, and events that occurred in the past. The key to

16. Collingwood, *The Idea of History*, 53.

17. Ibid., 52–56.

18. Ibid., 126–33.

19. Ibid., 132–33.

writing history, he argues, is grasping what happened in the past from the inside, internally, not viewing history as a series of divine spectacles (medieval historiography) or scientific phenomena (positivist historiography) to be observed, but as a series of human actions to be understood. This involves grasping the thought of the historical agent, understanding the agent's actions by means of a "re-enactment of past thought in the historian's own mind."[20] The task of the historian is "not a passive surrender to the spell of another's mind; it is a labor of active and therefore critical thinking." In other words, "the historian not only re-enacts past thought," but "re-enacts it in the context of his or her own knowledge and therefore, in re-enacting it, criticizes it, forms his own judgment of its value, corrects whatever errors he can discern in it."[21] For example, from the outside we can say simply that Julius Caesar crossed the Rubicon, but from the inside, we can go on to depict this action as a defiance of Republic law or as a clash of constitutional policy between Caesar and his adversaries. Grasping historical events from the inside entails a different and more complex concept of causality than that of the natural sciences. As Collingwood explains, a scientist finds out why a piece of litmus paper turns pink, what causes this to happen, from the outside. But an historian, answering the question, Why did Brutus stab Caesar?, must search for what Brutus thought in stabbing Caesar, and it is this thought or series of thoughts that can be regarded as a cause.[22] Historians converse with people of the past based on what can be known of them from what they said, did, and wrote, from the historical context in which they lived. It is like the work of a detective. Writing history involves actively and critically engaging the subject—whether Julius Caesar, Napoleon, Plato, Aristotle—on matters, we might say, of mutual importance.[23] Indeed, Collingwood suggests that writing history entails an inquiry into human nature itself, by means of which we learn not only about actors and events in the past but also about ourselves.

More can be said about Collingwood's *The Idea of History*, but this is enough to see its relevance in writing a history of Dorothy Day and the Catholic Worker. For one thing, it stresses the importance of empathizing with Day so as to reenact, in the historian's research and writing, her understanding of God, Christ, the church, the sacraments, the works of mercy, capitalism, the modern state, and the struggle for social justice and genuine peace. For another thing, it stresses the importance of an historian allowing

20. Ibid., 215.
21. Ibid.
22. Ibid., 213–15.
23. Ibid., 228–31.

his or her own worldview—*his or her* understanding of God, Christ, the church, economics, politics, social change, and so on—to engage with and, indeed, be challenged by Dorothy Day's worldview so as to bring about a kind of conversation and a debate in the mind of the historian about human activity, human life, and human nature. And then there is Collingwood's refutation of the notion that writing history is a neutral, scientific, fact-gathering activity. He cogently rebuts the claim that historians simply ascertain facts and then let the facts speak for themselves. This claim, he contends, is not neutral as regards philosophy; rather, it is dependent on a definite and deeply flawed philosophy, namely, positivist philosophy. Collingwood's argument here is important because this positivist philosophy shaped the historiographical framework that prohibited theological narrations of historical events, including those espoused by Day and her followers. At this point, we need to turn to Day's alternative vision of history, which was drawn from the historiography, so to speak, of her intellectual mentor, Peter Maurin, and her spiritual advisor and confidante, Fr. John J. Hugo.

Note IV: History to What End?

Not long after their first encounter, Peter Maurin told Dorothy Day she needed a Catholic education, beginning with "a Catholic outline of history."[24] From Day's report in *The Long Loneliness* and the general themes of Maurin's *Easy Essays*, we can piece together this historical outline as follows: the central event, of course, was the incarnation of Christ, out of which flows the life and witness of the early church, the conversion of the Roman Empire, the conversion of Europe and the preservation of classical culture by the Benedictine and Irish monastics, and the creation of a society imbued with faith and reason in the thirteenth century. From this high point in history, the plotline takes a downturn, due to the disintegrating effects of the Reformation: the waning of church authority, the onset of capitalism, the rise of the nation-state, and the spread of false philosophies and erroneous trends of thought, such as individualism, collectivism, nationalism, utilitarianism, and (worst of all) atheism, which separated every aspect of modern life from God. All these events created a pervasive crisis that was religious, moral, intellectual, economic, political, and cultural in character: the crisis of modernity. In the early 1930s, this sense of crisis was reinforced by a series of ominous events and developments that had recently unfolded: the Great War, the communist revolution, the rise of fascism, worldwide

---

24. Day, *Long Loneliness*, 170, 172.

economic depression, an arms race in Europe and Asia, and the looming threat of another catastrophic world war.[25]

It should be noted that much of Maurin's "Catholic outline of history" was not unusual at the time. Catholic thinkers typically envisioned history in these terms, and the names and themes that Maurin cited in his *Easy Essays*—Catholic action, the common good, Thomas Aquinas, Pius XI, Charles Péguy, Jacques Maritain, Bede Jarrett, and Christopher Dawson— were standard ones in Catholic intellectual life. But even so, Peter Maurin was unique among Catholic thinkers in that he did not believe "social reconstruction," as it was called at the time, could be accomplished merely by economic and political reforms, however far-reaching. Maurin was not a liberal. He was a radical. He believed the ills of modernity had to be treated at the roots. Anything less was superficial and ineffective.[26] In one especially blunt essay, he states that modern society is stuck in an alley with no way forward; the only way out is to back the car up until we find the point in history at which we took a wrong turn. Then, and only then, will we be able to move forward, make real progress.[27] On this score, Maurin parted company with most Catholic thinkers of his day: with John Ryan, for example, whose prescriptions for economic reform were not enough to counter the acquisitiveness in capitalist society; with Maritain, whose belief that a "new Christendom" could be embodied in modern democratic states was illusory; and with George Shuster, who referred him to Day but whose vision of America and Catholicism as perfectly fitted for each other was a symptom of, rather than a cure for, modernity's ills. Drawing on an edgier, more critical group of thinkers—the English distributists Chesterton and Belloc, the Russian anarchist-personalists Kropotkin and Berdyaev, and the French personalist Mounier—Maurin disavowed all large-scale, state-centered approaches to social change. He called for constructing a *new* society, not repairing the old society's crumbling shell. For him, this meant turning back to Christ, adhering to his teachings and example, taking up with renewed fervor the apostles' mission of bringing Christ to all nations, retrieving the synthesis of faith and reason that integrated European society of the thirteenth century.

25. Maurin, *Easy Essays*. On Christ and the early church, see 45, 65–66, 110. On the Benedictine and Irish monastics, see 29, 17, 58–59, 71–72, 142. On the Middle Ages as the high point of cultural unity and the synthesis of faith and reason, see 28, 132–33, 168–69, 198. On the Reformation, see 139. On the onset of capitalism in the wake of the Reformation, see 18–20, 199–202. On the emergence of the modern state, see 6–7. On World War I, see 18, 81–82. On the economic depression of the 1930s, see 18, 20, 82. On the chaos of the situation in the 1930s, see 125–26. For this overall historical plotline, see 78–83.

26. Ibid., 61–63, 108, 156–57.

27. Ibid., 25–26.

His vision was deeply historical, in that it attempted to reach back in history, before the rise of modernity, to the ancient and medieval period, in order to retrieve a form of society guided by the principles of justice and enlivened by the works of mercy. Practically speaking, what this entailed was the three-pronged program that became the hallmark of the Catholic Worker movement: roundtable discussions for the clarification of thought, houses of hospitality for workers and the poor, and agrarian communities for a life on the land. While Maurin has often been accused of being a pessimist, his vision of social transformation was actually profoundly hopeful, predicated on the belief that, with God's help, the Catholic Worker could become a movement of world-historical significance.

By all accounts, including her own, Day was the one with the gift to translate this ambitious plan into practical action. But she never lost sight of Maurin's comprehensive historical vision, nor his belief that the movement would be sustained by God's care and providential guidance. She continually talked and wrote about it. In fact, in *The Long Loneliness*, Day described meeting Peter Maurin as itself providential, the answer to a heartfelt prayer.[28] When she asked Peter how his three-part program would be financed, he assured her that "in the history of the saints, capital was raised by prayer. God sends you what you need when you need it."[29] Looking back on the remarkable growth of the Catholic Worker—the newspaper, the houses of hospitality, the farms, the people coming to help—she explains it as the work of God. And near the end of *The Long Loneliness,* she tells how the community in New York was recently forced to move from a rental on Mott Street to a property on Christie Street that they had to buy; so they pray a novena, explain their plight in the paper, and come up with enough money to make the purchase. "As I write this," she reflects, "there is less than a hundred dollars in the bank, the line of men stretches to the corner, and our households here at Maryfarm and Peter Maurin farm comprise seventy-five people or more. How can we go on? We are as sure as ever that God can multiply the loaves, as He has sheltered the homeless these many years."[30] For Day, the central reality, in her life and in the Catholic Worker, is divine providence: God always provides. Moreover, as she saw it, God's providence is the central reality, not just for her history and the history of the Catholic Worker, but for all history, beginning to end.

28. Day, *Long Loneliness*, 166.

29. Ibid., 173.

30. Ibid., 284.

Day's understanding of divine providence in history is clearly articulated in *The Long Loneliness* in the chapter titled "Retreat."[31] The title refers to the retreat given by the French-Canadian Jesuit priest Onesimus Lacouture and two of his disciples who had extensive contact with Day: Fr. Pacifique Roy, a Josephite from Quebec who worked in Baltimore, and Fr. John Hugo of the Diocese of Pittsburgh. At the theological core of the retreat was the injunction to supernaturalize our lives by aligning our will, motives, and intentions with God's will. The point was not only to avoid sin, nor even merely to do good, but to seek "the better" through a ceaseless striving for union with Christ. This required a spirit of detachment, a readiness to set aside natural goods and gifts—"sowing" in the parlance of the retreat—so as to receive and embody the sanctifying grace of a supernaturalized life.[32] Trusting in providence was crucial in this effort, for it entailed the practice of foregoing the natural goods of, for example, economic and political security in order to embrace the poverty and pacifism that lay at the heart of the gospel. "You will get back your hundredfold," Fr. Roy used to assure his listeners, when it comes to "sowing" their time, money, or other natural goods.[33] Similarly, Fr. Hugo would exhort his readers to this trust in providence as they embraced the call to conscientious objection to war; war may be just on the natural plane, he conceded, but Christians must strive for a supernatural ethic, for "we are all called to be saints" (a phrase that served as something of a mantra for Day).[34] Day acknowledged that the "radical Christianity" of the retreat was criticized by certain theologians for being rigorist or Jansenist, in other words for denigrating nature.[35] But in Day's mind, the purpose of dying to nature ("mortification") was to transform nature and so unleash the power of love in the world.[36] In arguing about the supernatural, she wrote, we are talking about "spiritual capacities far more powerful than the atom."[37] This image of the atom (a pressing and poignant one in the early fifties) underscores how trusting in divine providence has far-reaching effects, not only on individuals or small communities, but on all nations and empires, all history.

31. Ibid., 243–63.

32. I am relying here on an excellent summary of the Hugo retreat in Peters, "Nature and Grace in the Theology of John Hugo." See also his recently published book, *Called To Be Saints*.

33. Day, *Long Loneliness*, 252.

34. Day, *By Little and By Little*, 102–3.

35. Day, *Long Loneliness*, 253.

36. Ibid., 257.

37. Ibid., 252.

Perhaps the clearest, and certainly the most provocative, illustration of a marginal movement like the Catholic Worker being turned into an instrument of sweeping social transformation comes early on in *The Long Loneliness*. Looking back on her youth, Day recalls the thrill she and her coworkers at *The Call* felt at the time of the Russian Revolution. "On March 21, 1917, at Madison Square Garden," she writes," I joined with those thousands in reliving the first days of the revolt in Russia. I felt the exultation, the joyous sense of victory of the masses . . ." The event celebrated how "revolutionary striving, with all its human aspirations, longing for liberty, human love, and justice, had culminated in a tremendous fact. The Russian masses, living on one-sixth of the world's surface, had overthrown the Czar." Day went on to reflect on how Lenin's widow, Krupskaya, was grateful when, in Paris before the Revolution, she and her husband managed to muster up a workers' meeting of forty people. "Forty people!" Day observed. "And now, not many years later, these little bands were taking over the destiny of one-sixth of the world."[38] This sense that small efforts can lead to great things, endeavors with no apparent effect igniting a chain reaction of events with world-historical significance, gave credence to her hopes and aspirations for the Catholic Worker. The difference was that now, in *this* revolution—this Christ-centered, Green Revolution—history unfolds not according to the laws of dialectical materialism, but to the designs of self-sacrificial love. In this sense, Day saw the Catholic Worker as part of God's providential work in history.

Note V: Sacred or Secular?

One way to capture Day's understanding of providence and history is to say that she places "history under the norm of Christ." This phrase comes from Hans Urs von Balthasar's brief treatise *A Theology of History*.[39] In his typically Christocentric manner, Balthasar shows how the primary task is not to show how Christ is included within history but how history is included within the life of Christ.[40] As the Divine Logos, Christ's existence is eternal, but as one born in Israel under the law, Christ lives within history; not, however, in submission to the confines of history, but in order to redefine history, to reshape history from within, as its source and center.[41] By remaining obedient to the will of the Father unto death, Christ breaks the

38. Ibid., 66.

39. Balthasar, *A Theology of History*, 113–54.

40. Ibid., 51.

41. Ibid., 24, 75–76.

cycle of sin that dominated Israel and ushers in the possibility of fulfilling the law in genuine freedom. A new space is created. A new norm is given. A new measure of human possibility is established by Christ, and reestablished in the church, by those who reenact Christ's limitless self-surrender in faith, prayer, and discipleship.[42] The prototypes of this new possibility are Mary and the saints. The movement of this possibility is an "outpouring of the 'seed of God' (1 John 3:9) into the womb of the world" which occurs "in the innermost chamber of history," a "begetting and conceiving" that takes place "in utter, reckless self-surrender."[43] When shaped by this receptive posture, the activity of the church reveals the true meaning of history. Indeed, this is what *makes* history. As Balthasar puts it, "the act of corresponding to what God wills for world history . . . is the central core which makes history happen."[44] The dynamics of this Christ-formed grace making history happen may be obvious, as with the "volcanic eruption" of Francis of Assisi into thirteenth-century Europe; or they may remain out of view, ensconced within the drudgery of ordinary events. In either case, these grace-created events, large and small, occur *within* history: "The law of the incarnation requires that the meaning of history should not be imposed from above, from outside . . . The meaning of history must emerge from the union of what God destines for it with its own interior line of development."[45] Thus, at the end of time, it will be fully revealed that the historical life, death, resurrection, and ascension of the Logos has been, all along, "the living center of history itself," "the source of history, the point whence the whole of history before and after Christ emanates: its center."[46]

Balthasar's theological-historical vision brings into relief key aspects of Dorothy Day's understanding of divine providence and the supernatural life. For one thing, by locating Christ at the center of history, it shows that Day and the Catholic Worker are by no means marginal; rather, our understanding of what is marginal and central in history is defined in light of Christ. For another thing, it gives an account of how Day and the others at the Catholic Worker, unlikely as they may appear to be as important historical actors, have the freedom as disciples "to make history happen" and to create with their lives a history-making space. And then there is the assurance enjoyed by Day and company, as disciples of Christ, that their life and work will be vindicated at the end of history. They persevere in performing

42. Ibid., 51–79.
43. Ibid., 121.
44. Ibid., 123.
45. Ibid., 126.
46. Ibid., 24.

the works of mercy, in working for justice and witnessing for peace, because for them the end of history is in sight.

But even though Day's understanding of divine providence in history is warranted in light of Balthasar's theology, the question arises, how are we to think about this gap between the ultimate meaning of history revealed at the end of time and history in the here and now? Balthasar answers this question by invoking a distinction between secular and sacred history, but he uses these terms tentatively. A full separation of sacred and secular history must be rejected as Averroistic, he maintains, for it would imply the existence of two separate sets of truths, one for secular scholarship and one for theology. At the same time, he argues against absorbing secular history into sacred history, as if what we know of history can be left to theology alone.[47] Instead, the task, as Balthasar sees it, is to relate the truths of sacred history—the truths of Israel, Christ, the church—with what we know of secular history—world history or the histories of the nations—so as to account for the particular facts and patterns ascertained by "secular" historical research while at the same time showing their "sacred" significance in the radiating light of Christ.[48]

But Balthasar does not offer anything more specific, so the question remains: how can a theologically grounded "sacred" history of Dorothy Day and the Catholic Worker inform and reshape a "secular" history of Dorothy Day and the Catholic Worker? To begin answering this question, I want to turn to a philosophical tradition that lends credibility to the historical vision of Dorothy Day and the Catholic Worker, namely, the Aristotelian tradition set forth by Alasdair MacIntyre in *After Virtue*.

Note VI: Can History Have Reasonable Ends?

What MacIntyre provides in *After Virtue* is a way to understand and defend the vision of history espoused by Dorothy Day and Peter Maurin on the basis of reason. For Balthasar's theology of history is an argument from faith, and it can be readily dismissed (mistakenly) by academic historians for its "confessional" or "sectarian" perspective. The same cannot be said of MacIntyre's argument concerning history in *After Virtue*.

The theoretical core of this argument comes in a key chapter in *After Virtue*, where MacIntyre claims that human action is intelligible only in light of the end to which it is directed.[49] Showing his indebtedness to

47. Ibid., 18–19.
48. Ibid., 133–45.
49. MacIntyre, *After Virtue*, 204–25.

Collingwood (and also to Ludwig Wittgenstein and G. E. M. Anscombe), he uses everyday examples—gardening, writing a book, conversing at a bus stop—to advance three interrelated claims: one, that intention is indispensible for understanding an agent's action; two, that a given human action can be understood only in sequence with other actions; and three, that human agents always act within the context of other agents who, therefore, interact with each other such that all actions must be placed in their particular social setting. Taken together, these three claims make clear that human action must be understood narratively.[50] For MacIntyre, it is important to note, a narrative conception of human action does not lead to a Nietzschean perspectivism that has marked much recent scholarship in a number of fields, including history.[51] Rather, for MacIntyre, a narrative understanding of human action is an irreducible part of his broader Aristotelian argument that human action aims at happiness and should be construed in terms of the good life and the virtues needed to attain it. This means not only that human life is shaped narratively, but also that the narrative is about the search for the good life, in which case life is understood as a drama that unfolds as a comedy, tragedy, or farce depending on whether or not, or to what extent, one possesses the virtues needed to attain the good one has been seeking all along.[52]

The implications of this Aristotelian vision for our purposes are far-reaching, for it entails that the writing of history involves evaluative judgments made on the basis of first principles and final ends of human life. But this philosophical argument runs counter to the protocols of academic history. Employing a substantive account of the good in order to judge whether or not, or to what extent, historical actors attain that good is not readily accepted in the writing of academic history. For instance, the events of World War II can be narrated, victories and defeats described, and a particular perspective can even be offered and defended. But the justice of the war and the actions in it, judged on the basis of a philosophical conception of the good, is not allowed within the scope of an historical account. How do we deal with this conflict between Aristotelian moral philosophy and modern academic history?

50. Ibid., 206–20.

51. I am thinking here of Michel Foucault's far-reaching influence, not only among theorists of history or historians of science, but on the writing of history more broadly in terms of power, resistance, and individual emancipation. For more on this trend, see Gregory, *The Unintended Reformation*, 127–28.

52. MacIntyre, *After Virtue*, 211, 218–19.

For an answer, we should look to the "disquieting suggestion" at the outset of *After Virtue*.[53] In this scenario, a know-nothing group has destroyed science, making it almost impossible later to reconstruct scientific knowledge from what is left. Because no one (or almost no one) comprehends genuine science as it existed, what is recovered is only partial and fragmentary, little more than a simulacra of science. MacIntyre uses this opening scenario to argue that a similar disintegration has befallen moral discourse and that a recovery of a prior vision is needed to restore coherence to our moral lives. As the book unfolds, we are gradually shown that what is missing in modern moral discourse is a teleological conceptual scheme within which action, reason, passion, rules, and moral and intellectual habits can be placed in order to display the transformation that occurs as humans acquire the virtues entailed in realizing the good life. What makes it difficult to recover this concept of a *telos* is that we live in an emotivist culture where morality is reduced to individual preference, so that we do not see the need for a moral vision grounded in a natural *telos* or end of human life. And even if we were to see the need, we do not think it is possible to regain it, due to the pluralistic character of modern society, which itself comes part and parcel with modern capitalism and the modern liberal state.

One might suppose that we could overcome our blindness to the loss of a human *telos* by means of historical investigation, but MacIntyre argues that our dilemma is compounded by the nature of "history" in modernity. "History by now in our culture means academic history," MacIntyre explains,

> and academic history is less than two centuries old. Suppose it were the case that the catastrophe of which my hypothesis speaks had occurred before, or largely before, the founding of academic history, so that the moral and other evaluative presuppositions of academic history derived from the forms of the disorder which it brought about. Suppose, that is, that the standpoint of academic history is such that from its value-neutral viewpoint moral disorder must remain largely invisible. All that the historian . . . will be allowed to perceive by the canons and categories of his discipline will be one morality succeeding another: seventeenth-century Puritanism, eighteenth-century hedonism, the Victorian work-ethic and so on, but the very language of order and disorder will not be available to him. If this were to be so, it would at least explain why what I take to be the real world and its fate has remained unrecognized by the academic curriculum. For the forms of the academic curriculum

53. Ibid., 1–5.

would turn out to be among the symptoms of the disaster whose occurrence the curriculum does not acknowledge.[54]

Academic history, in other words, with its alleged value-free methodologies and morally neutral standpoint, is not at all value-free and morally neutral, not from the Aristotelian tradition out of which MacIntyre advances the argument in *After Virtue*.

Granted, most historians—"working historians," as they often call themselves—would insist that such an argument does not fall within their domain, which is limited to making considered judgments based on established facts based on the historical record and leaving to others the task of evaluating those facts. But, as MacIntyre argues in *After Virtue* (again showing his indebtedness to Collingwood), this response is predicated on a post-Enlightenment fact-value dichotomy that has shaped the academic fields of history (and the social sciences) since their origin.[55] By historicizing academic history, he shows its blindness to the possibility of writing a history that accounts for the good to which humans are drawn and directed by nature. He shows that academic history rules out an account of the *telos* of human life, precludes writing history with humanity's end in sight.

By now I hope it is clear that MacIntyre's critique of modern moral philosophy and proposed recovery of the Aristotelian tradition of the virtues opens a way to thinking about writing the history of Dorothy Day and the Catholic Worker *from the perspective of Dorothy Day and the Catholic Worker*. For one thing, MacIntyre's account of the history of moral philosophy aligns with Peter Maurin's "Catholic outline of history." Indeed, in *After Virtue*, he locates the loss of the tradition of the virtues in the sixteenth and seventeenth centuries, when the new Protestant and Jansenist Catholic theologies held that reason cannot supply any genuine comprehension of humanity's true end because the power of reason was completely destroyed by Adam's fall.[56] For another thing, MacIntyre articulates on philosophical grounds the importance of constructing local forms of community in order to sustain virtuous practices and resist the corrosive effects of the market and the state, precisely the task set forth by Peter Maurin and carried out by Dorothy Day. This is no coincidence. Like Day and, to a lesser extent Maurin, MacIntyre too was at one point deeply shaped by a Marxist critique of capitalism and the modern state, but later came to see that the site of genuine social change is to be found in a localist politics and economics. And then there is the fact that, since publishing *After Virtue*, MacIntyre has

54. Ibid., 4.

55. Ibid., 79–108.

56. Ibid., 52–54.

extended and developed his Aristotelian argument by integrating it within a Thomistic account of the theological virtues (faith, hope, and charity) as the gifts that enable humanity to recover from the debilitating effects of the Fall and realize its final end.[57] Locating his argument in the context of Pope Leo XIII's call in *Aeterni Patris* (1879) for a return to the philosophy of Thomas Aquinas, MacIntyre is careful to cast his argument in philosophical terms, yet he is careful to show that reason does not negate the truths of revelation that are known by faith. As a result, MacIntyre advances, on grounds of reason, a philosophy that supports the unusual combination of a doctrinally traditional theology and a radical vision of social transformation—an unusual combination that has been the hallmark of the Catholic Worker from the beginning.

Note VII: Catholic History with the End in Sight

A host of important philosophical issues go well beyond the scope of these brief notes, the most important of which, perhaps, is the relation of efficient, formal, and final causality in narrating historical events. Still, from what I have noted about MacIntyre's Thomistic Aristotelianism and writing a history of Dorothy Day and the Catholic Worker out of that philosophical tradition, we can say that it will be a history that goes against the grain of any historiographies shaped by Weberian assumptions about the possibilities of social transformation within the constraints of modern politics and economics, including Americanist historiographies. In the United States, the lineage of these Weberian (and Troeltschian) historiographies goes back to H. Richard Niebuhr, whose writings had a field-shaping influence on Christian social ethics and also on American religious history,[58] and indirectly, through the influence of his brother Reinhold Niebuhr, on U.S. political and diplomatic history. At the theoretical core of this Weberian historiography is the notion that religious movements can only exert an initially powerful, but short-lived, impact on society, one that dissipates as the movements grow and evolve from an early stage of charismatic leadership and heroic morality to a later stage of routinized religious practice and policies designed to preserve institutional stability. This historiography tells the story of religious idealism succumbing to the hard realities of economic and political life—a story that fit nicely into the ethos and exigencies of the Cold War, with the United States defending "the Christian West" or "Christian civilization," but only (as Reinhold Niebuhr persuasively insisted) by set-

---

57. MacIntyre, *Whose Justice? Which Rationality?*, especially 140–42.

58. See Niebuhr, *The Social Sources of Denominationalism*; and *Christ and Culture*.

ting aside the teaching and example of Jesus. Within the strictures of such a story, a gospel-based radical movement like the Catholic Worker could only be seen as, at best, hopelessly unrealistic and marginal, at worst, as subversive and un-American. Day wore such labels openly, adopted them in editorials and columns in *The Catholic Worker*, as a way of resisting the ideology of the Cold War.

What I have said about this Weberian historiography and its attending ideology is important for our purposes because it is clearly evident in what is still the most well-researched, well-written, and highly regarded history of Day and the Catholic Worker. I refer to Mel Piehl's *Breaking Bread: The Catholic Worker and the Origin of Catholic Radicalism in America*. Piehl covers the beginning of the Catholic Worker, the people and the thinking involved, the controversies that arose regarding peace and the struggle for justice, and he places it in the context of religious and social thought in the United States in the twentieth century, thereby giving the movement an importance not often acknowledged by scholars when his book was published in 1982. And yet, the narrative of *Breaking Bread* is structured so that the Catholic Worker turns out to be an interesting, inspiring, heroic effort in the cause of justice and peace that was doomed to ultimate failure. As Piehl tells it, the Catholic Worker pursued "a radical Gospel ethic," to use Ernst Troeltsch's phrase, that was more concerned with purity of intention than with social effectiveness.[59] It operated out of "the ethic of ultimate ends," in Max Weber's terms, which Weber and Piehl contrast with an ethic of responsibility.[60] In maintaining the pacifist stand, it failed to take seriously the moral ambiguities of political power and international relations, as urged by Reinhold Niebuhr.[61] It never allowed for the flexibility needed for political compromise, for which reason, like many idealistic movements, it remained "unable to effect any significant transformation in American political attitudes or institutions."[62] It did not, in other words, adopt H. Richard Niebuhr's Christ-transforming-culture approach to social change.[63] Interestingly, Piehl observes that "the Catholic Worker's most measurable success" in having an impact in the United States "probably came with the

---

59. Piehl, *Breaking Bread*, 41–42.

60. Ibid., 241. The source of the phrase, not cited by Piehl, comes from Weber, "Politics as a Vocation," especially 120–21.

61. Ibid., 238.

62. Ibid., 242.

63. Piehl does not cite Niebuhr's *Christ and Culture* here, but it is clear that he is drawing on the categories set forth in the book. See ibid., 242, and Niebuhr, *Christ and Culture*, 190–229.

publication of Michael Harrington's *The Other America*."[64] But this was because Harrington left and was free to pursue a "practical politics" that was not available "at the utopian Catholic Worker."[65] Later on, Harrington had to deal with the tension between his socialist ideals and the realities of politics, but he was willing to make the necessary compromises—for example, not even mentioning socialism in *The Other America*—whereas Day and company were not.[66] Hence the curious, and somewhat patronizing, last line of the book. After admitting it will be thirty years before a sound historical judgment is possible, Piehl writes of the Catholic Worker, "in the meantime, in a world that sensitive and timid natures still had to regard with a shudder, it was one small sign of hope."[67]

The problem with Piehl's narrative is that it oscillates between description and prescription, not only telling us what happened, but what *had* to happen. The Catholic Worker was fated to be ineffective, marginal, in Piehl's Weberian universe. But Day and Maurin and others in the Catholic Worker did not see the universe in this way—not because of their "timid natures" (few who knew Dorothy Day regarded her as timid), but because they knew that God created the universe, and created humanity for an end, and that we can live in light of that end.

At the outset, we noted Michael Harrington's astonishment that the U.S. Catholic bishops extolled Dorothy Day in their 1983 pastoral letter *The Challenge of Peace*. Her condemnation of nuclear weapons was swift and unswerving until the end of her life. Her editorial in September 1945 ("Mr. Truman was jubilant") was an interruption. Her arrests in the late fifties for protesting civil defense drills were godly events. These put her on the margins. But by the 1980s the margins shifted. They can shift further, inasmuch as we are willing to live in accord with the end for which we are created. And we can aid in that process inasmuch as we are willing to write history with the end in sight.

64. Piehl, *Breaking Bread*, 241–42.

65. Ibid., 175–76.

66. Ibid., 176–77.

67. Ibid., 250.

15

Holiness in History

Learning to Pray with
Father McSorley

SANDRA YOCUM

William Portier's *Divided Friends: Portraits of the Roman Catholic Modernist Crisis in the United States* tells the story of four men, all priests, caught up in the intellectually inflected spiritual and ecclesial crisis known as Modernism. Portier captures the personal pathos of this theological controversy through the prism of two friendships—Denis O'Connell and John Slattery, William Sullivan and Joseph McSorley. While all four men saw the givens of their Catholic faith called into question and even uprooted in some cases, each man responded differently to the theological challenges posed by modern historical criticism. One friend in each pairing eventually left the church (Slattery and Sullivan) and called into question the integrity of the one who stayed. Of the two who remained, O'Connell decisively turned away from theological controversy and succeeded in his ecclesial ambitions to the episcopacy. Despite the differences among these three, the weight of the modernist crisis marked their lives with the tragic quality that accompanies profound spiritual upheaval and loss. As Portier states, "For Slattery, Sullivan, and even for O'Connell, the story ended with Pius X."[1]

In Portier's telling, therefore, McSorley emerges as the most intriguing figure among the four. He navigated his way through turbulent waters in the wake of Pius X's condemnation of Modernism and did far more than survive

1. Portier, *Divided Friends*, 14.

the storm. After 1907, he remained an active Paulist priest, ministering to the poor, especially Italian immigrants at St. Paul's parish in Manhattan, serving as Paulist superior general from 1924–1929, and giving retreats to diverse groups of lay and religious over a number of years. In contrast to the other three men, "for McSorley, as for many of the rest of us, the story continues."[2] Although clearly chastened in the aftermath of the Modernist crisis, the faithful cleric also continued his intellectual work, which resulted in a number of publications.

Two of these publications appeared in multiple editions. Their longevity brings into sharp relief just how apt William Portier's phrase, "holiness and history" is in characterizing McSorley's response to and influence after surviving the Modernist crisis.[3] The first, published in 1934, is brief. *A Primer of Prayer* went through nine unrevised printings with the publisher, Longman Green, and reappeared in 1961 under Deus Books of Paulist Press. The 1961 version, evidently unchanged from the first edition, is a 4" x 7" paperback, which explains its topic in a mere 120 pages. His other multiple-edition text appeared in 1943, bearing the title, *An Outline History of the Church by Centuries (From St. Peter to Pius XII)*. It also went through ten editions, but its form and content stand in sharp contrast to the *Primer*. The last seven editions are listed as revised, with the tenth edition, published in 1957, appearing as a 6.5" x 9.5" cloth text of 1,174 pages.

Given its breadth and scope, *An Outline* completely overshadows *A Primer of Prayer*. In fact, *A Primer* receives no mention in the *Divided Friends* index entry listing Joseph McSorley's works. In its brevity, however, the book offers the purest distillation of McSorley's Hecker-charged theological vision of the path to holiness. Its appearance in the form of practical instructions on how to pray seems particularly apt given Hecker's spiritual inspiration for his own mission, i.e., the conversion of ordinary Americans to an active Catholic faith.

McSorley translated that conviction into basic instructions on how to pray. His recollection of the book's inspiration sheds some light on why he calls it a "primer," a beginner's textbook.

> I could still remember my own confusion at the novitiate on the subject and how quickly most of it vanished when I began to see that prayer is essentially an inner relationship between the individual soul and God; that one who is trying to adjust his will to the Divine Will is praying; and that, when a soul is exerting its free will to give everything it possesses, or will possess, back

2. Ibid.

3. Ibid., 322.

to God from Whom it came, this is true prayer, this is ador-
ing. When that idea dominates, we soon discover that various
approaches, recommended by different writers on prayer, serve
the same simple end. Convinced that an outline of the principles
involved would help to clear up much confusion on the subject
of prayer, I wrote a small book and offered it to Longmans who
published it, reprinting it eight times, *Primer of Prayer (1934)*.[4]

A quick scan of the table of contents suggests nothing remarkable in the
organization and content. The book is divided into three parts: "Three Ways
of Praying," "What to Say to God," and "Helps and Hindrances." McSorley's
plain style suits his purposes: to convey how intimacy with God is accessible
to anyone who prays—an assurance also proclaimed in Hecker's writings.

The Office of Encouragement: Duty and Prayer

McSorley's *A Primer of Prayer* is an encore to "the office of encouragement"
first performed in *The Sacrament of Duty and Other Essays*.[5] As if to justify
the 1909 publication of revised *Catholic World* articles which he had written
prior to 1907, the Paulist vividly describes the need for this office in introducing the selection of essays: "It is no small blessing to the weak, in the
darkness and din of battle, to hear an encouraging cry from some friendly
voice, to receive assurance that the fight is really worth while."[6] *The Sacrament of Duty and Other Essays* was to be that "cry," a striking word choice,
which conveys the confusion, even desperation felt by many after *Pascendi
Dominici Gregis*. The 1907 encyclical described Modernism as "the synthesis of all heresies" and implicated anyone who sought an alternative to neo-
scholastic objectivity as succumbing to theological immanentism that led
inevitably to agnosticism or worse.[7] As Portier explains in exquisite detail,
The Sacrament of Duty was this American priest's most explicit defense of
his fidelity to the Catholic Church in the face of the ensuing crisis.[8] Yet,
as McSorley makes clear in his introduction, his cry is not of distress but of
encouragement and reassurance, delivered by an ally who apparently plans
to continue the fight. The essays make clear that he intends to rely not on

4. McSorley, "Reverend Joseph McSorley, CSP," 266–67.

5. McSorley, "Introduction," in *The Sacrament of Duty*, 7.

6. Ibid.

7. Portier, *Divided Friends*, xx–xxi.

8. The practical effects on McSorley's work are discussed in Portier, *Divided
Friends*, 294–95, and the significance of *The Sacrament of Duty and Other Essays* in
ibid., 364–67.

neo-scholastic objectivity, but in his conviction that "God's care for man is the basis of all valid idealism, and the Lord Christ its best exponent."[9]

A Primer of Prayer shows little evidence that McSorley's deeply held faith had waned in the twenty-five years between the two publications. The effects of praying align so closely with those enjoyed in frequenting the "sacrament of duty" that they become almost indistinguishable. In the 1909 essay, he asserts: "Duty is a sacrament, because it is an expression of the will of God and a means of entering into communion with Him."[10] In his *Primer*, prayer too culminates in "conversation, communion," which he explains in more personal terms. "Aware of God, looking at Him with the eyes of my soul, I reach toward Him—to converse with Him, to give Him what I have, to identify my will with His."[11] As presented in the earlier essay, performing the sacrament of duty creates an interior sacred space, "the meeting-place and marriage-chamber of the human will and the divine."[12] Echoing the image of the "marriage-chamber," *A Primer's* opening paragraph concludes with this declaration: "Intercourse of spirit with spirit, of man with God,— this is prayer."[13] His instructions on prayer, like his argument for duty as a sacrament, convey an expansive understanding of the human capacity for intimacy with God, clearly reminiscent of Isaac Hecker's optimistic theological anthropology.[14] *humanity, though harmed by Original Sin is not depraved of*

A reader who finds inspiration in *A Primer's* identification of "spirit" *virtuous citizens* as the point of connection between humans and God has already received a share in Isaac Hecker's spiritual legacy. In *Devotion to the Holy Spirit in American Catholicism*, Joseph P. Chinnici, OFM, describes Isaac Hecker as "the most important indigenous source for devotion to the Holy Ghost in the United States." He explains that Hecker identified the Holy Spirit as the "fullness of Christian perfection, union, and communion, for which he [Hecker] longed." The human spirit seeks relationship with "the Spirit" which Hecker understood as "a *outside nature* transcendental principle of synthesis, the *combination of ideas* reality of God's life in which action and contemplation, the person and the world, the individual and society, faith and reason, authority and liberty were united."[15] By comparison, Hecker's spiritual descendent communicated a tempered awareness of the Holy Spirit's activity, especially evident in

intuitive + spiritual above experience + material

9. McSorley, "Introduction," in *The Sacrament of Duty*, 8.

10. Ibid., 11–12.

11. McSorley, *A Primer of Prayer*, 1.

12. McSorley, *Sacrament*, 12.

13. McSorley, *A Primer of Prayer*, 1.

14. See O'Brien, *Isaac Hecker*, 339–44.

15. Chinnici, *Devotion to the Holy Spirit in American Catholicism*, 25.

his constant emphasis on duty and prayer, first and foremost, as a means of uniting one's will with God's will.

McSorley's preoccupation with duty, obedience, and submission, earned him the reputation as a rigorist among his Paulist confreres;[16] and, as will be seen, *A Primer* provides evidence enough for this charge. He made painfully clear that spiritual communion exacts a price. In the *Primer*, "Part III, Helps and Hindrances," the chapter, "Daily Conduct," reaffirms the non-negotiable demands of duty. In explaining how "to practice recollection in the routine of ordinary life," he emphasizes the importance of guarding "our inner consciousness" from anything "inconsistent with the peaceful worship of God, unless perchance it wears the badge of duty." This singular exception "may disturb us for the moment, but it cannot really hurt us, so long as we hold fast loyally to the will of God." Perhaps he is speaking from past experience, but McSorley assures his readers that enacting duty "will serve as a life-line to the soul tossed about by distractions or temptations; in fact, it would be very difficult to find a spiritual principle more steadying and comforting."[17]

As evident in the previous quotes, even twenty-seven years after *Pascendi*, duty's demands cast a long shadow over the "office of encouragement." In the passage from his *Primer*, duty appears as both a potential threat to "peaceful worship" and "a life-line" thrown to a soul in distress. In the essay, "The Sacrament of Duty," McSorley's conviction about duty's priority becomes crystal clear with his startling claim: "The habit of frequenting the sacrament of duty is not only an effective way of attaining to God, but the only way."[18] Opportunities to develop the habit occur through the daily offer of "grace in our everyday routine . . . the worth of the infinitely little."[19] For those who struggle in obscurity and face life's inevitable difficulties, know- *(Not being understood)* ing that their fidelity to ordinary duties possesses a sacramental dimension "saves [them], because it makes clear the worth of unsuccessful striving and tells the enduring triumph of every blameless defeat."[20] The poignancy of such salvation practically leaps off the page, and the essay's conclusion offers no escape from duty's unrelenting demands. "Nothing can take its place."[21] *Duty!* In the essay's final sentence, McSorley's rigor appears in full force with little of the softening effects of Hecker's signature optimism. He counsels the

16. Portier, *Divided Friends*, 323.

17. McSorley, *A Primer of Prayer*, 96.

18. McSorley, *The Sacrament of Duty*, 18.

19. Ibid., 20.

20. Ibid., 22–23.

21. Ibid., 27.

reader: "School carefully, therefore, your vision and your will; and when there occurs a struggle in the choosing between what is painful and what is wrong, set your will resolutely to the receiving of the sacrament of duty."[22] Twenty-five years later, a textbook suitable for that schooling appeared under the guise of *A Primer of Prayer*.

Praying: A Natural Expression of Intimacy with God

A Primer of Prayer communicates what McSorley had learned as a novice: "That prayer is essentially an inner relationship between the individual soul and God." In the "Introductory," he makes this relationship seem quite natural. His response to "such questions as 'How, and when, and why shall I pray?'" is simple, unassuming, reassuring. He considers "how" first, with a disarming question: "How shall I converse with my dearest and most intimate friend?" Then with a gently worded answer: "No one needs elaborate instruction. . . . The heart of a man—his natural instinct—tells him how, and when, and why to speak, when dealing with a friend; it is the same in dealing with God." He next compares conversing with God to talking with "my mother," with a comforting twist—"that His love of me surpasses even hers."[23] He counsels those feeling unworthy that God "delights to have me tell Him whatever is on my mind, or in my heart."[24] The natural connection between God and the individual is a recurring theme in this beginner's text on prayer.

Similar responses to questions of "When?" and "Where?" convey divine availability. "Obviously, at any time and at any place. For I am always in His presence and His attitude towards me is ever the same."[25] Humans change; God remains constant in every age. "The Psalmist found Him present in heaven and in hell and in the uttermost parts of the sea; and the modern man meets Him 'in every London lane and street.'"[26] The divine indwelling makes prayer, like duty, a non-negotiable. In his reply to the question: "Why shall I pray?," he leaves no room for doubt: "'Because without prayer I dare not face life.' Out of touch with God, I can neither carry my burdens nor do my work; I surely cannot hope to fulfill my destiny." McSorley tempers this stark claim: "Spiritual life and health and achievement are dependent upon communion with my Heavenly Father; and it is literally no less natural, nor

22. Ibid.

23. McSorley, *A Primer of Prayer*, 1–2.

24. Ibid., 2.

25. Ibid.

26. Ibid., 3.

should it be more difficult, to talk to Him than to talk to my own mother or father."[27] All these responses, beginning with his simple definition of prayer as "lifting up of mind and will to God," serve the office of encouragement well. "To get that definition clear and to hold it fast will greatly help us to learn the art of prayer."[28] The subsequent instructions make clear that each person holds the God-given potential to become a virtuoso in spiritual arts.

[handwritten: 1. Right Attitude 2. Sincerity]

Common Sense: A Prerequisite for Learning to Pray with Father McSorley

McSorley's first lesson in "Three Ways to Pray" explores the many possibilities of "Vocal Prayer." The first section, "The Worth of Words," delineates *[handwritten: show the form of]* two simple criteria for discerning authentic prayer: "We must understand what we are saying, and must have the attitude toward God which our words imply."[29] Of the two, right attitude takes pride of place since words receive their worth from the will's intent, and one can certainly rely on a multitude of "printed prayers" for words to say. McSorley offers simple advice on selecting among the many mass-produced options: "If it [a prayer] works well, it is good."[30] His common sense advice communicates confidence in the spiritual capacities of ordinary individuals to figure out what "works" for them.

McSorley continues in this same vein when he extols the virtues of composing prayers. He calls them, "home-made prayers," locating their production not in a monastery, rectory, convent, or even university, but in a place most readers know, their homes. Consistent with his previous prioritizing of attitude or sentiment, the Paulist reasons that "a prayer poured out in one's own words, has the best chance of being personal, sincere, real." To make his point, he observes that no one converses with "a dear human friend" by reading eloquent passages from someone else's writings. "Neither solidity of thought, nor graceful expression, is the most desirable quality of a conversation between intimates, but sincerity; and this, essential element of all affectionate communion, is also the essential element of prayer." Even those unable to pray can make that lament their prayer "in their own words," since the expression will come from "the fullness of one's own heart."[31]

27. Ibid.
28. Ibid., 1.
29. Ibid., 7.
30. Ibid., 10.
31. Ibid., 11.

The Paulist offers several examples in which he expresses in his own words, "adoration," "contrition," "faith," "consecration," "trust," and "love"—themes explained more fully in Part II of *A Primer*. His "home-made prayers" communicate his humble assent to spiritual vulnerability, here exemplified in this simple act of love:

> You, O God, I choose—
>
> As I am privileged to choose—
>
> For my Lover and my Beloved;
>
> You are and always shall be First.
>
> All else is but a means
>
> Of pleasing You. And for Your sake, O God
>
> I love my neighbor.
>
> Every one of my fellow creatures I love,
>
> Especially the unfortunate,
>
> And most especially
>
> Those who seem not to love me.[32]

Perhaps his prayer serves as a confession of his post-*Pascendi* faith commitment, a choice rooted in the will, recognized as grace—i.e., a privilege—understood first and foremost as an act of love that enfolds and ultimately transcends an assent of the intellect. The prayer certainly affirms the close connection between prayer and the sacrament of duty. Obeying Jesus' commandment to love God and the neighbor, including "those who seem not to love me," seems to be simultaneously the very essence of the sacrament of duty as well as a near-perfect expression of prayer.

McSorley's presentation of his own home-made prayers lends credibility to his subsequent suggestion to create "a private prayer-book." He introduces the novel idea in his usual fashion by making it sound perfectly ordinary. He compares the project to "the common impulse to collect curios" or the desire to "make notes and memoranda to help in the preservation of precious memories."[33] Favorite Scripture passages, familiar prayers, spiritual writings are suitable content, but so are "prayers composed by oneself, the things we have grown accustomed to say in the sacred privacy of conversation with God, our nearest and best Friend, so infinitely understanding, so much more generous and helpful than any other."[34] He casually

32. Ibid., 16.
33. Ibid.
34. Ibid., 17.

observes that in one's prayer-book, "possibly the most beautiful part will be that gathered from the saints. . . ." He continues, contrasting the "beautiful" with the "useful," which ultimately reveals the more ubiquitous beauty of the soul. "But not improbably the most useful part of our prayer-book will be that which records our inner feelings and aspirations when communing with our Heavenly Father, with His Son, our Saviour, and with the indwelling Holy Spirit, Life of our life, and Soul of our soul."[35] He anticipates that private prayer-books will reveal "the abundance of our inner life" in displaying distinctive personal patterns. "They seem to be and really are in a special sense our own, for they have been woven out of the very texture of our souls."[36] His faith in the human soul's spiritual capacity rests not in human abilities but in an ever-accessible and loving God dwelling within that soul.

[handwritten margin note: present everywhere @ once]

McSorley attributes to prayer a central role in all dimensions of human development. In introducing the Ignatian method of "praying slowly," he emphasizes how prayer, as "the central activity of the Christian's life . . . unifies all his scattered acts."[37] These acts engage the intellect as well as the will. In one example, McSorley explains how praying slowly may inspire an exploration of a word from a prayer or Scripture as exhaustive as Melville's discussion of "white" in *Moby Dick*. He emphasizes the give-and-take between a person's praying and his or her intellectual explorations which, as his example suggests, include a broad range of resources: "[Prayer] bears upon, and is in turn affected by his growth in knowledge, the development of his ability to compare facts and deduce conclusions, in a word all his intellectual progress."[38] His final comments, however, undercut any corrosive effects of intellectual elitism. "Probably the hymn, 'Good-night, Sweet Jesus,' would be endorsed by no critic of music or of verse; but it has served millions for purposes of prayer, just as 'Rock-a-bye, Baby' and other famous lullabies have soothed generations of children to sleep without benefit of criticism."[39] Common sense once again prevails. Any text that lifts one's mind and will to God is worthy of the name "prayer."

McSorley's final lesson in "vocal prayer" offers numerous examples of "short prayers" or "aspirations." One sentence, in particular, conveys the warmth and charm that helps to explain the book's multiple reprints. He describes a simple, but potentially quite meaningful task: "It would be a profitable exercise to go through the pages of the New Testament with a

35. Ibid., 17–18.
36. Ibid., 18.
37. Ibid., 22.
38. Ibid.
39. Ibid., 24.

pencil, copying out those brief cries of loving souls at the moment of close contact with God."[40] One can easily imagine sitting down, pencil in hand, copying in one's private prayer book the "brief cries of loving souls," and suddenly recognizing familiar Scripture phrases as pathways into "close contact with God."

Spiritual Rigor: A Necessary Component in Learning to Pray with Father McSorley

McSorley's reputation as a rigorist finds frequent confirmation in *A Primer of Prayer*. Though it has its dark side, his rigorism has more than one dimension and, in many respects, served him well. It gave him a way of embracing his deeply held faith in the wake of the Modernist crisis, and it made his intellectual work possible after 1907. After all, he committed a decade to gathering and organizing the material to write a century-by-century church history. The consistency in his methodical approach to filling out the details in a complex outline which he created is truly "remarkable," as Portier shows in examining the work.[41] *A Primer of Prayer's* chapter on meditation offers another striking example of how McSorley's instructions on prayer require a rigorous use of the intellect to guide the will toward accepting the rigors of Christian living.

McSorley's intent in this chapter is to remove the veil of mystery surrounding meditation. He first sets the reader at ease, emphasizing how natural and flexible meditation is. He compares it to a pianist warming cold hands, an athlete loosening muscles, or someone collecting thoughts prior to an interview. After offering this final example, he assures his reader, "Meditation is essentially nothing more than that—a process of collecting one's thoughts, of focusing one's attention, of recalling pertinent facts and principles and circumstances."[42] This simple description offers little preparation for the intricate steps involved in learning to meditate with Father McSorley. Acknowledging his dependence on St. Ignatius, the Paulist identifies "three powers of soul" critical for meditating. He describes the first two powers in simple terms: "The memory recalls; the intellect considers." McSorley attributes a wider range of activity to the third power: "The will embraces, chooses, decides, resolves, aspires, protests, loves."[43] Upon

---

40. Ibid., 24–25.

41. Portier, *Divided Friends*, 339–43.

42. McSorley, *A Primer of Prayer*, 33.

43. Ibid., 34.

further reading, however, what "the intellect considers" is equally expansive, evident in his long list of potential questions for the intellect to consider.[44]

The Paulist's thorough application of the Ignatian method in his examples rivals his systematic organization of his *Outline History of the Church*. Multiple meditations on the last judgment include written reflections under "memory," "understanding," and "acts" or "will." First, McSorley remembers the inevitability of the Last Judgment and then explores the question: "Who is Here?" using two basic responses: "God is Here" and "I am here."[45] From that starting point, McSorley next considers God as "All-Knowing" and as "All-Loving"[46] and then scrutinizes "I, the fortunate one," "I, the sinner," "I, the survivor," and "I, the promiser."[47] His penchant for thoroughness in understanding is evident in his further suggestions for "who," including family members, friends, enemies, guardian angels, and Mary.[48] The reader has little choice but to accept his claim of meditation's endless options.

McSorley's actual meditations on the last judgment are, at times, painful to read in their self-accusatory tone. An undergraduate student, who read this section in a 2014 college course exploring prayer, exclaimed, "It seems as if he thinks that he can't do anything right!" Evidence abounds for this conclusion. His use of the first person intensifies a sense of harsh self-judgment, especially striking in his many accusations of betrayal. What he "understands" about "God the All-Knowing," for example, highlights the divine judgment determining his status as "one of His good and faithful servants, or as one of his betrayers."[49] In the next meditation, he directly addresses "God, the All-Loving," acknowledging his judge is also his benefactor, providing "sight and hearing, intelligence and free-will, the gift of faith, the love of friends, every joy that has ever been mine." An expression of his will follows: "I accuse myself of having repaid love with indifference, coldness, treachery."[50] Similar accusations appeared earlier in a "home-made prayer" on contrition and reappear in a subsequent chapter on the theme of contrition. In the latter, he insists that nothing substitutes for writing one's own prayer of contrition since "no one but myself can reproduce the exact story of my treachery and measure the precise depth of my baseness in

44. Ibid., 39.
45. Ibid., 40, 43.
46. Ibid., 40–43.
47. Ibid., 43–47.
48. Ibid., 47–49.
49. Ibid., 40–41.
50. Ibid., 42.

misusing God's gifts to displease and disobey him."[51] Identifying one's story with "treachery" conveys a gravity of alienation from God most closely identified with Judas.

Similar emphases appear under his "I" meditations. The most intriguing is "I, the promiser," in which McSorley derides himself as someone "who so often and so fervently promised to amend my ways." This self-ridicule reaches a fevered pitch in "Acts." He begins with a warning: "Let me never again be tempted to pride!" He then gives his reasons that surely make the reader wonder about the author's past: "Shall I ever forget that God has pardoned me, a convicted liar, a friend forsworn, a perjured traitor?" And as if anticipating what the reader is thinking, he continues: "None of these names is too harsh for me,—I am indeed a weakling, a broken reed." His conclusion follows with an unrelenting logic. "Pride is crushed, self-confidence shattered, as I review the past." Then, as if taking his cue from the Psalms, McSorley turns from self-accusation to a confession of faith. "From now on, my confidence and my strength must come entirely from You, O God of mercy." His final line in "Acts" is the concluding Latin line of the *Te Deum*: "*Non confundar in aeternum*'—Trusting You, I shall never be confounded."[52] His profession of trust in God as "I, the promiser" echoes his other expressions of trust, perhaps most evident in his "encouraging cry" after Modernism's condemnation.

The repeated appearance of "treachery" in *A Primer* raises questions about the extent to which *Pascendi* reconfigured McSorley's sense of his own sinfulness. Whether he perceived himself as a traitor in light of his involvement with those eventually identified as Modernists remains unknown to anyone except, perhaps, his confessor. At the same time, his prayers and meditations make clear that even "treachery" does not escape God's mercy nor eradicate God's indwelling in a soul who seeks forgiveness. After 1907, McSorley had staked his very life on such trust in God's mercy and fidelity.

Four subsequent meditations on the "Holy Ghost" demonstrate how McSorley's rigorism inspired more than harsh self-judgments. As he notes, these examples are "less methodical and more spontaneous,"[53] though each includes the requisite sections on memory, understanding, and will. In the first, he simply recalls God's mercy that allows him to be in a "state of grace."[54] This recollection leads to the realization that "I bear God with me

[handwritten margin note: "Pascendi" Encyclical of Pius X on the Doctrines of the Modernist]

51. Ibid., 76.

52. Ibid., 47.

53. Ibid., 50.

54. Ibid.

as truly as Mary did."[55] Or "This flesh of mine is a true Holy of Holies."[56] His concluding prayer exclaims: "I recognize Thee within me, O Hidden God—and I adore Thee."[57] The second example recalls that his God-given destiny is holiness: "Like the flames of a fiery furnace which heat and color iron, the love of God is transforming me into His true likeness."[58] His concluding prayer directly addresses the Holy Spirit: "Pour Thyself into me more and more abundantly, until this blessed consummation is realized."[59] These devotions resound with Hecker's fervent love of the Holy Spirit.

The third meditation acknowledges "that frequently the voice of the Holy Ghost speaks within my soul." Of the four points attributed to this inner voice, the first two seem unexceptional: "Resist temptation . . . be constant in prayer." The next two bear a distinctive McSorley quality. He hears, on the one hand, the demand "to perform unpleasant duties faithfully," and on the other, "to remember the intimate tender relationship established between Him and me." He admits that he fails far more than he succeeds: "There are ten, or a hundred, or perhaps thousands [of times], when I pay no attention to Him whatever." His prayer ends directly addressing God: "O Father and Brother; O Friend and Lover; Thy will is mine."[60] These meditations suggest the deepest source of McSorley's rigor: the divine intimacy that comes with the Holy Spirit indwelling the soul. An awareness of this intimacy, both acknowledged and, perhaps more importantly, carelessly overlooked, evokes McSorley's rigor. His rigor seeks to intensify this intimacy.

The Paulist's final meditation exposes the loving attentiveness of "God within" who is "ever awaiting a whispered word, a loving glance, an act of service, or of adoration."[61] This recollection leads him to "realize" his relationship with God transcends the limits of ordinary human communication. "I need not take a single step in order to put myself in His presence. I need not ever speak aloud in order to be heard by Him."[62] To convey the sacramental quality of this indwelling, he compares his heart to a "tabernacle lamp" steadily burning with a "flame of love," signaling a real presence within each human, analogous to Christ's body reserved in a

55. Ibid., 51.
56. Ibid.
57. Ibid.
58. Ibid., 52.
59. Ibid.
60. Ibid., 53–54.
61. Ibid., 55.
62. Ibid.

church's tabernacle.[63] Given this realization, he proclaims a readiness to en-dure every hardship, no matter the severity. His final prayer acclaims: "God of Beauty, God of Might, God of Sweetness and Peace and Love, I adore Thee."[64] Such images highlight McSorley's profound awareness of a loving God that informs his rigorist tendencies.

Praying with Father McSorley

McSorley returns frequently to intimate images of God to encourage pray-ing from one's situation in life. He introduces his tutorial on "What to Say to God" with a simple reminder that those "admitted to private audience with the King Who is moreover the Perfect Friend . . . have many things to say to Him."[65] Topics for conversation with the King-Friend include petition, thanksgiving, contrition, adoration, abandonment, and consecration. Mc-Sorley's conversational approach makes an intimate relationship with God seem entirely possible.

The first lesson considers the most familiar prayer with an unvarnished reassurance. "Petition"—the prayer of the supplicant soul—needs no defense. "Children ought to ask their Father for what they need, or think they need; and the Father is pleased, if His children trustfully ask Him."[66] He makes his case with an unassailable example, Jesus' praying. After all, Jesus nestles a request for daily bread in the Our Father. More dramatically, Jesus prays for deliverance from the cross in Gethsemane. Of course, he then offers the most perfect prayer: "Thy will be done, not mine."[67] McSorley encourages a trust in God that allows any request and accepts any answer, however puz-zling on this side of eternity.

McSorley turns next to thanksgiving, a logical progression after af-firming prayers of petition. Though an obvious theme for prayer, McSorley gives it attention, "if for no other reason than because it is so frequently overlooked."[68] To counter the inattention, McSorley assigns another task requiring "pencil and paper," in this case, to list "all the gifts we owe to God."[69] From such an exercise, "we should see ourselves to be enjoying quite casually a thousand privileges which many of our fellow-creatures

63. Ibid.
64. Ibid., 56.
65. Ibid., 65–66.
66. Ibid., 67.
67. Ibid., 68.
68. Ibid., 70.
69. Ibid., 71.

would give years of life to share." The privileges he mentions have little to do with exceptional favors: "To hear and see and walk, to breathe easily and to be free from acute pain, these and other propensities of our present comfortable estate to which we ordinarily advert not at all, might well be the inspiration of many a fervent prayer of thanksgiving for God's gifts to us."[70] McSorley observes the transformative effects of grateful awareness. "In various ways, then, the grateful soul tends to grow prayerful. Every creature becomes to him 'a mirror of life and a book of holy doctrine.' Almost constantly his mind and will are lifted up to God."[71] Such a vision shares much in common with St. Francis's praise of all creation which, in turn, led the saint to a profound awareness of his sinfulness in the face of so generous a God. A Primer follows a similar spiritual logic and examines "contrition" next, which this essay already considered in connection with McSorley's many other acts of contrition.

A Primer covers three more themes: adoration, abandonment, and consecration. In McSorley's telling, the trio forms a complex spiritual dynamic that leads into the very heart of holiness. The Paulist identifies adoration as "an act apart, unique, transcendent, a voluntary setting up of the proper relationship between God and the creature made in His image."[72] Here, "the art of simple prayer" comes into full focus. Repeating "My God and My All" or similar phrases duly honors the One "who is essentially Other than all the finite universe, actual and possible."[73] He imagines "many a holy soul" using such prayers of adoration not only "in church, before a crucifix," but also "in the open field, or at the seaside, or standing beside a running stream, or walking along a city street."[74] McSorley even ranks "Adoro Te" above "Amo Te," because adoration "offers to God that great and peculiar thing which can be offered to no one else." To drive home his point, McSorley identifies "I adore" as "a complete prayer-book; or indeed a whole liturgy in itself."[75] "The art of simple prayer" is unpretentiously minimalist and completely portable.

Adoration has its negative spiritual corollary, "abandonment." McSorley, following Hecker's lead, finds inspiration in Jean Pierre de Caussade's text Abandonment to Divine Providence. In his Primer, McSorley specifically recommends the Frenchman's spiritual treatise as worthy of careful

70. Ibid., 73.
71. Ibid.
72. Ibid., 78.
73. Ibid., 79.
74. Ibid., 80.
75. Ibid., 81.

attention: "One who reads this little book will obtain a very simple ideal of holiness and a very clear notion of the dispositions necessary for spiritual progress."[76] The Paulist readily admits that "it takes heroic courage to realize this ideal."[77] Yet, as he has done so many times in his *Primer,* he situates even this loftiest of spiritual aspirations within the familiar routines of daily life. The myriad of frustrations, disappointments, and interruptions "provide us with opportunities to practice this sort of prayer,—the weather, the unexpected visitor, the telephone, the furnace, the radio, a peddler, a tradesman, a servant, an employer, a child, a neighbor, someone's rudeness, poor cooking, delays, accidents, misfortunes, illness." He identifies these mundane events as "the raw material of holiness, if we have the eyes to see and the wills to utilize these providential opportunities."[78] Prayers of abandonment become quite ordinary, even if demanding ways to heed his warning issued in "The Sacrament of Duty," to "school carefully" the vision and will.

The spiritual logic, introduced in the pairing of adoration and abandonment, culminates with consecration. "To the Christian, no form of spiritual activity should be more spontaneous than that of offering self to God."[79] The church-sanctioned movement, "the Apostleship of Prayer," makes a perfectly fine morning offering available, but the personal nature of consecration naturally leads McSorley to suggest composing a prayer using "the various materials presented by daily duties, problems, burdens, trials, misfortunes, inclinations, opportunities, dangers, temptations, attractions."[80] What he offers to the imagination in describing self-offering gives way to the fantastic. "It is as if I stand upon the pinnacle of all the world and then, looking into His eyes, I make the leap; and, for one splendid instant, I am a saint, caring for nothing in the universe but the fulfilling of His will, believing in Him wholeheartedly, trusting Him absolutely, loving Him with all my soul."[81]

At the same time, given all the discussion that has preceded this moment, the fantastic seems within reach precisely because it is the stuff not of fantasy but of God Incarnate. He concludes with a lesson on assisting at Mass as a unique opportunity for self-offering in union with Christ. Confessing sins through the *Confiteor* serves as preparation "until at the Elevation we too are consecrated, transformed, lifted up and given to God without

76. Ibid., 83.
77. Ibid., 84
78. Ibid., 85.
79. Ibid., 86.
80. Ibid., 87.
81. Ibid.

reserve. '*Consummatum est.*'" It is consummated. I have been given to God with a finality attainable in no other way. Simply then, as if inevitably, I go to Communion and to Thanksgiving."[82] Consecration, like every other prayer, brings "intercourse of spirit with spirit" through the graciousness of a loving God here made manifest in the Holy Communion of the Catholic Church.

The Worth of the Infinite Little

McSorley gathers the last few topics under the straightforward heading, "Helps and Hindrances," which opens with an overview of "Daily Conduct." He respects "the routine of ordinary life" enough to take seriously the genuine challenges it poses to deeper forms of prayer. "It is not easy, at a moment's notice, to escape from all this and enter into the spaceless, timeless, invisible world where the soul and God commune alone as lover and Beloved."[83] One can, however, take deliberate steps to make the transition easier by controlling what enters into "our stream of consciousness."[84] McSorley cautions against being "too reckless in keeping the doors of the mind always so wide open that our soul resembles a country without laws, an army without discipline, a school with no rules."[85] The disruptive distractions of everyday modern urban life require constant monitoring. One ought "to withhold attention—at least in part—from advertisements and newspapers and shop windows and crowds and street scenes and interesting incidents and queer passersby; from rowdy songs and vulgar music and silly chatter; from profanity and scandal and irreverent speech."[86] A subsequent chapter, "Resisting Distractions," reiterates the special challenges posed by consumer capitalism, especially "if we go to prayer, fresh from the market place, with the world's shouting still in our ears, with a thousand high-lights from its gaudy pageant still dazzling in our eyes."[87] Perhaps he has in mind his confreres' distaste for his rigorism when he assures his readers, "One may be normal, serene, a good companion and a pleasant conversationalist and yet maintain a high idealism in daily behavior."[88] In other words, one can still be a regular guy, or even gal, and maintain a life conducive to intimacy with God.

82. Ibid., 88.
83. Ibid., 91.
84. Ibid., 92.
85. Ibid., 93–94.
86. Ibid., 95.
87. Ibid., 110.
88. Ibid., 95

    Daily life involves much more than avoiding the near occasion of distractions; it requires cultivating the good. With this positive end in mind, even disruptive influences can be "the raw material of holiness for the soul bent upon doing the will of God."[89] Even more important is actually performing good works. He first suggests reviewing "the list of the Corporal and the Spiritual Works of Mercy," and then adds an oddly worded suggestion: "Incidently, it might not be useless to commit them to memory, so as to impress their value on our consciousness."[90] Throughout his discussion on daily conduct, "the worth of the infinitely little" is apparent, but especially so in a delightfully concrete suggestion. He gives instructions on "the art of making spiritual use" of those many in-between moments of modern life, such as waiting in line or for an appointment. Such moments, however brief, become opportunities for "redeeming the time" through activities like examining the conscience, composing a prayer, reflecting on a gospel scene.[91] To identify such fleeting moments with redemption conveys clearly and simply the hidden potential in "the infinitely little" as a passageway to contemplation.

    Immediately after considering the importance of "daily conduct in praying," McSorley turns to "immediate preparation," offering a realistic assessment of the need for "a certain degree of solitude."[92] The quiet enables one "to see clearly the underlying principles of ideal conduct, to work out solutions for the puzzles of life, perhaps to taste some of the sweetness of God."[93] McSorley then presents a montage of suitable prayer sites, beginning with the bucolic and finally acknowledging the chaotic: "The woods, the seashore, the bank of a running stream, an open meadow" have inspired the likes of saints in their prayer. More typical places of prayer include "a quiet corner, a church or chapel, a dim or darkened room, or some other place where friends will hesitate to intrude." Then he continues with comforting reassurance that "if no such conditions can be secured, God may, and doubtless will, make up the lack."[94] His subsequent description dramatizes his point: "For who can doubt that also in the crowded quarters of a hovel, in a tenement, beside wash-tub or kitchen stove, alongside the whirring wheels of a factory, souls have entered into close and loving communion

---

89. Ibid., 96.
90. Ibid., 97.
91. Ibid., 98.
92. Ibid., 99.
93. Ibid., 100.
94. Ibid., 100–101.

with God?"[95] Such reassurance seems more convincing, given McSorley's repeated assurance of God's presence within every soul.

A definite "help" for Catholics at prayer is "the consoling doctrine of the Communion of Saints," which finally receives explicit attention in the chapter, "Invoking the Saints." McSorley states flatly, "The Catholic program of worship can never be a narrow, individual affair. It is social, collective." Catholics pray for the living and the dead; and some of the dead, i.e., the saints "intercede for us with God. Thus is kept alive the family spirit which binds together the brothers and sisters of Jesus Christ, under the Fatherhood of God and the motherhood of our Blessed Lady."[96] He offers a relatively lengthy discussion of Marian devotion and concludes with a remarkable example of the consoling nature of Catholic collectivity. He promotes "the habit of frequently invoking the holy men and women mentioned in the litany, for their names are among the last earthly sounds we shall hear, when loving friends escort us to the gates of death and leave us there, calling upon the saints to intercede with God for us before it is too late."[97] McSorley's vivid characterization of the moment of death may be one more clue for understanding why McSorley remained firmly within the Catholic fold.

Learning to pray with Father McSorley offers more than communion with other saints; it offers the possibility of communion with God. In "Three Ways to Pray," the third way with the non-descript title, "Beyond Meditation," introduces contemplative or silent prayer. Although a somewhat unusual topic in 1934, McSorley emphasizes its commonplace quality. He describes silence as "a fine human instinct" and "love's favorite language."[98] He borrows from modern physics to convey both the intensity and brevity of this experience beyond meditation. "This movement of the soul toward God can begin and end in the fraction of a split second; it can flash from earth to heaven with a quickness greater than the speed of light."[99] The intensity, however, can produce lasting effects. McSorley associates it with a familiar practice: "It resembles what we experience in the church on a First Friday, when in our mental background looms up incessantly that Sacramental Presence ever on the altar." The experience may be called "recollection, or sense of the presence of God, or contemplation, or silent prayer. Whatever its name, it is one of God's greatest gifts to the soul.*" The asterisk signals that an explanatory comment appears on bottom of the page. "*Fur-

95. Ibid., 101.
96. Ibid., 102.
97. Ibid., 104.
98. Ibid., 61.
99. Ibid.

ther discussion of the higher degrees of union with God does not seem to be called for here."[100] Whether his hesitancy arises from his assumption of its irrelevance to imagined readers of *A Primer* or his desire to avoid any hint of the Modernist threats associated with spiritual immanence or Quietism remains a matter of speculation.[101] However, caution does not undercut his clearly encouraging message of trust in the person of goodwill to receive the gift of contemplation through attentiveness to God's presence in the practices of everyday living.

The epilogue reinforces "how easy it is to pray when one has good will. No learning is needed, no fluency of speech, no mental quickness, no fervor of feeling."[102] McSorley recalls the gospel story of the "Widow's Mite" to emphasize "our smallest offering is acceptable to God and, if it is our all, it becomes at once precious beyond appraisal."[103] Consistency is critical. "Life as a whole must be no crazy quilt, nor puzzle picture, but a plain pattern." Praying promises this harmonizing effect and leads us "on our way to happiness and holiness, once we have fitted the rest of life into those aims and aspirations which are ours when we 'lift up minds and wills to God.'"[104] McSorley speaks from experience, given his life's "crazy quilt" moments which became "the raw material of holiness." *A Primer of Prayer* really does involve learning to pray *with* Father McSorley, joining him in the struggle to remain on the pathway, first blazed by Isaac Hecker, and recognizing "the worth of the infinitely little," where God's call to holiness reveals itself as the true end in our fidelity to the sacrament of duty that comes in the daily living of even the most modern among us.

William Portier's lifework may appear more like a "crazy quilt," but no doubt one of great beauty, whose underlying "plain pattern" comes in his fidelity to the sacrament of duty. For over four decades, William Portier has entered his classroom ready to engage his students in the Catholic tradition's theological riches. His care for his students and colleagues is rarely hidden from view, and this essay collection is but a small indicator of those who share in his intellectual legacy. His proficiency in the historical-theological task, evident in years of careful and wide-ranging research, commitment to honoring his sources, and respecting those whose story he seeks to tell, finds many expressions; certainly one of its finest is *Divided Friends*. This book does far more than give us an account of the past, as important as that

---

100. Ibid., 62.

101. See Portier, *Divided Friends*, 310, 365.

102. McSorley, *A Primer of Prayer*, 114.

103. Ibid.

104. Ibid., 115.

is. It reminds us that the Christian theologian's task is guided by all those who have gone before us marked with the sign of faith, especially those who, like Father McSorley, guide and accompany us on the way of holiness, in the midst of intellectual and spiritual trials and tribulations arising not only from our culture but also our church. Dr. William L. Portier is a guide and companion for our own day, helping us to chart a way forward together in the precious faith given us in Christ, and for that, we owe him an enormous debt of gratitude.

The Writings of William L. Portier

Graduate Work

"An Examination of the Contemporary Theological Task: Toward a Suitable Method for a Specifically American Theology." Master's thesis, Washington Theological Union, 1972.
"Providential Nation: An Historical-Theological Study of Isaac Hecker's Americanism." PhD diss., University of St. Michael's College, 1980.

1972

"Of Folk Masses and Woodstock—American Pie and Explo '72." *Liturgy* 17.7 (August–September 1972) 15–17.

1974

"The Visions of Androphilos Theoreticus: An Apocalypse for Renewal Refugees." *U.S. Catholic* 39.1 (January 1974) 34–37.

1980

"Isaac Hecker and Americanism." *Ecumenist* 19 (November–December 1980) 9–12.

1982

"Theology and Authority: Reflections on *The Analogical Imagination*." *The Thomist* 46 (October 1982) 593–608.

1983

"Isaac Hecker and *Testem Benevolentiae*: A Study in Theological Pluralism." In *Hecker Studies: Essays on the Thought of Isaac Hecker*, edited by John Farina, 11–48. New York: Paulist, 1983.

"Schillebeeckx' Dialogue with Critical Theory." *Ecumenist* 21 (January–February 1983) 20–27.

"Catholic Theology in the United States, 1840–1907: Recovering a Forgotten Tradition." *Horizons* 10.2 (Fall 1983) 317–33.

1984

"Edward Schillebeeckx as Critical Theorist: The Impact of Neo-Marxist Social Thought on his Recent Theology." *The Thomist* 48 (1984) 341–67.

1985

Isaac Hecker and the First Vatican Council. Studies in American Religion 15. Lewiston, NY: Mellen, 1985.

"A Note on the Unpublished *Biographie de J.R. Slattery* in the Papiers Houtin." In *Historiography and Modernism*, edited by Ronald Burke, Gary Lease, and George Gilmore, 74–75. Working Papers of the Roman Catholic Modernism Group of the American Academy of Religion. Mobile, AL: Spring Hill College, 1985.

"*Ancilla Invita*: Heidegger, the Theologians, and God." *Studies in Religion/Sciences Religieuses* 14.2 (1985) 161–80.

"Isaac Hecker and the First Vatican Council." *Catholic Historical Review* 71.2 (1985) 206–27.

"Ministry from Above and/or Ministry from Below: An Examination of the Ecclesial Basis of Ministry according to Edward Schillebeeckx." *Communio* 12.2 (1985) 173–91.

1986

"Modernism in the United States: The Case of John R. Slattery (1851–1926)." In *Varieties of Modernism*, edited by R. Burke, G. Lease, and G. Gilmore, 77–97. Working Papers of the Roman Catholic Modernism Group of the American Academy of Religion. Mobile, AL: Spring Hill College, 1986.

"John R. Slattery's Vision for the Evangelization of American Blacks." *U.S. Catholic Historian* 5.1 (1986) 19–44.

Review of *Does God Change?: The Word's Becoming in the Incarnation*, by Thomas G. Weinandy, OFMCap. *Theological Studies* 47.4 (1986) 708–9.

1987

"The Future of Americanism." In *Rising from History: American Catholic Theology Looks to the Future,* edited by Robert Daly, SJ, 49–51. College Theology Society Annual Volume 30. Lanham, MD: University Press of America, 1987.

"Two Generations of American Catholic Expansionism in Europe: Isaac Hecker and John J. Keane." In *Rising from History: American Catholic Theology Looks to the Future,* edited by Robert Daly, SJ, 53–69. College Theology Society Annual Volume 30. Lanham, MD: University Press of America, 1987.

"John R. Slattery (1851–1926), Missionary and Modernist: The State of My Current Research Project." *American Catholic Studies Newsletter* 14.1 (1987) 8–11.

1988

Editor, *The Inculturation of American Catholicism, 1820–1900: Selected Historical Essays.* New York: Garland, 1988.

Review of *Tradition and Transformation in Catholic Culture: The Priests of St. Sulpice in the United States from 1791 to the Present,* by Christopher J. Kauffman. *Records of the American Catholic Historical Society of Philadelphia* 99 (March–December 1988) 75–77.

Review of *Tranquillitas Ordinis: The Present Failure and Future Promise of American Catholic Thought on War and Peace,* by George S. Weigel. *Horizons* 15.2 (1988) 429–31.

Review of *John XXII and Papal Teaching Authority,* by James Heft, SM. *The Thomist* 52 (1988) 763–68.

1989

"Church Unity and National Traditions: The Challenge to the Modern Papacy." In *The Papacy and the Church in the United States,* edited by Bernard Cooke, 25–54. New York: Paulist, 1989. [College Theology Society's Best Article Award, 1989]

"Interpretation and Method." In *The Praxis of Christian Experience: An Introduction to the Theology of Edward Schillebeeckx,* edited by Robert J. Schreiter and Mary Catherine Hilkert, 18–34. San Francisco: Harper & Row, 1989.

Review of *Catholic Intellectual Life in America,* by Margaret Mary Reher. *Theological Studies* 50.3 (1989) 597–99.

Review of *Triumph in Defeat: Infallibility, Vatican I and the French Minority Bishops,* by Margaret O'Gara. *Catholic Historical Review* 75.4 (1989) 718–19.

1990

"Americanism," "Birth Control," "Gibbons, James," "Humanae Vitae," "Keane, John Joseph," "*Longinqua Oceani*," "Nativism," "Protestant-Catholic Relations, Contemporary," "Slattery, John Richard," "Spellman, Francis Joseph," "*Testem Benevolentiae,*" "Vatican-U.S. Catholic Church Relations." In *Dictionary of Christianity in America,* edited by Daniel G. Reid, 53–56, 155–57, 480–81, 560–61, 607–8, 667–68, 801–2, 951–52, 1092, 1120, 1166, 1219–21. Downers Grove, IL: InterVarsity, 1990.

1990 *(continued)*

"The Mission of a Catholic College." In *Theology and the University*, edited by John V. Apczynski, 237–54. College Theology Society Annual Volume 33. Lanham, MD: University Press of America, 1990.

"Missionary As Philanthropist: A Social and Economic Portrait of John R. Slattery (1851–1926)." In *Religion and Economic Ethics*, edited by Joseph P. Gower, 199–217. College Theology Society Annual Volume 31. Lanham, MD: University Press of America, 1990.

1991

"Mysticism and Politics and Integral Salvation: Two Approaches to Theology in a Suffering World." In *Pluralism and Oppression: Theology in World Perspective*, edited by Paul F. Knitter, 255–78. College Theology Society Annual Volume 34. Lanham, MD: University Press of America, 1991.

1992

"Catholic Evangelization in the United States from the Republic to Vatican II." In *The New Catholic Evangelization*, edited by Kenneth Boyack, CSP, 27–41. New York: Paulist, 1992.

Review of *A Century of Catholic Social Thought*, edited by George Weigel and Robert Royal. *Records of the American Catholic Historical Society of Philadelphia* 103 (Spring 1992) 72–73.

"A Look at the History of American Catholic Evangelization." *Catholic World* (July–August 1992) 148–55.

1993

"American Spirituality." In *New Dictionary of Catholic Spirituality*, edited by Michael Downey, 34–38. Collegeville, MN: Liturgical, 1993.

Review of *Desegregating the Altar: The Josephites and the Struggle for Black Priests, 1871–1960*, by Stephen J. Ochs. *U.S. Catholic Historian* 11.1 (1993) 144–45.

"Inculturation as Transformation: The Case of Americanism Revisited." *U.S. Catholic Historian* 11.3 (1993) 107–24.

Review of *Isaac Hecker: An American Catholic*, by David J. O'Brien. *Theological Studies* 54.2 (1993) 356–57.

Review of *Salt, Leaven and Light, the Community Called Church*, by T. Howland Sanks, SJ. *Religious Studies Review* 19.3 (1993) 237.

1994

Tradition and Incarnation: Foundations of Christian Theology. Mahwah, NJ: Paulist, 1994.

Review of *Being Catholic: Commonweal from the Seventies to the Nineties*, by Rodger Van Allen. *Horizons* 21.1 (1994) 146–48.
Review of *Cane Ridge in Context: Perspectives on Barton W. Stone and the Revival*, by Anthony J. Dunnavant. *Horizons* 21.1 (1994) 191–92.

1995

"Americanism," "Great Awakening," "Modernism," "Social Gospel." In *HarperCollins Dictionary of Religion*, edited by Jonathan Z. Smith, 44, 393, 725, 1007. San Francisco: HarperSanFrancisco, 1995.
"Response to Reviewers of *Tradition and Incarnation*." *Horizons* 22.1 (1995) 120–28.
Review of *Mystery and Promise: A Theology of Revelation*, by John F. Haught. *Religious Studies Review* 21.2 (1995) 115.

1996

"Dialogue Between Gospel and Culture: Historical Perspectives." *Current Issues in Catholic Higher Education* 16.2 (1996) 73–90.
Review of *Essays in Critical Theology*, by Gregory Baum. *Religious Studies Review* 22.1 (1996) 49–50.
"Are We Really Serious When We Ask God to Deliver Us From War?: The Catechism and the Challenge of Pope John Paul II." *Communio* 23.1 (1996) 47–63.
"Spirituality in America: Selected Sources." *Horizons* 23.1 (1996) 140–61.
"Democracy at the Catholic Crossroads?," review of *Soul of the World: Notes on the Future of Public Catholicism*, by George Weigel. *Washington Times* (20 July 1996) A13.
"'Catholics in the Promised Land of the Saints' Revisited: Cultural History and its Irony." *U.S. Catholic Historian* 14.4 (1996) 141–54.

1997

Editor, with Sandra Yocum Mize. *American Catholic Traditions: Resources for Renewal*. College Theology Society Annual Volume 42. Maryknoll, NY: Orbis, 1997.
Reply to Michael Baxter, "America All Too Much with Us." *Our Sunday Visitor* 86.1 (4 May 1997) 10.
"What Does It Mean To Be *Ex Corde Ecclesiae*?: Toward an Alternative Academic Culture." *Delta Epsilon Sigma Journal* 42.3 (1997) 77–84.
"George Marsden and American Catholic Higher Education." *Delta Epsilon Sigma Journal* 42.3 (1997) 110–14.

1998

Review of *Christology: A Biblical, Historical, and Systematic Study of Jesus Christ*, by Gerald O'Collins, SJ. *Modern Theology* 14.1 (1998) 153–55.
Review of *Thank You, St. Jude: Women's Devotion to the Patron Saint of Hopeless Causes*, by Robert A. Orsi. *Cross Currents* 48.1 (1998) 119–21.

Review of *Being Right, Conservative Catholics in America*, edited by Mary Jo Weaver and Scott Appleby. *Pro Ecclesia* 7.4 (1998) 503–4.

1999

"Judge, Thomas A.," "Slattery, John R.," and "Sullivan, William L." In *American National Biography*, edited by John A. Garraty, 12:303–4, 20:81–82, 21:127–28. New York: Oxford University Press, 1999.

Review of *Catholic Converts: British and American Intellectuals Turn to Rome*, by Patrick Allitt. *Catholic Historical Review* 85.1 (January 1999) 117–18.

"Père Just's Hero-Martyr Secularized: John R. Slattery's Passage from Self-Sacrifice to 'Honest Manhood.'" *U.S. Catholic Historian* 17.2 (1999) 31–47.

"Reason's 'Rightful Autonomy' in *Fides et Ratio* and the Continuous Renewal of Catholic Higher Education in the United States." *Communio* 26.3 (1999) 541–56.

2000

"Isaac Hecker" and "William Laurence Sullivan." In *Biographical Dictionary of Christian Theologians*, edited by Patrick W. Carey and Joseph T. Lienhard, 237–49, 484–85. Westport, CT/London: Greenwood, 2000.

Review of *Catholics and American Culture: Fulton Sheen, Dorothy Day and the Notre Dame Football Team*, by Mark S. Massa. *Cross Currents* 49.4 (1999–2000) 568–71.

"Mandates at the Mount." *Mountaineer Briefing* (Winter 2000) 11–13.

"In Defense of Mount Saint Mary's: They Are Evangelical, not Conservative." *Commonweal* 127.3 (11 February 2000) 31–33.

"Americanism and Inculturation: 1899–1999." *Communio* 27.1 (2000) 139–60.

"Isaac Hecker and American Catholicism." *Catechist* 34.3 (2000) 34–38.

2001

Review of *Inventing Catholic Tradition*, by Terrence W. Tilley. *Horizons* 28.1 (2001) 108–11.

"Queen of Victory, Pray for Us: A Tribute to Al McGuire." *Commonweal* 128.5 (9 March 2001) 47.

Review of *The Early Works of Orestes Brownson*, Volume 1, *The Universalist Years, 1826–29*, edited by Patrick W. Carey. *Catholic Historical Review* 87.3 (2001) 530–31.

"Fundamentalism in North America: A Modern Anti-Modernism." *Communio* 28.3 (2001) 581–98.

"Le fondamentalisme aux États-Unis: Un anti-modernisme moderne." Translated into French by Xavier Morales. *Communio* 26.6 (November–December 2001) 29–43.

2002

"Interpretation and Method." In *The Praxis of the Reign of God: An Introduction to the Theology of Edward Schillebeeckx*, 2nd ed. with introduction by Edward

Schillebeeckx, edited by Mary Catherine Hilkert and Robert J. Schreiter, 19–36. New York: Fordham University Press, 2002.

"Slattery's O'Connell: Americanism and Modernism in the *Biographie de J.R. Slattery.*" In *Personal Faith and Institutional Commitments, Roman Catholic Modernist and Anti-Modernist Autobiography*, edited by Lawrence Barmann and Harvey Hill, 91–112. Scranton, PA: University of Scranton Press, 2002.

Review of *Senses of Tradition: Continuity and Development in Catholic Faith*, by John E. Thiel. *Modern Theology* 18.1 (January 2002) 136–37.

"The Genealogy of Heresy: Leslie Dewart as Icon of the Catholic 1960s." *American Catholic Studies* 113.1–2 (2002) 65–78.

"George Tyrrell in America." *U.S. Catholic Historian* 20.3 (2002) 69–95.

"Dorothy Day and her First Spiritual Director, Fr. Joseph McSorley, CSP." *Houston Catholic Worker* 22 (September–October 2002) 1, 5, 7.

2003

"'The Eminent Evangelist from Boston': Father Thomas A. Judge as an Evangelical Catholic." *Communio* 30.2 (Summer 2003) 300–319.

"Two Freedoms," review of *Catholicism and American Freedom*, by John T. McGreevy. *U.S. Catholic Historian* 21.4 (Fall 2003) 104–6.

2004

Editor, with R. Scott Appleby and Patricia Byrne, CSJ. *Creative Fidelity: American Catholic Intellectual Traditions*. Maryknoll, NY: Orbis, 2004.

"Here Come the Evangelical Catholics." *Communio* 31.1 (2004) 35–66. [College Theology Society's Best Article Award, 2004]

Review of *Goodbye Father: The Celibate Male Priesthood and the Future of the Catholic Church*, by Richard Schoenherr. *The Journal of Religion* 84.2 (2004) 287–88.

Review of *The Two Wings of Catholic Thought: Essays on 'Fides et Ratio,'* edited by David Ruel Foster and Joseph W. Koterski, SJ. *The Thomist* 68.2 (2004) 325–28.

Review of *The Lion and the Lamb: Evangelicals and Catholics in America*, by William M. Shea. *Horizons* 31.2 (2004) 418–20.

Review of *A People Adrift: The Crisis of the Roman Catholic Church in America*, by Peter Steinfels. *Theological Studies* 65.3 (2004) 657–58.

2005

"Foreword." In *New Wine, New Wineskins: A Next Generation Reflects on Key Issues in Catholic Moral Theology*, edited by William C. Mattison III, ix–xii. Lanham, MD: Sheed & Ward, 2005.

"Confessions of a Fractured Catholic Theologian." *Horizons* 32.1 (2005) 117–22.

"From Historicity to History: One Theologian's Intergenerational American Catholic Narrative." *U.S. Catholic Historian* 23.2 (2005) 65–72.

2006

Editorial Symposium: "Response to Avery Dulles on Catholicism 101: Challenges to a Theological Education." *Horizons* 33.2 (2006) 308–10.

"Theology of Manners as Theology of Containment: John Courtney Murray and *Dignitatis Humanae* Forty Years After." *U.S. Catholic Historian* 24.1 (2006) 83–105.

2007

"*Pascendi*'s Reception in the United States: The Case of Joseph McSorley." *U.S. Catholic Historian* 25.1 (2007) 13–30.

Review of *The Early Works of Orestes A. Brownson.* Volume VI, *Life By Communion, 1842*, edited by Patrick W. Carey. *Catholic Historical Review* 93.1 (2007) 210–11.

2008

"Does Systematic Theology Have a Future? A Response to Lieven Boeve." In *Faith in Public Life*, edited by William J. Collinge, 135–50. College Theology Society Annual Volume 53. Maryknoll, NY: Orbis, 2008.

"Heartfelt Grief and Repentance in Imperial Times." In *Love Alone is Credible: Hans Urs von Balthasar as Interpreter of the Catholic Tradition*, edited by David L. Schindler, 349–60. Grand Rapids: Eerdmans, 2008.

"The Way Ahead," review of *The Priority of Christ: Toward a Postliberal Catholicism*, by Robert Barron. *Commonweal* 135.2 (31 January 2008) 24–26.

"Thomist Resurgence," review of *Twentieth-Century Catholic Theologians*, by Fergus Kerr. *Communio* 35.3 (2008) 494–504.

2009

"Genealogy of a Metaphor: Evolution and the 'Warfare' Between Science and Religion." In *Tradition and Pluralism: Essays in Honor of William M. Shea*, edited by K. L. Parker, P. A. Huff, and M. J. Pahls, 201–19. Lanham, MD: University Press of America, 2009.

"Preface." In *Modernists and Mystics*, edited by C. J. T. Talar, ix–xi. Washington, DC: Catholic University of America Press, 2009.

"The Mystical Element of the Modernist Crisis," with C. J. T. Talar. In *Modernists and Mystics*, edited by C. J. T. Talar, 1–22. Washington, DC: Catholic University of America Press, 2009.

"Rising to the Evangelical Moment." *Current Issues in Catholic Higher Education* 26.1 (2009) 49–57.

"Paul Hanly Furfey: Catholic Extremist and Supernatural Sociologist, 1935–1941." *Josephinum Journal of Theology* 16.1 (2009) 24–37.

"Divided Friends: Portraits of the Roman Catholic Modernist Crisis in the United States." *American Catholic Studies* 120.1 (2009) 105–12.

"'Good Friday in December,' World War II in the Editorials of *Preservation of the Faith Magazine*, 1939–1945." *U.S. Catholic Historian* 27.2 (2009) 25–44.

"The Transfigured World," review of *Atheist Delusions: The Christian Revolution and Its Fashionable Enemies*, by David Bentley Hart. *Commonweal* 136.9 (8 May 2009) 33–34.

"Restrung," review of *A Pilgrim in a Pilgrim Church: Memoirs of a Catholic Archbishop*, by Rembert G. Weakland. *Commonweal* 136.13 (17 July 2009) 22–25.

Review of *Jesus: Word Made Flesh*, by Gerard S. Sloyan. *Horizons* 36.2 (2009) 351–52.

Review of *Recovering American Catholic Inculturation: John England's Jacksonian Populism and Romanticist Adaptation*, by Lou F. McNeil. *Catholic Historical Review* 95.4 (2009) 878–79.

2010

"Angling for Anglicans." *Religion in the News* 12.3 (2010) 8–10, 21.

"A Three-Cornered Struggle," review of *Redeeming the Enlightenment: Christianity and the Liberal Virtues*, by Bruce K. Ward. *Commonweal* 137.7 (9 April 2010) 24–25.

2011

"Stability First," review of *Unlearning Protestantism: Sustaining Christian Community in an Unstable Age*, by Gerald Schlabach. *Commonweal* 138.4 (25 February 2011) 36–37.

Review of *When Values Collide: The Catholic Church, Sexual Abuse, and the Challenges of Leadership*, by Joseph P. Chinnici. *U.S. Catholic Historian* 29.2 (2011) 5–7.

"Twentieth-Century Catholic Theology and the Triumph of Maurice Blondel." *Communio* 38.1 (2011) 103–37.

"Geezer Rock for the Summer," review of *Big Man, Real Life and Tall Tales*, by Clarence Clemons and Don Reo. dot Commonweal (13 July 2011). Available at https://www.commonwealmagazine.org/blog/geezer-rock-summer.

"Challenging Caesar," review of *God in Action: How Faith in God Can Address the Challenges of the World*, by Cardinal Francis George. *Commonweal* 138.14 (12 August 2011) 24–26.

Review of *Maurice Blondel: A Philosophical Life*, by Oliva Blanchette. *Horizons* 38.2 (2011) 363–66.

Review of *Were the Popes against the Jews?*, by Justus George Lawler. *U.S. Catholic Historian* 29.4 (2011) 101–7.

2012

Contribution to "A Modus Vivendi?: Sex, Marriage, & the Church." *Commonweal* 139.1 (13 January 2012) 13.

"What Kind of a World of Grace?: Henri Cardinal de Lubac and the Council's Christological Center." *Communio* 39.1–2 (2012) 136–51.

"A Centurion's Story," review of *Reborn on the Fourth of July, The Challenge of Faith, Patriotism & Conscience*, by Logan Mehl-Laituri. dotCommonweal (6 August 2012). Available at https://www.commonwealmagazine.org/blog/centurions-story.

Review of *Infinity Dwindled to Infancy: A Catholic and Evangelical Christology*, by Edward T. Oakes, SJ. *Horizons* 39.2 (2012) 322–24.

2013

Divided Friends: Portraits of the Roman Catholic Modernist Crisis in the United States. Washington, DC: Catholic University of America Press, 2013.

"Assembly Required: Christ's Presence in the Pews." *Commonweal* 140.5 (8 March 2013) 12–14.

Contribution to "Regime Change: Benedict and His Successor." *Commonweal* 140.6 (22 March 2013) 18.

"More Mission, Less Maintenance," review of *Evangelical Catholicism: Deep Reform in the 21st-Century Church*, by George Weigel. *Commonweal* 140.7 (12 April 2013) 29–31.

"The First Encyclical of Francis?: Signs of a New Voice in 'Lumen Fidei.'" dotCommonweal (22 July 2013). Available at https://www.commonwealmagazine.org/first-encyclical-francis.

"Response to Reviewers of *Divided Friends*." *U.S. Catholic Historian* 31.4 (2013) 118–21.

"Street Pope: Francis and the Pastoral Rhetoric of Invitation." dotCommonweal (7 October 2013). Available at https://www.commonwealmagazine.org/street-pope.

"Here Come the Nones!: Pluralism and Evangelization after Denominationalism and Americanism." *Horizons* 40.2 (2013) 275–92.

2014

Editor, with Matthew Lewis Sutton. *Handing on the Faith*. College Theology Society Annual Volume 59. Maryknoll, NY: Orbis, 2014.

"Hauerwas on Hauerwas," review of *Approaching the End: Eschatological Reflections on Church, Politics, and Life*, by Stanley Hauerwas. *Commonweal* 141.4 (21 February 2014) 32–34.

"Claiming Civic Space," review of *America's Church: The National Shrine and Catholic Presence in the Nation's Capital*, by Thomas A. Tweed. *Sacred Architecture* 25 (2014) 35.

2015

"Doing Theology in the Enigmatic Rift," contribution to review symposium on *Saving Karl Barth: Hans Urs von Balthasar's Preoccupation*, by D. Stephen Long. *Pro Ecclesia* 24.2 (2015) 141–47.

Review of *The Catholic Studies Reader*, edited by James T. Fisher and Margaret McGuinness. *The Catholic Historical Review* 101.2 (2015) 390–91.

"Just a Gang of Sinners?" review of *The Future of the Church with Pope Francis*, by Garry Wills. *Commonweal* 142.6 (20 March 2015) 24–26.

"Are You a Catholic Historian?," contribution to review symposium on *The Past As Pilgrimage: Narrative, Tradition, and the Renewal of Catholic History*, by Christopher Shannon and Christopher O. Bloom. *U.S. Catholic Historian* 33.3 (2015) 132-34.

Contribution to review symposium on *Contesting Catholicity: Theology for Other Baptists*, by Curtis W. Freeman. *Horizons* 42.2 (December 2015) 421–27.

2016

"Newman, Millennials, and Teaching Comparative Theology." In *Comparative Theology in the Millennial Classroom: Hybrid Identities, Negotiated Boundaries*, edited by Mara Brecht and Reid B. Locklin, 36–49. New York: Routledge, 2016.

Contribution to "A Balancing Act: Reading *Amoris Laetitia*." *Commonweal* 143.9 (20 May 2016) 16–18.

Review of *Shaping American Catholicism: Maryland and New York, 1805-1915*, by Robert E. Curran. *Revue d'Histoire Ecclésiastique* 111.1–2 (January–June 2016) 338–40.

Response to "A Scary Resurrection." In *Preaching Conversations with Scholars: The Preacher as Scholar*, by Rodney Wallace Kennedy, 36–38. Eugene, OR: Wipf & Stock, 2016.

"Jesus and the World of Grace, 1968-2016: An Idiosyncratic Theological Memoir." *Horizons* 43.2 (December 2016) 374–96.

Forthcoming Works

"Every Catholic an Apostle": A Life of Thomas A. Judge C.M., 1868-1933. Washington, DC: Catholic University of America Press.

Catholicism in America. Malden, MA: Wiley-Blackwell.

Bibliography

Ahlstrom, Sydney. "The Radical Turn in Theology and Ethics: Why it Occurred in the 1960s." *Annals of the American Academy of Political and Social Science* 387 (January 1970) 1–13.

Aitken, James. "Lexical Semantics and the Cultural Context of Knowledge in Job 28, Illustrated by the Meaning of *ḥaqar*." In *Job 28: Cognition in Context*, edited by Ellen van Wolde, 119–37. Biblical Interpretation Series 64. Leiden: Brill, 2003.

Alba, Richard, and Dalia Abdel-Hady. "Galileo's Children: Italian Americans' Difficult Entry into the Intellectual Elite." *Sociological Quarterly* 46 (2005) 3–18.

Alba, Richard, and Robert Orsi. "Passages in Piety: Generational Transitions and the Social and Religious Incorporation of Italian Americans." In *Immigration and Religion in America: Comparative and Historical Perspectives*, edited by Richard Alba, Albert J. Raboteau, and Josh DeWind, 32–55. New York: New York University Press, 2009.

Alba, Richard, Albert J. Raboteau, and Josh DeWind, eds. *Immigration and Religion in America: Comparative and Historical Perspectives*. New York: New York University Press, 2009.

Alcaraz Varó, Enrique, and Brian Hughes. *Diccionario de términos jurídicos*. 6th ed. Barcelona: Ariel, 2001.

Alighieri, Dante. *The Divine Comedy, Volume 2: Purgatory*. Translated by Mark Musa. New York: Penguin, 1985.

Allen, John L., Jr. *The Future Church: How Ten Trends Are Revolutionizing the Catholic Church*. New York: Image, 2009.

Altman, Ida. "The Revolt of Enriquillo and the Historiography of Early Spanish America." *The Americas* 63 (2007) 587–614.

Anderson, Bernard, ed. *Creation in the Old Testament*. Issues in Religion and Theology 6. Philadelphia: Fortress, 1984.

Applebaum, Yoni. "How Columbus Day Fell Victim to Its Own Success." *The Atlantic*, online (8 October 2012). http://www.theatlantic.com/national/archive/2012/10/how-columbus-day-fell-victim-to-its-own-success/261922.

Appleby, R. Scott. *Church and Age Unite!: The Modernist Impulse in American Catholicism*. Notre Dame, IN: University of Notre Dame Press, 1992.

————. "In Pursuit of Coherence: Catholic Formation, 1950–2000." Catholic Daughters of America Lecture, Catholic University of America, Washington, DC, 2001.

————. "The Triumph of Americanism, Common Ground for U.S. Catholics in the Twentieth Century." In *Being Right: Conservative Catholics in America,* edited by Mary Jo Weaver and R. Scott Appleby, 37–62. Bloomington: Indiana University Press, 1995.

————, and John H. Haas. "The Last Supernaturalists: Fenton, Connell and the Threat of Catholic Indifferentism." *U.S. Catholic Historian* 13.2 (1995) 23–48.

————, and Mary Jo Weaver, eds. *Being Right: Conservative Catholics in America.* Bloomington: Indiana University Press, 1995.

Arrupe, Pedro, SJ. "Letter to the Whole Society on Inculturation." *Studies in the International Apostolate of Jesuits* 7 (June 1978) 1–9.

Balthasar, Hans Urs von. *A Theology of History.* 1963. Reprint, San Francisco: Ignatius, 1994.

Barber, Michael Patrick. "Jesus as the Davidic Temple Builder and Peter's Priestly Role in Matthew 16:16–19." *Journal of Biblical Literature* 132 (2013) 935–53.

Baxter, Michael. "In Service to the Nation: A Critical Analysis of the Formation of the Americanist Tradition in Catholic Social Ethics." PhD diss., Duke University, 1996.

————. "Writing History in a World Without Ends: An Evangelical Catholic Critique of United States Catholic History." *Pro Ecclesia* 5.4 (1996) 440–69.

Bea, A. "Progress in the Interpretation of Sacred Scripture." *Theology Digest* 1 (1953) 67–71.

Béchard, Dean P., ed. *The Scripture Documents: An Anthology of Official Catholic Teachings.* Collegeville, MN: Liturgical, 2002.

Bell, Daniel. *The End of Ideology: On the Exhaustion of Political Ideas in the Fifties.* Glencoe, IL: Free Press, 1960.

Benedict XVI, Pope. "Homily for Vespers at the Cathedral of Aosta" (24 July 2009). http://w2.vatican.va/content/benedict-xvi/en/homilies/2009/documents/hf_ben-xvi_hom_20090724_vespri-aosta.html.

————. *Verbum Domini.* 2010. http://w2.vatican.va/content/benedict-xvi/en/apost_exhortations/documents/hf_ben-xvi_exh_20100930_verbum-domini.html.

Beretta, Francesco. "Les Congrès scientifiques internationaux des catholiques (1888–1900) et la production d'orthodoxie dans l'espace intellectuel catholique." In *Le catholicisme en Congrès (XIXe–XXe siècles),* edited by Claude Langlois and Christian Sorrel, 155–203. Lyon: Resea-Larhra, 2009.

————. "La Doctrine romaine de l'inspiration de Léon XIII à Benoît XV (1893–1920): La production d'une nouvelle orthodoxie." In *Autour d'un petit livre: Alfred Loisy cent ans après,* edited by François Laplanche, Ilaria Biagioli, and Claude Langlois, 47–60. Turnhout: Brepols, 2007.

Bergsma, John S. *The Jubilee from Leviticus to Qumran: A History of Interpretation.* Vetus Testamentum Supplements 115. Leiden: Brill, 2007.

————, and Scott Walker Hahn. "Noah's Nakedness and the Curse on Canaan (Genesis 9:20–27)." *Journal of Biblical Literature* 124 (2005) 25–40.

Bernardi, Peter J., SJ. *Maurice Blondel, Social Catholicism, and Action Française: The Clash over the Church's Role in Society during the Modernist Era.* Washington, DC: Catholic University of America Press, 2009.

Bernardin, Joseph Cardinal. "The Catholic Moral Vision in the United States: Georgetown University, September 9, 1996." In *A Moral Vision for America*, edited by John P. Langan, SJ, 144–57. Washington, DC: Georgetown University Press, 1998.

———. "A Consistent Ethic of Life: An American-Catholic Dialogue: Gannon Lecture, Fordham University, December 6, 1983." In *A Moral Vision for America*, edited by John P. Langan, SJ, 7–16. Washington, DC: Georgetown University Press, 1998.

———. "The Consistent Ethic of Life and Public Policy: USCC Diocesan Social Action Directors' Conference, Washington, DC, February 10, 1988." In *A Moral Vision for America*, edited by John P. Langan, SJ, 51–58. Washington, DC: Georgetown University Press, 1998.

———. "Faithful and Hopeful: The Catholic Common Ground Project: October 24, 1996," In *A Moral Vision for America*, edited by John P. Langan, SJ, 158–68. Washington, DC: Georgetown University Press, 1998.

———. "Religion and Politics: Stating the Principles and Sharpening the Issues: Woodstock Forum—Georgetown University, October 25, 1984." In *A Moral Vision for America*, edited by John P. Langan, SJ, 37–50. Washington, DC: Georgetown University Press, 1998.

Blanchette, Oliva. *Maurice Blondel: A Philosophical Life*. Grand Rapids: Eerdmans, 2010.

Blondel, Maurice. *The Letter on Apologetics & History and Dogma*. Translated by Alexander Dru and Illtyd Trethowan. Grand Rapids: Eerdmans, 1994.

Bourget, Paul. *Outre-Mer: Impressions of America*. New York: Scribner, 1895.

Bravo, Francisco. *Christ in the Thought of Teilhard de Chardin*. Notre Dame, IN: University of Notre Dame Press, 1967.

Bredin, Jean-Denis. *The Affair: The Case of Alfred Dreyfus*. Scranton, PA: Braziller, 1986.

Brown, Frederick. *For the Soul of France: Culture Wars in the Age of Dreyfus*. New York: Anchor, 2010.

Brown, Mary Elizabeth. *Churches, Communities, and Children: Italian Immigrants in the Archdiocese of New York, 1880–1945*. New York: Center for Migration Studies, 1995.

———. *The Scalabrinians in North America, 1887–1934*. New York: Center for Migration Studies, 1996.

———. *Shapers of the Great Debate on Immigration: A Biographical Dictionary*. Shapers of the Great American Debates 1. Westport, CT: Greenwood, 1999.

Brown, Raymond E. *The Virginal Conception & Bodily Resurrection of Jesus*. New York: Paulist, 1973.

Brown, William P. *Character Is Crisis: A Fresh Approach to the Wisdom Literature of the Old Testament*. Grand Rapids: Eerdmans, 1996.

Browne, Henry J. "The 'Italian Problem' in the Catholic Church of the United States, 1880–1900." *Historical Records and Studies* 35 (1946) 46–72.

Brownson, Orestes A. "An Address Prepared at the Request of Guy C. Clark, with the Intention of Having It Delivered to the Assembly on the Day of His Execution, February 3, 1832." In *The Early Works of Orestes A. Brownson*, vol. 2, *The Free Thought and Unitarian Years, 1830–35*, edited by Patrick W. Carey, 174–82. Milwaukee: Marquette University Press, 2001.

———. *The American Republic: Its Constitution, Tendencies, and Destiny*. Edited by Gregory S. Butler. Wilmington, DE: ISI, 2003.

————. "The Laboring Classes." *Boston Quarterly Review* 3 (1840) 358–95.

————. "Leroux on Humanity." In *The Early Works of Orestes A. Brownson*, vol. 6, *Life By Communion, 1842*, edited by Patrick W. Carey, 217–76. Marquette Studies in Theology 46. Milwaukee: Marquette University Press, 2005.

————. "The Mediatorial Life of Jesus." In *The Early Works of Orestes A. Brownson*, vol. 6, *Life By Communion, 1842*, edited by Patrick W. Carey, 186–216. Marquette Studies in Theology 46. Milwaukee: Marquette University Press, 2005.

————. "The Mission of America." In *The Collected Works of Orestes A. Brownson*, vol. 11, edited by Henry F. Brownson, 551–84. Detroit: Nourse, 1884.

————. "Remarks on Universal History." In *The Early Works of Orestes A. Brownson*, vol. 7, *Life By Communion Years, 1843–1844*, edited by Patrick W. Carey, 177–237. Marquette Studies in Theology 46. Milwaukee: Marquette University Press, 2007.

————. "Theodore Parker's Discourse." In *The Early Works of Orestes A. Brownson*, vol. 6, *Life By Communion, 1842*, edited by Patrick W. Carey, 280–386. Marquette Studies in Theology 46. Milwaukee: Marquette University Press, 2005.

Brueggemann, Walter. *In Man We Trust: The Neglected Side of Biblical Faith*. Richmond, VA: John Knox, 1972.

Cadegan, Una M. "Running the Ancient Ark by Steam: Catholic Publishing." In *A History of the Book in America*, vol. 4, *Print in Motion: The Expansion of Publishing and Reading in the United States, 1880–1940*, edited by Carl F. Kaestle and Janice A. Radway, 392–409. Chapel Hill: University of North Carolina Press, 2009.

Camp, Claudia V. *Wisdom and the Feminine in the Book of Proverbs*. Bible and Literature Series 11. Decatur, GA: Almond, 1985.

————. "Woman Wisdom as Root Metaphor: A Theological Consideration." In *The Listening Heart: Essays in Wisdom and the Psalms in Honor of Roland E. Murphy*, edited by Kenneth G. Hoglund, 46–76. Sheffield, UK: JSOT, 1987.

Carey, Patrick W. *Catholics in America: A History*. Lanham, MD: Sheed & Ward, 2004.

————. "College Theology in Historical Perspective." In *American Catholic Traditions: Resources for Renewal*, edited by Sandra Yocum Mize and William L. Portier, 242–71. Maryknoll, NY: Orbis, 1997.

————. "Introduction." In *The Early Works of Orestes A. Brownson*, vol. 6, *Life by Communion, 1842*, edited by Patrick W. Carey, 1–54. Marquette Studies in Theology 46. Milwaukee: Marquette University Press, 2005.

————. *Orestes A. Brownson: American Religious Weathervane*. Grand Rapids: Eerdmans, 2004.

Carter, Michael S. "'Under the Benign Sun of Toleration': Mathew Carey, the Douai Bible, and Catholic Print Culture, 1789–1791." *Journal of the Early Republic* 27 (2007) 437–69.

Catholic Peace Fellowship, "The Life and Witness of Ben Salmon." *Sign of Peace* 6.1 (2007). http://www.catholicpeacefellowship.org/nextpage.asp? m=2524.

Center for Applied Research in the Apostolate. "CARA Catholic Poll 2011: Fordham Center on Religion and Culture Questions." Washington, DC: Center for Applied Research in the Apostolate, 2011. http://www.fordham.edu/images/undergraduate/centeronreligionculture/faith_citizen_poll%20crc-cara.pdf.

Cerase, Francesco. "Nostalgia or Disenchantment: Considerations on Return Migration." In *The Italian Experience in the United States*, edited by Silvano M. Tomasi and Madeline H. Engel, 217–39. New York: Center for Migration Studies, 1977.

Chamberlain, Robert S. "The Concept of the Señor Natural as Revealed by Castilian Law and Administrative Documents." *Hispanic American Historical Review* 19.2 (1939) 130–37.

———. *The Conquest and Colonization of Yucatan, 1517–1550.* Washington, DC: Carnegie Institute of Washington, 1948.

———. *The Pre-Conquest Tribute and Service System of the Maya as a Preparation for the Spanish Repartimiento-Encomienda in Yucatan.* Miami, FL: University of Miami Press, 1951.

"Characteristics of Italian Immigrants." *New York Times* (18 May 1902) SM12.

Charbonnel, Victor. *Congrès universal des religions en 1900. Histoire d'une idée.* Paris: Colin, 1897.

Chenu, Marie-Dominique, OP. *La 'Doctrine sociale' de l'Église comme idéologie.* Paris: Cerf, 1979.

Chinnici, Joseph P., OFM, ed. *Devotion to the Holy Spirit in American Catholicism.* Mahwah, NJ: Paulist, 1985.

Ciani, John L. "Across the Wide Ocean: Salvatore Maria Brandi, SJ, and the 'Civiltà Cattolica,' from Americanism to Modernism, 1891–1914." PhD diss., University of Virginia, 1992.

Cohen, David A. "Secular Pragmatism and the Thinking of Pere III *el cerimoniós.*" In *Crusaders, Condottieri, and Cannon: Medieval Warfare in Societies around the Mediterranean,* edited by Donald J. Kagay and L. J. Andrew Villalon, 19–55. History of Warfare 13. Leiden: Brill, 2003.

Coleman, John, SJ. "Vision and Praxis in American Theology: Orestes Brownson, John A. Ryan and John Courtney Murray." *Theological Studies* 37 (1976) 3–40.

Colin, Pierre. *L'Audace et le soupçon: La crise moderniste dans le catholicisme français, 1893–1914.* Paris: Desclée de Brouwer, 1997.

Collinge, William J. Review of *Tradition and Incarnation: Foundations of Christian Theology,* by William L. Portier. *The Living Light* 31.4 (1995) 77–79.

Collingwood, R. G. *The Idea of History.* London: Oxford University Press, 1956.

Commager, Henry Steele. "That Sturdy but Erratic Reformer, Orestes Brownson." *New York Times* (23 April 1939) 88.

Connell, Francis J., CSsR. Review of *Applied Christianity,* by John J. Hugo. *American Ecclesiastical Review* 113 (July 1945) 69–72.

Connor, Joseph J., SJ. "The Catholic Conscientious Objector." *Ecclesiastical Review* 108 (February 1943) 125–38.

Corbishley, Thomas. *The Spirituality of Teilhard de Chardin.* New York: Paulist, 1971.

Cosco, Joseph P. *Imagining Italians: The Clash of Romance and Race in American Perceptions, 1880–1910.* Albany: State University of New York Press, 2003.

Cox, Harvey. "Afterword." In *The Secular City Debate,* edited by Daniel Callahan, 179–203. New York: Macmillan, 1966.

———. *The Secular City.* New York: Macmillan, 1965.

Crenshaw, James. "In Search of Divine Presence (Some Remarks Preliminary to a Theology of Wisdom)." *Review and Expositor* 74 (1977) 353–69.

———. *Old Testament Wisdom: An Introduction.* Rev. ed. Louisville: Westminster John Knox, 1998.

———, ed. *Theodicy in the Old Testament.* Issues in Religion and Theology 4. Philadelphia: Fortress, 1983.

Cuddihy, John Murray. *No Offense: Civil Religion and Protestant Taste*. New York: Seabury, 1978.

Curran, Charles. *American Catholic Social Ethics: Twentieth-Century Approaches*. Notre Dame, IN: University of Notre Dame Press, 1982.

Curtis, Georgina Pell. *The American Catholic Who's Who*. St. Louis, MO: B. Herder, 1911.

D'Agostino, Peter. Review of *The Lion and Lamb: Evangelicals and Catholics in America*, by William Shea. *Cithara* 54 (November 2004) 73.

Dailey, Thomas. "The Wisdom of Job: Moral Maturity or Religious Reckoning?" *Union Seminary Quarterly Review* 51 (1997) 45–55.

Dall'Olio, Alessandro, SJ. "Teilhard de Chardin: Thinker Wedded to Wisdom." In *Jesuits: Year-book of the Society of Jesus, 1972–1973*, English ed., 81–86. Rome: Curia Generalizia, 1972.

Davidson, David M. "Negro Slave Control and Resistance in Colonial Mexico, 1519–1650." In *Maroon Societies: Rebel Slave Communities in the Americas*, edited by Richard Price, 82–103. Baltimore: Johns Hopkins University Press, 1996.

Davis, Ellen F. *Proverbs, Ecclesiastes, and the Song of Songs*. Westminster Bible Companion. Louisville: Westminster John Knox, 2000.

Day, Dorothy. *By Little and By Little: The Selected Writings of Dorothy Day*. Edited by Robert Ellsberg. New York: Knopf, 1983.

———. *Dorothy Day: Writings from* Commonweal. Edited by Patrick Jordan. Collegeville, MN: Liturgical, 2002.

———. *The Long Loneliness*. New York: Harper & Row, 1952.

———. "Our Country Passes from Undeclared War to Declared War; We Continue Our Christian Pacifist Stand." *The Catholic Worker* (January 1942) 1. Reprinted in *A Penny A Copy: Readings from* The Catholic Worker, edited by Thomas Cornell, Robert Ellsberg, and Jim Forest, 37–39. Maryknoll, NY: Orbis, 1995.

Deagan, Kathleen, and Jose Maria Cruxent. *Columbus's Outpost Among the Tainos: Spain and America at La Isabela, 1493–1498*. New Haven: Yale University Press, 2002.

de Chabrol, Comte. "Un Prêtre américain: le Révérend Père Hecker." *Le Correspondant* 187 (1897) 893–912.

de Concilio, Januarius. *Sullo stato religioso degli italiani negli Stati Uniti d'America*. New York: Carbone, 1886.

de Hartog, Leo. *Genghis Kahn: Conqueror of the World*. London: IB Tauris, 1989.

Delattre, Alphonse J. *Un Catholicisme américain*. Namur, Belgium: Auguste Godenne, 1898.

———. *Un Congrès d'intellectuels à Gand en février, 1897*. Louvain: Imprimerie Polleunis et Ceuterick, 1897.

de Lubac, Henri, SJ. *At the Service of the Church: Henri de Lubac Reflects on the Circumstances that Occasioned His Writings*. Translated by Anne Elizabeth Englund. San Francisco: Ignatius, 1998.

———. *Corpus Mysticum: The Eucharist and the Church in the Middle Ages*. Translated by Gemma Simmonds, CJ, Richard Price, and Christopher Stephens. Notre Dame, IN: University of Notre Dame Press, 2006.

———. *Surnaturel: Etudes historiques*. 1946. Reprint, Paris: Desclée de Brouwer, 1991.

———. *Teilhard Posthume: Réflexions et Souvenirs*. Paris: Fayard, 1977.

————. *Theology in History.* Translated by Anne Englund Nash. San Francisco: Ignatius, 1996.

————. "The Total Meaning of Man and the World." Translated by D. C. Schindler. *Communio* 35 (2008) 613–41.

de Meaux, Vicomte. *L'Église catholique et la liberté aux États-Unis.* Paris: Lecoffre, 1893.

de Oviedo y Valdes, Gonzalo Fernández. *Historia general y natural de las Indias, islas, y tierra-firme del mar océano.* Madrid: Biblioteca de Autores Españoles, 1959.

DeVito, Michael. *The New York Review (1905–1908).* New York: United States Historical Society, 1977.

di Donato, Pietro. *Christ in Concrete.* 1939. Reprint, New York: Signet, 1993.

Doak, Mary. "Table Fellowship in a Land of Gated Communities: Virgilio Elizondo as Public Theologian." In *Faith in Public Life,* edited by William J. Collinge, 202–17. College Theology Society Annual Volume 53. Maryknoll, NY: Orbis, 2008.

Dolan, Jay. *The American Catholic Experience: A History from Colonial Times to the Present.* Notre Dame, IN: University of Notre Dame Press, 1992.

Donahue, John R., SJ. "Joseph A. Fitzmyer, SJ: Scholar and Teacher of the Word of God." *U.S. Catholic Historian* 31 (2013) 63–83.

————. "A Journey Remembered: Catholic Biblical Scholarship 50 Years After *Divino Afflante Spiritu.*" *America* 169.7 (1993) 6–11.

Donovan, Leo. "Was Vatican II Evolutionary?: A Note on Conciliar Language." *Theological Studies* 36 (1975) 493–502.

Douthat, Ross. *Bad Religion: How We Became A Nation of Heretics.* New York: Free Press, 2012.

Doyle, Dennis M. "The Concept of Inculturation in Roman Catholicism: A Theological Consideration." *U.S. Catholic Historian* 30.1 (2012) 1–13.

Drummond, John. "Downstream from Pittsburgh." *Delta Epsilon Sigma Journal* 42.3 (1997) 84–89.

Dulles, Avery. *Models of the Church.* 1974. Reprinted with new introduction. New York: Image, 2002.

Dumont, Martin. *Le Saint-Siège et l'organisation politique des catholiques français aux lendemains du Ralliement, 1890–1902.* Paris: Champion, 2012.

"Editorial: That Encyclical." *First Things* 15 (August–September 1991) 11–12.

Edwards, John. *The Spain of the Catholic Monarchs, 1474–1520.* Malden, MA: Blackwell, 2000.

Elliott, Walter. *The Life of Father Hecker.* New York: Columbus, 1891.

————. *Le Père Hecker: Fondateur des "Paulistes" américains, 1819–1888.* Translated by Félix Klein. Paris: Lecoffre, 1897.

Ellis, John Tracy. *American Catholicism.* 2nd ed. Chicago: University of Chicago Press, 1969.

————. *The Formative Years of The Catholic University of America.* Washington, DC: American Catholic Historical Association, 1946.

Ellsberg, Robert, *All Saints: Daily Reflections on Saints, Prophets, and Witnesses for Our Time.* 1997. New York: Crossroad, 2012.

————, ed. *All the Way to Heaven: The Selected Letters of Dorothy Day.* Milwaukee: Marquette University Press, 2010.

Ellwood, Robert S. *The Sixties Spiritual Awakening: American Religion Moving from Modern to Postmodern.* New Brunswick, NJ: Rutgers University Press, 1994.

Elsbernd, Mary. "What Ever Happened to *Octogesima adveniens?*" *Theological Studies* 56 (1995) 39–60.

Estepa, Carlos. "The Strengthening of Royal Power in Castile under Alfonso XI." In *Building Legitimacy: Political Discourses and Forms of Legitimacy in Medieval Societies*, edited by Isabel Alfonso, Hugh Kennedy, and Julio Escalona, 179–222. Medieval Mediterranean 53. Leiden: Brill, 2004.

"Evolution, Science and Religion." *Jubilee* (May 1960) 48–51.

Fanning, William. "Plenary Councils of Baltimore." In *The Catholic Encyclopedia*, vol. 2. New York: Appleton, 1907. http://www.newadvent.org/cathen/ 02235a.htm.

Faricy, Robert L., SJ. *Teilhard de Chardin's Theology of the Christian in the World.* New York: Sheed & Ward, 1967.

"Father Richard John Neuhaus on the Iraqi Crisis." *ZENIT* (10 March 2003). http:// www.zenit.org/en/articles/father-richard-neuhaus-on-the-iraqi-crisis.

Faudree, Paja. "How to Say Things with Wars: Performativity and Discursive Rupture in the *Requerimiento* of the Spanish Conquest." *Journal of Linguistic Anthropology* 22.3 (2013) 182–200.

Femminella, Francis X. "The Impact of Italian Migration and American Catholicism." *American Catholic Sociological Review* 22.3 (1961) 233–41.

Fenton, Joseph Clifford. "Nature and the Supernatural Life." *American Ecclesiastical Review* 114 (1946) 54–68.

Fernández, Luis Suárez. *Fernándo el Católico y Navarra: El proceso de incorporación del reino a la Corona de España.* Madrid: Rialp, 1985.

Ferraiuolo, Augusto. *Religious Festive Practices in Boston's North End: Ephemeral Identities in an Italian American Community.* SUNY Series in Italian/American Culture. New York: State University of New York Press, 2009.

Ferraro, Thomas J. *Feeling Italian: The Art of Ethnicity in America.* New York: New York University Press, 2005.

Finney, Torin R.T. *Unsung Hero of the Great War: The Life and Witness of Ben Salmon.* Mahwah, NJ: Paulist, 1989.

Fisher, James T. *The Catholic Counterculture in America, 1933–1962.* Chapel Hill: University of North Carolina Press, 1989.

———. *A Communion of Immigrants: A History of Catholics in America.* Oxford: Oxford University Press, 2008.

———. "Seeking a Way Home: The Mystical Body of Christ and the Beloved Community." Keynote Address at Benedictine Pedagogy Conference, Saint Vincent College, Latrobe, PA, 22 May 2015.

Floyd, Troy S. *The Columbus Dynasty in the Caribbean, 1492–1526.* Albuquerque: University of New Mexico Press, 1973.

Fogarty, Gerald P., SJ. *American Catholic Biblical Scholarship: A History from the Early Republic to Vatican II.* San Francisco: Harper & Row, 1989.

———. "American Catholic Biblical Scholarship: A Review." *Theological Studies* 50 (1989) 219–43.

Fontaine, Carol. "The Social Roles of Women in the World of Wisdom." In *A Feminist Companion to Wisdom Literature*, edited by Athalya Brenner, 24–49. Feminist Companion to the Bible 9. Sheffield, UK: Sheffield Academic, 1995.

Forest, Jim. *All is Grace: A Biography of Dorothy Day.* Maryknoll, NY: Orbis, 2011.

"For Uniform Divorce Laws." *New York Times* (21 February 1906) 8.

Francis, Pope. "Meeting with the Bishops of the United States: Address of the Holy Father." http://w2.vatican.va/content/francesco/en/speeches/2015/september/documents/papa- francesco_20150923_usa-vescovi.html.

———. "*Incontro con i rappresentanti del V Convegno Nazionale della Chiesa Italiana.*" http://w2.vatican.va/content/francesco/it/speeches/2015/november/documents/papa-francesco_20151110_firenze-convegno-chiesa-italiana.html.

Francoeur, Robert. "A Call to Greatness." *Commonweal* 72.19 (1960) 441–43.

———, ed. *The World of Teilhard.* Baltimore: Helicon, 1961.

Fretheim, Terence. *God and World in the Old Testament: A Relational Theology of Creation.* Nashville: Abingdon, 2005.

Furfey, Paul Hanly. *Fire on the Earth.* New York: Macmillan, 1936.

———. "The New Social Catholicism." *Christian Front* 3 (1936) 184. Reprinted in *Prayer and Practice in the American Catholic Community,* edited by Joseph Chinnici, OFM, and Angelyn Dries, OSF, 156–59. Maryknoll, NY: Orbis, 2000.

Gaillardetz, Richard. "Ecclesiological Foundations of Modern Catholic Social Teaching." In *Modern Catholic Social Teaching,* edited by Kenneth R. Himes, OFM, 72–98. Washington, DC: Georgetown University Press, 2004.

Gallo, Patrick J. *Old Bread, New Wine.* Chicago: Nelson-Hall, 1981.

Garlan, Yvon. *War in the Ancient World: A Social History.* London: Chatto & Windus, 1975.

Gauthreaux, Alan G. *Italian Louisiana: History, Heritage and Tradition.* Charleston, SC: The History Press, 2014.

Geller, Stephen A. "'Where Is Wisdom?': A Literary Study of Job 28 in Its Settings." In *Judaic Perspectives on Ancient Israel,* edited by Jacob Neusner, Baruch Levine, and Ernest S. Frerichs, 155–88. Philadelphia: Fortress, 1987. Reprint, Eugene, OR: Wipf & Stock, 2004.

George, Francis Cardinal. "How Liberalism Fails the Church." *Commonweal* 126.20 (19 November 1999) 24–29.

Gesualdi, Louis. "A Comparison of the Attitudes and Practices of the Irish American and Italian American Catholics." In *Models and Images of Catholicism in Italian Americana: Academy and Science,* edited by Joseph A. Varacalli, Salvatore Primeggia, Salvatore J. LaGumina, and Donald J. Elia, 40–51. Stony Brook, NY: Forum Italicum, 2004.

Gibson, Charles. "Conquest, Capitulation, and Indian Treaties." *American Historical Review* 83.1 (February 1978) 1–15.

Gigot, Francis E., SS. "Divorce in the New Testament." *New York Review* 2 (1906–1907) 479–94, 610–23, 749–60; *New York Review* 3 (1907–1908) 56–68, 545–60, 705–21.

———. *General Introduction to the Study of the Holy Scriptures.* New York: Benziger Bros, 1900.

———. *General Introduction to the Study of the Holy Scriptures.* Abridged ed. New York: Bengizer Bros, 1904.

———. "The Higher Criticism of the Bible: Its General Principles." *New York Review* 2 (1906–1907) 158–61.

———. "The Higher Criticism of the Bible: The Name and the Thing." *New York Review* 1 (1905–1906) 724–27.

———. Letter to James Driscoll. 7 March 1903. Record Group 10, Box 9, Sulpician Archives, Baltimore.

———. "The Study of Sacred Scripture in Theological Seminaries." *American Ecclesiastical Review* 23 (1900) 227–35.

———. "The Virgin Birth in St. Luke's Gospel: The Genuineness of Luke 1:34–35." *Irish Theological Quarterly* 8 (1913) 123–43, 412–34.

Gilligan, Bernard. Review of *The Phenomenon of Man,* by Pierre Teilhard de Chardin. *New Scholasticism* 34 (1960) 515.

Gillis, Chester. *Roman Catholicism in America.* Columbia Contemporary American Religion Series. New York: Columbia University Press, 1999.

Ginzburg, Carlo. *The Cheese and the Worms: The Cosmos of a Sixteenth-Century Miller.* Baltimore: John Hopkins University Press. 1991.

Gleason, Philip. *Contending with Modernity: Catholic Higher Education in the Twentieth Century.* New York: Oxford University Press, 1995.

———. "In Search of Unity." *Catholic Historical Review,* 65 (1979) 198–99.

———. "The New Americanism in Catholic Historiography." *U.S. Catholic Historian* 11.3 (1993) 1–18.

Goizueta, Roberto S. "The Symbolic Realism of U.S. Latino/a Popular Catholicism." *Theological Studies* 65 (2004) 255–74.

Grannan, Charles P. *A General Introduction to the Bible.* 4 vols. St. Louis, MO: B. Herder, 1921.

Gray, Donald. "The Phenomenon of Teilhard." *Theological Studies* 36.1 (March 1975) 19–51.

Gregory, Brad S. *The Unintended Reformation.* Cambridge, MA: Harvard University Press, 2012.

Griffith, Sidney and Monica Blanchard. "Henri Hyvernat (1858–1941) and the Beginning of Syriac Studies at The Catholic University of America." *ARAM* 5 (1993) 181–96.

Guglielmo, Jennifer and Salvatore Salerno, eds. *Are Italians White?: How Race Is Made in America.* New York: Routledge, 2003.

Gutiérrez, Gustavo. *Las Casas: In Search of the Poor of Jesus Christ.* Translated by Robert R. Barr. Maryknoll, NY: Orbis, 1993.

Gutjahr, Paul C. *An American Bible: A History of the Good Book in the United States, 1777–1880.* Stanford: Stanford University Press, 1999.

Habel, Norman. "The Implications of God Discovering Wisdom in Earth." In *Job 28: Cognition in Context,* edited by Ellen van Wolde, 281–97. Leiden: Brill, 2003.

———. "Of Things Beyond Me: Wisdom in the Book of Job." *Currents in Theology and Mission* 10 (1983) 142–54.

———. "The Symbolism of Wisdom in Proverbs 1–9." *Interpretation* 26 (1972) 131–57.

Hahn, Scott W. "Biblical Theology and Marian Studies." *Marian Studies* 55 (2004) 9–32.

———. "A Broken Covenant and the Curse of Death: A Study of Hebrews 9:15–22." *Catholic Biblical Quarterly* 66 (2004) 416–36.

———, ed. *Catholic Bible Dictionary.* New York: Doubleday Religion, 2009.

———. *Covenant and Communion: The Biblical Theology of Pope Benedict XVI.* Grand Rapids: Brazos, 2009.

———. "Covenant, Cult, and the Curse-of-Death: Διαθήκη in Heb 9:15–22." In *Hebrews: Contemporary Methods, New Insights,* edited by Gabriella Gelardini, 65–88. Biblical Interpretation Series 75. Leiden: Brill, 2005.

———. "Covenant, Oath, and the Aqedah: Διαθήκη in Galatians 3:15–18." *Catholic Biblical Quarterly* 67.1 (2005) 79–100.

————. *Kinship by Covenant: A Canonical Approach to the Fulfillment of God's Saving Promises.* New Haven: Yale University Press, 2009.

————, and John Sietze Bergsma. "What Laws Were 'Not Good'? A Canonical Approach to the Theological Problem of Ezekiel 20:25–26." *Journal of Biblical Literature* 123 (2004) 201–18.

————, and Benjamin Wiker. *Politicizing the Bible: The Roots of Historical Criticism and the Secularization of Scripture 1300–1700.* New York: Herder & Herder, 2013.

Hartdegen, Stephen J. "The Influence of the Encyclical *Providentissimus Deus* on Subsequent Scripture Study." *Catholic Biblical Quarterly* 5 (1943) 141–59.

Haught, John. "More Being: The Emergence of Teilhard de Chardin." *Commonweal* 136.11 (5 June 2009) 17–19.

Hébert, Marcel. *Religious Experience in the Work of Richard Wagner.* Translated by C.J.T. Talar and Elizabeth Emery. Washington, DC: Catholic University of America Press, 2015.

Hefner, Philip J. *The Promise of Teilhard: The Meaning of the Twentieth Century in Christian Perspective.* Philadelphia: J.B. Lippincott, 1970.

Hehir, J. Bryan. "A Catholic Troeltsch? Curran on the Social Ministry of the Church." In *A Call to Fidelity: On the Moral Theology of Charles E. Curran,* edited by James J. Walter, Timothy E. O'Connell, and Thomas E. Shannon, 191–208. Washington, DC: Georgetown University Press, 2002.

————. "Murray's Contribution." In *The Catholic Church, Morality, and Politics,* edited by Charles E. Curran and Leslie Griffin, 5–11. Mahwah, NJ: Paulist, 2001.

————. "Papal Foreign Policy." *Foreign Policy* 78 (Spring 1990) 26–48

————. "Reordering the World: John Paul II's *Centesimus Annus.*" *Commonweal* 118.12 (14 June 1991) 393–94.

————. "The Social Role of the Church: Leo XIII, Vatican II and John Paul II." In *Catholic Social Thought and the New World Order,* edited by Oliver F. Williams, CSC, and John W. Houck, 29–50. Notre Dame, IN: University of Notre Dame Press, 1993.

————. "The Unfinished Agenda." *America* 153.16 (30 November 1985) 386–87, 392.

Heineman, Kenneth. *A Catholic New Deal: Religion and Reform in Depression Pittsburgh.* University Park: Pennsylvania State University Press, 1999.

Hennesey, James J., SJ. *American Catholics: A History of the Roman Catholic Community in the United States.* New York: Oxford University Press, 1981.

Herberg, Will. *Protestant-Catholic-Jew: An Essay in American Religious Sociology.* Garden City, NY: Anchor, 1960.

Heyer, Kristen E. *Prophetic & Public: The Social Witness of U.S. Catholicism.* Washington, DC: Georgetown University Press, 2006.

Hill, Harvey. "Leo XIII, Loisy, and the 'Broad School': An Early Round of the Modernist Crisis." *Catholic Historical Review* 89.1 (2003) 39–59.

————. *The Politics of Modernism: Alfred Loisy and the Scientific Study of Religion.* Washington, DC: Catholic University of America Press, 2002.

Hill, Robert. "Job in Search of Wisdom." *Scripture Bulletin* 23.2 (1993) 34–38.

Hill, William F., SS. "Reverend Edward P. Arbez, SS." *Catholic Biblical Quarterly* 23 (1961) 113–24.

Hillgarth, J. N. *The Spanish Kingdoms, 1250–1516,* vol. 2. Oxford, UK: Clarendon, 1978.

Himes, Kenneth R., OFM. "To Inspire and Inform." *America* 192.20 (6 June 2005) 7–10. http://americamagazine.org/issue/534/article/inspire-and-inform.

Hogan, John B. *Clerical Studies*. Boston: Marlier, Callanan, 1898.

Hogan, Michael. "Quiet Gestures, Heroic Acts: A Conversation with Robert Ellsberg." *Monthly Review* (17 May 2006). http://mrzine.monthlyreview.org/2006/hogan170506.html.

Hogard, René. *Quarante-cinq ans d'episcopat: Mgr Turinaz évêque de Nancy et de Toul 1838–1918*. Nancy, France: Vagner, 1938.

Hollenbach, David. "Christian Social Ethics after the Cold War." *Theological Studies* 53.1 (March 1992) 75–93.

Hooper, J. Leon, SJ. "Murray and Day: A Common Enemy, a Common Cause?" *U.S. Catholic Historian* 24.1 (Winter 2006) 45–61.

Huff, Peter. *Allen Tate and the Catholic Revival: Trace of the Fugitive Gods*. Mahwah, NJ: Paulist, 1996.

Hugo, John. *Applied Christianity*. New York: The Catholic Worker, 1944.

———. "Catholics Can Be Conscientious Objectors." *Catholic Worker* (May 1943) 6–8; (June 1943) 6–8.

———. *A Sign of Contradiction: As the Master, So the Disciple*. Published by author, 1947.

Hügel, Friedrich von. *The Mystical Element of Religion*. 2 vols. New York: Dutton, 1908.

Ireland, John. *The Church and Modern Society: Lectures and Addresses*. 2 vols. Chicago: McBride, 1897.

———. *L'Église et le siècle: Conférences et discours de Mgr Ireland*. Translated by Félix Klein. Paris: Lecoffre, 1894.

"The Italian Problem: Some Suggestions About It But No Solution." *New York Times* (4 July 1888) 3.

"Italian Society Uplifts Immigrants." *New York Times* (20 February 1910) 15.

Jenkins, Philip. *Decades of Nightmares: The End of the Sixties and the Making of Eighties America*. New York: Oxford University Press, 2006.

John, Helen James. *The Thomist Spectrum*. New York: Fordham University Press, 1966.

John XXIII, Pope. *Journal of a Soul: The Autobiography of Pope John XXIII*. New York: Image, 1999.

John Paul II, Pope. *Redemptor Hominis*. 1979. http://w2.vatican.va/content/john-paul-ii/en/encyclicals/documents/hf_jp-ii_enc_04031979_redemptor-hominis.html.

———. *Sollicitudo Rei Socialis*. 1987. http://w2.vatican.va/content/john-paul-ii/en/encyclicals/documents/hf_jp-ii_enc_30121987_sollicitudo-rei-socialis.html.

Juliani, Richard N. *Priest, Parish, and People: Saving the Faith in Philadelphia's 'Little Italy.'* Notre Dame, IN: University of Notre Dame Press, 2007.

Kamp, Albert. "World Building in Job 28: A Case of Conceptual Logic." In *Job 28: Cognition in Context*, edited by Ellen van Wolde, 307–19. Leiden: Brill, 2003.

Kauffman, Christopher J. *Tradition and Transformation in Catholic Culture: The Priests of Saint Sulpice in the United States from 1791 to the Present*. New York: Macmillan, 1988.

Kennedy, John F. "Address to the Houston Ministerial Association, September 1960." In *Public Voices: Catholics in the American Context*, edited by Steven M. Avella and Elizabeth McKeown, 361–64. Maryknoll, NY: Orbis, 1999.

Kerlin, Michael J. "Maurice Blondel: Philosophy, Prayer, and the Mystical." In *Modernists & Mystics*, edited by C. J. T. Talar, 62–81. Washington, DC: Catholic University of America Press, 2009.

Kicza, John E. "Patterns in Early Spanish Overseas Expansion." *The William and Mary Quarterly* 49.2 (April 1992) 229–53.

"Klein, Félix." In *Dictionnaire du monde religieux dans la France contemporaine*. Vol. 9, *Les Sciences religieuses: Le XIXe siècle 1800–1914*, edited by François Laplanche, 359–60. Paris: Beauchesne, 1996.

Klein, Félix. *Americanism: A Phantom Heresy*. Atchison, KS: Aquin Book Shop, 1950.

———. "Anglicans et romans." *Revue du clergé français* 6 (1896) 385–407.

———. *Au pays de "la vie intense"*. Paris: Plon, 1904.

———. *Autour du dilettantisme*. Paris: Librairie Victor Lecoffre, 1895.

———. *Cardinal Lavigerie et ses oeuvres d'Afrique*. Paris: Librairie Ch. Poussielgue, 1890.

———. "Catholicisme américain: Le P. Hecker, fondateur des Paulistes de New York." *Revue française d'Edimbourg* 5 (September-October 1897) 305–14.

———. "La Démocratie et l'Église." In *Nouvelles tendances en religion et en littérature*, 77–133. Paris: Librairie Victor Lecoffre, 1893. Originally published as "La Démocratie et l'Église," *Le Correspondant* 130 (1892) 401–24.

———. *In the Land of the Strenuous Life*. Chicago: A. C. McClurg, 1905.

———. "Le movement néo-chrétien dans la littérature contemporaine." In *Nouvelles tendances en religion et en littérature*, 3–73. Paris: Librairie Victor Lecoffre, 1893. Originally published as "Le movement néo-chrétien dans la littérature contemporaine," *Le Correspondant* 130 (1892) 454–85.

———. Preface to *L'Église et le Siècle: Conférences et discours de Mgr Ireland*, by John Ireland, 1–18. Translated by Félix Klein. Paris: Victor Lecoffre, 1894.

———. *La route d'un petit Morvandiau*. 7 vols. Paris: Aubier, 1946–1952.

———. "Un grand mystique aux États-Unis." *Revue du clergé français* 11 (1897) 5–20.

Knighton, Tess and Carmen Morte García. "Ferdinand of Aragon's Entry into Valladolid in 1513: The Triumph of a Christian King." *Early Music History* 18 (1999) 119–63.

Koch, Klaus. "Gibt es ein Vergeltungsdogma im alten Testament." *Zeitschrift für Theologie und Kirche* 52 (1955) 1–42.

Komonchak, Joseph. "John Courtney Murray and the Redemption of History: Natural Law and Theology." In *John Courtney Murray & The Growth of Tradition*, edited by J. Leon Hooper, SJ, and Todd David Whitmore, 60–81. Kansas City, MO: Sheed & Ward, 1996.

LaGumina, Salvatore J. "Anti-Italian Discrimination." In *The Italian American Experience: An Encyclopedia*, edited by Salvatore J. LaGumina, Frank J. Cavaioli, Salvatore Primeggia, and Joseph J. Varacalli, 16–19. New York: Garland, 2000.

———, ed. *WOP!: A Documentary History of Anti-Italian Discrimination in the United States*. Ethnic Prejudice in America Series. San Francisco: Straight Arrow, 1973.

Lane, David. *The Phenomenon of Teilhard*. Macon, GA: Mercer University Press, 1996.

Las Casas, Bartolomé de. *Historia de las Indias*. Edited by Augustín Millares Carlo y Lewis Hanke. México, D.F.: Fondo de Cultura Económica, 1951.

Lears, Jackson. *Rebirth of A Nation: The Making of Modern America, 1877–1920*. New York: Harper Collins, 2009.

Leo XIII, Pope. *Providentissimus Deus*. 1893. http://w2.vatican.va/content/leo-xiii/en/encyclicals/documents/hf_l-xiii_enc_18111893_providentissimus-deus.html.

———. *Quam Aerumnosa*. 1888. http://w2.vatican.va/content/leo-xiii/en/encyclicals/documents/hf_l-xiii_enc_10121888_quam-aerumnosa.html.

————. *Testem Benevolentiae.* 1899. http://www.papalencyclicals.net/Leo13/l13teste. htm.

Linkh, Richard M. "Catholic Attitudes Toward the 'New' Immigrant with Particular Reference to the Italian and Pole." In *American Catholicism and European Immigrants,* 35–48. New York: Center for Migration Studies, 1975.

Loisy, Alfred. *Mémoires pour servir à l'histoire religieuse de nôtre temps tome premier: 1857–1900.* Paris: Nourry, 1930.

Lombardo, Michael F. *Founding Father: John J. Wynne, S.J. and the Inculturation of American Catholicism in the Progressive Era.* Jesuit Studies: Modernity Through the Lens of Jesuit History. Leiden: Brill, 2017.

Lonergan, Bernard. "The Transition from a Classicist World-View to Historical Mindedness." In *A Second Collection,* edited by W.F.J. Ryan, SJ, and B.J. Tyrell, SJ, 1–9. Philadelphia: Westminster, 1974.

Lukacs, John. *The Last European War: September 1939–December 1941.* New Haven: Yale University Press, 1976.

Lysaught, M. Therese. "From *The Challenge of Peace* to *The Gift of Peace*: Reading the Consistent Ethic of Life as an Ethic of Peacemaking." In *The Consistent Ethic of Life: Assessing Its Reception and Relevance,* edited by Thomas A. Nairn, 109–31. Maryknoll, NY: Orbis, 2008.

Lytle, Mark Hamilton. *America's Uncivil Wars: The Sixties Era from Elvis to the Fall of Richard Nixon.* New York: Oxford University Press, 2006.

Maas, Anthony, SJ. *The Life of Jesus Christ According to the Gospel History.* St. Louis, MO: B. Herder, 1892.

Machacek, David W. "The Problem of Pluralism." *Sociology of Religion* 64.2 (2003) 145–61.

Macdonald, Dwight. "Profiles: The Foolish Things of This World." Part 1: *The New Yorker* (4 October 1952) 37–60; Part 2: *The New Yorker* (11 October 1952) 37–58.

Machiavelli, Niccoló. *The Prince.* Translated by Christian E. Detmold. Edited by Lester G. Crocker. New York: Simon and Schuster, 1963.

MacIntyre, Alasdair. *After Virtue.* 2nd ed. Notre Dame, IN: University of Notre Dame Press, 1984.

————. *Whose Justice? Which Rationality?* Notre Dame, IN: University of Notre Dame Press, 1988.

Maignen, Charles. *Nouveau catholicisme, nouveau clergé.* Paris: Victor Retaux Librairie-Éditeur, 1902.

————. *Le Père Hecker: Est-il un saint?* Paris: Librairie de Victor Retaux, 1898.

————. *La Souveraineté du peuple est une hérésie.* Paris: Roger Chernovitz, 1892.

"Making American Farmers of Italian Immigrants." *New York Times* (4 December 1910) SM11.

Martin, Maria Gratia, IHM. *The Spirituality of Teilhard de Chardin.* Westminster, MD: Newman, 1967.

Marty, Martin. *The Pro and Con Book of Religious America: A Bicentennial Argument.* Chicago: Word, 1975.

Maurin, Peter. *Easy Essays.* Chicago: Franciscan Herald, 1977.

————. "Purpose of the Catholic Workers' School." In Peter Maurin, *Easy Essays,* 36–37. Chicago: Franciscan Herald, 1977.

————. "What the Catholic Worker Believes." In Peter Maurin, *Easy Essays,* 76–77. Chicago: Franciscan Herald, 1977.

Maye, Frances. *Under the Tuscan Sun: At Home in Italy.* New York: Broadway, 1996.

McAvoy, Thomas T., CSC. *The Great Crisis in American Catholic History, 1895–1900.* Chicago: Henry Regnery Company, 1957.

McCann, Dennis P. *New Experiment in Democracy: The Challenge for American Catholicism.* Kansas City, MO: Sheed & Ward, 1987.

McCarraher, Eugene. *Christian Critics: Religion and Impasse in Modern American Social Thought.* Ithaca, NY: Cornell University Press, 2000.

———. "The Church Irrelevant: Paul Hanly Furfey and the Fortunes of American Catholic Radicalism." *Religion and American Culture* 7 (Summer 1997) 163–94.

McCreesh, Thomas P. *Biblical Sound and Sense: Poetic Sound Patterns in Proverbs 10–29.* Journal for the Study of the Old Testament Supplement Series 128. Sheffield, UK: JSOT, 1991.

McDonald, Patricia M., SHCJ. "Biblical Brinkmanship: Francis Gigot and the *New York Review.*" In *American Catholic Traditions: Resources for Renewal,* edited by Sandra Yocum Mize and William L. Portier, 222–41. Maryknoll, NY: Orbis, 1997.

———. "Biblical Scholarship: When Tradition Met Method." In *The Catholic Church in the Twentieth Century: Renewing and Reimaging the City of God,* edited by John Deedy, 113–30. Collegeville, MN: Liturgical, 2000.

McGreevy, John T. *Catholicism and American Freedom: A History.* New York: Norton, 2003.

McKenzie, John L. "American Catholic Biblical Scholarship, 1955–1980." In *The Biblical Heritage in Modern Catholic Scholarship,* edited by John J. Collins and John Dominic Crossan, 211–33. Wilmington, DE: Michael Glazier, 1986.

McKevitt, Gerald. *Brokers of Culture: Italian Jesuits in the American West, 1848–1919.* Stanford: Stanford University Press, 2007.

McKinlay, Judith. *Gendering Wisdom the Host: Biblical Invitations to Eat and Drink.* Sheffield, UK: Sheffield Academic, 1996.

McLeod, Hugh. *The Religious Crisis of the 1960s.* New York: Oxford University Press, 2007.

McNeal, Patricia. *Harder Than War: Catholic Peacemaking in Twentieth-Century America.* New Brunswick, NJ: Rutgers University Press, 1992.

McSorley, Joseph, CSP. *A Primer of Prayer.* 1934. New York: Deus, 1961.

———. "Reverend Joseph McSorley, CSP." In *The Book of Catholic Authors,* Sixth Series, edited by Walter Romig, 263–69. Gross Pointe, MI: Walter Romig, 1960. http://www.catholicauthors.com/mcsorley.html.

———. *The Sacrament of Duty and Other Essays.* New York: Columbus, 1909.

Merton, Thomas. *Love and Living.* Edited by Naomi Burton Stone and Patrick Hart. New York: Farrar, Straus and Giroux, 1979. Reprint, New York: Harcourt Brace Jovanovich, 1985.

———. *The Road to Joy: Letters to New and Old Friends.* Edited by Robert E. Daggy. New York: Farrar, Straus and Giroux, 1989.

Meyers, Carol. *The Tabernacle Menorah: A Synthetic Study of a Symbol from the Biblical Cult.* Missoula, MT: Scholars, 1976.

Miller, James J. *An Environmental History of Northeast Florida.* Gainesville: University of Florida Press, 1998.

Misner, Paul. *Social Catholicism in Europe: From the Onset of Industrialization to the First World War.* New York: Crossroad, 1991.

Montagnes, Bernard. *Le Père Lagrange (1855–1938): L'éxégèse catholique dans la crise moderniste.* Paris: Cerf, 1995.

Morrow, Jeffrey L. "Alfred Loisy's Developmental Approach to Scripture: Reading the 'Firmin' Articles in the Context of Nineteenth- and Twentieth-Century Historical Biblical Criticism." *International Journal of Systematic Theology* 15 (2013) 324–44.

————. "Evangelical Catholics and Catholic Biblical Scholarship: An Examination of Scott Hahn's Canonical, Liturgical, and Covenantal Biblical Exegesis." PhD diss., University of Dayton, 2007.

————. "The Politics of Biblical Interpretation: A 'Criticism of Criticism.'" *New Blackfriars* 91 (2010) 528–45.

Moses, Paul. *An Unlikely Union: The Love-Hate Story of New York's Irish and Italians.* New York: New York University Press, 2015.

Murphy, John M. "'A Time of Shame and Sorrow': Robert F. Kennedy and the American Jeremiad." *Quarterly Journal of Speech* 76.4 (1990) 401–14.

Murphy, Roland. "The Hebrew Sage and Openness to the World." In *Christian Action and Openness to the World,* edited by Joseph Papin, 219–44. Volumes 2–3 of the Proceedings of the Theology Institute of Villanova University. Villanova, PA: Villanova University Press, 1970.

————. *The Tree of Life: An Exploration of Biblical Wisdom Literature.* New York: Doubleday, 1990.

Murray, John Courtney, SJ. "War and Conscience" in *A Conflict of Loyalties: The Case for Selective Conscientious Objection,* 19–30, ed. by James Finn, (New York: Gegasus, 1968).

————. *We Hold These Truths: Catholic Reflections on the American Proposition.* New York: Sheed & Ward, 1960. Reprint, Lanham, MD: Rowman & Littlefield, 2005.

Nelli, Humbert S. "Italians." In *Harvard Encyclopedia of American Ethnic Groups,* edited by Stephen Thernstrom, Ann Orlov, and Oscar Handlin, 545–60. Cambridge, MA: Harvard University Press, 1980.

————. "Italians in Urban America." In *The Italian Experience in the United States,* edited by Silvano M. Tomasi and Madeline H. Engel, 77–107. New York: Center for Migration Studies, 1977.

Neuhaus, Richard John. *The Catholic Moment: The Paradox of the Church in the Postmodern World.* San Francisco: HarperCollins, 1987.

Newsom, Carol A. "Dialogue and Allegorical Hermeneutics in Job 28:28." In *Job 28: Cognition in Context,* edited by Ellen van Wolde, 299–307. Leiden: Brill, 2003.

————. "Re-considering Job." *Currents in Biblical Research* 5.2 (2007) 155–82.

————. "Woman and the Discourse of Patriarchal Wisdom: A Study of Proverbs 1–9." In *Gender and Difference in Ancient Israel,* edited by Peggy L. Day, 142–60. Minneapolis: Augsburg Fortress, 1989.

Niceforo, Alfredo. *L'Italia barbara contemporanea.* Milan: Remo Sandron, 1898.

Nichols, Aidan. *Reason with Piety: Garrigou-Lagrange in the Service of Catholic Thought.* Washington, DC: Catholic University of America Press, 2009.

Niebuhr, H. Richard. *Christ and Culture.* New York: Harper, 1951

————. *Radical Monotheism and Western Culture.* Louisville, KY: Westminster John Knox, 1960.

————. *The Social Sources of Denominationalism.* Cleveland, OH: World, 1929.

Noll, Mark A. "Bishop James Gibbons, the Bible, and Protestant America." *U.S. Catholic Historian* 31 (2013) 77–104.

Novak, Michael. *The Catholic Ethic and the Spirit of Capitalism*. New York: Free Press, 1993.

Novick, Peter. *That Noble Dream: The "Objectivity Question" and the American Historical Profession*. New York: Cambridge University Press, 1998.

Nuesse, C. Joseph. *The Catholic University of America: A Centennial History*. Washington, DC: Catholic University of America Press, 1990.

O'Brien, David J. "American Catholicism After 200 Years: On the Razor's Edge of History." *Origins* 3.41 (4 April 1974) 638–46. Also published as "Signs of Hope." *Chicago Studies* 13.2 (Summer 1974) 146–62.

———. "An Evangelical Imperative: Isaac Hecker, Catholicism, and Modern Society." In *Hecker Studies: Essays on the Thought of Isaac Hecker*, edited by John Farina, 87–132. New York: Paulist, 1983.

———. *Isaac Hecker: An American Catholic*. Mahwah, NJ: Paulist, 1992.

———. "Moderate Manifesto for Church's Future," review of *A People Adrift: The Crisis of the Roman Catholic Church in America*, by Peter Steinfels. *National Catholic Reporter* (29 August 2003). http://natcath.org/NCR_Online/archives2/2003c/082903/082903s.htm.

———. *Public Catholicism*. New York: Macmillan, 1989.

———. *The Renewal of American Catholicism*. New York: Oxford University Press, 1972.

O'Brien Steinfels, Margaret. "Defenders of the Faith!" *Commonweal* (3 December 2010). https://www.commonwealmagazine.org/defenders-faith.

———. "Is the Papacy Obsolete?" *Commonweal* 132.9 (6 May 2005) 12–14.

O'Callaghan, Joseph F. *A History of Medieval Spain*. Ithaca, NY: Cornell University Press, 1975.

O'Connell, Marvin R. *Critics on Trial: An Introduction to the Catholic Modernist Crisis*. Washington, DC: Catholic University of America Press, 1994.

———. *John Ireland and the American Catholic Church*. St. Paul, MN: Minnesota Historical Society, 1988.

O'Connor, Flannery. "Parker's Back." In Flannery O'Connor, *The Complete Stories*, 510–30. New York: Farrar, Straus and Giroux, 1971.

O'Connor, Thomas F. "American Catholic Reading Circles, 1886–1909." *Libraries and Culture* 26 (1991) 334–56.

O'Neill, William L. *Coming Apart: An Informal History of the United States in the 1960s*. Chicago: Quadrangle, 1971.

Orsi, Robert A. *The Madonna of 115th Street: Faith and Community in Italian Harlem, 1880–1950*. 2nd ed. New Haven: Yale University Press, 2002.

Osiek, Carolyn. *Kathryn Sullivan, RSCJ: Teacher of the Word*. St. Louis, MO: Society of the Sacred Heart, 2011.

O'Toole, George Barry. *War and Conscription at the Bar of Christian Morals*. New York: Catholic Worker, 1941.

Ouellet, Marc Cardinal. *The Relevance and Future of Vatican II: Interviews with Father Geoffroy de la Tousche*. Translated by Michael Donley and Joseph Fessio, SJ. San Francisco: Ignatius, 2013.

Pagden, Anthony. *The Fall of Natural Man: The American Indian and the Origins of Comparative Ethnology*. Cambridge: Cambridge University Press, 1982.

Parry, John, and Robert Keith, eds. *The Caribbean*. Vol. 2, *The New Iberian World: A Documentary History of the Discovery and Settlement of Latin America to the Early 17th Century*. New York: Times, 1984.

"Pastoral Letter of the Third Plenary Council of Baltimore." In *The Memorial Volume: A History of the Third Plenary Council of Baltimore, November 9–December 7, 1884*. Baltimore: Baltimore Publishing, 1885.

Paul VI, Pope. *Octogesima Adveniens*. 1971. http://w2.vatican.va/content/paul-vi/en/apost_letters/documents/hf_p-vi_apl_19710514_octogesima-adveniens.html.

Pavlischek, Keith J. *John Courtney Murray and the Dilemma of Religious Toleration*. Kirksville, MO: Thomas Jefferson University Press, 1994.

Pelotte, Donald E., SSS. *John Courtney Murray: Theologian in Conflict*. Mahwah, NJ: Paulist, 1976.

Peters, Benjamin. "'Apocalyptic Sectarianism': The Theology at Work in the Critiques of Catholic Radicals." *Horizons* 32 (2012) 208–29.

———. *Called To Be Saints: John Hugo, the Catholic Worker, and the Theology of Radical Christianity*. Milwaukee: Marquette University Press, 2016.

———. "Nature and Grace in the Theology of John Hugo." In *God, Grace & Creation*, edited by Philip Rossi, SJ, 59–78. College Theology Society Annual Volume 55. Maryknoll, NY: Orbis, 2010.

Piehl, Mel. *Breaking Bread: The Catholic Worker and the Origin of Catholic Radicalism in America*. Philadelphia: Temple University Press, 1982.

Pitre, Brant. *Jesus, the Tribulation, and the End of the Exile: Restoration Eschatology and the Origin of the Atonement*. Wissenschaftliche Untersuchungen zum Neuen Testament 2/204. Tübingen: Mohr/Siebeck, 2005.

Pius X, Pope. *Pascendi Dominici Gregis*. 1907. http://w2.vatican.va/content/pius-x/en/encyclicals/documents/hf_p-x_enc_19070908_pascendi-dominici-gregis.html.

Pontifical Biblical Commission. "De mosaica authentia Pentateuchi." *Acta Sanctae Sedis* 39 (1906) 377–78.

Portier, William L. "Adam Smith with Jesus Sprinkles or Jesus-Flavored Economic Life: A Response to Edward Oakes." Paper Presented at DeSales University, Allentown, PA, 28 April 2001.

———. "Americanism." In *Dictionary of Christianity in America*, edited by Daniel G. Reid, 53–56. Downers Grove, IL: InterVarsity, 1990.

———. "Americanism and Inculturation: 1899–1999." *Communio* 27 (2000) 139–60.

———. "Are We Really Serious When We Ask God to Deliver Us from War?: The Catechism and the Challenge of Pope John Paul II." *Communio* 23 (1996) 47–63.

———. "Catholic Theology in the United States, 1840–1907: Recovering a Forgotten Tradition." *Horizons* 10 (1983) 317–33.

———. "Confessions of a Fractured Catholic Theologian." *Horizons* 32 (2005) 117–22.

———. *Divided Friends: Portraits of the Roman Catholic Modernist Crisis in the United States*. Washington, DC: Catholic University of America Press, 2013.

———. "Does Systematic Theology Have a Future?: A Response to Lieven Boeve." In *Faith in Public Life*, edited by William J. Collinge, 135–50. College Theology Society Annual Volume 53. Maryknoll, NY: Orbis, 2008.

———. "Epithalamium." Song presented at his wedding, Silver Spring, MD, 29 May 1971.

———. "An Examination of the Contemporary Theological Task: Toward a Suitable Method for a Specifically American Theology." Master's thesis, Washington Theological Union, 1972.

———. "From Historicity to History: One Theologian's Intergenerational American Catholic Narrative." *U.S. Catholic Historian* 23.2 (2005) 65–72.

———. "The Future of 'Americanism.'" In *Rising from History: U.S. Catholic Theology Looks to the Future*, edited by Robert J. Daly, 49–51. College Theology Society Annual Volume 30. Lanham, MD: University Press of America, 1987.

———. "'Good Friday in December': World War II in the Editorials of *Preservation of the Faith* Magazine, 1939–1945." *U.S. Catholic Historian* 27.2 (2009) 25–44.

———. "Heartfelt Grief and Repentance in Imperial Times." In *Love Alone Is Credible: Hans Urs von Balthasar as Interpreter of the Catholic Tradition*, edited by David L. Schindler, 349–60. Grand Rapids: Eerdmans, 2008.

———. "Here Come the Evangelical Catholics." *Communio* 31 (2004) 35–66.

———. "Inculturation as Transformation: The Case of Americanism Revisited." *U.S. Catholic Historian* 11.3 (1993) 107–24.

———. "Interpretation and Method." In *The Praxis of the Reign of God: An Introduction to the Theology of Edward Schillebeeckx*, edited by Mary Catherine Hilkert and Robert J. Schreiter, 19–36. New York: Fordham University Press, 2002.

———. *Isaac Hecker and the First Vatican Council.* Studies in American Religion 15. Lewiston, NY: Mellen, 1985.

———. "Isaac Hecker and *Testem Benevolentiae*: A Study in Theological Pluralism." In *Hecker Studies: Essays on the Thought of Isaac Hecker*, edited by John Farina, 11–48. New York: Paulist, 1983.

———. "Jesus 2000! A Fresh Look at His Mission." Lecture, Father Judge Apostolic Center, Stirling, NJ, 7 March 1997.

———. "Jesus and the World of Grace, 1968–2014: Reading the Signs of the Times Then and Now." Paper presented at the annual meeting of the Catholic Theological Society of America, San Diego, CA, 7 June 2014.

———. "John R. Slattery (1851–1926), Missionary and Modernist: The State of My Current Research Project." *American Catholic Studies Newsletter* 14.1 (1987) 8–11.

———. "Mysticism and Politics and Integral Salvation: Two Approaches to Theology in a Suffering World." In *Pluralism and Oppression: Theology in World Perspective*, edited by Paul F. Knitter, 255–78. College Theology Society Annual Volume 34. Lanham, MD: University Press of America, 1991.

———. "Paul Hanly Furfey: Catholic Extremist and Supernatural Sociologist, 1936–1941." *Josephinum Journal of Theology* 16 (2009) 24–37.

———. "Providential Nation: An Historical-Theological Study of Isaac Hecker's Americanism." PhD diss., University of St. Michael's College, 1980.

———. "Reason's 'Rightful Autonomy' in *Fides et Ratio* and the Continuous Renewal of Catholic Higher Education in the United States." *Communio* 26 (1999) 541–56.

———. Review of *Inventing Catholic Tradition,* by Terrence Tilley. *Horizons* 28 (2001) 108–11.

———. "Theology and Authority: Reflections on *The Analogical Imagination.*" *The Thomist* 46 (1982) 593–608.

———. "Theology of Manners as Theology of Containment: John Courtney Murray and *Dignitatis Humanae* Forty Years After." *U.S. Catholic Historian* 27 (2006) 83–105.

―――. "Thomist Resurgence," review of *Twentieth-Century Catholic Theologians*, by Fergus Kerr. *Communio* 35 (2008) 494–504.

―――. *Tradition and Incarnation: Foundations of Christian Theology*. Mahwah, NJ: Paulist, 1994.

―――. "Twentieth-Century Catholic Theology and the Triumph of Maurice Blondel." *Communio* 38 (2011) 103–37.

―――. "What Kind of a World of Grace?: Henri Cardinal de Lubac and the Council's Christological Center." *Communio* 39 (2012) 136–51.

Prescott, William H. *The History of the Conquest of Peru*. Lawrence, KS: Digireads, 2011.

Primeggia, Salvatore. "La Via Vecchia and Italian Folk Religiosity: The Peasants and Immigrants Speak." In *Models and Images of Catholicism in Italian Americana: Academy and Science*, edited by Joseph A. Varacalli, Salvatore Primeggia, Salvatore J. LaGumina, and Donald J. Elia, 15–39. Stony Brook, NY: Forum Italicum, 2004.

―――, and Joseph A. Varacalli, "The Sacred and Profane Among Italian American Catholics: The Giglio Feast." *International Journal of Politics, Culture and Society* 9 (1996) 423–49.

Rad, Gerhard von . *Wisdom in Israel*. Translated by James Martin. Nashville: Abingdon, 1972.

Rao, John C. "Secular Italy and Catholicism, 1848–1915: Liberalism, Nationalism, Socialism, and the Romantic Idealist Temptation." In *Models and Images of Catholicism in Italian Americana: Academy and Science*, edited by Joseph A. Varacalli, Salvatore Primeggia, Salvatore J. LaGumina, and Donald J. Elia, 195–230. Stony Brook, NY: Forum Italicum, 2004.

Rahner, Karl, SJ. "Christian Living Formerly and Today." In *Theological Investigations*, vol. 7, *Further Theology of the Spiritual Life 1*, 3–24. Translated by David Bourke. New York: Herder and Herder, 1971.

―――. "The Present Position of Christians: A Theological Interpretation of the Position of Christians in the Modern World." In *The Christian Commitment: Essays in Pastoral Theology*, 3–37. Translated by Cecily Hastings. New York: Sheed & Ward, 1963.

Ratzinger, Joseph Cardinal. "Foundations and Approaches of Biblical Exegesis." *Origins* 17.35 (11 February 1988) 593–602.

―――. "Kirchliches Lehramt und Exegese. Reflexionen aus Anlass des 100-jährigen Bestehens der Päpstlichen Bibelkommission." *Internationale Katholische Zeitschrift: Communio* 32 (2003) 522–29.

―――. *The Nature and Mission of Theology: Essays to Orient Theology in Today's Debates*. Translated by Adrian Walker. San Francisco: Ignatius, 1995.

Reese, Thomas J., SJ, et al. "Georgetown Letter to Rep. Paul Ryan." https://docs.google.com/document/d/1JRLM7Jh9PnrxptafWYENXdAmxnXd4gQJMYTu3H4TFHA/.

Reher, Margaret M. "Phantom Heresy: A Twice-Told Tale." *U.S. Catholic Historian* 11.3 (1993) 93–105.

Restall, Matthew. *Seven Myths of the Spanish Conquest*. New York: Oxford University Press, 2003.

Riegle, Rosalie. *Dorothy Day: Portraits by Those Who Knew Her*. Maryknoll, NY: Orbis, 2003.

Riis, Jacob. *How the Other Half Lives: Studies Among the Tenements of New York.* Edited by Hasia R. Diner. New York: C. Scribner's Sons, 1901. Reprint, New York: Norton, 2009.

Rivera Pagán, Luis. *A Violent Evangelism: The Political and Religious Conquest of the Americas.* Louisville: Westminster John Knox, 1992.

Rocha, Biff. "'De Concilio's Catechism,' Catechists, and the History of the *Baltimore Catechism.*" PhD diss., University of Dayton, 2013.

Rodriguez, Richard. *Hunger of Memory: The Education of Richard Rodriguez.* New York: Bantam, 1983.

Roof, Wade Clark. *A Generation of Seekers: The Spiritual Journeys of the Baby Boom Generation.* San Francisco: Harper, 1993.

Ruiz, Teofilo F. *From Heaven to Earth: the Reordering of Castilian Society, 1150–1350.* Princeton, NJ: Princeton University Press, 2004.

———— "Unsacred Monarchy: The Kings of Castile in the Late Middle Ages." In *Rites of Power: Symbolism, Ritual, and Politics Since the Middle Ages,* edited by Sean Wilentz, 109–44. Philadelphia: University of Pennsylvania Press, 1985.

Ryan, John K. *Modern War and Basic Ethics.* Milwaukee: Bruce, 1940.

Ryan, Paul. "Full Text of Paul Ryan's Remarks at Georgetown University. *The Daily Caller* (26 April 2012). http://dailycaller.com/2012/04/26/full-text-of-paul-ryans-remarks-at-georgetown-university/.

Sacred Congregation of the Holy Office. *Warning Considering the Writings of Father Teilhard de Chardin.* 30 June 1962. http://www.ewtn.com/library/curia/cdfteilh.htm.

Salvaterra, David L. "Becoming American: Assimilation, Pluralism, and Ethnic Identity." In *Immigrant America: European Ethnicity in the United States,* edited by Timothy Walch, 29–54. New York: Garland, 1994.

Savary, Louis M. *The Divine Milieu Explained.* New York: Paulist, 2007.

Schindler, David L. "*Communio* Ecclesiology and Liberalism." *The Review of Politics* 60.4 (Fall 1998) 775–86.

Schineller, Peter. *A Handbook on Inculturation.* New York: Paulist, 1990.

Schlesinger, Arthur, Jr. *A Pilgrim's Progress: Orestes A. Brownson.* Boston: Little, Brown, 1966.

Schloesser, Stephen, SJ. *Jazz Age Catholicism: Mystic Modernism in Postwar Paris, 1919–1933.* Toronto: University of Toronto Press, 2005.

Schmid, Hans H. "Schöpfung, Gerechtigkeit und Heil: Shöpfungstheologie als Gesamthorizont biblischer Theologie." *Zeitschrift für Theologie und Kirche* 70 (1973) 1–19.

Second Vatican Council. *Dei Verbum* (Dogmatic Constitution on Divine Revelation). 1965. http://www.vatican.va/archive/hist_councils/ii_vatican_council/documents/vat-ii_const_19651118_dei-verbum_en.html.

————. *Dignitatis Humanae* (Declaration on Religious Freedom). 1965. http://www.vatican.va/archive/hist_councils/ii_vatican_council/documents/vat-ii_decl_19651207_dignitatis-humanae_en.html.

————. *Gaudium et Spes* (Pastoral Constitution on the Church in the Modern World). 1965. http://www.vatican.va/archive/hist_councils/ii_vatican_council/documents/vat-ii_const_19651207_gaudium-et-spes_en.html.

————. *Lumen Gentium* (Dogmatic Constitution on the Church). 1964. http://
    www.vatican.va/archive/hist_councils/ii_vatican_council/documents/vat-ii_
    const_19641121_lumen-gentium_en.html.

————. *Sacrosanctum Concilium* (Constitution on the Sacred Liturgy). 1963. http://
    www.vatican.va/archive/hist_councils/ii_vatican_council/documents/vat-ii_
    const_19631204_sacrosanctum-concilium_en.html.

Seed, Patricia. *Ceremonies of Possession in Europe's Conquest of the New World, 1492–
    1640.* New York: Cambridge University Press, 1995.

Shadle, Matthew A. *The Origins of War: A Catholic Perspective.* Washington, DC:
    Georgetown University Press, 2011.

Shaw, George Bernard. *Back to Methuselah.* Rev. ed. New York: Oxford University
    Press, 1947.

Shaw, Russell. "Americanism: Then and Now." *Catholic World Report* (May 1995).
    http://www.ewtn.com/library/ISSUES/AMERICAN.TXT.

Sheed, Wilfred. "Père Teilhard's View of Evolution," *Jubilee* 7.8 (1959) 42–49.

Shelley, Thomas J. *Dunwoodie: The History of St Joseph's Seminary, Yonkers, New York.*
    Westminster, MD: Christian Classics, 1993.

————. "A Somber Anniversary." *America* 198.11 (31 March 2008) 14–16.

Sherman, William L. *Forced Native Labor in Sixteenth-Century Central America.*
    Lincoln: University of Nebraska Press, 1979.

Silk, Mark, and Andrew Walsh. "A Past Without a Future?: Parsing the U.S. Catholic
    Vote." *America* (3 November 2008). http://americamagazine.org/issue/674/article/
    past-without-future.

Simpson, Lesley Byrd. *The Encomienda in New Spain: Forced Native Labor in the Spanish
    Colonies.* Berkeley: University of California Press, 1929.

Smith, Timothy L. "Religion and Ethnicity in America." *American Historical Review* 83
    (1978) 1155–85.

Socolow, Susan Migden. *The Women of Colonial Latin America.* New York: Cambridge
    University Press, 2000.

Sorrentino, Joseph M. "The Italian Question." *America* 12.5 (14 November 1914) 118–
    19.

Spalding, John Lancaster. "L'Education et l'avenir religieux." *Annales de philosophie
    chrétien* 43 (October 1900) 5–37.

————. *Lectures and Discourses.* New York: Catholic Publication Society, 1890.

————. *Means and Ends of Education.* Chicago: McClurg, 1895.

————. "Mission vitale de l'université." Translated by Félix Klein. *Revue du clergé
    français* 21 (February 1901) 597–619.

————. *Opportunité.* Translated by Félix Klein. Paris: Lethielleux, 1900.

————. *Opportunity and Other Essays and Addresses.* Chicago: A.C. McClurg, 1900.

Spalding, Thomas W., CFX. "Most Rev. John Carroll." In *The Encyclopedia of American
    Catholic History*, edited by Michael Glazier and Thomas J. Shelley. Collegeville,
    MN: Liturgical, 1997. https://www.archbalt.org/about-us/the-archdiocese/our-
    history/people/carroll.cfm.

Stallsworth, Paul T. "The Story of an Encounter." In *Biblical Interpretation in Crisis:
    The Ratzinger Conference on Bible and Church*, edited by Richard John Neuhaus,
    102–90. Grand Rapids: Eerdmans, 1989.

Steinfels, Peter. *A People Adrift: The Crisis of the Catholic Church in America.* New York:
    Simon and Shuster, 2003.

Stibili, Edward C. "The Italian St. Raphael Society." *U.S. Catholic Historian* 6.4 (Fall 1987) 301–14.

———. *What Can Be Done to Help Them? The Italian Saint Raphael Society, 1887–1923*. New York: Center for Migration Studies, 2003.

Stossel, Scott. *Sarge: The Life and Times of Sargent Shriver*. Washington, DC: Smithsonian, 2004.

Stratmann, Franziscus. *Church and War: A Catholic Study*. New York: P.J. Kennedy and Sons, 1928.

"Studio la materia e trovo lo spirito: Nel pensiero di Pierre Teilhard de Chardin," *L'Osservatore Romano* (28 December 2013). http://www.osservatoreromano.va/it/news/studi-la-materia-e-trovi-lo-spirito.

Sullivan, Mary Louise. "Mother Cabrini: Missionary to Italian Immigrants." *U.S. Catholic Historian* 6.4 (Fall 1987) 265–79.

Swierenga, Robert P. "The Religious Factor in Immigration: The Dutch Experience." In *Immigrant America: European Ethnicity in the United States*, edited by Timothy Walch, 119–40. New York: Garland, 1994.

Talar, C.J.T. "Innovation and Biblical Interpretation." In *Catholicism Contending with Modernity: Roman Catholic Modernism and Anti-Modernism in Historical Context*, edited by Darrell Jodock, 191–211. Cambridge, UK: Cambridge University Press, 2000.

———. "Seminary Reform and Theological Method on the Eve of the Modernist Crisis: Transatlantic Reception of J.B. Hogan's *Clerical Studies* (1898)." *U.S. Catholic Historian* 28.3 (2010) 1–17.

Tanner, Norman P., SJ., ed. *Decrees of the Ecumenical Councils, Volume Two: Trent to Vatican II*. Washington, DC: Georgetown University Press, 1990.

Taranto, Maria A. "Facets of Wisdom: A Theoretical Synthesis." *International Journal on Aging and Human Development* 29 (1989) 1–21.

Teilhard de Chardin, Pierre, SJ. *The Divine Milieu*. New York: Harper & Row, 1960.

———. "Ecumenism" In *Science and Christ*, 197–98. New York: Harper & Row, 1968.

———. *Human Energy*. Translated by J.M. Cohen. New York: Harcourt Brace Jovanovich, 1971.

———. Letter to Marguerite Teilhard-Chambon, 15 March 1916. Teilhard-Schmitz Moormann Collection, Box 7, Folder 20. Woodstock Theological Center Library, Washington, DC.

———. *The Making of a Mind: Letters of a Soldier-Priest, 1914–1919*. Translated by René Hague. New York: Harper & Row, 1965.

———. *The Phenomenon of Man*. Translated by Bernard Wall. Introduction by Sir Julian Huxley. New York: Harper, 1959.

———. *Science and Christ*. Translated by René Hague. New York: Harper & Row, 1968.

———. *Writings in Time of War*. Translated by René Hague. New York: Harper & Row, 1965.

"The Teilhard Phenomenon After 20 Years." *America* 132 (12 April 1975) 270.

Tentler, Leslie Woodcock. "On the Margins: The State of American Catholic History." *American Quarterly* 45 (1993) 104–27.

Third Plenary Council of Baltimore. *De Clericorum Educatione et Instructione*. In *Acta et Decreta Concilii plenarii Baltimorensis tertii*, 69–98. Baltimore: Murphy, 1886.

Thomas, Hugh. *Conquest: Montezuma, Cortés, and the Fall of Old Mexico*. New York: Simon & Schuster, 1993.

————. *Rivers of Gold: The Rise of the Spanish Empire, from Columbus to Magellan.* New York: Random House, 2003.

Tomasi, Silvano M. "Scalabrinians and the Pastoral Care of Immigrants in the United States, 1887–1987." *U.S. Catholic Historian* 6 (1987) 253–64.

————, and Edward C. Stibili, eds. *Italian Americans and Religion: An Annotated Bibliography.* 2nd ed. New York: Center for Migration Studies, 1992.

Tosi, Arturo. *Language and Society in a Changing Italy.* Multilingual Matters 117. Clevedon, UK: Multilingual Matters, 2001.

"Toward Omega." *Time* 74.24 (1959) 62–63.

United States Catholic Conference. *A Century of Catholic Social Teaching: A Common Heritage, A Continuing Challenge.* Washington, DC: United States Catholic Conference, 1990.

————. *Faithful Citizenship; Civic Responsibility for a New Millennium: A Statement on Political Responsibility.* Washington, DC: United States Catholic Conference, 1999.

————. *Political Responsibility: Choices for the Future.* Washington, DC: United States Catholic Conference, 1987.

————. *Political Responsibility: Choices for the 1980s.* Washington, DC: United States Catholic Conference, 1984.

————. *Political Responsibility: Proclaiming the Gospel of Life, Protecting the Least Among Us, and Pursuing the Common Good.* Washington, DC: United States Catholic Conference, 1996.

————. *Political Responsibility: Revitalizing American Democracy.* Washington, DC: United States Catholic Conference, 1991.

————. *Sharing Catholic Social Teaching: Challenges and Directions.* Washington, DC: United States Catholic Conference, 1998.

————. "Victory and Peace." In *Pastoral Letters of the United States Catholic Bishops*, vol. 2, edited by Hugh J. Nolan, 38–43. Washington, DC: United States Catholic Conference, 1984.

United States Catholic Conference Administrative Board. "Political Responsibility: Reflections on an Election Year." *Origins* 5 (1976) 565–70.

————. "Statement on Political Responsibility." *Origins* 9 (1979) 349–55.

United States Conference of Catholic Bishops. "Forming Consciences for Faithful Citizenship: A Call to Political Responsibility from the Catholic Bishops of the United States." *Origins* 32 (2007) 389–403.

————. *Forming Consciences for Faithful Citizenship: A Call to Political Responsibility from the Catholic Bishops of the United States with Introductory Note.* Washington, DC: United States Conference of Catholic Bishops, 2011.

United States Conference of Catholic Bishops Administrative Committee. "Faithful Citizenship: A Catholic Call to Political Responsibility." *Origins* 33 (2003) 321–31.

————. "Federal Budget Choices Must Protect Poor, Vulnerable People, Says U.S. Bishops' Conference." News release, 17 April 2012. http://www.usccb.org/news/2012/12-063.cfm.

Vahanian, Gabriel. *The Death of God: The Culture of Our Post-Christian Era.* New York: George Braziller, 1961.

van der Coelen, Peter. "Pictures for the People?: Bible Illustrations and their Audience." In *Lay Bibles in Europe, 1450–1800*, edited by M. Lamberigts and A.A. den Hollander, 185–205. Leuven: Leuven University Press, 2006.

Van Dusen, Hugh. Letter to "Friends of Father Teilhard." 7 April 1960. Robert Francoeur papers, Box 1, Folder 6. Lauinger Library Archives, Georgetown University, Washington, DC.

Van Hecke, Pierre J.P. "Searching for and Exploring Wisdom. A Cognitive-Semantic Approach to the Hebrew Verb *ḥaqar* in Job 28." In *Job 28: Cognition in Context*, edited by Ellen van Wolde, 139–62. Leiden: Brill, 2003.

Vann, Gerald. *Morality and Just War*. London: Burns, Oates, and Washbourne, 1939.

Vecoli, Rudolph J., ed. *Italian Immigrants in Rural and Small Town America*. Staten Island, NY: American Italian Historical Association, 1987.

———. "Prelates and Peasants: Italian Immigrants and the Catholic Church." *Journal of Social History* 2.3 (Spring 1969) 217–68.

Viéban, Anthony. "Ecclesiastical Seminary." In *The Catholic Encyclopedia*, vol. 13. New York: Robert Appleton, 1912. http://www.newadvent.org/cathen/13694a.htm.

Voegelin, Eric. "The Mongol Orders of Submission to European Powers, 1245–1255." *Byzantion* 15 (1940–1) 378–413.

Vollert, Cyril. "Teilhard in the Light of Vatican II." In *Dimensions of the Future*, edited by Bernard Brown, SJ and Marvin Kessler, SJ, 139–76. Washington, DC: Corpus, 1968.

Walch, Timothy. "The Ethnic Dimension in American Catholic Parochial Education." In *Immigrant America: European Ethnicity in the United States*, edited by Timothy Walch, 141–59. New York: Garland, 1994.

Walter, Kenneth. "Thoreau and Orestes Brownson." *Emerson Society Quarterly* 51 (1968) 53–74.

Ward, James E. "The Algiers Toast: Lavigerie's Work or Leo XIII's?" *Catholic Historical Review* 51.2 (July 1965) 173–91.

Weatherford, Jack. *Genghis Khan and the Making of the Modern World*. New York: Crown, 2004.

Weaver, Mary Jo, ed. *What's Left?: Liberal American Catholics*. Bloomington: Indiana University Press, 1999.

Weber, Max. "Politics as a Vocation." In *From Max Weber: Essays in Sociology*, ed. H.H. Gerth and C. Wright Mills, 77–128. New York: Oxford University Press, 1946

Webster, Jane. "Sophia: Engendering Wisdom in Proverbs, Ben Sira, and the Wisdom of Solomon." *Journal for the Study of the Old Testament* 78 (1998) 63–79.

Weigel, George. "Catholicism and the American Proposition." *First Things* 23 (May 1992) 38–44.

———. *Catholicism and the Renewal of American Democracy*. New York: Paulist, 1989.

———. "An Eminent Distortion of History." *First Things*, online (16 July 2014). http://www.firstthings.com/web-exclusives/2014/07/an-eminent-distortion-of-history.

———. *Evangelical Catholicism: Deep Reform in the 21st Century Church*. New York: Basic, 2013.

———. "The Evangelical Reform of Catholic Advocacy." *First Things* 218 (December 2011) 27–33.

———. "Telling the American Catholic Story." *First Things* 7 (November 1990) 43–49.

———. *Tranquillitas Ordinis: The Present Failure and Future Promise of American Catholic Thought on War and Peace*. New York: Oxford University Press, 1987.

———. "What Popes Can and Can't Do." *First Things*, online (14 January 2014). http://www.firstthings.com/web-exclusives/2014/01/what-popes-can-and-cant-do.

Weithman, Paul. "John Courtney Murray—Do His Ideas Still Matter?" *America* 171.13 (29 October 1994) 17–21.

Westermann, Claus. *The Structure of the Book of Job*. Philadelphia: Fortress, 1981.

Wills, Garry. *Bare Ruined Choirs: Doubt, Prophecy and Radical Religion*. Garden City, NY: Doubleday, 1971.

Wilson, Samuel M. *Hispaniola: Caribbean Chiefdoms in the Age of Columbus*. Tuscaloosa: University of Alabama Press, 1990.

Wisniewski, Mary. "Most Catholics Vote for Obama, but Latinos and Whites Divided." *Reuters* (8 November 2012). http://www.reuters.com/article/2012/11/08/us-usa-campaign-religion-idUSBRE8A71M420121108.

Witherup, Ronald D., SS. "Raymond E. Brown, SS, and Catholic Exegesis in the Twentieth Century: A Retrospective." *U.S. Catholic Historian* 31 (2013) 1–26.

Yocum Mize, Sandra. "Defending Roman Loyalties and Republican Values: The 1848 Italian Revolution in American Catholic Apologetics." *Church History* 60.4 (December 1991) 480–92.

———. *Joining the Revolution in Theology: The College Theology Society, 1954–2004*. Lanham, MD: Sheed & Ward, 2007.

Zahn, Gordon. *Another Part of the War: The Camp Simon Story*. Amherst: University of Massachusetts Press, 1979.

Zavala, Silvio, ed. *Las doctrinas de Palacios Rubios y Matías de Paz ante la conquista de América*. Mexico City, DF: Fondo de Cultura Económica, 1954.

Index